D1436349

The County Books Series
GENERAL EDITOR: BRIAN VESEY-FITZGERALD, F.L.S.

SKYE
AND THE
INNER HEBRIDES

THE COUNTY BOOKS SERIES

*A series comprising 58 volumes. It covers every county
in England and there will be three books on the mainland
of Scotland, two each on the Hebrides, Ireland and Wales,
and one each on Orkney, Shetland, the Isle of Man and
the Channel Islands*

THE FOLLOWING FIFTY-SEVEN VOLUMES HAVE NOW BEEN PUBLISHED

Bedfordshire . . . . *Laurence Meynell*
Berkshire . . . . *Ian Yarrow*
Buckinghamshire . . . . *Alison Uttley*
Cambridgeshire and Huntingdonshire . . . *E. A. R. Ennion*
The Channel Islands . . . . . . *Wilfred D. Hooke*
Cheshire . . . . *F. H. Crossley*
Cornwall . . . . *Claude Berry*
Cumberland and Westmorland . . . . *Norman Nicholson*
Derbyshire . . . . *Crichton Porteous*
Devonshire . . . . *D. St. Leger-Gordon*
Dorset . . . . *Eric Benfield*
Durham—2 Vols. . . . . *Sir Timothy Eden*
Essex . . . . *C. Henry Warren*
Gloucestershire . . . . *Kenneth Hare*
Hampshire and Isle of Wight . . . *Brian Vesey-FitzGerald*
Herefordshire . . . . *H. L. V. Fletcher*
Hertfordshire . . . . . *Sir William Beach Thomas*
Highlands of Scotland . . . . . . *Seton Gordon*
Isle of Man . . . . . . *Canon E. H. Stenning*
Kent . . . . *Richard Church*
Lancashire . . . . *Walter Greenwood*
Leicestershire . . . . *Guy Paget and Lionel Irvine*
Leinster, Munster and Connaught . . . *Frank O'Connor*
Lincolnshire . . . . *John Bygott*
London—The City . . . . . . *Claud Golding*
London—The Northern Reaches . . . *Robert Colville*
London—The Western Reaches . . . . *Godfrey James*
London—West of the Bars . . . . *Douglas Newton*
East London . . . . *Robert Sinclair*
South London . . . . *Harry Williams*
Lowlands of Scotland—Glasgow and the North *Maurice Lindsay*
Lowlands of Scotland—Edinburgh and the South *Maurice Lindsay*
Middlesex . . . . *N. G. Brett-James*
Monmouthshire . . . . . . *Olive Phillips*
Norfolk . . . *Doreen Wallace and R. P. Bagnall-Oakeley*
North-East Lowlands of Scotland . . . *John R. Allan*
Northumberland . . . . . *Herbert L. Honeyman*
Nottinghamshire . . . . *Christopher Marsden*
Orkney . . . . *Hugh Marwick*
Oxfordshire . . . . *Joanna Cannan*
The Shetland Isles . . . . . *Andrew T. Cluness*
Shropshire . . . . *Edmund Vale*
Skye and the Inner Hebrides . . *Alasdair Alpin MacGregor*
Somerset . . . . *M. Lovett Turner*
Staffordshire . . . . *Phil Drabble*
Suffolk . . . . *William Addison*
Surrey . . . . *Eric Parker*
Sussex . . . . *Esther Meynell*
Ulster . . . . *Hugh Shearman*
Wales—2 Vols. . . . . *Maxwell Fraser*
Warwickshire . . . . *Alan Burgess*
The Western Isles . . . . *Alasdair Alpin MacGregor*
Wiltshire . . . . *Edith Olivier*
Worcestershire . . . . *L. T. C. Rolt*
Yorkshire—East Riding . . *John Fairfax-Blakeborough*
Yorkshire—North Riding . . . . *Oswald Harland*
Yorkshire—West Riding . . . . *Lettice Cooper*

PLEASE WRITE TO THE PUBLISHERS FOR FULL DESCRIPTIVE PROSPECTUS

SKYE
AND THE
INNER HEBRIDES

by

ALASDAIR ALPIN MACGREGOR

Illustrated and with a Map

Robert Hale Limited
63 Old Brompton Road London S.W.7

First published 1953

PRINTED IN GREAT BRITAIN BY
NORTHUMBERLAND PRESS LIMITED
GATESHEAD ON TYNE

PREFACE

A L B E I T many books have been written in recent years about the Gaelic islands of Scotland, it would seem as though no volume has yet appeared dealing exclusively with those comprising the Inner Hebrides, which embrace Skye. The present volume seeks to supply any such deficiency.

On some of the islands now falling to be considered a great deal has been written, particularly during the last few decades: on others the amount of correlated material has been somewhat scanty. It has therefore been of our purpose to devote more generous attention to the latter, rather than to the former. Thus the chapters dealing with such islands as Ulva and the Garvellachs contain certain matter not hitherto recorded between the covers of a single volume.

It may be objected that a more thorough survey of the region defined by our title should have ensured the inclusion of the Treshnish Isles, and of Skerryvore, Dubh Heartach, Hyskeir, and so on. My omission of these I seek to excuse on the pretext that they are more appropriate to a volume on the *Farthest* Hebrides, which we hope to publish in due course.

ALASDAIR ALPIN MacGREGOR

78 SWAN COURT
CHELSEA, S.W.3
June, 1952

CONTENTS

Chapter		Page
I	SKYE	1
II	RUM	28
III	EIGG	38
IV	CANNA	50
V	MUCK	60
VI	TIREE	67
VII	COLL	84
VIII	LISMORE	96
IX	KERRERA	109
X	THE SLATE ISLANDS	118
XI	THE GARVELLACH ISLES	131
XII	SCARBA	141
XIII	ISLAY	148
XIV	JURA	174
XV	COLONSAY AND ORONSAY	194
XVI	GIGHA	214
XVII	CARA	224
XVIII	MULL	233
XIX	IONA	258
XX	STAFFA	281
XXI	INCH KENNETH	293
XXII	ULVA'S ISLE	302
	INDEX	315

vii

ILLUSTRATIONS

1 The Bens of Jura from Knockrome   *frontispiece*

                                                     facing page
2 Neist Point, westernmost reach of Skye   4
3 Where the cliffs of the Bioda Mor, in western Skye,
   drop 1,000 feet to the sea   5
4 Dunvegan Castle, Isle of Skye   20
5 Rory Mor's Drinking-horn, the Dunvegan Cup, and the
   Faery Flag   21
6 The Singing Sands of Laig Bay, Isle of Eigg, with Rum
   enshrouded in storm   36
7 The Old Harbour at Scarinish, Isle of Tiree, with the
   Mary Stewart at her last anchorage   37
8 *Above:* Ruins of Breachacha Castle, Coll   52
   Below: The Post Office, Lismore   52
9 Bell-shrine from Kilmichael-Glassary, believed to be
   St. Moluag's   53
10 Ruins of Castle Coeffin, Isle of Lismore   60
11 *Above:* The Parish Church, Lismore   60
   Below: Port Ellen, Isle of Islay   60
12 Horse Shoe Bay, Isle of Kerrera. (Note the lobster-rafts
    moored offshore.)   61
13 On the lobster-farm in Horse Shoe Bay, Isle of Kerrera,
    in the Firth of Lorne   61
14 Gylen Castle, Isle of Kerrera   68
15 Ellanbeich, Isle of Seil, from Isle of Easdale   69
16 Christina MacKenzie lime-washing her cottage at Culli-
    pool, Isle of Luing   84
17 *Above:* Seil and the Cuan Ferry from Luing   85
   Below: The swirling tides of Fladda, in the Firth of
    Lorne   85
18 The Garvellach Isles—Eileach an Naoimh—seen from
    A' Chùli   100
19 *Above:* The Landing-place at Garbh Eileach   101
   Below: Beehive structure on Eileach an Naoimh
    (Clochain)   101
20 Isle of Scarba from Cullipool, Isle of Luing   116
21 Donald MacDougall's Smithy, in Lennox Street, Port
    Ellen, Isle of Islay   117
22 Ruins of Dun Naomhaig, stronghold of the Lords of the
    Isles, Isle of Islay   132

facing page

23 *Above—Left:* Sanctuary Stone at Kilchomain, Islay   133
       Right: Ancient Cross at Kilnave, Islay   133
       Below—Left: Mary MacCrain's tombstone at Inver-
       lussa, Jura   133
       Right: Kildalton Cross, Islay   133
24 *Above:* The Donkey-cart at Bowmore, Isle of Islay   148
       Below: Portaskaig, Isle of Islay   148
25 *Above:* Crofting township of Keills, Isle of Jura   149
       Below: Old Burial-place of Earnadail, Isle of Jura   149
26 Kiloran Bay, Isle of Colonsay   156
27 Robert Meechan, shepherd, on the tidal sands between
       Colonsay and Oronsay   156
28 The Rev. Dr. Kenneth MacLeod in his boat in the
       Minister's Creek, just below his manse on Gigha   157
29 The ferryboat leaving the mail-steamer off Craignure,
       Isle of Mull, on an autumn morning   157
30 Ruins of Aros Castle, Isle of Mull   164
31 Ben Buie, Isle of Mull, on a summer morning, with the
       Memorial Cairn to Edward VII, raised by MacLaine
       of Lochbuie   165
32 The jetty at Iona, with the Ross of Mull seen beyond
       the Sound of Iona   180
33 Iona: the Abbey, with the ruins of St. Oran's Chapel to
       the right, and the Refectory (restored 1951) to the
       left   181
34 Two of the natives of Iona removing, as a labour of
       love, lichen and riotous valerian from the Nunnery
       walls   196
35 West side of St. Martin's Cross (tenth century), with the
       Sound of Iona in the middle-distance, and Fiona-
       phort, in the Ross of Mull, beyond   197
36 Doorway of St. Oran's Chapel, Iona   212
37 The Abbey's Sacristy Door, Iona   213
38 Tomb of Abbot MacKenzie flanking the Holy Table in
       Iona Abbey. Behind are the Sedilia where, in
       Roman days, sat the Celebrant and his two assistants   228
39 *Above:* The Reliquary of St. Columba   229
       Below: St. Columba's Bay, Iona   229
40 Island Pastorale—Iona, with Ulva in the distance   244
41 Ann MacArthur and her pet lambs, Isle of Iona   245
42 Fingal's Cave, Staffa   260
43 Staffa: the Great Face and the entrance to the Boat
       Cave   261

ILLUSTRATIONS

facing page

44 *Above:* The Anchorage, Inch Kenneth   276
    Below: The house on Inch Kenneth (1951)   276
45 Ruins of ancient Chapel on Inch Kenneth, with
    Gribun, Isle of Mull, in the background   277
46 Ulva Ferry with Mull in the background   292
47 Basalt columns by the southern shore of Ulva's Isle,
    with Mull in the distance   293
48 Ulva House in autumn, with Ben More (Mull) in the
    distance   308
49 The road through Ulva. Mull in the distance   309
    Folding map   at end

Present-day difficulties do not permit of a comprehensive map of the area being included in this book. For more detailed information, readers are referred to the respective Ordnance Survey sheets.

ACKNOWLEDGMENTS

All the above illustrations are reproduced from photographs taken by the author.

What shall we tell you? Tales, marvellous tales
    Of ships and stars and isles where good men rest,
Where nevermore the rose of sunset pales,
    And winds and shadows fall towards the west.

JAMES ELROY FLECKER
The Golden Road to Samarkand

CHAPTER I

SKYE

Eilean a' Cheo, Isle of the Mist, as the Gaels call Skye, is perhaps the most remarkable of all the islands of Britain. Together with Raasay and Rona, Scalpay and Soay, and a number of lesser islets, all of which are situate in proximity to it, and have been closely identified with it throughout the centuries, it has an area of roughly 650 square miles, and a population of between 8,000 and 9,000. A century ago, the population was considerably more than double this figure.

Skye is by far the largest of the Hebrides; and it is also the nearest to the mainland of Scotland. Its coast-line, owing to the entry of several wide and splendid sealochs, and thrice as many narrow and penetrating fiords, is enormous. A glance at a map will convey more of its extraordinary shape than would many pages of words, however carefully chosen. Suffice it to say that isthmuses but a few miles across, between certain of its sealochs, link considerable areas which, otherwise, would form separate islands. No more than half a mile of relatively low ground intervenes, for example, between the inmost reach of Loch Eishort and Loch na Dal, an inlet of the Sound of Sleat. But for this narrow belt, Sleat, the southernmost peninsula (sometimes called the Garden of Skye, because of its being so much more fertile than the rugged rest) would be an island by itself. The six miles of glen known as the Strath Mor, between Lochs Ainort and Slapin, intervene to prevent another extensive insulation. Lochs Bracadale and Dunvegan may still be striving to join hands in the isolation of Duirinish, Skye's most westerly province. The headwaters of Little Loch Snizort reach within five miles of the eastern seaboard at Portree, metropolis of this remarkable isle. But for these few miles, the vast, northern territory of Trotternish would be detached. Expressed in another way, so enormous and sinuous are the sealochs and fiords of Skye that no part of this great island is more than half a dozen miles from salt water. The eastern coast-line is far more regular—far less interrupted, one should say—than the western. Northward from Portree harbour it runs nearly 25 miles, with but one minor inlet—Staffin Bay, overhung by the mighty battlements of the Quirang. Compared with the enormous inroads made by the sea elsewhere, this is quite a minor curve. Southward from Portree the coast sweeps round in a great arc toward the east. This arc is indented slightly by the little bay of Tianavaig, by the fiords of Loch Sligachan and Loch Ainort, and the rectangular form of Broadford Bay. The islands of Raasay and Scalpay, and to a lesser extent the islet of Pabbay, shelter this coast considerably. Thus the short sea-journey from Kyle of Lochalsh to Portree is in waters largely enclosed.

On the west coast one finds an endless series of cliffs rising loftily and precipitously, terminating in mighty headlands such as Dunvegan Head and the Bioda Mor. These, for the most part, are shoreless except for the narrow fringe of detritus at their base, often scarcely visible at high water. The cliffs of the Bioda Mor, among the most amazing of the many characterising Skye's western reaches, fall nearly a thousand feet to the sea, in a region of primitive grandeur. Only near the head of many of the sealochs can a landing be effected without incurring an element of danger.

The Bioda Mor has a fascination of its own. If at any time you should find yourself ascending the curved cliff-edge to its summit, see that you keep a few feet farther inland than may be your inclination, since the rabbits have burrowed so extensively here as to have made unsafe the track one used to adopt. A stumble or a false step hereabouts will assuredly precipitate you over the cliff's edge to the Atlantic, several hundreds of feet below. Having reached the summit, look down on Loch Mor Vaterstein, which you will have passed an hour or so previously, to see how tiny—how insignificant—it appears at this distance and altitude. The day I did so, recently, the white pony grazing by its fringe seemed from the Bioda Mor's summit like the water-horse for which this Loch was eschewed in ancient days. If you pursue your way southward toward Ramasaig, following the old moorland road to the ruined homesteads there, you will find yourself in territory now seldom trodden except when the folks of Milovaig and Glendale are busy there at the peats, or when the sheep are being gathered for dipping or shearing in the hirsel lying in the green valley where the road quietly dies away. In summer you can gather, upon this wild country, so much white heather that you will experience difficulty in carrying it home, unless you have some receptacle for its conveyance. And, if hunger should overtake you during the gathering, you may refresh yourself amply with water-cress. A stretch of a hundred yards or more of one of

2

the many rills up there is covered with two kinds of water-cress, cool and refreshing.

.   .   .   .

These westerly reaches of Skye are still remote; and one recalls that they were the seat of much of the disaffection among the peasants which led to the agitation of 1883. It was at Glendale, in western Skye, that John MacPherson (the Glendale Martyr, as he is called) incited the people to action against the landlords. In this he was greatly helped by an old clergyman I knew many years ago—the Rev. Donald MacCallum, a Gaelic bard of no mean account, who was a native of Glendale, and who, after much persecution and imprisonment, retired there to spend the last years of his life. Donald himself told me much of the Highland Clearances, and how, in the end, his own persistent advocacy of the cottars' cause brought into the sealochs of Skye the man o' war, *Sea Horse*. It happened that at this time the weather was very boisterous, with the result that the *Sea Horse* was unable to effect the landing of those aboard her who had been directed to arrest Donald and the more rebellious of his associates.

I shall always remember Donald MacCallum's vivid description of his apprehension. He was on a visit to the schoolhouse, in close proximity to his home, when a little girl came running in to inform the company that the police had arrived in the glen, from Portree, in a horse-drawn vehicle. Soon the charge against David was read aloud, that all might hear and take heed—"inciting the lieges to violence". He was hastily removed to the island's gaol at Portree, and lodged there until liberated on bail for a hundred pounds. In the meantime, his manse at Vaternish was raided by officials, in the hope of finding incriminating literature. Only matter written in the Gaelic could be found, however. As the searchers did not know a word of that language, they removed all his Gaelic MSS., firmly believing them to have been of a seditious nature. He used to tell me that it was always one of the great regrets of his life that these MSS. were never returned to him. Nevertheless, if it were some consolation to discover, on his return to Glendale after his detention, that various crown officials had visited the crofting communities of western Skye to elicit from them the real cause of the disaffection, it was complete triumph to learn that the Report, in 1886, of the Royal Commission set up to investigate these matters produced the Crofters' Act. True, subsequent modifications limited to some extent the recommendations of that Commission; but the measure of freedom gained from arbitrary eviction certainly exceeded the most sanguine expectations of the land reformers in Skye.

In the years intervening, Glendale has been the focal point of several minor revolts. In 1947, grave exception was taken by a considerable section of the population to the fact that a licence for the sale of intoxicating liquor had been granted to the hotel at Dunvegan. The temperance party, who had attributed to the lack of a licence in the locality the exemplary behaviour of its inhabitants, were incensed that a letter from Flora, Mrs. MacLeod of MacLeod, addressed imposingly from Dunvegan Castle, and strongly urging the granting of the licence, was read at the Licensing Court, whereas a petition signed by more than two hundred householders who, it was held, had good cause to fear the adverse effects of the granting of such a licence, was not even mentioned in court! So much for democracy in the Isles! A solicitor appearing on behalf of the applicant for the licence declared that it was required primarily in order to attract tourists. In short, people cannot be expected to visit this wondrous isle unless they are guaranteed such drink as they may want.

It was pointed out, and not altogether irrelevantly, that Flora had heartlessly departed from the attitude to drink adopted by her uncle, the late Norman Magnus, XXIIIrd Chief of the Dunvegan MacLeods, according to the reckoning during his lifetime. Norman and his wife, Emily MacLeod, did much to promote the cause of temperance in Skye. At the time of his death, his widow wrote to an acquaintance of mine a letter containing the following passage:

"What would have pleased him most was that he needed no monument. That was seen in the No-Licence Hotel, for all went home quiet and sober, which would not have been so under other circumstances. I am sure he was the first Chief ever buried without a lot of whisky, and that is such a dreadful custom. He did all in his power for the cause of Temperance, not only in Skye, but everywhere; and his memory will long be honoured for it. The young of Dunvegan have grown up away from temptation. They may well bless his name for this. I think he will always be remembered in Skye as 'MacLeod the Good'."

The more sober residents in the district were, indeed, indignant that the niece of MacLeod the Good should have backed the introduction of drink into Dunvegan.

4

Neist Point, westernmost reach of Skye

The crofting community of Glendale was embroiled in further controversy in 1948, when it was proposed to erect, under the auspices of the Scottish Council of Social Service and of the Inverness County Education Committee, a village hall. Both of these bodies regarded the matter as important, because of their activities in the Highlands and Islands. The young people of Glendale, many of whom had returned from the war a year or two previously, felt that some such centre was necessary for the social life of the community. The Free Presbyterians, led by their minister, fiercely opposed the project on the grounds that it would lead to such excesses as immorality, drinking, gambling, card-playing, and other recognised expressions of the devil. The minister declared that any such support to organised amusement would lead to "orgies and community sins which baffle description". The young folk replied that they were not going to be stifled by the narrow bigotry of the 'traditionalists', and that they meant to assert themselves, if obliged to live in a glen so devoid of entertainment. In the end, a meeting of local crofters was convened to discuss the matter. The heated controversy of several months' standing over-boiled; and the minister left, protesting, followed by his sectarians. The residue decided to proceed with the proposal, and to raise funds for it. "We cannot sing a song," said a retired schoolmaster, recently returned to his native glen. "We cannot whistle a tune, or play the pipes. And yet they say there is music in heaven!" The county's Director of Education declared in favour of the hall, adding that the authorities would not desert the young people of Glendale. The minister and his supporters were right, however, when they remarked, in their petition against the hall, that many in Skye already had too much leisure, and that they would fare better if they did a little work. It is as true of many of the natives of Skye that they are an indolent lot as it is of many of the natives of the Outer Hebrides, whom I criticised in our companion volume. On the other hand, how can anyone imagine that a hall at Glendale is going to do anything more than arrest *temporarily* the drift of young people from the glen?

. . . .

Skye's Norse associations are innumerable. In crossing to the island by the ferry plying between Kyle of Lochalsh and Kyleakin, the trim village on the opposite shore, one instantly feels oneself in a land where the Norse tradition, rather than the Celtic, predominates. Kyleakin is simply Haco's Strait, or Kyle—Haco, that king of Norway whose expedition against the Scots in the reign of

Where the cliffs of the Bioda Mor, in western Skye, drop 1,000 feet to the sea

Alexander III met with disaster off Largs in 1263. Until the cession of the Hebrides to the Scottish Crown three years later, Skye, for centuries, had been completely under the suzerainty of Norway.

Here, as elsewhere throughout their former dominions in Scotland, the Norse have left a legacy in place-names. Very few place-names in Skye are not of Norse origin. Of this foreign domination the stranger arriving in these parts for the first time is immediately reminded when he enquires about the ruined keep standing conspicuously, and in a position so commanding in olden times, above the shore at Kyleakin. He will be told that its name—Castle Maol —originated with the *maol*, or tribute—with the toll—exacted from ships passing through these narrows by Saucy Mary, the Norwegian princess who occupied this keep. Tradition has it that a great chain slung across the sound held up shipping here until the dues were paid; and the natives of Kyleakin, to this day, point out to one the marks this chain wore in a pillar-like rock by the shore, not far from Castle Maol. To this rock, says tradition, the Skye end of the chain was attached.

Whatever may have been the origin of this castle, it is certainly very ancient. Its oldest walls, believed to date from the tenth century, are ten feet thick; while its more recent parts are probably fifteenth century. Upon a time, the castle was occupied by the Clan Fingon—the MacKinnons—who owned for centuries that region of Skye known as Strath.

Saucy Mary is by no means the only Norwegian princess remembered in Skye. One recalls another of her line, commemorated in the cairn crowning the summit of Beinn na Caillich, one of that lovely group of mountains known as the Red Hills, or the Red Coolins, thus named in order to distinguish them from their darker and more illustrious brethren, the Black Coolins. Beinn na Caillich is the peak which Dr. Johnson is careful to tell us he did not ascend while he and Boswell tarried in its shadow with Old MacKinnon of Corrie, at Corrie Chatachan. The cairn on its summit is said to mark the grave of a Norwegian princess who died at Ord, and who, at her own request, was buried there, in the wake of the winds from Norway.

．　　．　　．　　．　　．　　．　　．　　．　　．

And now I must confess to this chapter's being as arduous a piece of writing as I have yet undertaken—arduous not through any lack of knowledge or of enthusiasm for the subject, but arduous in that one can say, within its limits, so very little about an island which is so well known, and upon which so very much has been written. I must therefore confine myself, though perhaps somewhat arbitrarily, to such matters as I think may produce upon the reader unfamiliar with Skye the best general conception of this wonderful isle, as regards its natural features, its inhabitants and their customs, its history, and its traditions. My omissions and commissions must necessarily be equally open to criticism. I excuse them on the pretext that others have dealt with the subject so very fully.

One of the earliest references to Skye is that contained in Adamnan's *Life of Columba*. There we learn that the saint, while staying for some days on the island, which he calls Scian, baptised at a place near the sea called Dobur Artbranani (thought to be Totarder, in the Bracadale district of the island) the aged heathen, Artbranan. Ever since that early reference, Skye has been finding its way with increasing acceptance to the printed page. It is doubtful whether there has been accorded to any other of the islands of Great Britain or of Ireland so much literary attention. Its bibliography is considerable. This has grown steadily since 1865, the year in which Alexander Smith's memorable book, *A Summer in Skye*, was published. In 1905 the island again received loving treatment, this time at the pen of the late Canon John Arnott MacCulloch, D.D., who died at his home in Edinburgh as recently as 1950, at the age of 82. His book, *The Misty Isle of Skye*, went through several editions. It was re-issued in 1948.

During recent years no one has done more to publicise Skye than Seton Gordon. Where this isle is concerned, his persistent pen has never been at rest since he went to live at Upper Duntulm, in the far north of the island. He is one of the luminaries responsible for the recently inaugurated annual fête known as the Skye Week.

And I might mention as modestly—as unvainly—as possible, and without claiming for the work any special merit, that in 1926 a chiel named Alasdair Alpin MacGregor wrote, under the title of *Over the Sea to Skye*, what, from a sales point of view, has probably been the most successful book on Skye published this century.

With the formation of the Scottish Mountaineering Club in 1892, Skye was destined to receive well merited treatment, certainly so far as its peaks and pinnacles were concerned; and it is indeed proper that the Club should have seen fit to include, in the introductory chapter of its accurate and intimate *Guide* to the island, Professor Norman Collie's fine tribute to the Coolins.

With perhaps the exception of the Cairngorms, the Coolins are the best known, best beloved, and most frequented of all the

7

mountains of Britain. Their rugged grandeur, as well as their dangers, attract serious mountaineers and rock-climbers from every part of the world. Their popularity arises from their affording some splendid climbing, from their possessing some of the finest rocks, some of the wildest corries, and some of the most interesting peaks. They consist of two groups, the Red Coolins and the Black Coolins, divided from one another by Glen Sligachan, probably the most impressive of Skye's glens. The enormous mountain masses on each side of it, with their eerie silences, make one feel that laughter here would be irreverent. The scenery of Glen Sligachan, as Alexander Smith himself wrote, drives one in on oneself. It is certainly a place where one might well engage in a little self-examination.

It is only within comparatively recent times that mountains such as these have attracted, rather than repelled. Was it not Dr. Johnson who remarked that a walk upon ploughed fields in England was as a dance upon carpets when compared with the toil and drudgery of wandering in Skye? If, at the age of sixty-four, he felt thus about the easiest mode of transport then in vogue in the island, he cannot have felt very enthusiastic about its mountains, which he mentions but once. "Here are mountains that I should have climbed," he wrote to Mrs. Thrale, "but to climb steeps is now very laborious, and to descend them is dangerous." Other writers viewed mountains, such as the Coolins, with something akin to horror and dread. The year before Johnson and Boswell visited Skye, Pennant described the Coolins as a savage series of red mountains. Blaven, one of the finest of Skye's many peaks, affected him with astonishment.

Largely owing to the influence of Sir Walter Scott, the mountainous territory of Scotland began to assume in our literature a place more felicitous. Scott endowed our highlands with romance and mystery. Literature since his day shows how completely the attitude to mountainous country has altered. The Coolins of Skye, and the wild, lofty fastnesses of Trotternish, its northern peninsula, have now acquired a dignity which makes the adventurous anxious to explore them.

For the fame which the Coolins have enjoyed in recent years, no small measure of gratitude must be assigned to Sheriff Alexander Nicolson, a native of Skye. Quite early in their climbing history, Nicolson ascended many of their peaks. It is known that in 1873 he made the first recorded ascent of Sgurr Dubh and of Sgurr Alasdair. The latter, hitherto, had been without a name, although some of the natives used to refer to it as Sgurr Sgumain. This is the highest peak in Skye. It is also one of the most comely.

So sharp is its summit at 3,251 feet (the Ordnance Survey's altitude of 3,309 feet is wrong, I think!) that there is room upon it only for a small cairn. It received its name from the Sheriff, Alasdair being the Gaelic for Alexander.

.   .   .   .

The more inaccessible, precipitous, and perilous reaches of the Coolins have urged the boldest and hardiest to amazing feats of courage and endurance, many of which are duly recorded in mountaineering annals. To me, the most remarkable physical achievement connected with them is that of the Goorkha named Herkia. Toward the close of last century, the barefooted Herkia sped from the bridge near Sligachan Inn to the summit of Glamaig (2,537 feet), and back—in fifty-five minutes! This astonishing feat was witnessed by MacLeod of Macleod, and by others, some of whom are still alive. I remember being told at Sligachan some years ago, and by an eye-witness, that Herkia made straight for the summit, without any deviation. He descended likewise, finally making for the river by the bridge, that he might steep his nimble feet.

The simplest way of conveying to the reader what Herkia's feat entailed is to add that most people would take twice fifty-five minutes merely to reach the *base* of Glamaig, from Sligachan, for so very broken and swampy is the ground intervening.

Herkia's remarkable athleticism was brought to mind the other day when, accidentally, I came upon a letter written to me some years ago by a certain Percy Caldecott. The letter, I feel, is sufficiently apposite to warrant quoting in full:

> The Old Mill House,
> Cowley,
> Uxbridge.
> Nov. 24, 1936.

Dear Mr. MacGregor,

    I feel almost as if I knew you personally. Owing to my love of the West Highlands, and Skye in particular, your book, " Over the Sea to Skye ", came as a great joy to me. On page 262 I notice a paragraph about a barefooted Goorkha who, from the bridge at Sligachan, climbed to the top of Glamaig, and back, in 55 minutes. You are perfectly correct, for it was *I* who timed him, and as I write I have in my pocket the very watch— a gold compensated watch which is also a stop watch—and the time was 55 minutes, and I think either 5 or 25 seconds. (Anyhow, I remember there was a 5 in the seconds.) As you will know even better than I do, the land between the bridge and Glamaig is very rough going—heather, water-courses, pools, etc. To this day I can see in my mind the spray thrown high up by Herkia as he ran along, regardless of pools or any other obstruction. The speed with which he climbed Glamaig was incredible, more like a spider than anything else. On reaching the top he waved his arms to us, and then immediately started the descent, which he made at the run.

As you probably know, on that side of Glamaig there is much fine loose scree. He came down this in what one might call a series of jumps, and each time his foot landed, he slid for some distance as the scree moved with him. The most wonderful thing about it was that he arrived at the bridge barely out of breath.

You are quite right. He did step into the river on his return, but only for a short time, to wash his feet.

I can envisage the whole scene perfectly to this day. We were standing on the bridge, General (as he now is) Bruce on my right, and The MacLeod on my left. And all the time Bruce kept looking at my watch to see how the time was going. MacLeod was such a kindly man, and such a perfect gentleman. It has always grieved me to think that he had, later on, to come to England and let Dunvegan Castle.

Bruce told me that he considered Herkia the finest Goorkha in the army—a man of iron nerve and utterly without fear of any kind. Once, when climbing high up in the Himalaya with Bruce (Conway was, I think, the other), Bruce was leading in the climb, then Herkia. On coming to a very bad place, Bruce went ahead and anchored himself well, in case of accident, watching Herkia, when suddenly a piece of rock gave way and he went over the precipice which had some 3,000 feet drop. Herkia never even dropped his ice axe. He at once started chipping for his toes, and with Bruce's help came up over the edge, and immediately went on with the climb as if nothing had happened. He held the Star for bravery in action. (In those days the Victoria Cross was not awarded to coloured troops.) And he gained it again on a subsequent occasion.

Bruce told me that on one campaign, when camped in a valley, many men were lost by sniping from the hills around, and that Herkia volunteered to go out at night, and with only his kukri. After dark he would watch for the flame when a rifle was fired, carefully stalk that spot, and before daybreak would return to camp with, possibly, one or more severed heads.

10

I pleased Herkia very much by photographing him, and giving him a few copies of it.

Bruce (with Dr. Norman Collie for part of the time) and Herkia were staying at the Sligachan Hotel for some weeks, as they were climbing in the Coolins; and, as I had also been staying there for a month or so, I got to know Herkia well, and took an interest in hearing about him, though our conversations were somewhat limited as at that time he knew very little English.

I hope I have not bored you with this long and rambling letter; but, as you seem to take an interest in this particular climb, I thought you might like to have a few more details of it.

Yours sincerely,

PERCY CALDECOTT.

. . . .

The backbone of the Sleat peninsula is lofty, rugged, and bare. Where the shores of Loch Eishort wash its western side, however, vegetation thrives to a degree justifying Sleat's being regarded as the Garden of Skye. The little valleys running down to this splendid sealoch are filled with birches and hollies. The sloping croft-lands at Tokavaig and Tarskavaig bear grain crops as heavy as any in the most fertile of the Inner Hebrides. Here the harvest of summer hay is one of the islanders' major delights. The old fruit-trees in the garden at Ord, a couple of miles north of Toka-vaig, look insignificant in comparison with its palm, aspiring at least twenty feet. Incidentally, it was as the result of a succession of summer holidays, spent with the MacIans on their farm at Ord, that Alexander Smith wrote the classic already alluded to. His rhapsody on the lofty peak of Blaven, dominating the view of Strathaird as seen across Loch Eishort from Ord, epitomised his love for the native isle of Flora MacDonald, his wife.

. . . .

And this brings to mind another Flora MacDonald, and the Prince whom she succoured.

It was while Prince Charlie's prospects seemed least hopeful that a strange and secret message was delivered to him from Captain Hugh MacDonald of Armadale, in Skye, who at the time was in Benbecula, at the head of a company of militiamen, but who is said to have been in profound sympathy with the Jacobite cause. The message came "from an enemy in appearance, yet a true friend in heart". It advised the Prince to reach Skye, where he should endeavour to obtain the help of Lady Margaret Mac-

Donald. It proposed that Flora MacDonald, Hugh's step-daughter, then on a visit to her relatives in South Uist, should return to her mother in Skye, taking with her, in the guise of her maidservant, the hapless Prince.

About midnight on Midsummer's Eve, 1746, Prince Charles Edward, in company with MacEachain and O'Neil, the last of his companions, wandering in fugitive fashion among the wilds of the Hebrides, came over the hills to a shieling near Ormacleit, not far from the Atlantic coast. The shieling belonged to Angus MacDonald of Milton. There, for the first time, the Prince met Flora MacDonald, Angus's sister: there it was suggested to her how she might help the Prince to evade his pursuers. Flora, herself a native of Uist, was then about twenty-three years of age. Unhesitatingly, she assented to do all she could in the matter. She hastily made preparations to visit her step-father, then in the neighbouring isle of Benbecula, to seek his guidance. Her own father, Ronald MacDonald of Milton, a cadet of Clan Ranald, died when she was but a year old; and the property of Milton had passed to her brother, Angus. Shortly after her own father's death, she was taken to Armadale, where she lived with her mother and step-father. It was indeed fortunate for the Prince that, while he was skulking in the Outer Hebrides, Flora should have been on a visit to her brother there.

During her temporary absence, the Prince and his two companions remained concealed among the bushes above Coradale, a few miles away. After much hardship and vicissitude, they reached Rossinish, in Benbecula. There the final plans for the Prince's escape to Skye were made. He was to adopt the name of Betty Burke, and assume the rôle of an Irish maidservant. His apparel, coarse in texture as in appearance, consisted of " a calico gown with a light coloured pettycoat, a mantle of dun camelot made after the Irish fashion with a hood joined to it ". The Prince found the hood very irritating. MacEachain tells how he was continually adjusting it, and how " he cursed it a thousand times ". Eventually, however, he was able to comport himself properly. About eight o'clock on the evening of June 28th, having said farewell to the faithful O'Neil, who was so anxious to accompany them, Flora, Betty Burke, and MacEachain, with five boatmen whose names we know, set out on their hazardous voyage, ' over the sea to Skye ', hoping to reach safety there before daybreak. The oarsmen pulled with vigour through calm water until about midnight, when a storm overtook them. The Prince, we are told, in the hope of sustaining the crew's spirits, sang songs throughout the night at sea, and recounted amusing tales. Early in the morning, the coast of Skye was sighted; but by this time the wind had veered to a direction less favourable. For two hours the rowers pulled without making any appreciable headway. The Prince himself offered from time to time to take a spell at the oars to afford each, in turn, a little respite. At last they reached Vaternish. Here they disembarked to eat, in the shadow of inhospitable cliffs, a frugal meal of bread and water. They then resumed their course as close inshore as was compatible with safety. On rounding Vaternish Point, they found a couple of MacLeod sentries watching them. In order to avoid identification, they pulled out to sea a little. One of the sentries now challenged them to stop. As they did not heed him, he discharged his musket at them. His companion would appear to have hastened off to raise the alarm. "Do not be afraid of the villains!" said the Prince, by this time inured to danger. Encouraged by his self-control, the rowers rowed the more resolutely, urging that their anxiety was for *him* rather than for themselves. As the boat gradually drew away, the other sentry was seen to return to the shore, accompanied by fifteen militiamen. Since the fugitives were now out of their range, all they could do was to fire blankly in their direction, in the hope of hitting someone. In the end, the Prince was landed near Monkstadt, the house of Sir Alexander MacDonald, in Trotternish. Here Flora's coolness and courage were no less necessary than they had been in the early stages of her perilous undertaking.

Prince Charlie, after his adventures in Skye, as well as on the neighbouring island of Raasay, finally found his way to the Inverness-shire mainland. It was strange that, on September 19th, he should have sailed away to France from the very loch, on the shore of which he had disembarked the previous year, hopeful of regaining, in his father's name, the throne now lost to the Stuarts forever.

Flora MacDonald was destined to have further associations with Skye. In 1750 she married Alan MacDonald, elder son of Alexander MacDonald of Kingsburgh, who was chamberlain to Sir Alexander MacDonald of Sleat. Her early married life was spent at Flodigarry. There she bore five of her seven children. After a stay of eight years at Flodigarry, she and her family moved to Kingsburgh, where, in September, 1773, they entertained Dr. Johnson and James Boswell. The *Journal* of the latter supplies us with a graphic description of their arrival there:

"I was highly pleased to see Dr. Johnson safely arrived at Kingsburgh, and received by the hospitable Mr. MacDonald, who, with a most respectful attention, supported him into the house. Kingsburgh was completely the figure of a gallant Highlander, exhibiting 'the graceful mien and manly looks', which our popular Scotch song has justly attributed to that character. He had his Tartan plaid thrown about him, a large blue bonnet with a knot of black ribband like a cockade, a brown short coat of a kind of duffil, a Tartan waistcoat with gold buttons and gold button-holes, a bluish philibeg, and Tartan hose. He had jet black hair tied behind, and was a large, stately man, with a steady sensible countenance."

The travellers were conducted to a comfortable parlour with a good fire; and a dram went round. At supper-time, Boswell continues, there appeared the lady of the house, the celebrated Flora MacDonald. "She is a little woman, of a genteel appearance, and uncommonly mild and well-bred. To see Dr. Samuel Johnson, the great champion of the English Tories, salute Miss Flora Macdonald in the isle of Sky, was a striking sight; for though somewhat congenial in their notions, it was very improbable they should meet here."

At Kingsburgh the worthy Doctor and his Scots factotum each had a bed, with tartan curtains, in an upper chamber. Their bedroom was already a historic one. The Doctor occupied the very bed in which the grandson of the unfortunate King James the Second lay one night, after the failure of his rash attempt to regain his kingdom. On the bedroom table in the morning, Boswell found a slip of paper on which Dr. Johnson had pencilled the words, *Quantum cedat virtutibus aurum*—With virtue weigh'd, what worthless trash is gold!

The following day, he and Boswell were to hear from Flora's own lips all that had occurred during the hazardous voyage which brought the Prince safely to Skye, disguised as her maidservant. Flora died in 1790; and she was buried away up there, in the Kilmuir of Trotternish, where a large, granite monument in the form of a Celtic cross commemorates her. Its inscription embraces Dr. Johnson's tribute to her—"a name that will be mentioned in history, and, if courage and fidelity be virtues, mentioned with honour".

Sleat is a peninsula of ancient castles as well as of crofts more productive than most. Here are the ruins of Knock Castle, of

Dunscaith, and of Castle Camus. Here, also, stands Armadale Castle, seat of the MacDonalds of Sleat, who, once upon a time, vied with the MacLeods in the blood-thirstiness of their vengeance. They were fond of giving to the flames the thatch of one another's homes, fond of suffocating one another in caves, much given to burning down one another's churches during worship.

It was at Armadale that Dr. Johnson, seated at Sir Alexander MacDonald's table, learned of the origin of the pipe-tune, *Cill Chriosd,* which the piper played during the meal. " As the bag-pipe was playing, an elderly Gentleman informed us, that in the former time, the MacDonalds of Glen Garry, having been injured or offended by the inhabitants of Culloden, and resolving to have justice or vengeance, came to Culloden on a Sunday, where, finding their enemies at worship, they shut them up in the church, which they set on fire; and this, he said, is the tune the piper played while they were burning." The tune is usually attributed, however, to the occasion on which a number of MacKenzies perished in this way in the church of Urray, near Strathpeffer.

Dunscaith is steeped in Ossianic associations. It was Cuchullin's headquarters. Here he himself learnt the arts of war; and here the Fingalian heroes assembled for instruction in those arts. It was to Dunscaith that Cuchullin sent Bragella for safety during his absence at the wars in Ulster. Nearby is a stone bearing a Gaelic name testifying to its having been the particular one to which Cuchullin, after a day's hunting, leashed Luath, his favourite hound. That Dunscaith was once a Norse fort, there is little doubt. Early in the sixteenth century, when the Mac-Donalds of Sleat occupied it, Alasdair Crotach (Alexander the Hunchback), one of the chiefs of the MacLeods of Skye and Harris, besieged it and took it. This is the chief whose tower still forms part of Dunvegan Castle, and whose sculptured tomb, on the south side of the chancel of St. Clement's, at Rodil, in Harris, was prepared by himself in 1528, nineteen years before he died.

. . . .

Wild and barren as is so much of Skye, there are sheltered valleys where vegetation grows luxuriantly. I have in mind that stretch between the village of Dunvegan and the Castle. There, by the roadside at Kilchoan Cottage, where lived that great Skye-woman, Frances Tolmie, who did so much for the folklore and folk-music of the Hebrides, the wild raspberry-canes bear an abundance of fruit; and I remember my astonishment at the enormous clusters of red currants which I saw in August, a year or two ago, clinging to some bushes in an old and almost completely neglected cottage garden at Milovaig, fanned by the winds stealing up from Loch Pooltiel, in the far west of the island.

Upon the sheltered spaces as one approaches Dunvegan Castle from the village, the raspberry bushes have their competitors—to wit, the foxglove, the willow-herb, and the privet. Never have I seen bushes more heavily weighted with flowers than those composing the untrimmed privets about Dunvegan.

Flowers bloom readily in the cottage gardens of Skye, provided they are given a little attention, and are not too often soused by heavy rains. In many of these gardens, in autumn-time, I have seen displays of phloxes as splendid as any in the sheltered gardens of the fertile and sunny south.

Skye abounds in wild flowers. I once spent a holiday at Milovaig, in a house surrounded by wild gentians. The wayside near at hand was deep in valerian and scabious, in meadow-sweet and hemlock, in cow-parsley and cow-parsnip, and in knapweed. The last named is persistent throughout Skye.

The adjoining moorlands are decked with bog-asphodel and bog-violet, with bog-cotton and bog-myrtle. The deep and dark ravines, usually so moist, harbour numerous ferns; and in the crannies of ancient walls one finds, in abundance, the Scots maidenhair fern. The entire walls of the roofless church of Kilmuir, in Dunvegan, where many of the MacLeod chiefs lie buried, are covered with the latter.

.   .   .   .

The less austere nature of Sleat is seen not only in its richer croft-lands but also in its being one of the few parts of this large island where trees grow to any appreciable size and maturity. Limes, firs, and ash-trees thrive at Armadale Castle. Dr. Johnson alluded to the last mentioned nearly 180 years ago, when they shaded the walled orchard. He learnt of the value of the species from Mr. Janes, a palæontologist. This plantation, he adds, was very properly noted in a recent account of the state of Britain, since it proved that Nature was not altogether responsible for the treelessness of the Hebrides. He also remarked favourably on the fir-trees sheltering the garden at Talisker, home of the MacLeods of Talisker, and now a name so widely known on account of the amber product of its distillery. These fir-trees grew so profusely in 1773 "that some, which the present inhabitant planted, are very high and thick". The sage found Talisker itself very depressing, however. All gaiety and joviality, he felt, were excluded from a place which a hermit might have selected as suitable for his growing old in meditation, free from all intervention or interruption.

Boswell does not appear to have found it much to his liking either. He complains of the way in which the court before the house was injudiciously paved with the round, bluish-grey pebbles brought from the seashore, so that one walked as if on cannon balls driven into the ground. The old house of Talisker is almost as remote nowadays as it was then; and its garden is still sheltered by these fir-trees.

Various parts of Skye have had proprietors who were interested in ameliorating the condition of their estates by way of planting trees. The result of this may be seen to-day in its woodlands, such as that at Skeabost, and in the immediate neighbourhood of Dunvegan Castle. Many of the trees have grown to a considerable height and girth, despite the fact that the soil supporting them has no great depth on its rocky foundation. The roots are often unable to penetrate sufficiently deep to allow of the trees' with-standing the gales sweeping the island in winter. In the policies of Dunvegan Castle one still sees evidence of the havoc among the trees caused by the great gale which swept the Hebrides in March, 1921, when no fewer than 40,000 are said to have been blown down at Dunvegan alone. Sir Reginald MacLeod, in the hope of making good this enormous loss, subsequently carried out an extensive re-planting.

Sylviculture about Dunvegan Castle was the happy concept of General MacLeod, toward the close of the eighteenth century. So rich and varied, to-day, is the vegetation of these policies that it is claimed that about a third of the British flora is to be found among them. According to the official *Guide* to the Castle, mosses, ferns, heaths, wild flowers, flowering shrubs, and forest trees are to be found in its immediate environs in teeming luxuriance.

Despite the great destruction these woodlands suffered in 1921, parts of them remain heavily embowered, especially where the stream drops in the cascade known as Rory Mor's Nurse, so close to the Castle itself. It was said of this prominent chief of the MacLeods of Dunvegan that he never enjoyed a night's rest when removed from the cascade's soothing lullaby. To it Sir Walter Scott refers in the lines:

> *I would old Torquil were to show*
> *His Maidens with their breasts of snow,*
> *Or that my noble liege were nigh*
> *To hear his Nurse sing lullaby.*
> *(The Maids—tall cliffs with breakers white,*
> *The Nurse—a torrent's roaring might.)*

17

It was at Dunvegan that Dr. Johnson, distressed with a cold, wore the large, flannel nightcap Miss MacLeod had made for him. Apropos the Castle's claim to being the oldest inhabited house in Britain (it is said to have been occupied continuously for roughly a thousand years), it is interesting to recall that the hostess of 1773 told Dr. Johnson of her ardent desire to build a house upon a farm she had taken, five miles away, where gardens and other amenities could be developed. She complained of Dunvegan's inconveniences—how Herculean a task was the preparation there of a dinner, for example, and how little suited was its rocky site for a garden. Boswell insisted that the family seat of the MacLeods should always be on this rock; and he was disturbed at finding in a lady diffusing so much of the old family spirit the taint of modern refinement.

'Madam, (said I,) if once you quit this rock, there is no knowing where you may settle. You move five miles first;—then to St. Andrews, as the late Laird did;—then to Edinburgh;—and so on till you end at Hampstead, or in France. No, no; keep to the rock: it is the very jewel of the estate. It looks as if it had been let down from heaven by the four corners, to be the residence of a Chief. Have all the comforts and conveniences of life upon it, but never leave Rorie More's cascade.'—'But, (said she,) is it not enough if we keep it? Must we never have more convenience than Rorie More had? he had his beef brought to dinner in one basket, and his bread in another. Why not as well be Rorie More all over, as live upon this rock? And should not we tire, in looking perpetually on this rock? It is very well for you, who have a fine place, and every thing easy, to talk thus, and think of chaining honest folks to a rock. You would not live upon it yourself.'—'Yes, madam, (said I,) I would live upon it, were I Laird of M'Leod, and should be unhappy if I were not upon it.'

Here Dr. Johnson interposed with a strong voice and in a determined manner to observe that Boswell, rather than quit the old rock, would have lived in a pit—"he would make his bed in the dungeon". The latter was greatly elated at having had his resolute, feudal enthusiasm so eminently confirmed.

. . . .

Among the most interesting of the numerous relics preserved at Dunvegan Castle is the Faery Flag. According to one version of its origin, a faery, clad in green apparel, entered the castle late one autumn evening, and made her way to the apartment known ever since as the Faery Room. There, sleeping in his cradle, she discovered the baby heir of MacLeod. When the nurse looked up, she was amazed to find a strange little woman seated by the cradle, rocking it gently. This faery visitor lifted the child in her arms, and swathed him in the Faery Flag, meantime crooning the Lullaby of the Faery Woman—in the Gaelic, of course. " Behold my child, limbed like the kid or fawn, smiting horses, grasping the accoutrements of the shod horses, the spirited steeds, *mo leanabh beag*, my little child! . . . Oh! that I could behold thy team of horses; men following them, serving women returning home, and the Catanaich sowing the corn! . . . Oh! not of Clan Kenneth [MacKenzie] art thou! Oh! not of Clan Conn. Descendant of a race more esteemed—that of Clan Leod of the swords and armour, whose fathers' native land was Lochlann."

These words are a translation of the Faery Woman's Croon, given me in Skye many years ago by that exquisite old lady, Frances Tolmie, of whom I saw a great deal at that time, and from whom I learned much of the folklore of the Highlands and Islands, particularly of Skye.

To return to the Faery Flag, the nurse sat spellbound during the faery's singing; and, when the singer had gone, she discovered that she had remembered every word of it, and also the melody to which it was sung. Lifting the child from his cot, where the faery woman had replaced him, she wrapped him in the famous banner now known as the Faery Flag. Down the stair still winding in the Faery Tower she hurried with him to the banqueting hall, where the MacLeods were assembled. Great was their surprise when they cast eyes upon this bequest, and listened to the nurse's strange account of what had occurred.

The MacLeods of Dunvegan used to insist that every nurse they employed knew the Lullaby of the Faery Woman, since they believed that it acted as a charm protecting from all ill any infant heir.

In olden times the Faery Flag had its hereditary custodian, just as the old Celtic croziers had. This custodian bore it into any conflict in which the MacLeods were involved. The chief maintained the bearer of this standard on a freehold near Bracadale, in return for his services in connection with it.

According to another version of the origin of the Faery Flag, it came into the possession of a young MacLeod warrior when at the Crusades. The name of the warrior is given as *Mac a' Phearson*, son of the parson. This doughty clansman, when wandering in Palestine, reached a broad river which he was prevented from crossing by a faery maiden, who wrestled with him. In the legendary struggle which ensued, the warrior overcame his faery adversary. When parting from her, she bequeathed to him the Faery Flag, assuring him that, when unfurled, it would give the appearance of a vast multitude of armed men. She warned him, however, that the banner should only be used on three particular occasions, and told him of the misfortunes which would arise from its misuse. Neither lambs nor calves would be born in MacLeod's Country, nor would any foals. The crops would fail, and the sealochs about Dunvegan would be devoid of fish. Worst of all, no children would be born unto MacLeod.

In Skye the most popular version of the origin of the Faery Flag is that one of the chiefs of MacLeod was betrothed to a faery who dwelt on earth only for a short space of time. In bidding him farewell on the eve of her return to faeryland, she presented him with the Faery Flag as a keepsake. At a spot about three miles from Dunvegan, there crosses a brook the bridge known to this day as the Faery Bridge. Here the Skye folks say the chief and the faery finally took leave of one another.

On two occasions, it is said, the unfurling of the Faery Flag averted disaster. On the former of these, it was waved during a cattle plague threatening to destroy MacLeod's vast herds. On the latter, Clan Ranald's fleet had arrived off the coast of Vaternish one holy day, his clansmen bent on vengeance. They disembarked in Ardmore Bay to hurry to the church at Trumpan, where the MacLeods were worshipping at the time. They fired the church, and put to the sword every occupant except an old woman, who managed to escape to Dunvegan with an account of what had occurred. MacLeod now mustered his clansmen, and set off for Vaternish, taking with him the Faery Flag. On arrival there, he unfurled it. The MacDonalds instantly beheld an enormous force, with which they dared not join issue. So they made a dash for their boats on the beach of Ardmore Bay, pursued by the MacLeods, who killed them to a man. When the strife was over, the MacLeods collected the corpses of their slain enemies, and placed them in a row along the base of an old dyke, which they now threw down upon them. And so, to this day, the conflict is referred to by a Gaelic name signifying The Battle of the Spoiling of the Dyke.

Many a famous visitor to Dunvegan Castle has seen this famous relic, and also the Dunvegan Cup, standing $10\frac{1}{4}$ inches in height, on four little silver feet. It seems odd that, though Pennant, Dr.

Dunvegan Castle, Isle of Skye

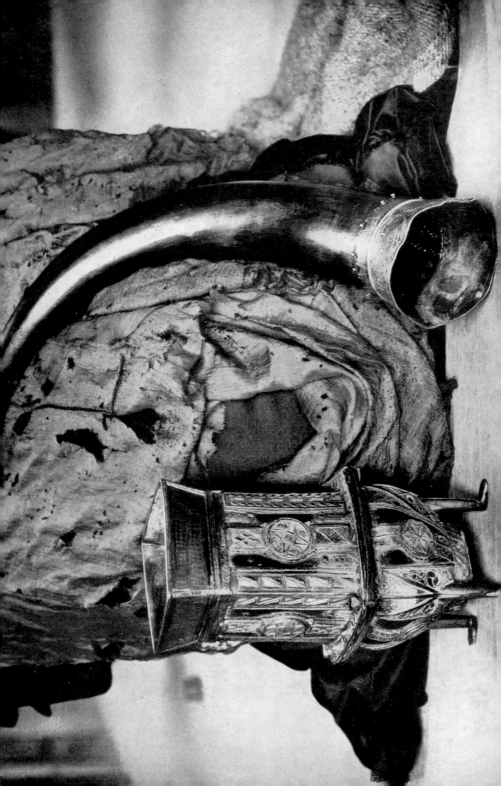

Johnson, and Boswell all visited Dunvegan Castle during the eighteenth century, not one of them mentions this famous heirloom, which Scott afterwards referred to as the "mighty cup . . . erst owned by Royal Somerled". The date of the cup is 1493. How it came into the possession of the MacLeods of Dunvegan is uncertain, though it is thought that during military operations in Northern Ireland, in which Dunvegan MacLeods participated, it may have been a trophy of war, or a reward for services rendered.

One could devote a small book to the relics housed at Dunvegan Castle; but we must be content here with mentioning but one more—the Drinking Horn of Sir Rory Mòr, one of the most illustrious of the Dunvegan chiefs. This is a large ox-horn, rimmed with a deep silver band, on which is engraved a familiar Celtic lacing pattern. It is said that, in olden times, every young heir, on succeeding to the chiefship, was required to prove his worth by draining to the lees, in a single breath, the overflowing horn. In times more recent, however, this ordeal was mitigated by the insertion within the horn of a wooden lining.

Many traditional tales are recounted in Skye of the origin of Rory Mòr's famous bumper. According to the most popular, it was taken from the head of a wild bull slain in the woods of Glenelg by Malcolm, third chief of the MacLeods. From this incident, it is said, originated both the bull's head cabossed between two flags which is the crest of the MacLeods, and their device, "Hold Fast". Another tradition as to the origin of the horn mentions MacLeod's having gone to Inveraray, where he found, within a fenced arena, a young man whom Argyll had condemned to be gored to death by a bull. To MacLeod's remark that the proposed victim was too fine a fellow to be killed in this way, Argyll answered that it was too late now to spare his life. "Will you give him to me if I save him?" asked MacLeod. "Yes, but you, also, go to your death," answered Argyll. Thereupon MacLeod leapt into the arena and seized the enraged bull by the horns. "Hold fast!" shouted the spectators, as MacLeod killed the bull with his dirk, and lopped off one of its horns. Incidentally, there lives in the village of Dunvegan to this day a family of the name of Campbell, claiming descent from the young man whom MacLeod of MacLeod rescued so valiantly.

At Boreraig, on Loch Dunvegan, the MacCrimmons, hereditary pipers to the MacLeods of Dunvegan, had their piping college, to which pupils came from all over Scotland, and even from Ireland.

Rory Mor's Drinking-horn, the Dunvegan Cup, and the Faery Flag

An early chief of the MacLeods endowed them there with a farm. There they remained until the late years of the eighteenth century. By this time the rental value of the farm is said to have increased so much that an avaricious chief sought to recover at least part of it. This so offended the MacCrimmons that they deserted Boreraig, where they had been, in unbroken succession, for ten generations. The MacLeods of Dunvegan claim that the Mac-Crimmons remained at Boreraig as hereditary pipers to their chiefs for three centuries—from 1500 until 1800. Near the site of their piping college, and in the presence of a great concourse of the island's people, the late Sir Reginald MacLeod unveiled, in August, 1933, a cairn to the memory of the MacCrimmons, "who were renowned as Composers, Performers, and Instructors of the classical music of the Bagpipe".

That the MacCrimmons and their piping school may have been on the decline some years before 1800 is suggested by Dr. Johnson's remark that "there has been in Sky beyond all time of memory, a college of pipers, under the direction of MacCrimmon, which is not quite extinct". He also tells us that the Rankins' piping school in Mull became defunct about sixteen years before he made his journey to the Hebrides—that is to say, about 1757. The Doctor must have heard a good deal of the pipes during his itinerary. He tells us that on no fewer than three occasions "I have had my dinner exhilarated by the bagpipe"—at Armadale, at Dunvegan, and again at Coll.

Among existing records of persons sent to Boreraig for the seven years' piping course is that concerning a certain David Fraser, servant of Simon, Lord Lovat—the very Simon who, years later, was beheaded on Tower Hill for his part in 'The Forty-five'. In 1743 he visited the MacCrimmons on behalf of this servant of his, "in order to have him perfected a Highland pyper by the famous M'Crimmn, whom his Lordship is to reward for educating the said David Fraser. And the said Simon, Lord Fraser of Lovat, binds and obliges himself, and his Lordship's heirs, executors, and successors whatsomever, to maintain this said David Fraser, his servant, during the space above mentioned, in bed, board, and washing, and to furnish and provide him with cloaths, shoes, and stockings, and likewise to satisfy and pay to him yearly and ilk year the sum of fifty merks Scots money in name of wages during the said space of seven years."

The same day in 1933 as that upon which Sir Reginald Mac-Leod unveiled the cairn at Boreraig, a memorial tablet to the MacCrimmon pipers, placed in the wall of the old, roofless church of Kilmuir, in Dunvegan, was unveiled. Here, at Kilmuir, some of the chiefs of the Dunvegan MacLeods are buried, and also a number of their MacCrimmon pipers.

Just as the MacLeods established, at Boreraig, the MacCrimmons, the MacDonalds established on a freehold at Peingown, in Trotternish, the MacArthurs, their own illustrious pipers. When they, as Lords of the Isles, occupied Duntulm Castle, situated but a few miles north of Peingown, the position of the MacArthurs was one of great dignity. Yet, they never quite achieved, as pipers, the reputation enjoyed by the MacCrimmons.

Many of the MacArthurs lie buried in the old churchyard of Kilmuir, not far from Peingown and the spot where stands the monument to Flora MacDonald. This Kilmuir, of course, is not to be confused with the Kilmuir at Dunvegan. On a weathered stone in the former churchyard one reads with difficulty the uncompleted inscription:

HERE LY THE REMAINS OF
CHARLES MACKARTER
WHOSE FAME AS AN HONEST MAN
AND REMARKABLE PIPER
WILL SURVIVE THIS GENERATION
FOR HIS MANNERS WERE EASY & REGULAR
AS HIS MUSIC & THE MELODY OF
HIS FINGERS WILL

When visiting Kilmuir some years ago, I made enquiries locally about this stone, and learnt that the man engaged on the inscription refused to finish it, on the pretext that he had not been adequately recompensed for the work he had already executed.

Of course, there is perpetuated about the Highland chiefs an enormous amount of nonsense. Take the position of the MacLeods of Dunvegan, for instance. The present chief is a Mrs. Walter, who lives at Dunvegan Castle, which she inherited from her father, the late Sir Reginald MacLeod. She likes to be styled Flora, Mrs. MacLeod of MacLeod. Her contribution to the controversy over our companion volume, *The Western Isles*, in 1949, was an endeavour to throw doubt upon statements made in that book of mine because, in her view, I had wrongly numbered the MacLeod chiefs! It would appear that the MacLeods have re-enumerated their chiefs recently. They now seek to include additional chiefs, two of whom were " young boys, accepted by the Clan as successors to their fathers, though they died young and never actually led or administered the Clan ". The quotation I give you is from a letter written me by Flora herself, in answer to my request for some guidance in the matter. I had not heard, at that time, that the MacLeods had discovered two or three additional chiefs!

But was the chiefship hereditary? Or did each clan select for its chief the clansman most likely to lead its armed men victoriously in battle? The numbering of these Highland chiefs is, of course, quite arbitrary and fanciful. It would not bear historical scrutiny. According to this new enumeration, Flora now describes herself as the 28th chief of the MacLeods.

It would seem as though we are going to have a surfeit of MacLeods during the next few generations, for only a few years ago we read a family announcement from Dunvegan that Flora's elder daughter, Mrs. Alice Macnabb, and her husband had assumed with Flora's consent, under the authority of the Lord Lyon King of Arms, the additional name of MacLeod, and were now to be known as Archibald Corrie Macnabb MacLeod and Alice Macnabb MacLeod of MacLeod. And, as if this were not enough to establish the survival of this clan nonsense, in May, 1951, John Wolrige Gordon, elder son of the late Captain Wolrige Gordon and of Joan, Flora MacLeod's younger daughter, had, " by the wish of his grandmother ", assumed the name of John MacLeod of MacLeod. We are given to understand that the Lyon King has also assented to *this* change. So you see how easy it is nowadays to perpetuate these arbitrary chiefships. But the important question is whether there is any serious historical basis at all for a woman being a chief.

To-day there are three main approaches to Skye. Until a few years ago, there were four. The fourth was the Scottish Airways plane which used to land in lone and lovely Glen Brittle, in the shadow of the Coolins. Regular flights to Skye have been discontinued, owing to the island's lack of any landing-ground fulfilling the minimum statutory requirements as to suitability and safety.

The oldest route to and from Skye is that by Kylerhea. Before the railway reached the seaboard of Wester Ross at Kyle of Lochalsh, within half a mile or so of the island, most of its external traffic passed through Kylerhea, by the ferry plying a channel half that width. In pre-railway days, the Skye drovers, landing on the Inverness-shire mainland at Bernera of Glenelg, travelled toward the head of Loch Duich, in Kintail, by way of the celebrated mountain-pass known as the Mam Ratagan. Thereafter they pursued their journey to those old-time cattle-markets, the Falkirk Trysts, by Glen Shiel and Cluanie and Tomdoun. In recent years this route has been opened again by the re-establishment of a ferry at Kylerhea, whence one travels the old drove-road through Glen Arroch to Broadford, one of the chief centres of population and activity in Skye—the Charing Cross, as it were, of its more southerly parts.

The traffic here is negligible compared with that between Kyle of Lochalsh and Kyleakin, but a few miles to the northward, where the amount of ferrying is increasing steadily year by year. During the holiday season the vehicular ferry here is one of the busiest in Britain.

The other approach to Skye is by way of Mallaig, another railway terminus. The ferry service operates all the year round between Mallaig and Armadale, in the Sleat of Skye. Some of the island's mails travel by this ferry. The sea trip of roughly five miles takes about half an hour in good weather. It is from Mallaig that most people visit such of Skye's phenomena as Spar Cave, described by Dr. Johnson as the greatest natural curiosity he had ever seen. Skye has many remarkable caves, but none so remarkable as this——

The mermaid's alabaster grot
Who bathes her limbs in sunless well,
Deep in Strathaird's enchanted cell.

From Mallaig, too, most people make their first acquaintance with the Coolins, sailing right up Loch Scavaig to disembark at its head, in order to see, so near at hand, one of the most dramatic spectacles, not only in Skye, but anywhere in Britain—Loch Coruisk, where

all is rock at random thrown—
Black waves, bare rock, and banks of stone.

Skye has no industries in the accepted sense. In addition to casual fishing and casual crofting, however, many of its inhabitants have been profitably engaged in recent decades in tweed-making; and one must not overlook, of course, the employment afforded by the Talisker Distillery.

Marble of a somewhat indifferent quality was once quarried in the Strath district; and the iron-ore deposits on the adjacent island of Raasay have been sporadically worked since the First World War. On the east side of Skye, diatomite works were started half a century or more ago, but were soon abandoned.

25

North of Portree, in the region of that mighty pillar of rock known as the Old Man of Storr, the hydro-electricians have been busy in recent years. By the roadside on the way to Bearreraig Bay are two fairly large sheets of fresh water—Loch Fada and Loch Leathan—lying within half a mile of one another, and originally at different levels. The overflow of both of them is carried to the sea by the Bearreraig River and its waterfall. The two lochs are replenished by a watershed of over five square miles, in a region where the annual rainfall is nearly 6o inches. In order to raise the level of Loch Leathan to that of Loch Fada, a dam 180 feet long, and 36 feet in height, has been built across its north end, where the river leaves it. Here a huge pipe-line now carries the excess water down to a generating station near the river's mouth, by the shore, 447 feet below. This station of the North of Scotland Hydro-Electric Board's Storr Lochs Project is now supplying power to about 9o per cent of Skye's inhabitants. The project, which is perhaps one of the Board's lesser known, received Parliamentary approval in 1948. The power-station houses two 8oo-kilowatt horizontal Francis turbines, with a joint annual output estimated at 5,500,000 units. Before long, power produced by the Storr Lochs plant will be carried to every corner of Skye, an undertaking which will require some 330 miles of high- and low-pressure distribution lines.

So Skye is being modernised. Yet, much persists that is ancient, both as regards physical features, and as regards customs and beliefs. Apropos the latter, in no isle do so many of the inhabitants believe in the faeries. And there are remote places where the dairymaid still pours out a libation of milk for the *gruagach*, or long-haired one. The water-horse, too, is still dreaded in the island; and in this context I cannot but recall an old man I knew, John MacRae by name. John lived near the old manse of Glenelg. In 1870, as a boy, he happened to be present when the loch in Sleat known as Loch nam Dubhrachan was systematically dragged for its alarming water-horse! His account of this astonishing enterprise, taken down *verbatim*, will be found in my book, *Somewhere in Scotland*.

And what of Skye's ghosts? Their number is legion. In 1947 an interesting one was added in the form of a ghost car, which began to manifest itself at night on the road between Sligachan and Sconser. Ever since the autumn of that year, this phantom vehicle has been seen at varying intervals. Its powerful head-lights signal its approach. All of a sudden, it stops; and out go the lights immediately. It has been neither seen nor heard twice on the same night.

But this locality, surprising to relate, has a ghost car *seen in the day-time.* On February 10th, 1948, the driver of a motor-lorry, proceeding toward Portree from Sconser, noticed a car approaching him. He drew up close to the roadside, in order to allow of its passing him. The car came on; but, at a point roughly sixty yards from the stationary lorry, it vanished. No fewer than five men in the lorry at the time saw the car approach. The driver made a sixth. This phenomenon is usually seen about the same place, though not necessarily at the same time of day.

Six weeks later—on March 24th, 1948, to be precise—four islanders living at Sconser Clachan hired a car to convey them to Portree. While travelling in broad daylight through Glen Varrigil, a car appeared to be coming toward them. Close behind this car was a motor-lorry. The driver of the Sconser car and his four passengers were all agreed that they had met and passed the oncoming lorry. Of that, no one had any doubt. *But not one of them had seen the other car pass.* There was no side-road, up which it could have gone. One and all declared that, somehow, somewhere, between their car and the lorry, the third vehicle vanished.

CHAPTER II

RUM

SOUTH of Skye, and west of the Arisaig and Morar districts of the Inverness-shire mainland, lies the diversified parish of the Small Isles, consisting of Rum, Eigg, Canna, and Muck. With Canna goes the adjacent isle of Sanday, so situated in relation to it as to afford it an excellent harbour of enclosed waters, well protected in time of storm. With the names of the four principal isles, the Scottish schoolboy familiarises himself at an early age: they provide him with ready material in the geography classroom for puns. (" I canna take rum and muck with my egg! " is an example of such frivolity as I have remembered since my backward days at George Watson's.) Nowadays the punners refer to them as the Cocktail Isles!

Apart from Skye, these are the only islands of the Inner Hebrides included in Inverness-shire. With the exception of Eigg, they were regarded formerly as part of Argyll. The year, 1726, saw them detached from the parish of Sleat, in Skye, to form an ecclesiastical parish of their own. Since then, they have been in the Presbytery of Sleat, in the Synod of Glenelg.

Eigg lies little more than seven miles west of the Inverness-shire mainland. The mouth of Loch Scresort, in Rum, is roughly eight miles in the same direction from the Point of Sleat, southernmost reach of Skye. Muck, smallest and most southerly of the group, lying three miles south-west of Eigg, is only five from the Argyllshire mainland at Ardnamurchan—which reminds one that, among the finest views of Eigg and Rum, is that to be had from the hill-track between Sanna and Achosnich, in Ardnamurchan, beyond a foreground of black skerries, and bays of very white sand. If the sun could be seen sinking behind these isles from the track I have mentioned, the view of them would be as famous as that from Morar at sundown.

Canna, third of the Small Isles in point of size, is little more than two miles north-west of Rum, and nine south-west of the Minginish district of Skye. In the days of the bitter clan feuds, these islands' situation, roughly equidistant between MacLeod properties in Skye and Clan Ranald properties on the Inverness-shire mainland, brought them their share of unrest, and even of disaster. They belonged for centuries to the colourful Clan Ranald. That, in itself, was sufficient to tempt the MacLeods to raid them from time to time, setting out from Skye in their galleys, across the Coolin Sound. But Clan Ranald would retaliate, mustering his birlinns—his war-galleys—in the splendid harbour of Canna, and sailing in dark stealth for the cattle-folds of Glen Brittle, so often taking its inhabitants by surprise that MacLeod of MacLeod was obliged to maintain at Rudh' an Dunain, the headland at the entrance to Glen Brittle, a hereditary Lieutenant of the Coast, whose duty it was to keep watch, and raise the alarum by beacon-fires, wherever Clan Ranald's galleys were known to be sallying forth from the cover of the Small Isles.

In good weather these isles are easily reached from Mallaig by motor-boat. All the year round, MacBrayne's Outer Islands mail-steamer, on her itinerary between Mallaig and Lochboisdale, calls regularly, though not very frequently, at Eigg, at Rum, and at Canna. Muck is not so favoured. Canna is the only island of the group with a pier alongside which the mail-steamer can berth. In the case of the others, a ferryboat plies in attendance. The trip from Mallaig to Galmisdale, in Eigg, takes about an hour and a half, allowing for the ferrying ashore; and a very pleasant trip it can be on a summer's afternoon. By motor-boat one can travel from Eigg to Rum—from Galmisdale to Kinloch, at the head of Loch Scresort—in about the same time, as does the minister of the Small Isles parish at least one Sunday in every month, in order to conduct a service there, in the building serving the dual purpose of church and school.

Stormy weather frequently delays by several hours the mail-steamer's arrival at islands like the Small Isles. Such lateness can be very trying indeed for the passengers aboard her, as also for those hanging about jetties and ferries in wind and rain, waiting to embark. The natives, though inured to such hardship, are critical of their steamer service when delays do occur. On the other hand, they are swift to resent any *stranger's* criticism of it. One recalls in this connection a crofter's reply to an impatient traveller who, in a reproachful way, had asked him how much longer he thought it might be ere the steamer did arrive. " Och, well," said the crofter, " she'll be coming sometimes sooner; and sometimes, maybe, she'll be coming earlier; and sometimes she'll be coming before that again."

Of the Small Isles' area of roughly 38,000 acres, wild and mountainous Rum occupies more than half. From north to south, as from east to west, this round and compact island measures about eight miles. For its size it is inordinately mountainous, a fact commented upon by nearly every writer who has referred to it during the last four centuries or thereabouts. An early annotator writes of it as being "all hillis and waist glennis". Dean Monro, writing in the middle of the sixteenth century, and referring to it as Ronin, mentions its being "ane forest of heigh mountainis, and abundance of litle deire in it". An account written about 1580 alludes to it as "ane Ile of small profit, except that it conteins mony deir". This was at a time when its population had fallen so low that it could raise for the wars no more than half a dozen men, while Canna could muster twenty, and Muck, then the property of MacIain of Ardnamurchan, as many as sixteen. Mull's capacity then was nearly a thousand. Thomas Knox, Bishop of the Isles, reporting on the state of his diocese in 1626, alludes to Rum as "a montanus barren iland containing tua touns. The landis are not sett nor valued".

Martin Martin (*circa* 1700) likewise refers to Rum's mountains, and to the hundreds of deer inhabiting them. The island at this time was owned by the MacLeans of Coll, who would appear to have come into possession of it about the middle of the sixteenth century, just when the aforementioned Donald Monro, High Dean of the Isles, was travelling through the Hebrides, and recording about them those contemporaneous facts to which reference is so often made.

Martin cites the interesting belief among the inhabitants of Rum that fatality would always befall the posterity of MacLean of Coll, then owner of the island, if he or any member of his family shot a deer on Fionn Chrò, a mountain on the west of the island, overshadowing Glen Seilisdeir. The discharge of such a shot meant that "he dies suddenly, or contracts some violent Distemper, which soon puts a period to his Life. They told me some instances to this purpose: whatever may be in it, there is none of the Tribe abovenamed will ever offer to shoot the Deer in that Mountain."

One assumes Rum's population to have been small at the time of Dean Monro's visit, since he mentions that the island's wild fowl "has few to start them except deir". To what species of fowl the Dean referred, we do not know. He does refer to solan geese. "Maney solan geise are in this ile," he writes. However, ornithologists—and among them Seton Gordon—incline to the view that the Dean mistook Rum's shearwaters for solans. Shearwaters occupy innumerable burrows in Allival, right up to its very summit at 2,365 feet above sea-level. These birds, whose habits and behaviour, in their fight for survival against the predatory gulls, I once studied on Skokholm, cannot fail to instil one with awe and admiration; and they may well have been the species on Rum disturbed, in the Dean's day, only by deer.

The location of the shearwaters' inland nesting-cliffs were among the major objectives of J. A. Harvie-Brown and his companions when they landed on Rum in 1881 from their yawl, *Crusader*. They managed to get ashore at a perilous spot in Guirdil Bay, on the west side of the island, under *Creag nan Stàrdean*, the Bloodstone Hill—thus named on account of the heliotropes or bloodstones so common here as to have been once quarried on its north side, just below the summit. This enterprise, one imagines, was abandoned owing to transport difficulties. The act of production, in the sense that Adam Smith uses the term, may well have rendered it wholly uneconomic. Incidentally, a proprietor of Rum presented Queen Victoria with a table-top made out of a single piece of bloodstone from this hill.

The population at the time must have been approximately what it was the year before, when Pennant put it at 325. "The inhabitants are fifty-eight families," wrote Dr. Johnson, "who continued Papists for some time after the Laird became a Protestant. Their adherence to the old religion was strengthened by the countenance of the Laird's sister, a zealous Romanist, till one Sunday, as they were going to mass under the conduct of their patroness, Mac-Lean met them on the way, gave one of them a blow on the head with a *yellow stick*, I suppose a cane, for which the *Earse* had no name, and drove them to the kirk, from which they have never since departed. Since the use of this method of conversion, the inhabitants of *Egg* and *Canna*, who continue Papists, call the Protestantism of *Rum* the religion of the *Yellow Stick*."

In 1826 Rum experienced depopulation on a vast scale, when no fewer than 400 crofters were obliged to emigrate to America. By 1828, as Hugh Miller relates in his *Cruise of the Betsy*, their place had been taken by a farmer and his sheep stock, plus the shepherds imported to look after the latter. "All was solitary," he wrote in 1858. "We could see among the deserted fields the grass-grown foundations of cottages razed to the ground. The valley, more desolate than that which we had left, had not a single inhabited dwelling. It seemed as if man had done with it for ever. . . . The island had been divested of its inhabitants to make way for one sheep-farmer and 8,000 sheep." The valleys and coastal strips, won so arduously for pastoral purposes, had already reverted to their pristine wildness.

Yet, it must not be assumed that the island's productive capacity

31

could sustain, except on the lowest subsistence level, a peasantry so numerous. Poverty and want there must have been; and here on Rum, as elsewhere, a situation may well have arisen which nothing short of emigration could have alleviated. Though, undoubtedly, much harshness attended the Highland Clearances and Evictions, there was another side to this agrarian problem which the more emotional of contemporaneous writers overlooked entirely.

The sites of the townships occupied by this peasantry are still clearly defined in the less barren parts of the island. One finds them in Glen Harris, in Glen Dibidil, at Guirdil, Kinloch, and Kilmory. The largest settlement would seem to have been at Kilmory, where, upon a time, as the name itself suggests, was a religious house, with a place of burial adjacent thereto. Though the island is singularly wanting in remains of a hagiological or ecclesiological origin, and the name of no particular saint appears to have been associated with it, its toponomy includes Kilmory and Papadil, indicative of *some* religious settlement there in olden times. Kilmory is the Gaelic equivalent of the cell or churchyard of Mary: Papadil is simply the Norse equivalent of the priest's dale. The name survives where the Papadil Burn, draining part of the watershed of Sgùrr nan Gillean, near the island's southern extremity, flows into the loch of the same name, by the side of which stands the little shooting-lodge of Papadil, built by Sir George Bullough.

A few years after the evacuation of 1826, one or two families from Skye were permitted to come to the island, and to settle in the locality of Loch Scresort. About 1845, the sheep, in turn, began to be displaced by deer. The island was soon converted into the vast deer-forest which it has been ever since.

In 1840 MacLean of Coll disposed of Rum to the Marquis of Salisbury. The island remained in that family's hands until 1880, when it was purchased by John Bullough, of Meggernie, a historic property in Glen Lyon. It was he who, in 1880, imported a number of stags and hinds from Windsor Great Park, with a view to improving the quality of the native herds. During the proprietorship of his son, the late Sir George Bullough, Rum became increasingly a private sporting preserve.

It was Sir George who introduced into the island, from Perthshire, a flock of wild goats. This flock, which throve well, was augmented later by a number brought over from the Sunart district of Argyll. To the steep rock-faces of so many of the island's summits, goats are admirably suited; and for the unnamed peak of some 2,475 feet, situated below Ashval and Sgùrr nan Gillean, an Oxford mountaineering party suggested the name of Sgùrr nan Gobhar, because of the presence upon it, the day they traversed it, of so many wild goats.

Although John Bullough inaugurated many schemes for the island's improvement, he did not live to see them carried to fruition. When the island passed to the late Sir George, aforementioned, it was almost entirely devoid of anything in the nature of a road, except in the immediate vicinity of Kinloch. Sir George, however, constructed a road across the island, from Kinloch to Glen Harris, on its west coast. His father loved greatly that part of Rum, hitherto so remote; and there he was buried, first in a chamber hewn out of the face of the rock, and subsequently in the centre of a field, near the shepherd's house. On a comparatively flat piece of ground near the mouth of Glen Harris, overshadowed by Rum's own Coolins, stands one of the most surprising monuments in all the Inner Isles. It is the memorial, in the form of a Greek temple, which Sir George Bullough caused to be erected to his father at the spot where he was buried. This mighty mausoleum consists of broad steps leading up on each of four rectangular sides to a base upon which stand eighteen round pillars supporting a massive roof. Like such monuments Grecian in design, it is open on all sides to every wind. The storms of winter bring the spindrift of the Atlantic right up to it when the gales rush, unhindered, between its pillars. Anybody coming ashore at Glen Harris from a shipwreck, there to be confronted by this monument, might well wonder where he was. He could be excused for imagining that he had landed where——

> *The mountains look on Marathon,*
> *And Marathon looks on the sea.*

Rum was an island of unusual activity while Sir George Bullough was building and plenishing, at the head of Loch Scresort, the mansion-house known as Kinloch Castle, and laying out in a lavish way the gardens, lawns, and policies surrounding it. Here, at Kinloch, are to be found almost the only trees on the island. No fewer than 80,000 are said to have been planted toward the close of the nineteenth century. A forest fire, unfortunately, destroyed a great number of these.

To-day all the splendour of those spacious times has vanished from Kinloch Castle. The lengthening shadow of decay would seem to have fallen upon it. Even the deer are now left comparatively alone, in consequence of which they have become emboldened. No longer do they confine themselves to the mountains, or to the succulent pastures of such remote glens as Glen Harris and Glen Dibidil. They now graze confidently in the lower reaches of the valley through which the Kinloch River flows eastward to Loch Scresort. By the river's mouth from time to time some of the older stags may be seen, feeding on the fresh herbage between road and river, little alarmed at human intrusion.

There is no accommodation on Rum for anyone who may wish to land and explore an island that, to all but the favoured few, in pursuit of its antlered denizens, remains *terra incognita*—no *official* accommodation, anyhow. The present population of roughly thirty consists of families whose men-folk are in the proprietor's employment—estate workers, as they are termed. For their convenience the mail-steamer calls at Loch Scresort, where there is no pier, but where the proprietor's ferryboat attends her. The anchorage here is excellent, though somewhat exposed to easterly winds. Loch Scresort is by far the best of the many places round the shores where a landing can be effected without much peril. Stormbound yachts and small, steam-propelled coasting craft frequently anchor here.

For all that, few lacking personal contact with the island, or with one of the families dwelling thereon, ever land, partly through fear of being warned off (unaware that, even in Scotland, there is no law of trespass, *as such*!), and partly owing to a deliberate scheme to render as inhospitable as possible the sojourn of any stranger who may be bold enough to disembark. The isle, as a modern writer so aptly puts it, is inhospitable by deliberate intent.[1] This is all to the bad, when it might be all to the good. I can think of no other island so accessible and compact where those genuinely interested in mountaineering and rock-climbing might receive training for the infinitely more arduous tasks which may await them in the later stages of their pursuit. The island might well be purchased by some public-spirited organisation, such as the National Trust for Scotland, for the promotion of the more strenuous and manly exercises.

Though in theory, of course, it is possible to land on Rum—at all events, on its foreshore—adventurers do arrive at this forbidden isle with the firm intention of pressing inland to explore its wild and alluring interior, bringing with them tent or bivouac, together with food. They might be well advised to bring with them a little milk too. That such persons do land is evident from contributions appearing from time to time in that admirable publication, *The Scottish Mountaineering Club Jour-*

---

[1] *Quest by Canoe*, by Alastair M. Dunnett (G. Bell & Sons, 1950).

34

nal. Rum provides excellent climbing. For evidence of this, one could not do better than consult the relevant passages in the *Guide*,[1] based upon data supplied in the main by M. B. Nettleton, at one time President of the Oxford University Mountaineering Club. In the summer of 1933, Nettleton and five other members of that organisation spent some weeks in the neighbourhood of Rum, having solved the problem of accommodation by sleeping aboard the motor-boat by which they had arrived. For the period during which they climbed and studied Rum's summits and precipices, their craft rode at anchor in Loch Scresort. They returned to it each night. Throughout their visit, they were favoured with excellent weather—a most unusual boon in one of the wettest of all our islands.

No one should land on Rum unprepared for rain, heavy and prolonged. Nor should anybody arrive intent on remaining any length of time without taking ashore with him a supply of food, in case of his being isolated or marooned. The burns, of course, will furnish him amply with the water he wants, even in the driest of seasons. Above all, he must bear in mind that Rum is primarily a deer-forest, and should therefore be given the widest berth at stalking time, if merely for reasons of personal safety. The mountains of this forbidden isle have an allure like the Coolins of Skye, towering in ancient splendour no more than a dozen miles away. Some of the finest distant views of the one are to be had from the summits of the other—the Coolins of Skye from the Coolins of Rum: the Coolins of Rum from the Coolins of Skye. Although the peaks of the former hardly compare with the loftier of the latter, they are certainly not negligible. As many as five of them, all grouped in close proximity to one another at the south and south-east of the island, stand well over 2,000 feet. They are Askival (2,659 ft.), Ashval (2,552 ft.), Sgùrr nan Gillean (2,503 ft.), Allival (2,365 ft.), and twin-peaked Trallval (approximately 2,300 ft.). The fine summit of Barkeval, rising in pyramidal fashion almost in the centre of the island, falls short of 2,000 feet by less than a hundred. A seventh mountain worthy of mention is Orval (1,869 ft.), a mighty uprising of granite dominating a lesser group of mountains in the west of the island, and separated from the loftier by Glen Harris.

Access to Rum's highest peaks is comparatively easy from Kinloch, whence one follows the course of the Slugan burn to the northern flanks of Barkeval. A ridge, easy of traverse, connects that hill with Allival. Precaution is necessary, however, when

---

[1] *The Islands of Scotland* (excluding Skye), published in 1934 by the Scottish Mountaineering Club.

moving about the island's higher reaches, since much of the ancient rock of which these peaks are composed stands shattered and loose. The careless placing of a foot or the rash grasp of the hand might readily dislodge masses of precariously poised material, and, with it, oneself. Concentration and self-discipline are therefore essential to personal safety in this domain of fretted ridges, of splintered pinnacles.

And what views are to be had from these summits on a clear day! Scottish mountaineers and rock-climbers, who know these crags and screes, these buttresses, pinnacles, and *arêtes*, declare that they are distracted from their main pursuit by the magnificence of the panoramas on every hand.

My attempts at photography on Rum have always been foiled by rain, during which the peaks themselves often remained invisible for several consecutive days. A few years ago, when staying on Eigg, I was offered an opportunity of landing on the island through the goodness of a fellow-traveller, the Rev. James Reid Christie, then minister of one of London's Presbyterian churches. He had offered to take the service at Kinloch on the ensuing Sunday, when the parish minister of the Small Isles was expected in any case. On a day of wind and rain and swelling seas, we set out from Eigg in the motor-boat graciously provided on one Sunday in each month by the proprietor of Muck, in order to take the parish minister to Rum and back. We were well and truly drenched by the time we sailed into the quieter waters of Loch Scresort, preparatory to disembarking at Kinloch. No sooner had we got ashore by dinghy than it became obvious that our arrival had been noticed. As we passed up from the shore toward the building serving the island as church and school, Mrs. Morrison, the head stalker's wife, came forth from her house near at hand to welcome us. She had sought to prepare food and warmth the instant our craft came into view in the misty loch. For her truly Christian offices, we were indeed thankful. Dry clothes, and especially dry footgear, were provided. Warm food was served by a warm fire; and in no time we were our vigorous selves again. I was in fettle for the mountains, had the day permitted: James was re-invigorated for his sermon. Soon we found ourselves in that half of the island's public building devoted on such occasions to non-secular uses. The entire population had turned out to hear James—men, women, and children, a dog or two, and a cat which refused to be dislodged from a corner she had selected under some ponderous benches. At the back of this

36

The Singing Sands of Laig Bay, Isle of Eigg, with Rum enshrouded in storm

packed apartment, I sat upon one of the infants' forms specially carried in from the adjoining schoolroom to accommodate the surplus congregation. Not for years had there been such a muster of the inhabitants. News of James's rhetorical powers had already been bruited; and, in any case, the parishioners were rather weary of their own minister, and anxious for a change.

In front of that part of the building used as a church towered the laird's pew. This large, high-backed piece of furniture rose like a wall before the eyes of the ordinary, common folk worshipping at this outpost of the Church of Scotland. Not only did it provide the laird and his guests with a front seat, but it also screened them from the vulgar gaze.

At the close of the service, we stepped out into the open to find the hills and cliffs of Rum and of Eigg clear of rain and of mist, and warmed with sunshine. For the first time for nigh a week, the peaks of Allival and Askval were free of cloud. But it was now too late to do much with the camera. The cataracts were swollen and noisy in their descent to the brine of Loch Scresort as we embarked, toward evening, for Eigg.

These mountains of Rum, with their beautiful Norse names, have a subtle enticement. They are indeed magnetic. Who can hear but whispered the name, Allival, without feeling a tug at the heart, and a restlessness in the feet?

The Old Harbour at Scarinish, Isle of Tiree, with the "Mary Stewart" at her last anchorage

Chapter III

EIGG

WITH an area of approximately 5,600 acres, *Eilean Eige,* as the Gaels call Eigg, is about a sixth the size of Rum, largest of the Small Isles. Its name, likewise of Norse origin, is thought to denote its being a notched or nicked isle; and this, doubtless, is the nick seen so conspicuously in its skyline about the centre of the island from certain directions, indicating the position of the glen running right across it from Kildonnan, in the south-east, to Laig Bay, in the north-west. This glen divides Eigg in two almost equal parts, the centre of each being mountainous. The island attains, toward its south-western end, its highest point in that famous landmark—that geological phenomenon—the Scuir of Eigg, one of the most fantastic rock formations in Britain. The Scuir, rising to a height of 1,289 feet, is an object of the greatest interest. From its summit may be had one of the most magnificent panoramas in all the Western Highlands. To the north-west, and at a distance of no more than eight miles, Rum's alluring peaks may be viewed to advantage. On the northern horizon, thrice as far away, the jagged range of the Coolins of Skye fret the skyline. Eastward lies that romantic region of Inverness-shire known as Prince Charlie's Country. Far away, on the western horizon, beyond the Minch, lie the Outer Hebrides, prominent among them being South Uist and Barra, Mingulay and Barra Head. The prospect from the Scuir, in *any* direction, is inspiring.

The Scuir itself, seen from the east, resembles the perpendicular walls of a gigantic fortress perched impregnably and defiantly on the edge of the island's loftiest ridge. Its bastions of columnar pitchstone porphyry rise mightily, like Suilven, in Sutherland, dwarfing everything in their vicinity. From the south it appears as a rampart of porphyry overlaid with a great mass of other rock, igneous in origin. Someone likened its appearance from this direction to that of an enormous, mute organ, shafted upwards by a tremendous upheaval in times primordial. The pitchstone columns stand on a base of fossiliferous oolite—remnant of a prostrate forest turned to stone. Whether any intrepid rock-climber, other than Professor Norman Collie, has scaled the Scuir's

38

southern face, which is perfectly vertical, I do not know. Collie's ascent, I believe, is the only one officially recorded. He reached his perilous objective a little to the west of the top. On the summit there are traces of an ancient fortification. In the appropriate Inventory of Monuments and Constructions,[1] the Scuir is described as being possibly the most impressive fort site in Scotland.

The precipices of the Scuir are not the only ones in Eigg providing tests of prowess. Cliffs for the adventurous, varying in height from a hundred to five hundred feet, extend for several miles, uninterrupted, in the north-east section of the island. These cliffs, set some little distance inland, define an old coastline. Experts report that in many places they are unscalable, but that, nevertheless, they offer to the surest of foot and the steadiest of head several routes by which they may be assailed.

The view of Eigg itself from its famous Scuir well merits the exertion entailed in ascending it. The summit, it might be added, is accessible from the north side without involving one in any peril. " There is no access to this Rock," writes Martin, " but by one passage, which makes it a natural fort." There, at the top, the same authority informs us, is a freshwater lake. One must conclude from this observation that Martin himself did not climb the Scuir, but recorded what he had been told. In point of fact, several lakes—several lochs and tarns—may be seen from it, dotted about the island's loftier regions, some of them lying deep and secluded in the hollows of the hills. I myself once counted from the summit of the Scuir no fewer than seven. A London correspondent, Donald Nicholas, who knows Eigg thoroughly, tells me that he has picked out as many as nine. Associated with at least two of these lochs are legends and traditions deeply rooted in the island's folklore.

Some of these lochs are fished by the Runcimans, the proprietors of Eigg. A boat-house stands by the edge of one of them. When descending north-westwards from the summit of the Scuir, toward Beinn Tighe, a distance of two miles, most of these lochs lie by one's track.

Below Beinn Tighe's summit is Loch Beinn Tighe, the largest sheet of fresh water on the island. The moorland between the Scuir and this loch, especially those parts of it where rock gives way to peaty vegetation, is inclined to be very boggy indeed, even during dry summers. Here springs and streams abound: here the heather reaches waist-high, often concealing deep pools, and stretches of streams where they run sinuously and silently. Here,

[1] Published by His Majesty's Stationery Office, Edinburgh, 1928.

springing up among the red mosses, one finds white heather and white heath in quantities sufficient to enable one to gather literally an armful in a few hours. Prominent among the moorland flowers are orchids of a heliotrope hue. And one day in late summer, when picking my way through these marshy acres, I was able to appease a little my hunger, among the clusters of wild strawberries largely screened from the view of frugivorous birds by the heather among which they throve. In the damp hollows everywhere around, waved great tufts of bog-cotton—the white, mystic *cannach* of Gaelic lore.

The Scuir, seen in daylight from the manse of Eigg, which it overshadows, and where I once spent a few days when exploring the island, resembles some primordial giant's castle. In the half-light of dawn or of dusk, its outline resembles that of an eerie monster. This aspect, I think, would depress me if I resided for any length of time in a part of the island where it predominated the scene. It had upon me an effect similar to that of Crogary Mor, in North Uist, after I had lived for some weeks in its shadow at Ahmhor. It became uncouth, and even repellent. Anyone sensitive to his environment might well experience this. The Scuir, one feels, dominates not merely the physical island of Eigg: it must needs dominate also, to some extent, those whose lives are spent in proximity to it. One can easily imagine how primitive man, overawed by such phenomena, attributed to them much that has survived in legend and folklore, in tradition and superstition.

As one walks over the island to Laig of the Singing Sands, and on toward Cleadale, the Scuir's aspect alters considerably.

.   .   .   .

Geologists come to Eigg to examine not merely its Scuir, but also its remarkable coast, and the many fine caves penetrating it. The coast-line is strewn with boulders and the talus from overhanging cliffs; and several of its caves are difficult of access except to those inured to scrambling among rocks and slippery seaweed, and accustomed to scaling when confronted with obstacles of inordinate size and precipitousness. On the south shore is a cave, the entrance to which is so imposing as to have entitled it to the name of the Cathedral Cave. A little farther on is the Pigeons' Cave, so called on account of the great number of rock-pigeons nesting or roosting on its lofty ledges. Parts of this cave's floor are covered with an accumulation of guano several feet deep.

Not far from the pier at Galmisdale, and in fact just below Galmisdale House, is the Cave of St. Francis, because of the following incident the most famous of Eigg's caves. In the sixteenth century (the actual year is supposed to have been 1577), the Mac-Leods of Skye, bent on vengeance for some wrong or indignity they had suffered at the hands of the MacDonalds of Eigg, set sail for the latter isle. Warning of their foes' approaching galleys had been given when they were still some distance off. The entire population of Eigg—some 395 men, women, and children, it is said—sought refuge in St. Francis's Cave, an enormous cavern which I explored some years ago. Though it penetrates to a depth of about 300 feet, its entrance is small, and usually so over-hung with ferns and drooping vegetation as to render its location difficult except to those who know precisely where to look for it. To enter, one must needs crawl on hands and knees.

When the MacLeods disembarked, they found on Eigg no human inhabitant. Without let or hindrance, they pillaged and sacked the homes of their MacDonald adversaries, who, in their haste to evade them, had been able to carry very little away with them to safety. In any case, nothing the least bulky could have been got through the cave's small entrance. How long the MacLeods took to their ravishing of Eigg, we do not know; and for this reason no one can say how long the MacDonalds remained ensconced in the cave. It is said that scarcely had the MacLeods quitted the island when the MacDonalds, anxious to breathe again the fresh air of heaven, sent forth from the cave a scout. This fellow's movement, unfortunately, was detected. The Skye galleys returned to renew their search. Footprints in a light fall of fresh snow instantly disclosed the MacDonalds' hiding-place.

To the enemies' demand that they should come out and sur-render, they paid no heed. The exasperated MacLeods, having loaded their vessels with all of value the isle could yield, were impatient to return to Skye with their booty. A final appeal to surrender having failed, they diverted from the entrance to the cave a waterfall spilling over it; and there, at the cave's mouth, they kindled a huge fire with heather, and possibly also with thatch from the roofs of the homes so recently ransacked. With unrelenting determination, they maintained this suffocating blaze until there remained in the cave no one alive.

Ever since that horrible occurrence, the cave has been known as the MacDonald, or the Clan Ranald, Cave. Sometimes it is called the MacLeod Cave, after those who thus destroyed the island's inhabitants. On Eigg, to-day, there resides only one family maintaining that its ancestors were there before the mas-sacre. Curiously enough, that family's name is MacLeod.

It may well have been in retaliation for what happened on

Eigg that the MacDonalds, a few years later, destroyed so many MacLeods by setting on fire their church at Trumpan, in Skye, while they were worshipping therein. However, this is a moot point, since authorities differ as to the date of the incident at Trumpan. Some say it took place *before* the MacDonalds perished in the Cave of St. Francis.

Many of the bones of the smothered MacDonalds were afterwards recovered from the cave, and interred in the old burying-ground at Kildonnan, a mile or two away, nearer the present-day church and what are now the ruins of the chapel of St. Donnan, Eigg's tutelar saint. The islanders have always held that by no means were all the bones of the victims retrieved, however. Falls of rock from the cave's roof in the intervening centuries, they declare, have now buried irretrievably many of them. One recalls that, when Sir Walter Scott visited the scene in 1814, he found the cave's floor strewn with bones and skulls as thickly as in any charnel-house he had ever seen. From the numerous specimens of mortality the cavern afforded, Scott carried off a skull as a souvenir. This the Highland boatmen regarded as an act of sacrilege; and to it they attributed the prolonged calm which, for some days thereafter, made progress at sea very slow.

Tradition has it that, somewhere in St. Francis's Cave, treasure in the form of gold lies buried—presumably the valuables brought to it by the MacDonalds.

The number I have given you as having perished in the cave is based on an account thought to have been compiled for King James VI by James Stewart of Appin, who died in 1595. This account, after mentioning that Eigg "will raise 60 men to the weiris", proceeds to relate that "there is mony coves under the earth in this ile, which the countrey folks uses as strengthis, hiding thame and thair gear therein". In March, 1577, we are told, the people of Eigg, along with "ane callit Angus John Mudzartsonne their captain", took refuge in one such cove. There the Mac-Leods "smorit the haill people thairin to the number of 395 personnes, men, wyfe, and bairnis".

Just beyond the cave's outer entrance runs a narrow, inner tunnel to the cave proper. Where this tunnel ends, the cave immediately expands. It requires little imagination to realise how easily those seeking refuge were stifled to death.

This cave is situated quite close to the Cathedral Cave, and to the point where a wooden stile assists one over the fence restraining the islanders' cattle and sheep from falling over the precipitous face of the adjacent cliffs. At this spot, two pathways threading through grass and, in summer and autumn, through masses of wild flowers, diverge in opposite directions toward the shore. The entrance to the Cathedral Cave may be seen from the stile, but not that of St. Francis's. The boggy patch in front of the latter is rank in summer with irises, kingcups, and Scots thistles, springing from a floor of yellow mosses. When I visited the scene a few years ago, a small stream trickled seaward down the face of the rock near at hand. A casual survey indicated that it might well have been the stream diverted from its original course by the bloodthirsty MacLeods, so as to allow of the fire's being kindled at the mouth of the cave, over which it formerly had spilled. Oozing from the cliffs above, and dripping from saturated ferns and mosses clinging to the rock-face, was a gentle drip of water which did actually fall in front of the cave's entrance, sustaining amply the irises clustered there.

I penetrated the cave to its inmost wall, whence the merest peep of daylight was visible, signifying the direction in which lay the entrance. As I emerged, I found one of the natives walking by. In the course of conversation with him, I discovered him to be the keeper in charge of the great number of hand-reared pheasants impounded nearby. He told me that he derived much delight from flinging into St. Francis's Cave from time to time—" for devilment's sake ", as he put it—the bone of some domesticated animal. Every bone thus deposited, he added, had been carried away by summer visitors to Eigg, in the belief that they were of the anatomy of the suffocated MacDonalds!

. . . .

Eigg had known an earlier massacre. Tradition says that, in the spring of 617, St. Donnan, the island's patron-saint, having arrived with fifty or sixty monks, sought to establish a mission. Who St. Donnan was, no one can say. He is believed to have been a young disciple of Columba. One imagines that it is he who also finds commemoration in Eilean Donan, in the MacRae Country of Kintail, as well as in the two or three Kildonans to be found elsewhere in Scotland. Be this as it may, the saint and his brethren are said to have been slaughtered on Eigg by Norse rovers. There is a local tradition, however, that they came to grief at the hands of a wrathful woman known as the Queen of the Pirates, whom their Christianising activities had offended. It may be apposite to add that in Martin's time the natives, when at sea, would not have dared to allude to their island as Eigg: they always spoke of it by a Gaelic name denoting Isle of the Big Women. The memory of these supposed amazonian inhabitants survives in *Loch nam Ban Mora*, Loch of the Big Women. In this loch is situated an islet upon which can be traced some very ancient ruins suggesting its use as a lake-dwelling. On this islet, according to local tradition, resided one or two of the Big Women.

The memory of St. Donnan is perpetuated in Eigg in the name, Kildonnan, in the ruined chapel there, and also in St. Donnan's Well, situated over at the township of Cleadale, and once held in great veneration by the natives, so many of whom are Roman Catholics.

Doubtless, it is to the bones of this saint and his slain companions that Martin refers where he writes that, thirty yards from the church, " there is a sepulchral urn under ground; it is a big stone hewn to the bottom, about four feet deep, and the diameter of it is about the same breadth; I caused them to dig the ground above it, and we found a flat thin stone covering the urn: it was almost full of human bones, but no heads among them, and they were fair and dry. I enquired of the natives what was become of the heads, and they could not tell; but one of them said, perhaps their heads had been cut off with a two-handed sword, and taken away by the enemy."

The ruins of St. Donnan's, at Kildonnan, are thought to be that of a church of post-Reformation origin. Indeed, it is believed to have been erected by John of Moidart, Captain of Clan Ranald, during the latter half of the sixteenth century. The building, oblong in plan, was of stone and lime and local rubble. The ruins measure 51 feet from east to west, and 18 feet within the walls, which are 3 feet 3 inches thick. At the eastern end of the side wall is a small, reconstructed, lintelled window. In the north wall occurs a tomb recess with a moulded archivolt of freestone. At the back of the recess are two freestone panels. The upper bears the date, 1641, with the initials, D R, joined by a Y-shaped ligature. The lower panel is armorial. Centred in the upper part of it is an eagle flanked on the dexter side by a hand holding a wheel cross. A lion rampant occurs on the sinister side. A galley occupies the lower dexter, and a triple-turreted castle the sinister corner. The church is utilised as a place of burial, some of the more recent graves being provided with cover-slabs and headstones removed from the sites of earlier burials.

On the west coast of Eigg, between the small township of Laig and the large township of Cleadale, where most of the island's inhabitants reside, is that splendid, semi-circular sweep of white

sand fringing the beautiful Bay of Laig. Here we find yet
another of Eigg's phenomena—its Singing, or Musical, Sands.
These sands creak and hum weirdly underfoot when trodden
upon. They are silent, however, when damp, or just after the
tide has receded from them. A shower of rain silences them at
once; and, since showers are often precipitated here from clouds
trailing their tresses over the peaks of Rum, so close at hand, one
may have to tarry an hour or two until sun and wind have
dried the damp out of their surface. A hot, calm day in summer,
with the tide well out, is the best time to hear them as one walks
upon them. Naturally, they are scarcely audible when breakers
are rolling noisily upon Laig Bay, before a westerly wind.

The musicality of the Singing Sands of Eigg has been somewhat exaggerated, of course, by various descriptive writers. Only
an access of poetic licence could justify the simile I read somewhere recently about them, where it was said that they emitted
a sound like an aeolian harp!

From time to time geologists arrive at Laig Bay to take away
with them a quantity of its sand for scientific examination. J. A.
Harvie-Brown and his companions, having visited the cliffy
haunts of the *fachachs*, or shearwaters, and duly applied the
geological hammer to the shoreland rocks, in order to obtain
specimens of pitchstone from a vein exposed near the Cave of
St. Francis, carried off a biscuit-tinful of singing sand—" tourist-
like ", as Harvie-Brown himself says.

The only other sounding sands, I believe, are those at Jabel
Nakous, three miles south of the Gulf of Suez, and at Reg-Rawan,
forty miles north of Cabul. Hugh Miller, writing of those in
Eigg, says they are composed of disintegrate sandstone of the
oolite period, and belong to the same era as those at Jabel Nakous.

. . . .

Vegetation is dense in the more favoured parts of Eigg. The
dark under the fir plantation at Galmisdale, the only woodland
on the island, would surprise anyone familiar with the treelessness
of the Hebrides, or of the Northern Isles. Over at Laig, in summer and autumn, the cart-track leading down to the shore is
itself smothered in the wild flowers thriving there in such profusion.

In bygone days, Laig was the seat of the island's MacDonald
lairds. The present laird's residence—the Lodge, as it is called—
is at Galmisdale, set amid the woodland just referred to, and less
than half a mile from the pier. This building, until 1840, was the
island's inn. That year, Alan MacLeod, its last proprietor, gave

up business. Eigg has been without licensed premises ever since. This is sometimes cited as the explanation for the steady decline in the island's population. It does not explain, however, how islands with licensed premises also show this decline.

Eigg was repopulated after the extermination of its inhabitants at the hands of the unrelenting MacLeods. To-day, with roughly 95 persons residing there, it is the most populous of the sparsely peopled Small Isles, the total population of which was 216 in 1951, showing a fall of 66 in the last twenty years. In 1795 Eigg alone carried a population of 400. The eviction of fourteen families from the Grulin district, about the middle of the nineteenth century, reduced this figure considerably. Grulin village at that time was included in territory belonging to the Laig estate which, it is said, a Border farmer bought in 1853, on the understanding that these families might be removed. They are believed to have emigrated to Nova Scotia. A family living at Cleadale treasures to this day the old spinningwheel from which its great-grandmother refused to be parted when about to board the emigrant ship at that time. Since the authorities would not let her take the spinningwheel with her, both she and the wheel remained behind.

. . . .

Such population as Eigg supports to-day is divided between Galmisdale, on the east, and Cleadale, in the north-west. Between the two lie the island's post-office and shop. Roughly midway between these two centres, moreover, is the island school, attended at the time of writing by fourteen 'scholars' conveyed hither each morning by the local carrier's motor-truck, and likewise transported home, each afternoon, along the track serving admirably the purpose of a road. This track is, in fact, the island's highway. It runs from Grulin, in the south-west, round by Galmisdale, and then through the island's main valley to Cleadale, in the north-west.

One of the most fascinating walks in Eigg is from Galmisdale, following this track through heather and bracken and pools, and over burns, to the shepherd's cot at Grulin, now the sole habitation in a part of the island once so populous. Grulin overlooks the Isle of Muck and Ardnamurchan Point. Faintly visible beyond is Coll. Up the steep hillside behind the shepherd's cot one can scramble to the gullies admitting the level-headed to the ridge terminating in the Scuir. The going is indeed steep, and the foothold uncertain. Nevertheless, the rocks hereabouts are easy on the soles, since they maintain a homogeneity making them

safe to tread upon, without their ever depriving one of the aware-
ness of the aeons since they were poured out here, in molten
form. One derives a like sense of timelessness from the steep cliffs
overhanging the crofts about Cleadale. Though on a scale so
much smaller, they are reminiscent of the Quirang, in Skye, and
of the terraced rock formation, so conspicuous in the northern
parts of that island.

At Cleadale are the chapel and the priest's house, since
approximately half the population of Eigg, as of Canna, is
Roman Catholic. This is explained through the adherence of
the Clan Ranald chiefs in olden times to the Old Faith. To this
day, most of the vast territories once owned by Clan Ranald have
remained preponderantly Catholic. Morar and Moidart, the
Small Isles, South Uist, Benbecula, and so on, all formed part of
Clan Ranald's Country. This accounted for the inhabitants'
allegiance to the Jacobite cause in the eighteenth century. To-
day it accounts for the survival among their descendants of so
many traditions concerning Prince Charlie and his followers.
Bishop Forbes, in *The Lyon in Mourning,* gives an account of
the kidnapping, by the notorious Captain Ferguson of the sloop,
Furnace, in July, 1746, of the men of Eigg. The lists of Jacobite
prisoners of 'The Forty-five' disclose the names of twenty-five
belonging to this island.

The memory of Eigg's long and proud association with the
Clan Ranald is perpetuated in some of its place-names. Roughly
half a mile from the pier at present in use at Galmisdale is the
old landing-place frequented in the time of the Clan Ranald, and
now used but seldom. The natives still call it Clan Ranald's
pier. At the base of Sgùrr Sgaileach, situated at the very north
of the island, are several caves, one of which goes by the Gaelic
name of the *Uamh Mhic 'ic Ailein nan Eilean,* Cave of the Son of
the Son of Alan of the Isles—the patronymic of the great Clan
Ranald. Here, in company with that resolute native of Eigg,
John Roy MacLellan, young Clan Ranald, son of the old chief,
is said to have spent a night, not too securely, on his return to
Eigg from the Jacobite rout at Culloden. The story goes that
the boulder in this cave, upon which young Clan Ranald rested
his weary head, was not affording him as much comfort as he
desired in the matter of a pillow. "How fond you are of your
ease! " John Roy is said to have replied to Clan Ranald's request
that he might procure for him a divot instead. "Will not a
stone be good enough for the head you may be losing before
morning? "

Hugh MacKinnon, a native of the island, descendant of Donald

47

MacQuarrie, Eigg's famous piper, relates the tradition that John Roy MacLellan, when on his way south to Edinburgh to draw a small pension granted him by the exiled Stuarts, got into conversation, while passing through Perthshire, with a man who had been 'out' in 'The Forty-five', but on the Hanoverian side. Receiving at the Battle of Falkirk a severe slash from a Highland claymore, he explained that he had been left for dead on the field. An unknown Highlander, he added, had helped him into Falkirk, and had thus saved his life. The Highlander turned out to have been Donald Roy MacLellan.

.   .   .   .

With the exception of the children too young to go to school, who speak and understand the Gaelic language only, the natives of Eigg are bi-lingual. Dr. Martha Devon, who for many years was the island's medical officer, tells us that the womenfolk are better educated and more progressive than the menfolk. This she attributes to so many of the former having been 'away' when young—that is to say, in service—in good situations in Glasgow and elsewhere. She was delighted with the cleanliness of their cottages. Never was there any dirtiness, she declares, and therefore never any need to scold or shame her patients into the use of soap and water, though the housewife often had to carry both a goodly way home.

The existence on Eigg of the majority of the population of the Small Isles explains why the doctor and the parish minister reside there. Dr. Devon attributed the parish's progressive outlook to the fact that, while she officiated there, women held the posts of parish clerk, inspector of poor, registrar, and parish doctor!

The islanders, incidentally, are most happy in their landlords, the Runcimans, who are exceedingly popular.

.   .   .   .

Eigg is rich in legendary and traditionary lore. It would indeed be remiss not to mention, in this connection, the island's most illustrious native—one who has done so much in our own day to preserve the old lore and folk-music, not only of Eigg, but also of Celtic Scotland as a whole. I refer to him whose name will be appearing frequently throughout the ensuing pages of this volume—the Rev. Dr. Kenneth MacLeod, D.D., now living in retirement in Edinburgh. His father was schoolmaster in Eigg many years ago.

It is Kenneth himself who tells of the faeries of his native isle, of the terrifying water-horse in the tarn known as Lochan Nighinn Dughaill, of the apparition seen at the spot where a stream is spanned by a plank upon which no islander dare place foot after dark, and of the ominous *bean-nighe*—the washer of the death-shrouds in the Glen Charadale burn.

Others relate the story of Eigg's monster, slain by Alan Mac-Donald, one of the last of his race to own the Laig property. Alan, a heavy drinker, was a man of great physical strength. They say in Eigg that he killed himself by refusing to desist from drinking neat whisky after a forced ride from Arisaig to Leith, whither he had gone to prevent his sister's sailing for India with a husband who ill-treated her.

One night, when on his way home from the inn at Galmisdale, he encountered, at the spot where now stands the island's post-office, the mighty monster. After a fierce struggle in the dark, he succeeded in killing it. Arriving home in the small hours, exhausted and bloodstained, he explained to the household how, at last, he had freed the island of its nocturnal terror. Daylight revealed that Alan had despatched his own prize bull!

CHAPTER IV

CANNA

THREE miles north-west of Rum, and twelve south-west of the nearest point of Skye, lies Clan Ranald's Isle of Canna, third of the Small Isles in order of size. Together with much the lesser Isle of Sanday, which almost joins it at its south-eastern end, it has an area of about 2,500 acres. Roughly a sixth of this is arable: the rest, for the most part, consists of green, hilly pastures supporting cattle reputed to be of a better quality than can be found on any of the neighbouring isles. From east to west, Canna measures $4\frac{1}{2}$ miles: nowhere from north to south does its breadth exceed a mile by more than a couple of hundred yards Sanday, on the other hand, is only a mile and a half long, while its greatest breadth is three-quarters of a mile.

With the exception of Carn a' Ghaill, Canna's highest point, rising to 690 feet near the north coast, and of Compass Hill, at its eastern extremity, most of its hills are about 400 feet high. Compass Hill, though only 458 feet, is much the better known, as its name might suggest. The deposits of iron in the basaltic rock of which it is composed deflect the magnetic needle of vessels sailing in proximity to it—a fact recognised ever since these waters have been navigated by compass. "There is a high hill in the north end," wrote Martin, more than two and a half centuries ago, "which disorders the needle in the compass: I laid the compass on the stony ground near it, and the needle went often round with great swiftness, and instead of settling towards the north, as usual, it settled here due east." Some years ago, when exploring Canna, I derived diversion from submitting my own pocket compass to the test when cruising about its harbour, and when actually climbing Compass Hill. And one memorable summer's evening, when Robert and Alan, sons of the late Mr. Thom, penultimate proprietor of Canna, took me in their motor-boat round the sea-cliffs below this eminence, I was able to observe for myself just how much magnetic disturbance it creates for those sailing within range of its influence. Here the cliffs, in a succession of terraces, fall sheer to the sea.

Browsing upon the grassy patches of each terrace, as if pur-

posely arranged in tiers for spectacular effect, were many of
Canna's mountain goats, long since left to their own inclinations.
I counted with ease about sixty of them. These creatures, I was
soon to learn, were encouraged to occupy the more precipitous
of the island's cliffs, since they kept away from them sheep less
able to look after themselves. The goats easily retain mastery
of the dangerous clefts and ledges, thereby reducing the number
of casualties among the many sheep pastured on Canna's uplands. About the innumerable caves, crevices, and rock buttresses of the coast-line, close to which we were able to cruise
owing to the absence of any swell, cormorants stood marshalled
in long, black rows. The still, shadowy sea around us was alive
with puffins—adult birds and their babies. Occasionally, a seal,
when coming up to breathe, showed his head within a foot or two
of our boat. Between us and the South Uist mountains, seen on
the sunset horizon, small fishing-boats were in process of drawing
their draughts of fishes. That the nets were full of herrings was
obvious from the cloud of gulls hovering about these boats, their
screaming audible even at our distance from them. The fineness
of the evening tempted us to steer out to those fishing-grounds.
On arrival there, we circulated the boats as they ladled hundreds
of thousands of live, silvery herrings out of the nets, to pour them
into each vessel's innards, preparatory to sailing away to the
morning's fish-mart at Mallaig.

The sheltered harbour of Canna, protected from winds and
high seas by the position of the satellite isle of Sanday, has been
used for centuries by vessels overtaken by tempests when in
this locality. Small coasting vessels, such as the Clyde puffers,
frequently anchor there. Yet, the channel offering admittance to
this safe harbour is a tricky one. The reefs running out at the
south side of the entrance are avoided by steering close to the
north horn of the bay, where one finds the island's pier—the only
pier in the Small Isles parish alongside which the mail-boat can
lie. The water here is not very deep. I have visited Canna at a
time when the tide was so low as to have necessitated the vessel's
cruising some little distance offshore, while passengers and cargo
were transferred to the pier by ferryboat.

To the west of the pier, and of that part of the harbour offering accommodation for ships of moderate draft, there stretches,
between Canna and Sanday, a considerable area of tidal sand.
This widens to conform with the shape of the coast-line on either
side, and then contracts to a channel so narrow as to admit the

services of a short bridge linking with Canna the north-west corner of Sanday. A track from the bridge runs round the bay of Sanday to the dwellings fringing it, and to the Roman Catholic Church beyond. In the season of the spring tides, one can wade with ease between these islands.

In the days before ships were fitted with the many modern aids to navigation, mariners and fishermen in these waters usually liked to know their position in relation to Canna's harbour, so that, in the event of sudden storm, they might find timely refuge therein. This led to the frequent representations made to various public authorities, such as the Commissioners of Northern Light-houses, for the better lighting of the fairway. The Canna people used to relate harrowing stories of disaster befalling those unable to avoid the reefs, when seeking the harbour's navigable entrance; and it was claimed that something should be done to improve matters, not merely for the safety of Canna's own seamen, but also for those strangers who might be glad of its security. Weight was lent to the suggestion when, about 1895, no fewer than fifty-seven fishing-boats, operating in the Minch off Barra and South Uist, were irresistibly blown eastwards from the fishing-grounds by a storm, and found haven here.

Canna, along its southern slopes and terraces, is rich and fertile. Those portions under cultivation yield a harvest abundant and, at times, surprisingly early. Much was done to improve Canna's agriculture during the nineteenth and twentieth centuries. By mid-June early potatoes, raised not in a garden, but in the open fields, are often ready. A week or so later, strawberries may be gathered among the open beds in one or other of the two gardens near the proprietor's residence.

In 1827 this old Clan Ranald property was sold by Reginald George Clan Ranald to a certain Donald MacNeil, who did a lot for its amenities. He was succeeded by his natural son, another Donald MacNeil. The latter sold Canna in 1882 to Robert Thom, grandfather of Robert and Alan, who so felicitously took me a-sea in their motor-boat. During the Thoms' proprietorship, the island flourished. Good husbandry was matched with good gardening. I shall never forget the fruit I saw, and indeed enjoyed, in their gardens. To one of these, during my sojourn on the island, the late Mr. Thom, aware of my being a vegetarian, gave me free access—gave me 'the run of my teeth', as the saying is. I spent a good deal of time among the currant-bushes and raspberry-canes, among the strawberry-beds and gooseberry-bushes; and, when leaving the island for Mallaig, my hospitable host insisted upon my taking away with me a huge

ABOVE: *Ruins of Breachacha Castle, Coll*
BELOW: *The Post Office, Lismore*

basket loaded with fruit and vegetables. Oh! the great, golden gooseberries of Canna! Never in my life have I seen gooseberries quite like them, quite so large, quite so luscious—not even at Shearn's, in Tottenham Court Road, which I visit at least once a week. Just fancy picking one's own strawberries in the Hebrides, and in the open, before midsummer's day! The Thoms, by the way, used to encourage in the crofters on Canna a sense of orderliness and of colour by presenting prizes each year for the best-kept cottage gardens.

Mr. Thom told me about his island many a thing, one of the most remarkable of which I now relate. In September, 1892, the little daughter of Canna's blacksmith, when collecting by the shore, near her home, driftwood for fuel, picked up, in a small bay, a piece of wood, out of which had been carved, obviously with a pocket-knife, the inscription, "Lachlan Campbell, Bilbao, March 23, 1892". She instantly brought it home to her mother, who became greatly perturbed. Lachlan Campbell was the name of a son of hers: Lachlan was a boiler-maker in Spain. She was certain that the child's find, so close at hand, was a portent of distressing news. The Thoms did their best to allay her fears, adding that she should await an explanation. She immediately wrote to her son, telling him of his little sister's find, yet never believing that her letter could be answered by him. Some weeks later, she was relieved to hear from him, and to learn of his astonishment that this piece of wood, on which he had idly carved his name and had thrown into the sea when holidaying at Bilbao, should have been picked up six months later by his own sister, within a couple of hundred yards of their home in Canna.

. . . .

Canna and Sanday are more Roman Catholic than Protestant; and it would appear, from the perusal of the various accounts of these islands, that the two religions have existed here, side by side, in a greater measure of amity than in most rural places where they occur in the same juxtaposition. Writing of Canna in 1769, Thomas Pennant remarks that, though it had 220 inhabitants, all of whom were Roman Catholics except four families, there was neither church nor manse. Nor was there a school. However, the island *did* have a catechist. He was paid nine pounds a year from the royal bounty. "The minister and the popish priest reside in Eigg; but, by reason of the turbulent seas that divide these isles, are very seldom able to attend their flocks. I admire the moderation of their congregations, who attend the preaching of either indifferently, as they happen to arrive."

E

Bell-shrine from Kilmichael-Glassary,
believed to be St. Moluag's

That something of the same amity existed in the Small Isles a century later is shown by Sir Archibald Geikie's recording that, although half the population of Eigg was still Catholic, and the other half divided between the Established and Free Churches, the three clergymen—one Catholic and two Protestant—were excellent friends, and were in the habit of having pleasant evenings together, talking over their toddy.

The Roman Catholic Church on Sanday, with its lofty tower, forms a conspicuous landmark at the entrance to Canna's harbour. Situated in a meadowy place not far from the pier on Canna itself is the Protestant Church, a unit of the Church of Scotland. It was built by the Thoms in 1914. Its architect was the late MacGregor Chalmers. When its foundations were being excavated in 1913, there was found a bronze Viking pin more than a thousand years old. This Church, including the round belfry tower attached to it, is of native stone. The roof, too, is of stone; but, as this stone was found not to be impervious to the rains of the Hebridean winter, it became necessary to cement over the roof's outer side. Prior to this church's erection, on the occasions when the parish minister came over from Eigg to attend to the spiritual needs of his Presbyterian flock on Canna and Sanday, the Thoms placed at his disposal, for purposes of public worship, their conservatory. The church is dignified, and (if one may add, without any suspicion of bigotry) more in harmony with its rugged surroundings than is St. Edward's R.C. place of worship at Sanday, on the opposite side of the harbour. The latter was erected privately by the late Marquis of Bute for the worship of the majority of the inhabitants, who still adhere to the R.C. persuasion.

One evening of lengthening twilight, in lingering home by the Protestant Church, with its round tower, its cluster of ivy and hedge of fuchsia and veronica, I realized how seemly an edifice it was, how in keeping with the Isles. Cast on the still tide was every line of the white house down by the shore—the house which, as the Canna folks tell, once belonged to the Clan Ranald. As I stood by the tide's edge, contemplating its reflection, an eider duck with a brood of wee chicks cruised in and out among the shadowy pools between the patches of seawrack again spreading themselves out on the rocks with the falling tide.

.   .   .   .

Canna is not without archæological remains. Of special interest are those situated at a very exposed part of the precipitous south coast, about two miles west of the bridge connecting Sanday with Canna. They are believed to have been a monastery, or, as seems more probable, a nunnery. Authorities differ as to which. Some contend that it was a Celtic monastic settlement of the cashel type. However, the name given to this day to the cliff beneath it—*Sgòr nam Ban Naomha*, Cliff of the Holy Women —would suggest the site's association with nuns rather than with monks. The site is particularly remote. It is accessible from the sea only in calm weather. From the landward it is cut off by basaltic escarpments. Such remains as are to be seen, despite the bracken concealing so much of them, consist of an enclosure forty yards in diameter, formed by a drystone wall five feet thick. The entrance is on the south or seaward side. Four structures, dry-stone throughout, are built against the outer wall, within the enclosure.

At a spot on the machar-land below the cliffs at Rudha Lan-ganinnis, on Canna's north coast, is a setting of stones forming, as it were, the kerb of a burial cairn similar to that excavated at Arran some years ago to reveal, among other relics, incinerated bones, a number of boat rivets, a ninth-century coin, and a styca of Wigmund (A.D. 831-854), Archbishop of York. Another such cairn excavated in Colonsay yielded remains both of human and of horse origin, boat rivets, clinker nails, weapons, and three stycas.

Of this particular burial cairn in Canna, only the kerb remains, the actual chamber having been despoiled. A group of three such cairns lies in the valley due south of Rudha Langaninnis. These burial cairns, three of which have been identified on Sanday, are Viking. Roughly oval in shape, they vary in height from 10 to 23 feet, and in breadth from 8 to 17 feet. The major axis runs approximately north-east and south-west.

When sailing out into the Minch with the Thoms one evening, the site of that marked by the kerb was pointed out to me; and I was informed of the local tradition that at this spot a Viking king lies buried, with a pot of gold at his feet. Every attempt to retrieve the gold, however, has been interrupted by the oncoming of a violent thunderstorm instilling such fear into the seekers as to result in the abandonment of their quest.

.   .   .   .

At the spot appropriately called A' Chill is the site of St. Columba's Chapel, marked by a finely-sculptured, free-standing sandstone cross of an unusual type, erected in the graveyard there, in a valley rather less than a quarter of a mile north of Canna's post-office. This cross is somewhat mutilated. It lacks its top and a side arm. Its present height is 6 feet 5 inches. When complete, its width across the arms was 4 feet 4. Each face and side is sculptured. On the front, which looks east, the sculptures are mainly in high relief. Then, close to the west boundary, within this graveyard at A' Chill, is a slab of micaceous schist covering a modern grave, and sculptured with a heterogeneous assemblage of objects.

Canna also has a standing-stone or two. One is to be found at A' Chill. Another, of basalt, is seen within the remains of an enclosure on a grassy terrace beneath the cliffs, three-quarters of a mile north-east of Garrisdale Point, Canna's westernmost reach.

Earth-houses are also to be found. Two of them lie exposed just below the summit of a grassy knowe on the southern slope of Beinn Tighe, midway between the island's eastern and western extremities. It is thought that others, not yet excavated, may occur in the same locality.

. . . .

What is perhaps the most spectacular of Canna's ancient monuments has still to be mentioned. A quarter of a mile east of the island's pier is the Coroghon Mòr, a stack of conglomerate rising on three sides above the sea, to a height of eighty feet. A narrow neck, twenty-five feet above the shore, links the stack with the land. Upward along this neck runs a narrower and dangerous track affording the nimblest and the levellest of head ascent to the ancient forework of two storeys, built of stone and lime, and roughly rectangular in shape, stuck on at a lofty corner of the stack, as it were, like the eyrie of some giant bird. Stout oak forms the entrance lintel, a little to the right of which there occurs, in the stone-work, an aperture resembling a gun loop.

A late sixteenth-century account of the Isles of Scotland contains no reference whatsoever to a structure on the Coroghon Mòr; but it does mention the "heich crag callit Corignan" as having been a place of refuge. This would seem to justify the assumption that the ruin now clinging to the stack is that of a stronghold built at a date subsequent to the end of the sixteenth century.

On one occasion I climbed the precipitous face of the Coroghon Mòr, anxious to examine this ancient structure from within, as well as from without. The ascent, though dangerous, was comparatively easy—until the last step, which only a person with exceptionally long limbs could take with confidence. As I haven't such limbs, I held on with my fingernails to the rough corners of the stones at the base of the outer wall, trusting that, since they had withstood the denuding agencies of two centuries and more, they might not feel inclined to give way under the force I now exerted upon them. One apartment of this truly remarkable eyrie seemed quite intact, except that the roof was wanting; and I could not but conjecture the age of the two short beams of oak forming the lintel of the entrance. Both beams were visible from within the building, and also from the shore below. Whoever raised these walls so airily, and upon a base so precarious, must indeed have been intrepid cragsmen!

In this inaccessible place, according to one tradition in Canna, a Clan Ranald chief—one of the Lords of the Isles—confined his wife in a fit of jealousy. This tradition inspired in Sir Walter Scott the lines:

> *Signal of Ronald's high command,*
> *A beacon gleamed o'er sea and land*
> *From Canna's tower that, steep and grey,*
> *Like falcon-nest o'erhangs the bay.*
> *Seek not the giddy crag to climb*
> *To view the turret scathed by time:*
> *It is a task of doubt and fear*
> *To aught but goat or mountain deer.*
>
> .   .   .   .   .   .
>
> *Stern was her lord's suspicious mind,*
> *Who in so rude a jail confined*
> *So soft and fair a thrall!*
> *And oft when moon on ocean slept,*
> *That lovely lady sat and wept*
> *Upon the castle wall;*
> *And turned her eyes to southern climes,*
> *And thought, perchance, of happier times,*
> *And touched her lute by fits, and sung*
> *Wild ditties in her native tongue.*

The ghost of the unfortunate lady, they say, may still be seen at times, high up among the ruins of her prison.

According to another tradition current in the island, the laird, "two hundred years ago, anyhow", had a beautiful daughter—his heiress—with whom Iain Ban Og (Young Fair John), one of the MacLeods of Skye, fell in love, when on a visit to Canna. She, likewise, fell for Iain, who was soon interviewing her father, pressing his suit with great fervour. The laird remained obdurate in his objection to his daughter's marriage, even after Iain had assured him that he could maintain her in a position in keeping with her station—indeed, even after he had offered to bring to him the heads of any twenty of his enemies he might like to name! However, young MacLeod swore that, somehow or other, he would abduct her, even though the accomplishment of this took him the rest of his life. Hearing this, the laird decided to incarcerate his daughter where he hoped the most intrepid man from Skye could not reach her. So he employed masons to erect loftily on the Coroghon Mòr a chamber for her reception. One dark night she was escorted there, together with a supply of provisions such as might last her for a considerable time. The key to the door of this prison the laird himself retained, never allowing it out of his own personal possession.

In course of time, Iain Ban Og MacLeod arrived in Canna with a band of fearless followers. Unable to find, anywhere, his heart's desire, he was told by the inhabitants that she had been sent away, no one knew whither. In retreating to his boat, he warned the islanders that, before long, he and his clansmen would be back to avenge himself for what the laird had done. An old woman, hearing this declaration of his, and fearing its consequences for herself and her household, whispered advice to Iain in the Gaelic. "Travel to north," she said; "and stand on the highest hillock. Look to south, and you will see something."

Accordingly, Iain and his followers embarked. Carrying out the old woman's directions, he soon saw the maiden sunning herself on the summit of the Coroghon Mòr, above the prison her heartless father had built for her. That night Iain sailed for the stack. Calling up to its lone occupant in the dark, he told her that he had a boat in readiness for her, if only she could get down from her impregnable keep. Characteristic of the resourcefulness of maidens in similar plight, as related in our story-books, she managed to pin together her blankets with pieces of wood thrust through their ends. Down from her prison she descended to her lover's embrace. By daybreak, they say, she was in Skye, well out of her father's reach. And there she lived happily ever after.

.   .   .   .

In conclusion, let me relate an incident connected with Canna, showing the Highlander's dire dislike of the idea that any part of him should be buried elsewhere than in the family grave, where he himself expects to lie one day. It was told me about 1930 by the late Mr. Robert Thom, who knew well the native it concerned. He was found dead by the shore in Canna sometime during the nineteen-twenties. I see that Sir Archibald Geikie gives a somewhat similar version in one of his books.[1]

While masons were engaged in building on Canna a high wall, composed of large boulders and blocks of basalt lying abundantly to hand, part of the structure collapsed, and fell on one of them, crushing his leg. His fellow-masons, on extricating him, realised the seriousness of his injury. Since there was no doctor nearer than Arisaig, they carried him to a boat; and two of them set out with him for Arisaig. On arrival there, they discovered the doctor was away from home, and was not expected back for some days. As the injured man's condition was urgent, they proceeded forthwith to Tobermory. There, thirty-six hours after the accident, he received surgical attention: the crushed limb was amputated.

A few weeks later, the patient was well enough to return to Canna. The two masons who had transported him, first to Arisaig, and then to Tobermory, turned up to bear him home across the sea. When they had carried him down to the pier at Tobermory and got him aboard their boat again, he exclaimed in great perturbation, " But where's my leg? "

" Your leg's in the kirkyard, to be sure! " they told him.

" Oh! but I must be taking my leg home to Canna! "

" Man, but I'm no' seeing how that can be possible now," one of them replied. " Your leg's been buried in the kirkyard for a fortnight anyway."

" Well, now," said the fellow bereft of his limb, " I'll no' move an inch till I get my leg back! No' an inch! Do you think that I'm going to be searching about on the Last Day for my leg? "

In the end it became necessary to exhume the decomposing limb, though the boatmen declined to have it with them in the boat. Eventually, a compromise was reached. A second boat was procured for the conveyance of the amputated leg. The boat was towed astern, at an agreed distance of not less than ten yards, all the way to Canna. There, with solemnity, accompanied with the usual ' honours ', the leg was re-interred.

[1] *Scottish Reminiscences* (1904).

Chapter V

MUCK

SMALLEST and most southerly of the four islands comprising the Parish of the Small Isles is Muck, an isle two miles long, and having an area of 1,586 acres. It lies about five miles to the northward of the Argyllshire peninsula of Ardnamurchan, and but half that distance in a south-westerly direction from Eigg, second largest of the group. Its name is derived from the Gaelic, *muc*, a pig. The island has been so called since ancient days, probably on account of its shape, rather than because of the presence upon it of pigs—creatures from which the Highlanders have long shown a peculiar aversion. They eat them all the same, when purveyed by others.

Buchanan refers to Muck as *Insula Porcorum* (Pigs' Island). Roughly half a century later (*circa* 1549), Donald Monro, High Dean of the Isles, was recording how " verey fertill and fruitfull of cornes and grassing for all store " was this island, and how " verey guid for fishing ". But the Dean would appear to have got his toponomy slightly confused, having mistakenly given to it the Gaelic name of its richly pastured satellite, *Eilean nan Each*, the Horses' Isle, " an ile guid for horse and uther store ", to which he already has alluded a few lines earlier. There is no doubt, however, to which isle he was referring, since the pertinent paragraph is headed with its English name—to wit, " Swynes Ile ".

Martin Martin, writing half a century later than the Dean, also remarks upon Muck's excellence in corn and grass, but makes no mention of swine in connection with it. Then, as in the Dean's time, this isle pertained to the Bishop of the Isles. Its name occasioned Johnson and Boswell mild diversion during their Hebridean tour in 1773. Commenting on the Scottish custom of addressing gentlemen territorially (a custom still so prevalent in Scotland, even where it signifies possession of no more than a couple of acres, and perhaps a handsome mortgage), the laird of Muck, deeming the name too coarse a one to be applied to his island, thought it even more so when used to denote himself. He therefore liked to be addressed as ' Isle of Muck '.

60

Ruins of Castle Coeffin, Isle of Lismore
ABOVE: *The Parish Church, Lismore*
BELOW: *Port Ellen, Isle of Islay*

It was somewhat droll, Boswell remarks, to hear him called by this fuller title. Muck, by itself, he adds, would have sounded ill.

The laird at this time retained half the island for his own use: the other half, according to the same authority, was occupied by seven score persons. The tenants paid their rents to the laird in corn. Just what quantity this meant, the travellers "could not easily inquire". The year before their visit, there had been something of a smallpox scare—the sort of nonsense we indulge in to this very day. So the laird had about eighty of the inhabitants—most of them children—inoculated, at half a crown a head, having brought a surgeon over to the island to perform this dangerous and superstitious rite.

Though Muck then supported a population so large in proportion to its size, and was thus cited as an example of an isle exceptionally fertile, it could hardly have been self-sufficing, except at a low standard of subsistence. Six times a year, the laird requisitioned the services of a tailor from the mainland; while from the neighbouring island of Eigg a good blacksmith was brought over when required. If the population then were actually seven score (incidentally, 160 is the figure Dr. Johnson gives), it must have increased considerably during the next thirteen years, assuming one can accept as accurate the number supplied by Bishop Knox at the time of his tour of the Highlands and Islands. "Muck," wrote the Bishop about 1786, "belongs to Donald MacLean, Esq., is nearly two miles in length, and one in width. It is mostly arable, and exports some barley, oats, potatoes, and cattle. The number of people amounts to 253, who pay £200 of rent, exclusive of twenty tons of kelp every third year."

.   .   .   .

Although favourably endowed as regards fertility, Muck has remained one of the more isolated of the Inner Hebrides. No steamer service reaches it, as it does in the case of Rum, Eigg, and Canna, which, along with it, comprise the Small Isles parish. Apart from such contact as may be maintained, somewhat spasmodically, by a boat owned by one of its lobster-fishermen, the only reliable mode of transport it has to and from the rest of the world is the motor-boat belonging to Mr. Lawrence MacEwan, proprietor of this island, which possesses no postal facilities whatsoever. Once or twice a week, throughout the year, this sturdy craft, so admirably suited to inter-island requirements, traverses six miles of open sea to the neighbouring Isle of Eigg, in order to

Horse Shoe Bay, Isle of Kerrera. (Note the lobster-rafts moored offshore.)
On the lobster-farm in Horse Shoe Bay, Isle of Kerrera, in the Firth of Lorne

collect mails and provisions, and to convey at the same time any-one leaving or returning to the island. In winter-time this com-munication is maintained at considerable inconvenience, and even hazard. The isolation of an isle having neither telegraph nor telephone one can imagine, in the event of the proprietor's motor-boat failing to function. The doctor and the clergy of the Small Isles, as we have seen, reside in Eigg, though there is a priest in Canna. Yet, it must be remembered that, until times comparatively recent, scores of islands off the coasts of Britain were in this isolated position, and had to cope, in periods of ill-ness and distress, with such limited resources as they could assemble. Some such remote isles are more favourably situated, of course, when there is a lighthouse upon them, since nowadays the lighthouse wireless transmitter can call up stations in time of emergency, thus being the means of bringing necessary relief.

Not so with Muck, which is entirely cut off. Even the visits of her seafaring natives to Ardnamurchan are now seldom. In the days when the islanders, having no peat of their own, trans-ported this fuel from the Ardnamurchan peat-mosses, they were somewhat less isolated. Now they burn coal and driftwood. The former is brought to them at intervals by puffer, to be discharged by the jetty at the Port Mòr, Muck's quiet harbour capable of accommodating fishing-boats and coasting vessels of shallow draught. Driftwood can be collected abundantly along the island's shores. The devastating years between 1939 and 1945 increased enormously the quantity of driftwood washed up on Muck; and the supply which accumulated then is by no means exhausted. In certain winds the shores are thickly littered with the flotsam and jetsam of Atlantic storms—tree-trunks from tropical forests, the masts and spars of doomed ships, and specimens of the more buoyant paraphernalia of navigation, such as canvas awning, cork mats, and bits of life-belts.

To-day the population of Muck is twenty-six. Apart from the proprietor and his household, it is distributed among five families occupying the few cottages scattered about the grassy lands fring-ing the Port Mòr. Many of the inhabitants are employed by the proprietor, who farms the island, and whose residence and farm-steadings are at Gallanach, by the island's northern shore. Law-rence MacEwan, aforementioned, if he does not happen to be ski-ing in Switzerland, is always delighted to escort round his rich acres anybody who may chance to land. A recent visitor to Muck was astonished at the crop of immense carrots he saw growing there, in soil upon which the winds distribute lime evenly and adequately, in the form of powdered shell-sand.

Close to the Port Mòr's pier is the island's little school, which at present has an attendance-roll of three. In the green hollow among the rocks and the bracken and the thistles, at no distance from the sites of the islanders' dwellings, are the ruined and turf-covered walls of earlier homesteads.

Muck has not much to offer the archæologist. Yet, one might mention the old graveyard at the head of the Port Mòr, surrounded by a tumbled wall. A ruined chapel having rounded corners abuts on the graveyard enclosure. It measures roughly 20 feet by 10, within drystone walls 5 feet thick. In the south wall is the entrance, only 2 feet 1 inch in width. The island also has the remains of an ancient defensive construction, occupying the summit of a stack at the south-west of the entrance to the Port Mòr. The wall round the edge of the summit, enclosing thereon an irregular area, is eight to ten feet thick. The site is marked on the Ordnance Survey map as that of *Caisteal an Duin Bhain*, Castle of the White Fort. No one on Muck could tell me anything about it when I stayed there a few years ago.

. . . .

A cart-track runs across the island from the pier to the laird's house at Gallanach, passing at one point between a rock planted with trees in their adolescence and a field that, in mid-July, is a mass of purple vetch and of tall cornflowers. Than the blue of the latter, seldom have I seen anything in colour more exquisite, more optimistic. They reminded one of the deep-blue of gentian—of the blue meadow-lands in the Austrian Tyrol in June. Not even the hue of the celebrated Bluebells of Scotland, the harebells, so plentiful on Muck, can compare with its cornflowers. Marigolds, one should also mention, flourish on this island too.

Much that is colourful will delight the eye of him who, in summer, lingers among the rocks and boulders and the fresh pastures fringing the southern bay known as the Camus Mòr, swinging round in a great arc but half a mile to the west of the Port Mòr. Here the white sheep of Muck browse amongst yellow irises in emerald hollows overlooking the sea and the low-lying Isle of Coll, four leagues to the south-west.

From the farmhouse and appurtenant buildings at Gallanach, a vagrant track leads to the island's north-westerly extremity, beyond which lie two small islands, both of them accessible on foot at low water. The nearer, and much the smaller, is *Eilean Ard nan Uan*, the Lambs' Lofty Isle. The other is that to which we already have alluded—*Eilean nan Each*, the Horses' Isle. Westward from the latter, at a distance of a couple of hundred yards, lies the rocky islet of Eagamol, its summit crowned with fine grass upon which three ewes or three wethers are grazed. All kinds of seabirds nest in numbers on this islet, much of which is a dense gullery.

From the Horses' Isle I once beheld a memorable sunset, during which glimpses of the Outer Hebrides appeared and disappeared every now and again as the clouds, with linings truly silver, streaked the western sky in orange and gold. Near at hand the waves, in crashing on the rocks, were shot through with the golden translucence of sunset. An oystercatcher hurried past with agitated call: a whaup piped in flight across the darkening moorland behind me. The scene, all too evanescent where its colourings were concerned, recalled passages in the penultimate chapter of Revelation.

.   .   .   .

The laird's residence—Gallanach House, as it is called—is situated less than a stone's-throw from the fringe of the sandy bay of the same name. This bay affords for small craft excellent anchorage between the two long, parallel reefs running seaward for some considerable distance. This anchorage has the additional advantage of lying in the lee of most winds. Gallanach House has an inspiring outlook toward Rum and Eigg, with the Coolins of Skye seen in the far distance between them. The view of Eigg from Gallanach is particularly fine. It shows to perfection the rugged nature of that island's southern end, its skyline rising gradually to the face of the Scuir, where it drops precipitously. One sees also, in the shadow of the Scuir, the wee house of the shepherd at Grulin. He is now the sole human habitant of that great, desolate hillside, once so populous. He shares it with the sheep, and with the seabirds winging up from the tides and the cavernous cliffs far below.

There lived at Grulin early in the eighteenth century a certain Donald MacQuarrie, a renowned piper. Donald was no more than married to Catriona, a lassie from Muck, when rumour had it that he was constantly ill-using her. Catriona's brothers were wild at this. They told Catriona that, if ever things became unbearable for her at Grulin, all she had to do was to kindle two fires at agreed spots by the shore. One night the brothers observed the signal fires; and off they sailed for Grulin to bring their sister home to Muck. Before departing with her, they gave their brother-in-law a sound thrashing. Ere long, the bereft spouse, regretting his conduct, was out with his pipes on the cliff-edge facing Muck, playing an especially mournful pibroch to denote his loneliness and penitence. This brought Catriona hurrying back to him across the Sound of Eigg. At Grulin, ever after, they lived happily.

Many stories about Donald MacQuarrie are related at the present day by Hugh MacKinnon, a descendant of his, living at Cleadale, in Eigg. Hugh tells one that, when Donald was being carried in his coffin along the hill-track between Grulin and the burying-ground at Kildonnan, the funeral party noticed a boat approaching Eigg from the Arisaig direction. At a spot now marked by a cairn, the party rested awhile, wondering who the occupant of the boat could be. No sooner had it touched shore than there were heard the bagpipe strains of a lament. It was the old Arisaig piper who had taught Donald the art of the pibroch. He had come to pay his last respects to a pupil whose piping had done him credit. The funeral party tarried with the coffin at this spot until the old piper, playing all the way a slow and mournful dirge, reached it; and there, before proceeding to burial at Kildonnan, it erected, beside the track, a memorial cairn in the traditional manner. To this cairn each passerby contributed a stone until at length, it became quite a wellknown landmark. Hugh MacKinnon relates that, when some workmen, early in the present century, were employed in repairing the hill-track at this point, they irreverently removed, for their purpose, a number of the cairn's stones, greatly to the annoyance of two of their number, one of whom was a MacQuarrie, who complained about this act of sacrilege to the factor. The factor promptly ordered that the stones be replaced on the cairn, lest anything untoward occurred.

.   .   .   .

A few years ago I spent some very happy days on Muck with a Mrs. MacDonald. She lived in a wee house at the head of the Port Mòr, just where great quantities of seaware, fringed by clusters of iris-flags, lie uncovered at the ebb. She was a delightful hostess; and I enjoyed to the full her oatcakes and scones and homemade butter—not to mention the excellent jam made from berries growing on bushes scrambling for their very existence, amid nettles and bramble trailers in an unkempt enclosure near at hand. Mrs. MacDonald was a native of Eigg; and our interest in one another was largely explained by a mutual regard for that great Celtic scholar and mystic, the Rev. Dr. Kenneth MacLeod, D.D., with whom she went to school in Eigg. Kenneth's father was schoolmaster there at the time.

It was Mrs. MacDonald who put me in tactful touch with her

neighbour, Colin Campbell—Colin, who had heard the faery music issuing from the brugh, or faery knoll, near his cottage; and it was the reticent Colin who, in turn, assured me that Sandy MacDonald's sons, Lachie and Eachunn, living with their parents in the cottage down by the jetty, a hundred yards away, were really entertained in their boyhood by the faeries, aboard their tiny boat, when they visited Muck some years ago.

"When you see our boat out at the Dubh Sgeir," said the faeries to Sandy's boys (referring to a black reef lying off the entrance to the Port Mòr), "you must return home." They did so, to relate how a faery woman had given them loaves, each the size of a walnut, and how very, very happy they had been when in the faeries' company.

CHAPTER VI

TIREE

"TIREE—The mild weather of October has continued right through November, and, so far, none of the severe gales has swept the shores of Tiree. Very little ground swell has been observed, and this is always a sure indication of calm conditions prevailing in the Atlantic. November has been exceptionally fine all through, and stock are getting a good chance. Even should bad weather set in now, stock of all kinds have benefited immensely, and will be better fit to stand the rigours of real winter when it comes. Seaware is coming ashore at intervals, and top-dressing of land is being taken in hand. This valuable asset from the sea is more appreciated now than later on in the year, when the ground becomes sodden with rain, and carting is heavy amongst ploughed land. A start has been made with the fencing of the new crofts on the farm of Crossapol, in accordance with the scheme for land settlement."

This paragraph of district news, appearing in the December columns of a Highland newspaper, gives one an excellent picture of life, during the winter months, on Tiree, the *Ethica terra* of Adamnan, westernmost of the Inner Hebrides.

The flat, sandy, treeless island-parish of Tiree (which, for parochial purposes, includes Skerryvore, that famous rock lying some eleven miles away in a southerly direction) is situated in the vast and varied county of Argyll, two miles south-west of Coll, and roughly fourteen north-west of Iona, part of the patrimony of which it appears to have been in Columban days. It measures fourteen miles in length, and has a breadth ranging from three-quarters of a mile to six miles. Its area is approximately 19,000 acres, or 30 square miles. At the census of 1931, its population was just over 1,400. In 1951 it was 1,200—a figure representing roughly 40 to the square mile. This is considerably less than it was in 1846, when the island supported a population of over 5,000.

Most of the natives are Gaelic-speaking; and none of them is without a good, working knowledge of English. They all embrace the Protestant Faith and, for the most part, are in com-munion with the Church of Scotland. Except for the very few belonging to the Free Church, the remainder are Baptists. An astonishing proportion graduates at our Scottish Universities. Tiree, like Lewis, is famous for the number of its sons who be-come ordained ministers and sea-captains. But I am told that, in recent years, its younger men prefer the police force to the minis-try, owing to better conditions in the former service as regards pay and pension—illustrative of the West Highlander's extra-ordinary adaptability. When the money is equally good, it is all the same to him whether he devotes his life to saving souls, or to incarcerating them!

Of all the isles of Scotland, Tiree, without a doubt, is the lowest and flattest. Apart from the three hills located at the south—Carn Mor, Beinn Heynish, and Beinn Ceann a' Bharra, none of which exceeds 500 feet—Beinn Hough, rising in the north-west of the island to an altitude of less than 400, is the only eminence worthy of note. Here and there, however, rocks protrude. These are usually covered with bent, pasture, or blown sand. They would scarcely be noticed, were it not for the remarkable flatness of their surroundings. Nowhere do these protuberances attain a height of more than fifty or sixty feet. The northernmost parts of the island, especially those fringing Gunna Sound (the channel dividing Tiree from Coll) are characterised by considerable accumulations of aeolian sand, much of which is held together in low sand-dunes by bent, or marram-grass.

At the south end of the island one finds cliffs, rather than sand-dunes. The seaward clefts and chasms of Ceann a' Bharra are the haunt of great numbers of seafowl. On the cliffs here, as upon those of St. Kilda in olden times, the island's cragsmen, when collecting birds and their eggs, competed in daring.

Tiree's bird-life is wonderful and varied. Its snipe-shooting is claimed to be the finest in Britain, if not actually in Europe. Though it is hardly the sort of thing which would attract *me* to the island, such wildfowling does attract others. The best snipe bogs lie round Barrapol, and in the moss south of Loch a' Phuill. In 1946, no fewer than 1,882 snipe were shot—massacred—bumper bags all the time, for those who enjoy this kind of thing.

Incidentally, Tiree has hares, but no rabbits. Neither has it what is termed ground vermin.

One of the best views Tiree offers is that from the slopes of Beinn Heynish, whence, on a clear day, one can pick out Islay, Jura, and Colonsay, Mull and Iona, Eigg and Rum, Ardnamur-chan and Skye, and even Barra and the Uists. When visibility

Gylen Castle, Isle of Kerrera

is particularly good, Ben Nevis may also be seen. I once located this mountain from Scarinish, at a distance of some seventy miles. Far out on the horizon, to the south-west, one may see the Skerryvore lighthouse, and those adjacent skerries known as MacKenzie's Rock and Stevenson's Rock. At Heynish itself stands the tower used as a signal-station for Skerryvore until some time during the First World War. Near the tower are the dwellings built by Alan Stevenson for the lightkeepers isolated in rotation on Skerryvore and Dubh Heartach. Since the transference of the shore-station for these famous lighthouses, first to Erraid, and now to Oban, these dwellings at Heynish have been let to islanders. When wandering hereabouts one day, I hailed the barefooted son of one of the tenants, and got into conversation with him, for, with a little patient handling, one may sometimes learn more about a locality from children than from their elders. He was seven years, three months, and three weeks old, he told me; and his name was John MacKay. On my asking him whether he belonged to Heynish, or was just there on holiday, he replied with a sad and wistful longing in his eyes, "No! We're just here for ever!" What he meant to convey, of course, was that he had never been anywhere else in his life. This trifling incident made such an impression on me, however, that I never hear of Tiree without my immediate recalling it. The laddie may be there yet, for all I know.

. . . .

Tiree, for all its sandiness and aridity, possesses at least a score of freshwater lochs. These occupy an area of between 600 and 700 acres. Three or four are of appreciable size: the remainder are negligible. Flocks of wild swans and of wild geese frequent them throughout the winter and early spring. In the south is Loch a' Phuill. In the north-west lies Loch Bhasapol, from which emerges the *Amhuinn a' Mhuilinn*, River of the Mill—the only running water on the island worthy of being regarded even as a stream. Until a year or two ago, this stream drove, at the clachan of Cornaigmore, Tiree's principal meal-mill. Prior to the war of 1914, which brought so many changes, it worked steadily throughout the year. As the inhabitants began to obtain their flour and meal direct by sea from Glasgow, its usefulness declined. Latterly, only a few resorted to it, so that, when the question of repairing the kiln plates arose, it was held that the cost involved was hardly warranted by expectations of revenue.

Scarinish, the island's port of call, might also be termed its capital. There one finds the post-office, a hotel, a golf-course, and

Ellanbeich, Isle of Seil, from Isle of Easdale

the old harbour of Tiree. The last mentioned, though still in existence, is little used nowadays except by puffers arriving with coal between the early spring and the late autumn. But a picturesque touch is added to it by the final anchorage there of the *Mary Stewart*, an old, two-masted, wooden vessel that, in her sailing prime, was a familiar voyager in Hebridean waters. The mail-boat calls at the pier in Gott Bay, just north of Scarinish proper. This pier was opened for traffic in the early days of the First World War. However, when the sea is running strongly from the south-east, it is not easily made, with the result that there are days when the mail-boat, unable to call, sails direct through Gunna Sound to Castlebay, the port of Barra.

The coast of Tiree is indented, but not deeply. Close inshore, there are no good anchorages in the accepted sense, for, owing to the very gradual slope of the sea's sandy floor, the water is at all times too shallow. In places where skerries and reefs are common, parallel ridges of black, low-lying rock, running out almost at right angles from the shore, separate adjacent bay-lets of sheen-white sands. In these *geos*, or creeks, craft of modest dimensions and shallow draught can berth with safety. The *Port Ban*, or White Harbour, situated in the north of the island, is typical of such creeks. The coast-line about the township of Caoles, on Gunna Sound, is interrupted by at least half a dozen inlets affording shelter to small fishing craft in bad weather and, at the same time, offering conditions in which, without undue risk, one may embark or come ashore.

Several islets and skerries beset the coast of Tiree. The only islet of any magnitude, however, is Soa, situated in Gott Bay, on the east side, not far from the tiny townships of Ruaig and Brock. It is separated from the main island by half a mile of channel which dries out at low water. The rocks and boulders strewn about it are covered with seaware that provided a fair source of revenue in the days when kelp was burned extensively in the Hebrides.

One sunny day, as I sat among the rocks hereabouts, waiting for the tide to recede sufficiently to allow of my reaching Soa dry-shod, I noticed a string of cows moving slowly toward me along the sands, at an interval of about fifty yards between each. They, obviously, had some destination in mind. Where can they be making for? I asked myself.

Suddenly the foremost cow branched off at right angles, followed by the others when each, in turn, arrived at this spot. On reaching the water's edge, the leader of the contingent paused for a moment, and looked round to see whether the others were bringing up the rear in their approved style. When satisfied that they were all ready to venture forth, she uttered a prolonged moo. At intervals as regular as were those separating them as they lingered along the sands, they moved out into the sea, and made straight for the track leading up from the shore at Soa to the best of its pasture, a hundred yards or so inland.

This seemed to me a very wonderful performance. Those cows were a couple of miles away when first I observed their trek in my direction. They must have calculated that, at their rate of progress, by the time they reached the spot at which they diverted, the tide would have fallen just enough to allow of their fording the channel at the earliest moment consistent with ease and comfort.

A few minutes later, another batch, accompanied by a number of calves, arrived leisurely on the scene from the opposite direction. For half an hour they loitered hereabouts, aware, doubtless, that the channel was still too full for their offspring. They appeared more chary about wetting their feet than did their precursors. Every few minutes, the older members turned an enquiring glance in the direction of Soa, and lowed to the herd already grazing there, to be answered back, in like manner, as if to imbue them with initiative.

At length they, too, set out, and duly arrived in their original order.

A day or two later, I witnessed the reverse procedure at this spot. The tide had been some little time at the flow when, rather than incur unnecessary isolation (although cows are excellent swimmers), these herds returned across the channel to wander back to the less luscious pastures about their respective townships. They exhibited a complete grasp of their own needs, which, surely, is the essence of living.

.   .   .   .

The larger sweeps of shoreland, such as are to be found in Gott Bay, Balephetrish Bay, and Heynish Bay, are as lovely as anything the eyes of mortal man ever beheld. Could any seascape be more beautiful than that embracing the three-mile arc of sand and land known as the *Traigh Mhor*, or Great Shore, of Gott Bay, or the Traigh Sorobaidh of Heynish, on a summer's day, with a ribbon of fleecy cloud stretched over the distant, low-lying land, and with the tide so far at the ebb that often, to the eye unassisted by any elevation from which the scene might be reviewed with greater precision, it is impossible to discern just where sand and shallow sea meet? Take, for instance, that stretch of Heynish Bay seen in the noonday sunshine of summer or early autumn, at low water, from the township of Balemartine, when the crofters' cows and sheep, anxious to avoid the stifling heat and the irritating flies, quit the more inland pastures for the cool sea breezes by the tide's margin, lying all day long, in groups, upon the damper sands, every now and then following the tide as it recedes, every now and then rising to retreat a little inshore as a flowing sea once again encroaches upon these vast expanses. For livestock, there is on Tiree neither natural bield from storm, nor shade from sun. The very sheep at times are driven seaward, in order to escape the heat when a brilliant sun pours from his zenith upon this unusual isle. A flock of sheep, sharing with the cattle, at ebb tide, the cooler reaches of sand, is no uncommon sight. At Gott Bay, under such conditions, one may even see the sheep standing with the brine well over their trotters, their nostrils turned seaward to inhale the cooling winds wafted inshore from the lofty mountains of Mull.

Apropos heat and sultry conditions, one should mention that Tiree is liable to thunderstorms. Some years ago, during a particularly violent visitation, lightning struck a house on the island, and ripped the toe off a native's boot, leaving the wearer unscathed. It played havoc with the pendulum clock standing on his mantelshelf, churning its works into the strangest contortions.

I remember wandering late one evening on this island when a curious sultriness suddenly overspread everything. Elusive clouds, with a touch of salmon-pink in them, filled the sky to the west. To the east the welkin had taken on the hue of the bluebells still nodding here and there on the machar and adjacent sand-dunes. About midnight, when scanning the horizon for the flashes from the more distant lighthouses, one sensed the coming storm. A few big blobs of rain, and the rumble of thunder somewhere in the direction of Barra, urged one to hasten home. Soon Tiree was encircled by a girdle of lightning that lit up the skyline in weird silhouette, and showed us that the cattle had wandered across the machar to our very doorstep for companionship. To them, as to so many human beings, thunder and lightning are a terrifying combination. But for the pealing thunder, and until the rains came, there was no sound except that of the low, sullen waves creeping in, sinuously, as if by stealth.

The flatness of Tiree is proverbial. Apart from the hills already named, its mean height above high-water mark is no more than eighteen feet. From the deck of a ship approaching pier at Gott Bay, it would seem as though, at any moment, a tidal wave of no great magnitude might sweep clean over it. After the wild and rugged grandeur of the Western Highlands—nowhere seen to better advantage than in the case of Mull, so much of which the mail-boat circumnavigates on her route from Oban— one's first impression of Tiree may be a little disappointing, if not actually depressing. The island appears to be lacking in any-thing of the picturesque. The wild and varied scene of but a couple of hours earlier has given way to monotony, and to flat-ness wellnigh unrelieved. Yet, no more than a day's sojourn serves to dispel any earlier sense of disappointment. The glisten-ing bays, the bird-haunted voes, the quiet and homely cattle browsing on the common grazing composed so largely of wild flowers in greater profusion and variety than anywhere else among the Isles of Scotland (some 400 varieties have been classified), the dunes and sand-banks, the creeks and caverns affording the bather more than every boon to be found in the most luxurious bathing-coach, and, above all, complete privacy and freedom from time-table—these joys, and many more, fall to one in ample recompense. And, if the day be hot and the body somewhat lan-guorous, one seeking exhilaration need do no more than ascend the highest sand-dune by the windward shore, and rock and sway there in the wind a-blowing from the wide ocean.

Until a few years ago, the narrow highway encircling the cen-tral portion of the island, and also those slightly inferior roads radiating from it to the more remote farms and crofting town-ships, stretched like a seared ribbon, the colour of rusting celery. In places it lay hidden ankle-deep, and sometimes even knee-deep, in sand-drift.

About the centre of the island, and occupying an area of roughly fifteen hundred acres, is the remarkable plain known as the Reef. Here the land is as flat as is the surface of a quiet mill-pond. From parts of this neighbourhood, much of which, with its neat hamlets, is strangely reminiscent of Flanders, the sea cannot be seen at all. On the east side, the Reef is penetrated by the tide where a long, narrow strip of brackish water, known locally as *Am Faodhail* (The Ford), marks its lowest stretch. Much of the Reef remains in a slightly marshy condition all the year round, and is characterised by such marshland vegetation as thrift and iris-flag, lady's smock or cuckoo-pint, orchid and marsh-mallow.

The Reef is devoid of the slightest swelling. Maintained until recently under perpetual pasture, it boasts not even what one might term a knoll. Its fertility in normal years was not too difficult to ensure, for it possessed, in the matter of humidity, a regularity seldom found in sandy territory. Part of it would even appear to lie a little below sea-level. It seems obvious that at one time the sea flowed over it, dividing the Tiree we now know into two separate islands, and that centuries of silting and sand-blowing have filled in this ancient seaway.

. . . .

To Tiree's flat and low-lying aspect must be ascribed at least one of the ancient names by which the island is referred to in folk-tales, namely, *An Rioghachd Barr fo Thuinn*, The Kingdom whose Summits lie beneath the Waves. One recognises in this singular title a whisper of those Celtic traditions associated with the Land-under-Waves, allusions to which, in more recent times, are scattered throughout *The Songs of the Hebrides*, that monumental piece of art and scholarship emanating from the years during which Kenneth MacLeod and the late Marjory Kennedy-Fraser collaborated in this field.

The source of the name, Tiree (or Tyree, as it is sometimes spelt), is much a matter of conjecture and speculation. But it may be held with a measure of probability that both elements of the word are of Celtic origin, signifying 'corn-land'. Certainly, the components would seem to indicate an origin based upon the island's fertility and its fame for corn. Amateur etymologists, however, like the idea of its being derived from *Tir-I*, Land of the Island—the island alluded to being, of course, Iona. Weight is lent to this, they maintain, by the tradition that in St. Columba's time Tiree, even then renowned for its excellent crops, was the granary of Iona, and remained for centuries in the closest touch with the ecclesiastical settlement there.

According to a sixteenth-century account of the Western Isles, Tiree was "commodious and fertil of corns, and store of gudes", and its pastures so rich that "the ky of this Ile abundis sa of milk that thai are milkit four times in the day".

It cannot be gainsaid that Tiree is the most fertile of the Hebrides, despite the fact that the islanders often have to contend with the ravages of the wind sweeping across their farmlands, uprooting vegetables, blowing the soil away from seed planted in the springtime, and not infrequently devastating the crops in autumn. Fishing, as generally understood, is scarcely pursued at all—certainly not commercially. On the other hand, some of the natives deal profitably in lobsters. These they despatch to southern markets, but on a scale too small to justify lobster-fishing's being included among the island's industries. But what the natives are denied by way of harvest from the sea is more than compensated for by what they derive, in normal years, from the land. The abundance of good pasturage, albeit blown sand at times threatens to render parts of it barren, ensures the raising of considerable stock; while those areas under the plough produce cereals the like of which are not often equalled elsewhere in the Hebrides. The salt spray of the Atlantic, together with the fertilising value of pulverised sea-shells constantly being blown in and about the island, have done much to improve the soil. Then, as indicated in our opening paragraph, seaware, torn from the rocks and the sea's floor by storm and ground-swell, and some-times driven ashore in considerable quantities, is used exten-sively as a top-dressing during the winter months.

The island possesses no moorland. Peat and heather are as scarce as are trees and shrubs. The natives have no peat-hags at hand, therefore, from which to obtain their fuel. Until a few years ago, they brought their peats over from Mull. Nowadays they burn coal. This they receive by flat-bottomed puffers re-quiring neither pier nor prop, since they are adapted for sitting upright on the sands when the tide recedes. A puffer's arrival in Heynish Bay, off Balemartine, prognosticates a couple of days' feverish activity for the able-bodied of the locality. Carts from farm and croft, now assembled on the sands, ply all day long, and often well into the night, between the puffer's derrick and the premises of those who have purchased the cargo.

Tiree at one time consisted of prosperous farms, as well as of a number of crofts. In 1914, some of the larger farms—Heynish, Heylipol, and Hough, to mention but three of them—were con-verted into smallholdings by the Department of Agriculture for Scotland, when the Scottish Land Court fixed the rents, defined the common grazings, and laid down what stock should be carried on each. In 1922 the farm of Balephetrish was broken up for the purpose of giving land to returned ex-servicemen. Agrarian disputes, which cannot be settled on the spot by the resident factor to the Duke of Argyll, owner of the island, are submitted by the smallholders, themselves, to the Land Court, at Edinburgh. Periodically, the Court visits islands like Tiree, in order to hear the parties concerned, and to carry out such inspection as may be deemed necessary. In course of time it issues its decision, or Final Order, as it is termed.

With the exception of the Reef, an area of 1,230 acres acquired by the Air Ministry for an aerodrome in 1943, Tiree belongs to the Duke of Argyll. Since 1937 the Reef has been used as a landing-ground for aircraft. It is now possible to leave Renfrew airport at 8.30 a.m., and be in Tiree about an hour later. A British European Airways plane calls every morning on its flight between Renfrew and the Outer Hebrides, returning early in the afternoon.

At the moment of writing (March, 1952), the Trustees of the 10th Duke of Argyll, whose funeral I attended at Inveraray in 1949, propose selling approximately 20,000 acres of the island— all of it, in fact, with the exception of the part belonging to the Air Ministry. They advertise, among the island's attractions, its forty miles of road, mainly tarred, and most of them either constructed or put into good order by the Air Ministry during the Second World War; the island's sunny and comparatively dry climate; and its status as an agricultural investment, having a gross rental of nearly £3,000, derived from smallholdings and crofts, on which the owner has no repair obligations, since the buildings belong to the holders or crofters themselves. The arable land is easily worked, and has an abundance of shell lime, which is reflected in its crops and grazings. The island has 4 farms, 7 statutory smallholdings, and 280 ordinary smallholdings or crofts. The last named are distributed among 32 townships; and all but two of them have common grazings. There are also about 150 squatters who, in recent years, have built their own houses, without paying stance rents or feu duties. Although they are recognised under Scottish Law, their buildings revert, on their death, to the landowner, unless there is a lease or feu duty. Of late, many squatters in Tiree have regularised their position by agreeing to pay a proper stance rent or feu duty to the Estate. As it is in their interests to do so, it is expected that others will follow before long. The average stance rent payable is about 30s. per annum.

It would be accurate to say that Tiree has no industry other than agriculture, which occupies about 80 per cent of the adult population. However, there are hopes that the seaweed industry, which, many years ago, the Western Islanders found a most profitable one, may be resuscitated.

Toward the close of the eighteenth century, a variegated marble (of somewhat inferior quality, one supposes) was quarried in the neighbourhood of Balephetrish farm by an association designating itself the Tiree Marble Company. A considerable quantity was removed in the few years during which operations continued. But transport difficulties and other handicaps necessitated the abandonment of this enterprise. During the Second World War, however, this quarry, and also one at Baugh, were

76

worked by the contractors who made the aerodrome runways and roads, meantime paying the Estate royalties.

To the north and west of Loch a' Phuill lie considerable deposits of iron ore. These were investigated recently by the British Iron and Steel Corporation.

Pharologists may like to know that the great blocks of granite quarried at the Ross of Mull for the building of the Skerryvore and Dubh Heartach lighthouses were first brought to Heynish, where more than a hundred quarriers and labourers were employed steadily during the summer months. At Heynish each stone was dressed; and there also every tier was built, prior to its transhipment to the lighthouse sites. The spot where the preliminary constructions were carried out is still clearly defined.

Before the Second World War, the island was becoming increasingly popular as a holiday resort. Many householders catered for visitors in the summer and autumn, thus adding considerably to their otherwise limited incomes. During the Glasgow Fair Week, the natives give themselves over to a spell of fun and frivolity. They hold a cattle-show and a regatta at Scarinish, sports on the Reef, and dances every evening. Their excursions usually conclude with a trip to the Mull Highland Games, held at Tobermory.

.   .   .   .

Tiree in olden times had an unenviable reputation for hard drinking and the excesses associated therewith. "Drinking of ardent spirits at funerals", according to the *New Statistical Account*, was a lamentable feature of social life on the island in 1843; and, indeed, it remained so until fairly recently. It cannot be said that, even yet, the practice has wholly disappeared. The chronicler instances poor families parting with their last horse or cow, so as to provide the wherewithal for funeral refreshments; "and thus," to proceed with our quotation, "what might have contributed to their support for a twelvemonth is wasted in a day, to keep up a savage and disgusting custom". This, together with smuggling (mainly from northern Ireland), clandestine stilling, and the abundance of "low, illicit tippling-houses", or shebeens, was responsible for much depravity during the first half of the nineteenth century.

At many a funeral in the Western Highlands and Islands the providing of a copious supply of whisky is still deemed a matter of prime honour, and one which the natives of Tiree observed to the full until very recently, when it was agreed that too much brawling and fighting took place afterwards, and that few of them could really afford the traditional dramming associated with burial.

Between death and committal to the earth, however, it is still customary for relatives and friends to send or take to the house of the deceased all sorts of provisions, such as butter, eggs, cheese, and biscuits. Those actually visiting the house are expected to sit with the corpse for some twenty minutes—not nearly so long, one might add, as in Lewis or Harris, where the formalities connected with the death-wake are observed with even greater strictness, and where the period between death and interment is sometimes protracted, owing either to the expected arrival of a near relative from afar, or to the time required to procure, for the funeral party, a sufficient supply of alcoholic beverages. On such occasions, soft drinks are conspicuous by their absence.

On the day of the funeral, the female mourners on Tiree gather in large numbers *inside* the house of the deceased. The male mourners, with the exception of ministers, dominies, and the like, wait *outside*, where, on arrival, they are treated to the traditional dram. When an adequate number of carriers for the coffin has assembled, a short service is conducted just outside the door of the house. The coffin, raised on two short poles, is then borne on the shoulders of four mourners. Two of the principal mourners, who are usually the deceased's nearest relatives, stand by the coffin, one in front of it, the other behind, each holding a black cord attached to it. The other mourners precede the coffin. A local worthy heads the procession and, at intervals of between forty and fifty yards, calls on the next four mourners to stand out. This they immediately do, in order to relieve the first four bearers, who now walk in front of the coffin, but in the rear of the main part of the procession. This direction is repeated until the island burying-ground is reached.

No matter how cold or wet the day, no matter how distant the burying-ground, most of the inhabitants of Tiree adhere to the practice of carrying the coffin. In cases where the burying-ground lies in close proximity to the house of the deceased, the mourners often enter into open competition with one another for a turn of carrying, if only the matter of a few yards. One funeral I witnessed on this island necessitated the fours' changing over every ten yards, to ensure that everyone had his spell before the graveside was reached—so numerous were the male mourners, and so near lay the cemetery.

Female mourners in this Presbyterian Isle follow the coffin for a short distance only. Before returning to their *own* refreshments at the house where the coffin has been carried, however, they observe the custom of kissing it, and of the laying on of hands.

On Tiree, nowadays, there is no halting between the deceased's house and the place of interment. Yet it is not so long since there were many, at each of which the funeral party indulged in a few rounds of the Best Scotch. A halt used to be made on the slightest pretext. Undue weariness of foot occasioned many a dram!

.   .   .   .

On arrival at the place of burial, the coffin is immediately lowered and covered with the earth. Those islanders, who are perhaps more expert in the use of spade and shovel than their neighbours, trim the sods, and generally tidy up the grave. This process occupies some twenty minutes, during which the main body of mourners lingers idly through the graveyard to re-read the inscriptions on its tombstones, or rests on the surrounding dyke.

When all is in order, a brief committal service is held—*brief* it certainly used to be, because by this time the cart conveying the refreshments had arrived on the scene, and the mourners were drouthy with their exertions! Biscuits and cheese were then distributed, and drams freely dispensed. The greater the number of rounds, the greater the honour the natives believed they were paying to the dead.

The mourners' homeward journey was often boisterous and hilarious. Not infrequently, the least sober of them were literally *carted* home in the horse-drawn vehicle that had brought the whisky to the scene of their revels. There was a day—and not so long ago either—when more than one cart accompanied the procession, in order to carry home those defeated in brawling, and overcome in dramming.

A good story is told on Tiree of the way in which the natives often vied one with the other in the quantity of alcohol consumed at their funerals. When X's wife died, she was honoured in eleven drams. Shortly afterwards, X's son returned home from a funeral at a neighbouring township with the disconcerting tidings that thirteen drams had been given. This so annoyed his father that he threatened to dig his wife up, " and we'll have *fourteen* rounds! "

While I was living on Tiree some years ago, there took place a memorable departure, when a local worthy had the coffin of his late sister conveyed to the graveyard *by motor-lorry*. The mourners numbered five—just as many as the lorry could accom-

79

modate, together with the coffin. In the chief mourner's own words, "*it was all over in ten minutes, with just one bottle.*"

It is not so very long since it was customary in the Highlands and Islands to attend a funeral armed with a good stick, in anticipation of the inevitable brawl. Clan feuds often broke out afresh at funerals!

A Tiree minister did inaugurate a petition with a view to putting an end to these pagan and unseemly observances; and a member of the Argyll family (the island, you remember, belongs to the Duke of Argyll) actually went so far as to offer the natives a hearse. However, the first funeral to take place after the signing of the petition happened to be that of a near relative of a 'pillar o' the kirk'—a prominent signatory who, when the crucial moment arrived, had not the heart to break away just so suddenly from age-long tradition. Liberal supplies of whisky were procured, therefore; and the humble petition became a very humble affair indeed!

When liquor was more plentiful, it was usual for the bill to amount to £20 for the whisky alone. Families have been known to sell their only cow, in order to provide ready cash for funeral refreshments. Can you imagine anything more idiotic than that crofters, who usually live fairly near the margin of subsistence even in the best of years, should have wasted so much in this way?

. . . .

These funerals in Celtic Scotland, quite often, are boisterous and irreverent, even at the present day. Solemnity, in any marked degree, is seldom exhibited at them. Animated conversation on earthly topics, such as the price for cattle and sheep at the Oban marts, absorbs the procession's attention until dramming-time. One recalls the case of a Western Islander, who had some odd pieces of furniture he wanted to dispose of. As his house lay close to the township's burying-ground, he arranged that the sale of it should take place immediately after an interment, in the hope that the mourners, now somewhat inebriated, might be attracted to it. A schoolmaster on this particular island assured me some time ago that never had there been such keen bidding. In the estimation of all present, it was a good funeral, and a very good sale. No one had anything to complain of.

Invitation to these island funerals is usually delivered orally. One or two respected members of the community are honoured with instructions to call with it at every house. A friend on Tiree told me that a voice in the dark, outside his front door or sitting-room window, always summoned *him*, and in the recognised terms: "The presence of your company is expected at the funeral of —— from —— to —— at twelve noon to-morrow." An hour or two after noon, the proceedings usually begin.[1]

I have heard it said, where the dramming at funerals is concerned, that it had some connection with an ancient ritual into which seven, the mystical number, entered. Seven drams were given before setting out with the corpse, seven each time the bearers halted with it, and seven at the graveside.

Two other occasions are regarded by the West Highlander as justifying the most liberal consumption of intoxicants—the celebrating of the New Year, and a marriage. The pagan tradition that there must be plenty of drink at marriages and funerals, and on New Year's Day, is dying hard in these parts.

.   .   .   .

Tiree formerly belonged to the MacLeans of Duart. Incidentally, MacLean remains the commonest surname on the island. In 1674 it passed into the ownership of the Earl of Argyll, who, according to the MacLean version of the transfer, usurped it. At the beginning of the seventeenth century, the Clan MacLean, under its Chief, MacLean of Duart, was perhaps the most powerful in the Hebrides. By the end of that century, however, it had lost, by one means or another, nearly all its vast possessions. The deadly feud between the MacLeans and the MacDonalds, which began in Mary's reign, presaged their decline. "In the reign of James VI and Charles I," writes Gregory, the historian, "many debts had accumulated against the barony of Dowart, which enabled the Marquis of Argyll and his successors to establish a claim to that estate, and this claim the MacLeans, owing to their exertions in favour of the Stewarts, had never an opportunity of shaking off." Argyll's claim to Tiree, the MacLeans say, resulted from the former's crafty purchase of all the undisputed debts, public as well as private, owed by Duart. Whatever the process of displacement, by the beginning of the eighteenth century, the Argyll family was well and truly established in Tiree.

[1] This public bidding to funerals persists in many parts of Britain. Not until June, 1950, did the Town Council of Pittenweem, in Fife, discontinue its ancient custom of issuing invitations to the public to attend local funerals. Up till then, it had been the town officer's job to go round every home in Pittenweem, delivering a verbal invitation to each household in a town of 2,000 inhabitants. This he did in his spare time; and he was recompensed with six shillings. "It was a homely custom which was, no doubt, very nice in the olden days, when there was only a few houses in the place," said Provost Lawson; "but it takes the town officer two days to go round the town, and it is unfair to expect him to do it."

In antiquarian interest the island is by no means lacking, though collectors have removed many an object of value. The sites of more than a dozen duns or ancient forts, ascribed locally to the Danes, are to be found about the coast. These are said to have been used as watch-towers. Then some old stone crosses and coffins have been unearthed at various times. A few standing-stones are also to be seen.

Situated between the public road and the beach at Crossapol, by the south-east shore of the island, is a small, artificial mound, in the centre of which stands a stone structure some five feet in diameter. This, according to local tradition, marks the grave of the "winsome lady" commemorated in Thomas Campbell's poem, *Lord Ullin's Daughter*. Her body is said to have been washed ashore nearby, and to have been buried there.

> 'Twas vain: the loud waves lashed the shore,
>   Return or aid preventing:
> The waters wild went o'er his child,
>   And he was left lamenting.

Then, on the north shore is a huge, ice-borne boulder poised on a base of rock, and weighing many tons. It is known as the Ringing Stone, because of the metallic resonance produced by it when struck with another stone. Experts declare that the deep indentations in its surface are the ancient cup-marking of pre-Druidical times.

On a peninsula in a freshwater lake near Heylipol stands Island House, the most presentable dwelling on Tiree, apart from the Lodge, situated a mile and a half from the pier, and overlooking Gott Bay. It was built in 1748 by Archibald, 3rd Duke of Argyll, to accommodate his factor. Indeed, it is still the factor's residence. In 1874 it was enlarged and considerably improved. It occupies the islet site of an ancient keep of Isleburgh which, according to local tradition, was accessible only by draw-bridge. Many years ago, the space between the islet and the nearest shore was filled in, so that Island House now stands picturesquely on a peninsula in the lake still retaining its original name—Loch of the Island. Across the loch from the back of the house there runs an old wall, said to have been contemporaneous with the keep, and designed to enable the occupants to escape in time of siege.

.   .   .   .

None of the Western Isles, one might add in conclusion, is

richer in folklore than Tiree. Here one still learns of faeries and of faery music, of faery dogs and faery cattle. Here, furthermore, the washing-woman, prognosticating bereavement, has been seen at the rinsing of the death-shrouds.

Then, a benevolent sprite of the *gruagach* species—a little woman with long, yellow locks, haunted Island House for many a day. She dwelt in the attics. Though a sight of her was had but seldom, she might be heard making preparations when guests were expected, and scolding, and even belabouring, the servants, when they neglected their duties, or performed them perfunctorily.

Of visits to Tiree I have many happy memories; and these always return when I get my bare feet on something pleasurable—on something soothing, such as cool, glistening seawrack, or sun-warmed turf. A few years ago, I spent some days at Ruaig with a family named Lamont, a member of which had married one of my distant MacLeod kinsfolk from Lewis. The house was a little, red-roofed one, on the machar, with the sea rolling in upon the sands of Gott Bay, on the one hand, and acres of wild flowers, on the other. Beyond, on the horizon, lay bent-covered sand-dunes. Here, surely, was one of the finest golf-courses ever designed by nature. The natural turf, so short and sweet, was its fairways: the great sand-dunes its bunkers. Though I seldom play golf (mainly because I haven't the time), I soon found this setting very tempting—so tempting, indeed, that every morning, long before breakfast, I wandered straight from bed, barefooted and in pyjamas, to follow a golf-ball in the morning sunshine through the catmint and the summer grasses upon sward so closely cropped by the crofters' livestock as to resemble a vast putting-green meticulously mown. Who, finding so excellent a course at his doorstep—at his very bedroom window—and balls and clubs always ready to hand on the hall-stand, could resist the call of the machar at Ruaig? The warm, velvety turf under the bare soles sent through one a current of wellbeing.

CHAPTER VII

COLL

A COUPLE of miles in a north-easterly direction from Tiree, and but seven to the west of Cailleach Point, in Mull, lies Coll, an island parish some twelve miles in length from east-north-east to west-south-west, and three-quarters of a mile to four miles in breadth. By sea from Oban, it is roughly sixty miles.

Composed of Lewisian gneiss, it might be described as flat, in the main, with rocky protuberances. In common with other isles of the Hebrides, it is treeless. It attains its highest point in Ben Hogh, 339 feet, situated near the western shore, about halfway between the island's longitudinal extremities. The total area of Coll has been estimated at about 18,000 acres, roughly a sixth of which is productive in a sense certainly not applicable to the Hebrides as a whole. Its soil is fairly fertile; and for many years the island's pasturage has maintained, in dairy produce, as well as in cattle and sheep, a profitable export trade. In the export of cheese, Coll holds the record for the Highlands and Islands. Half a century ago, it despatched, annually, to the southern markets, some sixty tons of this commodity. The islanders were, indeed, proud in the knowledge that Coll Cheese was to be found on the menu at the House of Commons! Owing mainly to depopulation, and the consequent decline in the numbers engaged in dairy-farming, the quantity exported in more recent years has fallen considerably. The island's population in 1931 was 322. Ninety years previously, it was nearly five times that number.

Oats, barley, rye and potatoes are Coll's main crops. Potatoes are even exported. Up till the closing years of last century, the island was noted for its shipments of garrons—sturdy, Highland ponies. At this time, moreover, ling-fishing was a thriving industry. The depletion of the Coll fishing banks, owing to a variety of causes, killed it. To-day lobster-fishing has largely taken its place. This lucrative calling is prosecuted in the rocky voes penetrating its coast-line, and among the islets and skerries lying off the north of the island, and known as the Cairns of Coll.

There are several freshwater lochs scattered about the island, many of which abound in trout. Boswell mentions that there

*Christina MacKenzie lime-washing her cottage
at Cullipool, Isle of Luing*

were some forty-eight when, in 1773, he and Dr. Johnson landed, and called upon the parish minister, the Rev. Hector MacLean, "a decent ecclesiastick, dressed in a full suit of black clothes and a black wig", who was then about seventy-seven years of age. But it all depends upon what one would regard as a loch, rather than as a pond. Boswell himself says that many of the forty-eight were "mere pools". In any case, several of them have been drained away since Boswell's time: their sites now form part of Coll's arable land, or of its common grazing. Extensive areas consisting of sand-dunes, or covered with a peaty soil supporting heath, afford a good deal of rough pasture. The peaty parts, of course, supply the inhabitants with fuel. The peat-hags seem almost inexhaustible, and must be the envy of the natives on the adjacent island of Tiree, which was 'skinned' of its top-soil many a generation ago.

Coll's watershed is not sufficient to support a river. Yet, its rainfall feeds a number of streams. Many of these, however, lose themselves in its sandy fringes ere they reach the sea.

The life of the island revolves mainly round Arinagour, the principal township, which, deriving its name from the Gaelic, signifies the Goats' Shieling. There are few goats on Coll to-day; but in olden times the island possessed many. It supported several when Johnson and Boswell arrived, to be entertained with "a primitive heartiness". Boswell's account of Coll is well worth reading, for, although he records a mass of superfluous observation and comment, he does give one a faithful picture of the island during the latter half of the eighteenth century. While he and his hero admired the minister's fine library, they deplored the poor accommodation he had for it, "being obliged to keep his books in large chests". A few days' confinement on Coll, owing to stormy weather, evoked from Dr. Johnson a note of despair: "I want to be on the mainland, and go on with existence!" Boswell reports him as having said; "This is a waste of life."

Yet, the Doctor seems to have been amply occupied during his stay. It was on Coll that he first mounted a little Highland steed—one of the low but strong and muscular animals to be found on so many of the Western Isles. In recording this feat of his, he observed that, had there been a lot of spectators, he would have felt somewhat ashamed of himself, "for a bulky man upon one of their backs makes a very disproportionate appearance".

Coll and Tiree at this time were united for parochial purposes.

G

ABOVE: *Seil and the Cuan Ferry from Luing*
BELOW: *The swirling tides of Fladda, in the Firth of Lorne*

The Rev. Hector MacLean was minister of the joint parish. Prior to 1618, each of these islands was a parish of its own. Not until 1866 did they again become separate parishes. In 1843, at the time of the Disruption, most of the natives left the Auld Kirk of Scotland, and joined the Free Kirk. Having for many years no building in which to worship, they held their services in the open, at Clabhach, within sight of their old church. Eventually they erected at Grishipoll, a mile or so away, a place of worship which remained in use until 1884, when it was superseded by a new church at Arinagour. Thus there are on Coll but two congregations, both of which, of course, are Presbyterian. The one is Church of Scotland: the other is *Free* Church of Scotland. Each has a Gaelic-speaking minister.

At Arinagour, where the mail-steamer calls thrice weekly, one finds all the institutions and personages requisite to the island's economy. There, in close proximity to one another, are the post-office, factor's office, the island's two churches, its principal shop, inn, smithy, and main school. There, also, live such important members of the community as the island doctor and the island carpenter. Most of Arinagour consists of two rows of cottages. One of these is known as High Street: the other as Main Street.

My first voyage to Coll I well remember. Though at times a glimpse of blue was to be had overhead, a thick fog so enveloped sea and land as to make navigation wellnigh impossible. As a means of keeping the mail-boat, *Lochmor,* in position until visibility improved, thirty fathoms of anchor cable rattled down into the still waters of Oban Bay a few minutes after our leaving the pier there. We were already more than an hour behind time, owing to the delayed arrival of the train from the south. "No bottom at twenty, sir," one heard the mate shout to the captain an hour or two later, when the vessel's engines were switched off, and the sounding-line dropped. We had been threading our way with extreme caution through the Sound of Mull when, in a twinkling, a fresh blanket of fog descended upon us. Just when it looked as though we might have had to remain indefinitely in this romantic fairway, a glint of sun struck our bows, showing that the tide had turned us right about. Everything around remained calm and subdued until the pantry-boy loitered through the ship, ringing the breakfast-bell with deafening determination, out-rung only by the fog-bell tolled intermittently by a seaman at the bow. There was no wind. The faintest breeze would have solved our trouble. From the ship's interior, the smell of good

Scots porridge ascended, and hung about the deck, enclosed about us, as it were, by the fog. Gulls, accustomed at this hour of the morning to the scraps of bread and leathery toast flung into the sea from the galley door, hovered about the foremast riggings. There was now no alternative but to drop anchor and wait. To the accompaniment of the gulls' squawking, and the flutter of a huge flock of duck skimming the tideway within a few feet of us, the fog-bell sounded yet again, as the black ball was hoisted to denote, at sight, a vessel riding at anchor. (In these days of inventions and contrivances, the black ball, as you are probably aware, is no longer a ball; and very frequently it is not even black. Nowadays it usually consists of two large, circular, metal discs intersecting one another at right angles, and hinged in such a way as to give, at a distance, the appearance, when open, of being a ball. So, to-day, the black ball is both a misnomer and an optical delusion).

It was some time ere the Lismore Lighthouse showed through the fog on the starboard bow, and direction was given for weighing the anchor. Then began a prolonged rattle of chains, indicating that below us lay a considerable depth of water. The ship had now to be swung about for Tobermory, our first port of call.

"The anchor's home, sir," shouted the mate to the skipper on the bridge, as the winchman, wiping his hands with cotton-waste, surveyed the batch of bored passengers gathered round the noisy capstan.

"When do we arrive at Tabbamackie or something?" a pronouncedly English passenger enquired of him.

"A quarter-to-nine *some* days," responded the laconic winchman.

"Is that a signal?" another passenger asked him, as he hauled down the black ball preparatory to our again attempting to steer a course through the Sound of Mull.

"No! It's a Chreesamus decoraashun," replied the harassed winchman who, all morning, had been raising and dropping anchor, and answering inane questions.

"Ship ahead!" cried the outlookman at the bow, as we came within sight of Duart Castle, vaguely visible to port as the mists began to roll off the great Mull mountains.

Sure enough, there lay a ship ahead—an Inverness herring-drifter beating southward at full steam to the fish-mart at Oban, cutting through the conflicting currents between Craignure and Morven as though they scarcely existed.

At this juncture there was added a touch of local colour. A

hen, in course of transit to Coll in a small sack, succeeded in getting free among the luggage in the hold, and in locating therein a basket containing her chicks. Her cackling soon attracted the attention of members of the crew, and so inspired two of her brood that they escaped from the basket, and hid themselves amid several tons of baggage and such impedimenta as is usually to be found in a ship's hold. A couple of spaniels leashed to a stanchion near at hand now joined in the general uproar with which the campaign to retrieve hen and chicks was conducted. Their owner, a young Coll girl, then came on the scene, not the least perturbed at the commotion. She stood among the passengers, watching the round-up quite dispassionately. Indeed, she did not seem to mind much whether the birds were caught or not. "Och, never mind her!" she was overheard saying to the A.B. who, in lunging at the hen, seized her in her flight from one suitcase to another, and with an air of triumph thrust her back into the sack. "She got out on me in a bus in Glasgow yesterday," the lassie went on to explain. "I put the sack up on the rack, thinking it would be all right, till I heard all the people screaming in the bus. The poor beast was just terrified with the screams, I think, because she got out in the train to Oban this morning, and was near out of the window."

"Well, she'll no' get away *this* time, whateffer!" the seaman assured her in tying the mouth of the sack with a new cord, and giving the knot an extra tug or two.

"Och, well," said the lassie in thanking him, "I'm no' minding if she gets away on me altogether, for she's been an aawful bother since leaving Glasgow. I'll never take a hen home again. No, not to please anyone!"

.   .   .   .

When eventually we reached Coll, it was bathed in sunshine. However, knowing well how fickle the weather can be in these parts, I resolved to cover as much of the island as possible before nightfall. From Arinagour, therefore, I set off, anti-clockwise, with a borrowed bicycle on a circular tour of the southern part of the island, by way of Arnibost and Grishipoll, Clabhach and Totronald, Arileod and Acha. For most of the way, the sandy road curved among grasslands, white and yellow and purple with summer flowers. The children were just coming out of the little local school by the roadside at Grishipoll as I passed by. Among them was a fair-haired boy of nine, bare-headed and bare-footed, in like manner trundling on a rickety bicycle along the island road toward Clabhach and the manse and parish church. For

some distance, and indeed until I dismounted at the manse gate
to call on Mr. Robertson, then parish minister, we rode abreast
and engaged in lively conversation. Slung by his side was a neat,
homemade school-bag consisting of no more than two pieces of
sacking, each about a foot square, and bound together with a
strip of black tape. "There's no' another like it in aall the
island!" he proudly informed me when I remarked upon it, and
congratulated him upon his originality.

The little boy told me that his name was Donald Bremner, and
that his father was the island roadman.

"Well, Donald," I said, "can't your father do anything about
these roads?"

"He's been doing something about them aall his days!"
Donald was quick to respond. "There's never much difference
on them. They're aalways this way."

"And what are *you* going to be when you grow up, Donald?"
I continued.

"A roadman too, likely," he replied with the most beautiful
Gaelic intonation you ever heard. "My father aalways says it's
the best life for a man. No botheraation at aall!"

I afterwards learnt that Donald's father, many years ago, came
to Coll from the mainland, acquired the Gaelic, married a woman
from Uist, and settled down in Coll where, doubtless, he still is.

My visit to Mr. Robertson at the manse of Coll was of short
duration, for, although he and his spaniel extended to me the
warmest of Highland welcomes, I still had much to see, and
much uneven ground to traverse before returning in the evening to Arinagour. Roughly a mile to the south of Clabhach, as
my map so faithfully showed, the road encircling the southern
half of the island petered out between a pond and the small
township of Ballyhaugh. As I was obliged to dismount at this
point, I emphasised the occasion by climbing Ben Hogh, so close
at hand, and so easy of ascent. I had but reached the summit
when the land became weirdly overcast. A squall could be seen
approaching from the open Atlantic; and in a matter of a few
minutes I found myself unprotected from a heavy shower of hail-
stones. From my notes I see this was on June 26th—midsummer
hail!

Soon I located, on the slope of Ben Hogh, the huge boulder
regarded by the natives as one of the more singular of their
island's natural features. This is the very large stone (probably
a boulder borne, erratically, to its present position during the Ice
Age) which, according to the tradition as given by Boswell, was
thrown at a giant by his mistress, in return for a similar one which

he, "all in sport", had pitched at *her*. Indeed, a vast weight for Ajax, as Boswell remarked, recalling Pope's allusion to that mighty Trojan—"When Ajax strives some rock's vast weight to throw". Dr. Johnson did not trouble to ascend Ben Hogh. He accompanied Boswell and young Coll (the laird's son) no farther than he could travel comfortably on horseback. There he "placed himself on the ground, with his back against a large fragment of rock. The wind being high, he let down the cocks of his hat, and tied it with his handkerchief under his chin. While we were employed in examining the stone, which did not repay our trouble in getting to it, he amused himself with reading *Gataker on Lots and on the Christian Watch*, a very learned book, of the last age, which had been found in the garret of Coll's house, and which he said was a treasure here. When we descried him from above, he had a most eremitical appearance; and on our return told us, he had been so much engaged by Gataker, that he had never missed us."

This strange boulder, resembling at a distance a large, plump mammal of pre-historic times, is poised so delicately on three small stones as to make it possible for one to rock it slightly with but little effort.

.   .   .   .

In due course I returned to the borrowed bicycle. After pushing it up steep sand-hills here and there, and cycling cautiously through bent-lands, I eventually reached the farm at Totronald and the corner of a field, by a cattle-trough, at which the island road resumes the appearance of something along which wheeled traffic might proceed less tardily. Among the bent and sand-dunes between Ballyhaugh and Totronald, one could easily lose oneself, if one missed the track and wandered toward the seashore, a mile or so away. In doing so one day, I came upon a brace of grouse that screamed noisily at me with anger, and ran round me in circles, with outstretched wings. Their odd behaviour halted my progress for a moment. In seeking the reason for it, I looked down at my feet to find a row of the most beautiful, brown chicks you ever saw. They were but a day or two old.

By the time one passes Arileod and bears eastward toward Acha, the going becomes easier. At Arileod several tracks divert from the main thoroughfare. For the most part these are passable: here and there, however, in their threading through bent-grass and wild flowers, they disappear. Undermined in places by rabbit-burrows, they demand caution from him who travels them, whether a-foot or a-wheel. On the flat stretches, where the bent is less belligerent, one finds, in summer, acres upon which the wild geranium flowers with astonishing profusion.

· · · · · · ·

A little to the south of Arileod, and situated not far inland from the almost circular bay known as Crossapol, is the mansion-house of Kenneth Stewart, proprietor of the greater part of Coll. Indeed, Stewart owns all Coll except the thousand-acre estate of Caoles, in the south; Gunna Isle, lying in the channel between Coll and Tiree; and the three-thousand-acre estate of Cornaig, at the north of the island. These belonged, until recently, to a certain Colin Buchanan Campbell, whose grandfather, Colin Campbell, a native of Mull, purchased them from his own relations about the middle of last century, on his return to Coll after many years' absence in Australia.

The said Colin Buchanan Campbell succeeded to these three estates in 1884, on the death of his uncle, Hector Archibald Campbell, having immediately complied with the primary condition laid down in his uncle's testamentary disposition that he should adopt the surname of Campbell, in place of Buchanan. In 1946 he sold the Cornaig estate to a Captain O'Connor who, in turn, disposed of it to a Major Jackson. Colin died in 1949; and Caoles and Gunna are now the property of my friend, Dr. John Buchanan, his brother.

The Stewart domains in Coll have also been contracting in recent years. In 1949, Kenneth Stewart, aforenamed, disposed of Gallanach to a certain James Paterson, who had been farming it for years; and I see that he is now (1952) endeavouring to sell some further property in Coll, but hopes to retain Breachacha and Crossapol.

The Stewarts came to Coll about the same time as the Campbells. In 1856 John, the first Stewart laird of Coll, bought from the last of the MacLeans the greater portion of the island. The MacLeans of Coll had been in possession for at least three centuries. They were a branch of the MacLeans of Duart, and were noted patrons of the pibroch, in the rendering of which their hereditary pipers, the Rankins, were regarded as being second only to the MacCrimmons of Skye. MacLean, by the way, is still the commonest surname in Coll. There are also several Mac-Kinnons and MacDonalds, and a few MacFadyens, MacInneses, and Campbells.

Close to the mansion-house just mentioned are the ruins of Breachacha Castle, the MacLeans' ancient keep. The name, which is obviously Gaelic in origin, signifies the Speckled Field.

"The Laird of Collow," writes a sixteenth-century chronicler, "has ane castell callit Brekauche, quhilk is ane great strength be reason of the situation thairof verie neir to the sea, quhilk defendis the half thairof, and hes three walls about the rest of the castell and thairof biggit with lyme and stane, with sundrie gude devices for defending of the tower. Ane uther wall about that, within the quhilk schippis and bottis are drawin and salvit. And the third and the uttermost wall of tymber and earth, within the quhilk the haill gudes of the cuntrie are keipit in tyme of troublis or weiris."

In olden times there was to be seen at Breachacha Castle (possibly over the doorway) a stone referred to by several who had seen it. The following is a literal translation of the Gaelic inscription it bore: "If any man of the Clan MacLonich should arrive at this castle, though it should be at midnight, and he have a man's head under his arm, he shall be admitted and given protection against all but the King."

Thereby hangs a tale, of which there are several variants. According to the best known of these, John, one of the earliest of the MacLean chiefs of Coll, accompanied by a band of followers, as well as by his wife, and she with child, went forth into Lochaber upon a warlike expedition on which he was killed, leaving his wife at the mercy of her husband's slayers, who placed her in charge of one, MacLonich. It was decided that, if she gave birth to a son, he was not to be allowed to survive. In due course a son was born to her.

About this time, MacLonich's wife had had a baby girl. In order to spare the life of the infant MacLean, MacLonich and his wife agreed with its widowed mother that, if only as a means of affording it temporary protection, the mothers would exchange children. In this way, MacLean's son and heir was saved. On attaining manhood, he landed in Coll with an armed force, recovered his patrimony, and took up residence at Breachacha, once his father's stronghold. In recognition for what the MacLonichs had done for him, he pronounced that no member of their clan should ever be denied asylum at Breachacha. Furthermore, he undertook to maintain and educate the MacLonich heir, and directed that his successors should do likewise where future heirs were concerned. The treaty between the MacLean lairds of Coll and the MacLonichs had been faithfully observed, according to Dr. Johnson, who mentions that he had read a demand of protection, made not more than thirty-seven years earlier, for a certain

MacLonich named Ewan Cameron. (The MacLonichs, by the way, were a branch of the Camerons: they swore fealty to Locheil.) It appears that Ewan, on account of his having been implicated in the murder of one of the MacMartins, had been exiled by Locheil for a stated number of years. At the end of this period he returned to Scotland, in the hope of settling down peacefully there. But the MacMartins still sought to avenge themselves upon him. So, in virtue of the old promise made to his ancestor, he applied to MacLean for protection against their comminations. This he was vouchsafed; and thus, for the remainder of his days, he found in Coll refuge from his enemies.

Dr. Johnson tells us that, though the guarantee of asylum had lapsed by the time he visited Coll, MacLean was still educating the MacLonich heir. "The power of protection subsists no longer," he remarks; "but what the law permits is yet continued."

Breachacha Castle at this time was still in a fair state of repair, since it had not long been discarded as the laird's residence in favour of the present mansion, nearby.

The Laird of Coll at the time of my sojourn there, a decade or so ago, was the late Brigadier-General Paul Stewart. "He's a clever sort of fellow! " I was informed by one of the islanders, with whom I got into conversation by the roadside, when actually on my way to pay the Laird a call.

"In what ways? " I enquired, desirous of being informed on such matters before crossing his threshold at the New Breachacha, as his mansion-house is called, to distinguish it from the Old.

"Well, he's a C.B. and all that sort of thing—a Commander of the Bath. And, what's more, he lives up to the honour by inviting the local school-teachers to Breachacha Castle for a bath at the week-ends."

Since the General's bath at Breachacha appeared to be the only one in the locality—certainly, the only one to which the island's teaching staff had access—it was an institution much appreciated by those qualified to use it. His tenantry referred to it as the Laird's Dipping!

．　　．　　．　　．　　．　　．　　．　　．　　．

Our mentioning Dr. John Buchanan, proprietor of Caoles and of Gunna Isle, recalls the gallantry, in 1798, of his great-great-grandfather, Malcolm Campbell, when he saved a naval vessel from disaster off Coll. The beautiful silver urn afterwards presented to him by the Lords Commissioners of the Admiralty has now reached Nova Scotia, where it resides in the possession of Samuel Campbell, Governor of St. Paul's Island, Malcolm's direct lineal descendant. The urn, surmounted by a silver anchor and chain, bears the inscription:

"From the Right Honourable the Lords Commissioners of the Admiralty to Mr. Malcolm Campbell, Cornaig, of the Island of Coll, as a mark of their Lordships' sense of Mr. Campbell's meritorious zeal and exertions in having, on the 29th November, 1798 (when no other person would venture to quit the shore) gone off to the assistance of His Majesty's ship 'Caesar' of 84 guns, commanded by Captain Reddam Home, when driven by stormy weather near that Island, and by whose local knowledge she was safely conducted into Tobermory Bay during the storm."

The *Caesar* was one of the Navy's largest ships. While cruising off the west coast of Scotland, she was driven by storm among the Inner Hebrides. The inhabitants of Coll, believing her to be a French vessel in distress, were greatly alarmed at her arrival in these waters. Several attempts made by her crew to effect a landing from their boats were unsuccessful, since none of the inhabitants would direct them to safe anchorage from the raging sea. Soon the ship drifted opposite Malcolm Campbell's home at Cornaig; and Malcolm, realising that she was in imminent danger of being wrecked, resolved that, whether vessel of friend or of foe, he would succour her. He rowed out to her, boarded her, and eventually brought her to safety at Tobermory, where captain and officers gave a great ball to commemorate their deliverance, and in recognition of Malcolm Campbell's bravery.

As Malcolm declined to accept from them any pecuniary reward, Captain Home brought his services to the notice of the Lords of Admiralty, who now presented him with the urn, and also with a letter stating that, if at any time he or his descendants should feel inclined to join the Navy, they would have special consideration. For his public services on this occasion, Malcolm also received the written congratulations of the Duke of Argyll.

.   .   .   .

Coll, like Tiree, is often cut off by storms. I have frequently been aboard the mail-boat sailing between Oban and Barra when she has been unable to make her customary call at either—which reminds me of the humorous incident recorded by Seton Gordon in his *Highways & Byways in the West Highlands.* Some women had come aboard at Tobermory. They were returning to Kilchoan, in Ardnamurchan, the first port of call thereafter, but three or four miles away, on the opposite side of the Sound of Mull. So stormy was it, however, that the Kilchoan ferryboat could not put out to meet the mail-boat. The latter, therefore, continued on her course to the Outer Hebrides, by way of Tiree and Coll. On reaching the former isle, it was discovered that conditions there were as unpropitious as they had been at Kilchoan some hours earlier. Since it was found impossible to go alongside at Scarinish, the boat sailed for Arinagour, in Coll, her next port. There these unfortunate women, more dead than alive, were put ashore by heaving, pitching ferryboat.

" Well," said the captain to Seton Gordon, " they have, I think, had their ninepence-worth! "

CHAPTER VIII

LISMORE

BETWEEN the Lynn of Lorne and the Lynn of Morven, at the wide entrance to Loch Linnhe, and in true alignment with the Great Glen of Scotland, from the south-western extremity of which it lies at no great distance, is Lismore, an island noted in olden days for its fertility. The memory of this fertility, due largely to the calcareous nature of its soil and to an even distribution of moisture, is perpetuated in its very name: Lismore, a word purely of Gaelic origin, signifies the Great Garden. One must concede, however, that scholars have interpreted it differently. Some have maintained, for example, that the first syllable of Lismore is from the Gaelic, *lios*, denoting a fortified enclosure.

The island, at its north-eastern end, comes well within half a mile of the Appin district of Argyllshire's mainland; while the centre of its east coast is less than a mile from the legend-haunted land of Benderloch. Lismore, throughout the centuries, has had the closest associations with Appin and with Benderloch. Largely for geographical reasons, its contacts with Morven, on the western shores of Loch Linnhe, have been less intimate. Between Port Appin and the jetty situated a little beyond Port Ramsay, in Lismore, plies a ferry enabling its natives to leave for or return from the mainland of Argyll almost at any hour, and almost in any weather. This amenity is appreciated by such of its 200 inhabitants as may wish to avail themselves of it in preference to the seven miles' sea journey between Oban and the pier at Achnacroish, their island's regular port of call, centre of its modest activities. All the year round, at least twice daily, Sundays excepted, MacBrayne runs between Oban and Achnacroish the *Lochnell*, a commodious motor-vessel of 31 tons, certificated to ply for short distances by sea during daylight, and in fine weather. In addition to this, the picturesque *Lochfyne* makes several calls during her summer and autumn cruisings between Oban and Fort William. This means that, in the matter of transport, the island is among the most favourably situated of the Hebrides. Take into consideration also the convenience of the North End Ferry, as it is called, and you will see that its inhabitants have little cause to complain of isolation. Yet, I know many of them maintain that, in the matter of communication with the mainland, their lot is inferior to that enjoyed by their great-grandparents a century ago. The younger and hardier members of the community, attending weekend functions at Oban, have no means of returning home thereafter except by taking the last bus thence to Appin, by way of Connel, and crossing therefrom by the North End Ferry. If their homes be at the Kilcheran extremity of Lismore, they will have as much as six miles to travel on foot, following such minor roads and tracks as diversify it. Of this they think nothing. They do it regularly, arriving home hilariously contented in the small hours. Even the older inhabitants will adopt this somewhat arduous and circuitous homeward route rather than that the scheduled time of the last ferry service direct from Oban to Achnacroish should deprive them of the occasion for those sprees in which so much of the male population of the Highlands and Islands indulges, especially at weekends.

In recent years the North End Ferry has found popularity among those who go a-hiking through the West Highlands. Bands of young people, seeking an excursion not too strenuous, will cross by the regular motor-launch from Oban to Achnacroish with their knapsacks and waterproofs (the latter always a wise precaution in these parts) and walk thence to the ferry which, in the matter of a few minutes, will transfer them to the Appin shore. Many come to Lismore from the opposite direction, crossing over from Appin, and returning to Oban from Achnacroish by the late launch. In time of fog or of darkness, one summons the ferryman to the Appin side by means of the horn enclosed in a box erected by the wayside as one approaches the pier there. Lower the lid and turn the handle to send forth the weird brayings which soon bring the ferryboat over from Lismore. In daylight and in clear weather, of course, a shout and a wave of the hand instantly attract this ready means of transport.

Lismore, at its south-western extremity, is a little over a mile from Duart Point, in Mull. Here intervenes that channel in which lies the Lady's Rock of dramatic association, the grey walls of Duart Castle rising above the tide on the one hand, and the Lismore Light on the other. This lighthouse stands prominently on an islet off Lismore's seaward extremity, and is passed by all vessels sailing north-westwards from Oban—a landmark familiar to everyone acquainted with such of the Inner Hebrides as are approached by way of the romantic Sound of Mull.

Lismore is about twelve miles in length, and has a maximum breadth of no more than a mile and a half. Its area of nearly 10,000 acres is covered for the most part with grass and bracken. Its surface is uneven, reaching in the Barr Mor, in the Kilcheran neighbourhood, its greatest height at 417 feet. There are no trees; and, since the island has never possessed but the meagrest quantity of peat (and that of poor quality), fuel has always been a problem with its inhabitants. From time immemorial, the *Liosaich*, as the natives of Lismore are called in the Gaelic, had peat-cutting rights about Kingairloch, in Morven, and in the Moss of Achnacree, that extensive peat deposit in Benderloch. From Kingairloch, too, they regularly brought home by boat quantities of timber from woods no longer in existence. To-day most of the inhabitants import coal, brought to them at stated intervals by a Clyde puffer.

For an island of no great altitude in relation to area, Lismore is copiously endowed with fresh water. Even in the driest season, its wells and springs have never been known to fail—a fact which prompted the parish's incumbent at the beginning of the nineteenth century to suggest that capital might be introduced to harness its water for manufacturing purposes! According to the Rev. Iain Carmichael, a native of Lismore, and its present parish minister, water is to be found where least expected, and is wanting just where one would hope to find it readily. It is to be found, for example, about the summit of the Barr Mor—obviously for geological reasons. Conversely, none can be located at the foot of slopes which one might reasonably suppose to be the lower parts of its watershed. Yet, water can be found in abundance on the higher reaches of these slopes. Quite recently, an amateur dowser on a visit to Lismore gave a few private exhibitions of his art. In order to test his power, he was conducted away from the beaten track to a spot near which it was known to all but himself that a well lay. Here the forked hazel twig reacted so violently that the dowser could not hold it. This readily convinced those accompanying him of his being a genuine dowser.

Another remarkable thing about the water on Lismore is that at times it gushes forth from the ground in a manner showing it to have been under considerable pressure. "There are twin fountains near Bailegarve, quaintly and poetically called *Fliuchaig* and *Fraingeag*," writes the Rev. Iain Carmichael, "which in their season can put the fountains of Trafalgar Square to shame."[1]

Considerable as is the rainfall in this part of Scotland, Lis-

[1] *Lismore In Alba,* by Iain Carmichael, D.S.O., M.C., Minister of Lismore (1947).

more's catchment is too limited to explain, alone, the quantity of water all the year round in each of its three freshwater lochs—in Lochs Fiart, Kilcheran, and Baile a' Ghobhainn. It is thought that these lochs derive much from springs within them, which are constantly active, and ensure for the brown trout, with which they are so amply stocked, their excellent condition.

It occurs to me that the unusual distribution of water may explain the mushrooms to be found so plentifully everywhere about Lismore—everywhere about its grasslands, and even among the hill-grazings which comprise so large a proportion of its area. In all my experience of islands, never have I seen one so abundant in mushrooms. When on a visit early in August, 1949, I could have gathered a bushel in a few minutes. The natives, unable perhaps to distinguish them readily from similar fungi known to be poisonous, are not too fond of them. But visitors to Lismore—and they are many in summer and autumn—make the most of a delicacy so plentiful here, and so fresh, conscious of the price demanded in the cities for mushrooms much inferior in quality, and anything but fresh.

.   .   .   .

Lismore shares with adjacent Benderloch its traditions of the ancient Fingalians. These survive in some of its Gaelic place-names—in the Port of the Great Heroes, for instance, in the Bay and in the Islet of Oscar, in Fingal's Hillock, and in the Hill of the Fingalian Women. The discovery of immense horns in Lismore gave weight to the tradition that it was one of the Fingalians' hunting-grounds. According to the compiler of the relevant section in the *Old Statistical Account of Scotland* (c. 1792), " the most remarkable curiosities in Lismore seem to be deer and perhaps elk horns of great size, and cow horns of a still greater size in proportion. The pith of one of the latter, though much shrivelled and withered, is 12 inches in circumference at the root. Tradition asserts that the Island was an old deer forest, and the number of deer horns and deer skeletons found, quite entire, confirm the assertion."

.   .   .   .

It was about the middle of the sixth century, when St. Columba was establishing himself at Iona, that there came to Lismore the saint whose name has been associated with the island ever since—Saint Moluag. Unlike his namely contemporary, who had at least three biographers, Moluag appears to have none, with the result that, apart from the few references to him scattered

99

throughout ancient Celtic annals, we know little of his work, either in Lismore or elsewhere. Local tradition, however, relates the circumstances of his arrival at Lismore. While sailing alone in his coracle in the Lynn of Lorne, close to the east coast of the island, looking for a suitable spot at which to disembark, lo! there suddenly emerged from the obscurity of the *Eilean Dubh*, or Black Isle, another coracle, the occupants of which also seemed to be looking for a convenient landing-place. Moluag soon recognised one of them to have been Columba. Knowing how masterful a man he was, he directed his sailors to row with all speed for the shore. It soon became obvious that he and Columba had decided to land at the same spot. A race between the coracles ensued; and it looked as though Columba's must win, and, in so doing, establish for that saint the prior right to Christianise the island's inhabitants. Moluag, determined to outbid him, picked up an axe, with which he severed, upon the gunwale, the little finger of his left hand. This he threw ashore, ahead of both coracles, with the pronouncement, " My flesh and blood have first possession of this island; and I bless it in the Name of the Lord."

According to a tradition cited by Iain Carmichael, whom we already have quoted, Columba did not take lightly Moluag's outwitting him in this way, and actually cursed him. " May you have the alder for your firewood! "

"The Lord will make the alder burn pleasantly," replied Moluag, in soothing tones.

" May you have the jagged ridges for your pathway! " Columba continued.

" The Lord will smooth them to the feet," answered Moluag, resolved not to lose his temper over an incident which had already lost him his little finger, and remembering that, although Columba and he were rivals in renown, they were still brethren in religion.

Commenting on these traditional and not too friendly exchanges between two saints, Iain Carmichael, who knows so intimately his native isle—the scene of his present ministry—says that the reference to the jagged ridges (another version of Columba's utterance. " The edge of the rocks be upwards! ") directs attention to a feature of Lismore's limestone formation, " which keeps appearing and disappearing in runs of sharp-edged ridges ". Alder, it is held, burns better in Lismore than anywhere else, as if in fulfilment of Moluag's pronouncement. Even more extraordinary is the fact that at Port Moluag, the inlet where the saint is believed to have landed nearly fourteen centuries ago, there is a little clump of alders. Probably Columba had noticed them.

The Garvellach Isles—Eileach an Naoimh— seen from A' Chùli

Most historians ascribe to St. Moluag the founding of the Christian Church in Lismore. When considering Columba's claim, they incline to the view that he "swallowed up into his own fame all the work of his predecessors, companions, and contemporaries, and deprived generations of pioneers and missionaries of their just fame".

It is natural that the natives of Lismore, in their hearts, should give pride of affection to St. Moluag, rather than to St. Columba, since they firmly believe it was the former who Christianised their pagan ancestors, and laid the foundations of the island's earliest place of Christian worship. They point out that, had Columba planted the first Church here, his name would have been perpetuated abundantly in the island's toponomy. It appears to be associated only with the remains of the ancient chapel on Bernera, an islet off Lismore's extreme south-west corner. At this chapel, says tradition, and in the shadow of a mighty yew-tree, Columba is said to have conducted a service or two when visiting Moluag. The name of the latter saint, however, survives in that of many of Lismore's natural features.

It is Professor Reeves who, notwithstanding the traditional connection between Columba and the yew at Bernera, demolishes so utterly the view that the saint so closely identified with Iona had anything to do with Lismore. "St. Columba," he writes, "had no more jurisdiction in Lismore than in Applecross or Kingarth."

If this be so, it seems a pity that the design of the two admirable stained-glass windows in the east gable of Lismore's parish church should include Columba so prominently as to foster and perpetuate the impression that he had had a directing hand in the island's early Christian affairs. These windows were designed by Miss M. I. Wood, in memory of Mrs. Gregorson. The figure on the right represents St. Columba blessing the Bernera yew-tree: that on the left portrays St. Moluag with his pastoral staff—his famous *Bachull Mor*—and the boat in which he reached Lismore. The windows' floral representations are those of flowers which grow exceptionally well in Lismore. They include the tormentil, that tiny, vivacious flower one finds growing wild upon our heathery and moorland parts, and by our Hebridean waysides—the little, yellow thing for which Columba is said to have had an especial affection.

The Gregorsons, by the way, are a family of Lismore origin. They were formerly MacGregors; and it is just possible that they were related to that illustrious member of my clan who had much to do with Lismore immediately prior to the Reformation. I refer to Sir James MacGregor, the Dean of Lismore—the island's last

H   101

Roman Catholic Dean, of whom you shall hear more a little later. A fragment of music—part of the Old 100th—incorporated in the window depicting St. Columba connects the Gregorsons with one to whom Iain Carmichael refers as a much abler man, namely, their scientific ancestor, the Rev. Colin Campbell (1667-1726), minister of Ardchattan. The fragment was copied from a music manuscript of his. Campbell was a mathematician and an astronomer, as well as a musician. "Were he among us," said Isaac Newton at a conference of scientists, " he would make children of us all."

．　　．　　．　　．　　．　　．　　．

Some maintain that the mass of tumbled stones at Port Moluag, the spot where Lismore's own belovèd saint first landed in ancient days, defines the site of his earliest place of worship there, and the *muinntir* or Christian fellowship he established shortly afterwards. His first cell or chapel probably took the form of those beehive structures in stone which are to be found all over Early Celtic Christendom, splendid examples of which survive in Ireland. The specimen nearest to Lismore is that on Eileach an Naoimh, the isle of the Garvellach group which scholars are prone to identify as Hinba.

It is with the neighbourhood of Clachan, rather than of Port Moluag, however, that Lismore's ecclesiastical history has been identified throughout the centuries. Here is the island's oldest Christian burial-place. No such place is to be found at or near the Port. Here, furthermore, situated just behind the smithy, is the well bearing Moluag's name. Here is the site upon which was built the Cathedral, and upon which, to-day, stands the Parish Church of Lismore. It is improbable that the Cathedral would have been raised on any site but that occupied, at least approximately, by some earlier religious building.

Moluag's death occurred on June 25th, 592. Its anniversary is commemorated in the Breviary of Aberdeen (c. 1509), one of the first books printed in Scotland by the printing-press, then recently introduced. There is some mention of the saint's death in Irish annals too. Tignernach records that in 592 there occurred "the death of Lugaid of Lismore, that is Moluoc". Accounts vary as to the place where he died, and as to where he was buried. Most of them give Ardclach, in Nairnshire, as the place where his death occurred; and most agree that he was buried at Rosemarkie. However, there exists in Lismore a tradition that the saint's remains were interred in the isle he knew well and loved so dearly, and that his relics were likewise conveyed there for preservation. The people of Lismore, according to this tradition, could not bear the idea that the corpse of their revered *anam-chara*, or soul-friend, should lie elsewhere. So they selected twenty of the doughtiest of their number to convey it home across Scotland to Lismore. Thus, says local tradition, " the gracious and decorous, the modest and white-haired, Moluag of Lismore in Alba " found a last resting-place among his very own people.

Unfortunately for tradition, there is absolutely no confirmatory evidence of Moluag's having been buried in Lismore. Yet, one must add that, when a lair in the centre of the churchyard, believed locally to be Moluag's, was opened at the end of the nineteenth century, a golden tripod candlestick, plain and beautifully proportioned, was discovered in it. Of this, Campbell of Lochnell took possession. Its whereabouts, to-day, is unknown. Perhaps, some reader of this volume may know where it reposes.

Those who claim Lismore as Moluag's place of burial point out that the saint's movable relics, so greatly revered, were there—his bell and its shrine, and his famous *Bachull*, or pastoral staff—his crosier. The bell, famed for its magical powers, is known to have been in Lismore at the close of the fifteenth century, and at the beginning of the sixteenth. The Aberdeen Breviary describes how Moluag, requiring a square iron bell, asked an artificer to make one for him. The artificer complained that he had no coals to enable him to do so. Thereupon Moluag gathered reeds and rushes which, when ignited, magically served the purpose. The bell thereby fabricated, says the Breviary, was greatly venerated in the Church of Lismore. That was in 1509.

In the National Museum of Antiquities of Scotland is a broken iron bell presented by John MacNeill in 1827, and believed to have been Moluag's. It is $3\frac{1}{2}$ inches in height, $2\frac{1}{2}$ inches by $1\frac{1}{4}$ inches across. It was unearthed in 1814, together with its shrine, in a ruined wall at a farm in the Argyllshire parish of Kirkmichael-Glassary.

The different parts of the bell-shrine are cast in bronze beautifully engraved. The style of the figure of the Crucified Christ and of some of the leaf ornament indicate a late twelfth-century date. The animal heads on the handle and feet, the leafy scrolls, as well as the interlacing ornament on the side, demonstrate Celtic taste in design. In this exquisite bell-shrine we find one of the many instances in which the intrinsic value of the object itself, both as regards its material and the workmanship it displays, far exceed that of the relic it was designed to enshrine.

More famous than Moluag's bell is his *Bachull Mor*—his crosier —a relic in the possession of the Duke of Argyll until 1951. It consists of a stick of blackthorn 34 inches in length, is a little curved at one end, and resembles a shinty-stick in miniature, which accounts for its being referred to in the Western Highlands as *An Caman*, the shinty, this being the name given in the Scottish Highlands to a game played like hockey with a club and ball. The name is also applied to the club with which it is played.

Moluag's Crosier shows signs of once having been covered over with a yellowish metal. This explains why it has sometimes been called the *Bachull Buidhe*, or Yellow Stick. Upon a time, says tradition, it was also inlaid with precious stones. It had its hereditary ' baron ' or custodian, who, in return for the protective services he rendered it, had a freehold near the sacred building in which it was kept. From time immemorial, this relic remained in Lismore, in the hereditary custody of a family named Livingstone. Consequently, the Livingstones were known as the Barons of Bachull.

The Crosier shared with many another relic the reputation of being endowed with miraculous powers. As was said of those ancient Celtic bells, if lost or stolen, it could return, of its own accord, to its rightful place. It was claimed that it vouchsafed immunity from danger at sea, that it ensured veracity on land, that it could stay the murrain among beasts, and that it brought relief to women in labour. There were occasions, too, when, after the fashion of a mace, it was borne as an emblem of authority.

In 1951, this pastoral staff, so greatly revered, but hitherto so seldom seen, was placed on view for three months in the Ancestry Room of the Livingstone Memorial, at Blantyre. In June of that year, the Duke of Argyll gave it to Dr. Hubert Wilson, grandson of David Livingstone, for temporary safekeeping. Dr. Wilson collected the staff at Inveraray Castle, where it had reposed for about a century. He was accompanied by Miss Nyasa Livingstone, representing her brother, Alistair Livingstone, who was abroad at the time. Alistair is joint custodian of the staff.

Among the natives of Lismore and their descendants in Britain and throughout the Dominions and Colonies, it was always a source of annoyance that St. Moluag's *Bachull* should have remained at Inveraray, in the possession of the Duke of Argyll, hereditary Chief of the Clan Campbell; and they regard as puerile the peat-stack explanation given by the Marquis of Lorne in

Adventures in Legend, published in 1898. " Now at Lismore," wrote the Marquis, " there was a very famous and holy relic, not of bones or dress, but the actual and true *Baculus* or Crozier which had of old belonged to Saint Moluac. . . . This holy pastoral staff, an undoubted crozier of the sixth century, was kept at Lismore where the saint had first landed to preach the Gospel to the Picts. For centuries it was held in such veneration that people came from far and near to be touched by it for the cure of their diseases. It was not lost or destroyed at the Reformation, but remained, guarded generation after generation, by the hereditary holder. Finally, after so many ages, a time came when the ' Baron' became too poor to have any safe place where it might remain, and he hid it behind a great peat-stack, unwilling that it should incur further perils. Its silver covering had been stolen piecemeal, and the lower portion of the staff itself is lost. It is now safe where it cannot be destroyed or stolen, in the hands of those who can preserve it. It was made in two parts, the upper fitting into the lower. One portion of the crook, and that the larger, has been broken off, leaving only the commencement of the curve at the top. It is of hard wood and is stuck full of little bronze tacks or headless nails, which in two places still retain portions of the inner bronze sheathing which originally covered it. Mutilated as it is, it is one of the most interesting relics of the Scots Irish Church, and is the most ancient of any . . ."

Nobody can say precisely how and why it came into the possession of the Argyll family. However, it was certainly fitting that, at the outset of its change of ownership in 1951, this ancient relic, so long hidden away at Inveraray Castle, should have been introduced to public view by its being exhibited at David Livingstone's birthplace, for David himself describes how his own ancestors were " made Protestant" in the Scottish Highlands " by the laird coming round with a man having a yellow stick". The Crosier at that time, he adds, was regarded as being of greater significance than the cleric who used it, and whose teaching thus went by the name of " the religion of the yellow stick".

Lismore retains in many of its place-names echoes of the centuries during which the Norsemen occupied it. Its ancient watchtowers are said to have been the vantage-points from which the more vigilant inhabitants looked out for those northern invaders, so as to give their neighbours sufficient time to conceal what otherwise might have been plundered. In Castle Coeffin, on the west side of the island, we see the ruins of a Norwegian fortress in which, says tradition, lived a prince and a princess, children of the King of Lochlann—of Norway. At Port Chaisteil, the little bay at Castle Coeffin, the prince, a young man of vigour and courage who permitted neither his galleys to rest nor his arms to rust, kept his galleys. Beothail, his sister, was a princess much loved by the people of Lismore, who shared with her the sorrow which carried her to an early grave. Her lover had died in distant Lochlann. Before long, the inconsolable Beothail was dead too. The islespeople buried her on the hill-top of Eirebal, in Lismore. But her spirit was soon to haunt her father and brother, urging them to exhume her remains and convey them across the seas to Lochlann, that they might be re-interred beside those of her lover. The Gaels, incidentally, have preserved in their own language, and in poetic form, Beothail's pleadings from the grave that her body might be taken to Lochlann. To these pleadings her relatives were eventually to give effect. Her remains were exhumed at Eirebal, and washed either in St. Moluag's Well, they say, or, as is more probable, in the well that to this day the natives refer to as the *Tobar Cnamh Bheothail*, the Well of Beothail's Bones. But there was still unrest, both in Lismore and in Norway, until it was discovered that, in the well in which the remains had been washed, there lay the bones of two of Beothail's toes. These were recovered and sent to Norway for burial with the rest of her, thus ensuring peace for the living as well as for the dead.

. . . .

The ecclesiastical history of Lismore is a long and complicated one, for the details of which one cannot do better than refer the reader to Iain Carmichael's admirable *Lismore in Alba*, which we have already mentioned. In 1249 there was instituted for Lismore a Cathedral Charter, which explains how, to this day, one sees references to the island's Cathedral. Its present Parish Church is regarded as having been its chancel or choir; and it is to be deplored that, in the restoration of the latter at various times, so little interest was shown in the architectural remains of the former. The systematic excavation of the site would probably yield much of historic and antiquarian interest.

The first Presbyterian minister of the Parish of Lismore and Appin, though he bore the title of Dean, is believed to have been Nicholas Campbell, installed in 1564. Perhaps the best known of its sixteen Presbyterian incumbents since that time, excepting the present incumbent, is the Rev. John Macaulay, Lord Macaulay's grandfather, who was translated to Lismore from North Uist in 1755. He owes his place in history to his violent anti-Jacobite activities—his endeavour to thwart the designs of, and even to capture, Prince Charles Edward.

Macaulay was succeeded in 1766 by the Rev. Donald MacNicol, Gaelic scholar and poet, and author of *Remarks on Dr. Samuel Johnson's Journey to the Hebrides.*

. . . .

My earliest knowledge of the existence of an island named Lismore was derived from my father's repeated allusions to the aforementioned Sir James MacGregor, its Dean between the years 1514 and 1551. Sir James, a descendant of the Vicar of Fortingall, Perthshire, was mainly responsible for that famous work, *The Book of the Dean of Lismore,* a quarto volume of 311 pages, first edited, with a translation and notes, in 1862, and the subject of two volumes published a few years ago by the Scottish Gaelic Texts Society. It reposes in the Scottish National Library. Except for a short Latin obituary and a few other fragments, it consists largely of a collection of Gaelic poetry written by Sir James and his brother, Duncan. The manuscript is in the Roman characters current during the early years of the sixteenth century, and not in Irish characters, as might have been expected. The spelling is phonetic, thus preserving the pronunciation of contemporary Gaelic.

Incidentally, Sir James MacGregor, Dean of Lismore, is regarded as having been the first to translate into Gaelic the Psalms of David.

Three and a half centuries after his time, Lismore was to be the birthplace of another man whose contribution to Celtic literature was considerable. I refer to Dr. Alexander Carmichael, author of that precious collection of Gaelic hymns, tunes, and incantations known as *Carmina Gadelica*, and father of the late Ella Carmichael, whom my own father ought to have married. Ella ultimately became the second wife of the late W. J. Watson, LL.D., Professor of Celtic at Edinburgh. Like her father, and certainly not unlike my own, Ella Carmichael was an enthusiastic Celtic scholar, and an indefatigable folklorist where Gaeldom was concerned. I have always thought it a great tragedy for Gaeldom, as well as for my late mother, and the rest of us, that my father, on his return from India, did not marry Ella. All five—Dr. Carmichael and Ella, Professor Watson, my father, and my mother—are now well and truly in heaven, where four of them, at least, will assuredly be parleying in the language of the Garden of Eden, and where the fifth—my mother—cannot have failed by this time to convince the other four of how suitable a wife Ella Carmichael would have made my father.

.   .   .   .

To-day Lismore has a rapidly decreasing population. The first large exodus was to North Carolina in 1775. Subsequent emigrations took place in 1789 and 1791. A population which, in 1831, was 1,790, had declined to 280 by 1931. Now it is about 200, and is still falling. Yet, the island is not without vigour. Get into conversation with some of its retired seafarers (it is noted, by the way, for the number of sea captains it produces), and you will learn much about adventure. Call on Captain James MacDonald, for instance (his house, *Glencoe*, is easily reached from the pier), and ask him to relate some of his experiences as master of one of the Nobel ships transporting explosives from Ardeer, by way of the Pentland Firth, to Heligoland, where his cargoes were transferred to German ships, and you will soon realise how much stranger than fiction is truth!

A surname wellknown on the island is MacColl. As far back as records go, a family of this name, residing at Achnacroish, has provided the north end with its postman. Through five generations, a John MacColl has succeeded a John MacColl in this capacity, delivering mails at farms and crofts scattered about the seven-mile stretch between the island's post-office, at Achnacroish, and the North End Ferry. The fifth John MacColl has just retired, after forty-five years' service; and he has been succeeded as postman by his nephew, Calum MacCaig.

Conclusively, a lovelier island than Lismore you will not find among the Inner Hebrides. Its colourings are truly exquisite. Often, when wandering among its inland rocks, you will see, against their grey lichen, an elusive blue—a drift of harebells— of the real Bluebells of Scotland. In springtime one sees another elusive hue in the heliotrope of the periwinkles growing profusely in its wayside dells.

CHAPTER IX

KERRERA

To the south-west of the Highland town of Oban, and separated from the mainland of Argyll by the narrow Sound of Kerrera, is the Island of Kerrera, almost the whole of which still belongs to the Dunollie Estates, the property of MacDougall of Mac-Dougall. It has a length of about four miles, and a breadth of two. Situated about the middle of the east side, between the bay known as the Little Horse Shoe and the farm of Ardachoirc (Height of the Cornfield), it reaches its highest point, at 617 feet, in *Carn Breugach*, the False Cairn. The summit of this modest eminence offers a wild diversion when travelling on foot, as one needs must on Kerrera, between the ferry and the ruins of Gylen Castle, to both of which we shall be alluding in a moment or two. On this hilltop stands an ancient cairn, increased in size throughout the centuries by observance of the custom whereby everyone reaching the summit picks up at least one stone on the way to add to it. At a spot some little distance below the summit, and overlooking the Horse Shoe Bay, there once stood the little wooden cross mentioned in more recent guide-books as commemorating a certain Miss MacRae, a visitor to the island who expired there in 1875, while climbing the False Cairn. When on Kerrera a year or two ago, I could not locate this cross, which I certainly had seen some years before. As it stood there unprotected in any way, it may have been blown down during a storm, and never re-erected.

Kerrera's coast-line, except on the east, is rocky and rugged. Its interior is rough and, in parts, difficult to traverse. From its uplands, however, may be obtained prospects of the Firth of Lorne and of some of the Inner Hebrides more than compensating for any fatigue entailed in reaching them. Away to the north stretches Lismore, firmly set between the Lynn of Lorne and the Lynn of Morven. To the suthard lie the Slate Islands, the Isles of the Sea, Scarba, and Jura. In fine weather the Paps of Jura are clearly visible. Eastward stretches that part of the continent of Argyll dominated by Ben Cruachan (3,689 feet). Westward, at a distance of but four miles across the Firth of Lorne, lies Mull, with Ben More (3,169 feet) on the far horizon.

I suppose that all of us, whose delight it is to wander the more strenuous byways, rather than the smooth highways, find from time to time, in our journeyings, panoramas which have remained in our inward vision with a peculiar clearness—panoramas which, perhaps, have been more spellbinding than others. During my wanderings among the Highlands and Islands, I have discovered many such, but none more lasting than that which filled me to overflowing one autumn morning some years ago, when the guest of the MacDonald family then tenanting the Kerrera farm of Upper Gylen. I had climbed the green steeps behind the farmhouse until I reached the high ground above the little farm and bay of Barrnamboc, beyond which stretched the sea, still and crystal-clear. That stretch of the Mull shore between Loch Don and the narrow entrance to expansive Loch Spelve seemed, in the shadowy distance, like a land of blues and purples in thrall— enchanted. There was no wind; and the heavens everywhere around one were cloudless, except for two puffy balls of white vapour hanging, motionless, above the hilly skyline. They instantly recalled the cloud Elijah's servant eventually beheld from Carmel, arising from the sea—"a little cloud out of the sea, like a man's hand". So still was the day that these fragments, suspended in the western sky, lingered long without any discernible change, either in size or in shape. They might well have been clouds anchored to an artist's canvas.

On my returning to the MacDonalds, I sought to explain my prolonged absence as having been due to something akin to enchantment. They expressed not the least surprise. "Were you sitting up there on the hill," they asked me, "gazing over to Mull?" The identical scene, on such a day as this, had bewitched members of their own household on more than one occasion. It was then that they told me how, in the days before Oban was either a seaport or a rail-head, cattle from Mull were transhipped across the Firth of Lorne to Barrnamboc, driven therefrom across Kerrera itself, and then swum over to the Argyllshire mainland. Since the development of Oban, and the establishment there of a cattle market (one of the most heartless and hideous of our institutions), the wretched beasts have gone direct from Mull to Oban by steamer. At Barrnamboc, however, may still be seen the pier, now greatly dilapidated, at which they were once landed, at the outset of their long and exhausting trail to the southern marts.

Originally the cattle were shipped from Loch Spelve, in Mull, to Slatrich, in Kerrera, or to Ardmore, a farm at the south of the island. "They were used to be kept alternately for three months at Ardmore and three months at Slattrach," runs an old account in the MacDougall's possession at Dunollie; but about the middle of the eighteenth century the MacDougall of the time, as pro-prietor of the ferry, realised "how troublesome this method proved to the leidges passing that way to Mull". So he sought to remedy the inconvenience occasioned them by fixing the ferry at Barrnamboc, "being not only the centre between the two fore-said ferrying-ports, but also a much safer and shorter run to Mull than either, as is known to the whole people". At Barrnam-boc may be seen the small creek blasted and cleaned out between the rocks in 1758, at a cost of fourteen pounds, to make this spot a safe place for the mooring and drawing up of boats—"a real advantage to the country and the whole leidges".

The cattle eventually left Kerrera from Ardentrive Bay, whence they were obliged to swim to the landing-place below Dunollie Castle, to be impounded in the Castle Park until they were herded off to the sales at Inveraray. At that time, Kerrera had at least two inns. These accommodated the Mull cattle-men marooned on the island when weather made ferrying impossible.

. . . .

Kerrera (the accent, by the way, is on the first syllable) is not always as easy of access as might be supposed, though its north-eastern extremity is no more than a few hundred yards from Dunollie, on the immediate outskirts of Oban. This is the part of the island sheltering Oban Bay, rendering it one of the safest of the more spacious anchorages of the Western Highlands. The protection Kerrera affords has been recognised by yachtsmen ever since these waters became popular with navigators in sail. Oban is not merely an important yachting station. It is also the head-quarters of the Royal Highland Yacht Club, instituted in 1881. Members of this select fraternity fly the blue ensign of the navy, and a blue badge depicting a crown on the Cross of St. Andrew. Anything more beautiful than the white wings of a yacht tacking on a colourful day through the Sound of Kerrera, between green hills, would be difficult to imagine.

Standing prominently on a hillock at the very north of Kerrera, just above the little bay of Ardentrive, is a monument in the form of an obelisk. It was erected by a grateful public in 1883 to com-memorate David Hutcheson, "by whose energy and enterprise the benefits of greatly improved steam communication were con-ferred on the West Highlands and Islands of Scotland". David Hutcheson & Co. were the predecessors of the firm whose name, to-day, is as wellknown as any in Celtic Scotland—David Mac-

Brayne, Ltd. The original firm of Hutcheson was founded in 1851. Twenty-eight years later, David MacBrayne, youngest of the three original partners, became sole partner, and gave to the enterprise his own name, which it has retained.

With the application of steam to ship-propulsion, David Hutcheson was swift to recognise the suitability of Oban as a base from which a steamship company might well operate a regular service to the Hebrides and the more distant communities of the Western and North-Western Highlands. So it is, indeed, fitting that this obelisk should stand precisely where it does, overlooking the deep but narrow channel between Kerrera and the mainland, used by the mail-boats and pleasure-cruisers plying constantly between Oban and the Hebrides, as well as by all manner of other vessels, such as warships, entering or leaving Oban's sheltered and commodious harbour.

The route usually adopted by those desirous of exploring Kerrera is that leading southward from Oban to Gallanach, and keeping close to the shore of the Sound of Kerrera. Roughly a couple of miles from Oban, and not far from the point where this shore-road terminates, is the Gallanach ferry, instituted by the grandfather of the present MacDougall of MacDougall, who owns it. Narrow though the crossing of the Sound of Kerrera is at this point, there are days when the ferry cannot be operated because of weather. If the ferryman and his boat be not on the landward side when one arrives at Gallanach with a view to crossing to Kerrera, one merely turns on its swivel a wooden board erected by the jetty. One side of this board is painted black, the other side white. The ferryman, who resides in the ferry-house some little distance above the shore on the Kerrera side, knows that his services are being requisitioned when he is unable to see, from his doorstep, the white side of the board. Should your arrival synchronise with any of his meal-times, you may have to await his pleasure. Otherwise, he is happy to come over for you immediately.

However, the most expeditious and satisfactory way of reaching Kerrera from Oban is by means of one of the motor-boats belonging to Mr. Alick Leslie, a personality widely known as the Lobster King of Kerrera. Alick's lobster depôt at Little Horse Shoe Bay has been going from strength to strength ever since he established his business here, early in the present century. One or other of his motor-boats is usually on the way between Kerrera and Oban in the lobster season, for he is then despatching these creatures all day long. For years, he has supplied with them such famous vessels as the *Queen Mary* and the *Queen Elizabeth*.

The lobsters are caught in the great expanse of the Firth of Lorne. Alick keeps an enormous reserve supply of them at his lobster farm at Cullipool, on Luing, one of the Slate Islands. Those destined for more immediate despatch, however, are retained in the spacious rafts moored offshore in the Little Horse Shoe, in a cottage by the fringe of which the Leslie family lives. Kerrera's proximity to the rail-head at Oban accounts for its successful participation in the lobster industry. Lobsters transported to Oban, often within a quarter of an hour of the receipt of a telegram, are placed on the southbound train that afternoon. Before breakfast-time the following morning, they are awaiting collection at Euston. Get on good terms with the Leslies, then, if you would pass free and freely between Oban and Kerrera! Otherwise, you may experience considerable difficulty in reaching or quitting the island, despite its nearness to Oban.

The other day I asked an active friend residing in Oban whether she could get someone to transport her over to Ardentrive, so near at hand, that she might be able to tell me, for our present purpose, the wording of the inscription appearing on the Hutcheson obelisk. "It seems a physical impossibility to get there," she wrote me in reply, "without having to spend several hours on the island, or walking miles, cross-country, which, meanwhile, the weather will not permit. It would be much easier to get from here to London, or even to America! The Provost tells me that he thinks he has a postcard somewhere with the wording; but he's not sure whether he can find it."

. . . .

Kerrera has ten good farms of moderate dimensions. These are devoted mainly to hill sheep. Quite good crops are raised on some of them, however. Nine of the farms belong to Mac-Dougall. The tenth—Ardentrive—he sold some years ago. Though farming has been reasonably prosperous, and the lobster-fishings in a thriving condition for several years, the island's population is not more than about 60. In 1931 it was 80. With a bit of a squeeze, as the saying is, the entire populace can be seated in the small building situated near the ferry—the building which serves as the island's church, school, and public hall. Here the local dances are held by those content with something of the kind less ambitious and expensive than Oban purveys.

The present school was built by the MacDougalls of Dunollie in memory of Alexander MacDougall, a nineteenth-century chief of the clan. It replaced an earlier school building situated by Balliemore farm. There a father and son of the name of Mac-

Intyre taught in succession for over a hundred years—for more than half a century each! The MacIntyres' teaching of mental arithmetic brought both them and their pupils renown. The son died at the close of the nineteenth century. He is remembered with affection by Kerrera's oldest inhabitants.

Kerrera has some salmon-fishing, in addition to its lobster-fishing and small-scale farming. At the Gylen end of the island resides the native who prosecutes his occupation so profitably as to be known in the district as the Salmon King. Almost everybody in Oban knows the Salmon King of Kerrera. Then, at the north end, on the fringe of Ardentrive Bay, is a small ship-building and ship-repairing yard, work at which appears to be suspended meantime. These premises have changed hands rather frequently during the past quarter of a century. The last tenant was the Oban Slipway Company, which abandoned its activities there some time ago. Quite recently, the yard was taken over by a Clydeside firm which has not, as yet, resumed operations.

Kerrera is not wanting in traditional and historical associations, though little remains of pre-historic structures. Ancient burial-places have been located at Barrnamboc, and also at Slatrach, some little distance to the north. At the island's north-west extremity, not far from the Hutcheson monument, there exists an old place of burial, even the approximate age of which no one seems to know. Of ecclesiological remains there would appear to be none—none identified so far, at all events. Yet, there lingers the tradition that St. Maolrubha had some connection with the island, and that an ancient altar, no longer extant, was dedicated to him. Tradition also has it that St. Columba, during one of his stormy journeyings among the Inner Hebrides, was obliged to anchor his galley in the Little Horse Shoe.

It is not improbable that the iconoclastic Northmen laid waste any early Christian institutions Kerrera may have had. That the island was known to the Norse kings and their seamen is a matter of history.

To Kerrera came King Alexander II of Scotland in the summer of 1249. He had arrived in the Sound with his galleys of war, prepared to give battle to the Norse, then dominating the Western Isles. But the King, on the eve of his proposed contest, took ill with the fever. He was carried ashore, and accommodated in a rudely improvised pavilion near a well by the beach of the Little Horse Shoe. There he died, and at a spot on the farm of Ardachoirc known ever since as Dalrigh—the King's Field. The Scots were thus obliged to abandon their hope of joining issue with the war-galleys of Norway. From Kerrera they bore their monarch's remains to Melrose for burial.

The well in the King's Field, by the beach of Little Horse Shoe Bay, was believed to have possessed curative properties. However, tradition says that Alexander died soon after his having drunk of it. Toward the close of the nineteenth century, this well, for some reason or other, was filled in with stones and earth. Yet, its water is still visible. To this day it goes by the name of the King's Well.

In 1263, just fourteen years after King Alexander's death on Kerrera, Haco's mighty fleet, through stress of weather, anchored in Horse Shoe Bay. Haco was on his way to subdue the late monarch's son and successor, Alexander III. Off Largs later that year, as we know, Haco's fleet suffered the disaster which precipitated the end of the Norse domination of the Scottish Isles. Ceded by Norway shortly afterwards, they now became part of the Kingdom of Scotland.

. . . .

Kerrera's outstanding antiquity—certainly outstanding in the literal sense—is Gylen Castle, an old stronghold of the Mac-Dougalls of Lorne, perched prominently and loftily on a mass of hard conglomerate at the south of the island. It was probably erected on the site of a watch-tower of Scandinavian times, commanding an extensive survey of the surrounding seas.

The building consists mainly of a square tower, well preserved, and rising to a height of three or four storeys. One or two corbelled bartizans, placed at corners high up in the gable, relieve what would otherwise be rather monotonous walls. On three sides, the walls fall steeply and unassailably to the seashore far below. On the fourth and north side, the castle's entrance is approached by a broad stretch of ground terminating in a narrow passage but a few feet long, on each side of which is a stone wall preventing the less steady of head from falling perpendicularly to the seashore. One may pass through the ruined castle to the very edge of the unfenced cliff-top beyond; but only those with the steadiest of nerves should venture as far.

When Dr. John Leyden visited Gylen Castle in 1800, he observed that, on a stone over the doorway, were carved three busts of the period of Mary Queen of Scots, and also the figure of a man playing the bagpipes. The stone's inscription was so obscured by lichen that Leyden could not read it, but thought such would have been possible, had he been able to get up to it. All he could distinguish from the ground was the date, 1587.

The inscription is on sandstone, in raised letters, unpunctuated in any way. Both lettering and spelling are Elizabethan. A few years ago, experts from Aberdeen University interpreted them as follows:

TRUST IN MY GOD AND NOT IN ME MY SON DO WELL AND LET THEM SAY.

The date stone seen by Leyden, and also one of the three figures he mentions, fell down some time ago. They are now preserved at Dunollie, as is also the castle's old kitchen grate, said by experts to belong to the period to which the castle belongs—the latter half of the sixteenth century.

Likewise preserved at Dunollie is yet another stone from Gylen. It bears the initials, D.M.D., said to represent Duncan Mac-Dougall of Dunollie, the fifteenth chief, who built it. The initials of his wife, Margaret MacLean of Duart, whom he married in 1587, are broken away. Below, and in Elizabethan character, are the initials, V.B.M. These are said to signify *Virgo Beath Maria*.

In the troublous years of the seventeenth century, the Mac-Dougalls held Gylen Castle for Charles I until 1647, when a detachment of General Leslie's army, commanded by Colonel Montgomery, took it for the Cromwellians. It was then that the Brooch of Lorne, which had been housed there for safe-keeping, was looted, afterwards coming into the possession of the Campbells of Bragleen, who occupied a little property of that name at the east end of Loch Scamadale, in North Argyll.

This famous heirloom had been in the MacDougall family ever since the 11th of August, 1306, that memorable day on which, in his skirmish with John, Lord of Lorne, son of MacDougall de Ergadia (of Argyll), at the Battle of Dalrigh, in Perthshire, Robert the Bruce was constrained to relieve himself of it by unfastening it, in order to shake himself free of his plaid, grasped by the hand of his slain adversary. Scott introduces into *The Tales of a Grandfather* and also into *The Lord of the Isles* the Bruce's loss of this brooch.

The Brooch of Lorne remained with the Campbells of Brag-leen until 1826, the year in which it passed to General Duncan Campbell of Lochnell, who graciously, and without reservation, presented it to the descendants of its original owner, the van-quished John of Lorne. Thus, to-day, it remains in the possession of MacDougall of MacDougall, Chief of the Clan MacDougall. Circular in shape, and measuring $3\frac{1}{2}$ inches across, it consists of a

large, central stone encircled by a number of pearls. Its centre unscrews to reveal, within, a small box which is said to have contained, at one time, a fragment of bone thought to have been the relic of some saint, or of some valorous ancestor, and which still enshrines a scrap of old, hand-woven, and much faded Mac-Dougall tartan. It is, in fact, a reliquary brooch, though many a year has slipped by since it enclosed any such relic as a bit of bone.

MacDougall was wearing the celebrated Brooch of Lorne in his plaid the day he steered, up Loch Tay, the royal barge conveying Queen Victoria. So greatly did Victoria admire it that he allowed her to wear it while the barge returned down the loch.

Donald MacDougall's Smithy, in Lennox Street,
Port Ellen, Isle of Islay

Chapter X

THE SLATE ISLANDS

The matter of differentiating between which islands should be included in the Inner Hebrides, and which excluded, must necessarily be arbitrary. This one certainly discovers when dealing with those scattered throughout the Firth of Lorne, off the west coast of the Argyllshire mainland. The Outer Hebrides, on the other hand, present no such problem. Their geographical situation in relation to the mainland of Scotland, and also their distribution in relation to one another, simplify their classification.

To all intents and purposes, however, most of the islands of Lorne lying south of Oban may be regarded as part of the Inner Hebrides. This, of course, includes Kerrera, with which we have just dealt. Most of the native population of these isles is still Gaelic-speaking; and many old social and agrarian customs survive there. So, too, do many old-world beliefs.

The highroad leading south from Oban in the direction of Kilninver brings one within easy reach of at least three of the wellknown Slate Islands of Lorne—Seil, Easdale, and Luing. In all of these, slate-quarrying has been going on, though somewhat intermittently, for a century or two.

At Clachan Seil one crosses from the Argyllshire mainland to Seil by a humpbacked stone bridge of a single arch, erected toward the close of the eighteenth century. This structure, known as Clachan Bridge, strides the strait where it is narrowest. The apex of its span of 78 feet is 26 above highwater mark. For a considerable distance to the north and to the south of this spot, the channel remains so constricted that the tidal waters streaming through it resemble more closely an impetuous inland river than a marine current.

Pictorial reproductions of Clachan Bridge are among the commonest to be seen in the Western Highlands. Postcards depicting it are always very popular, since they usually bear the fanciful legend of 'Bridge across the Atlantic'! Over this bridge passes all pedestrian and vehicular traffic for Seil and for Easdale, and indeed for Luing also. The road bearing southward from it,

through Seil itself, and skirting the slate-quarrying centre of Balvicar, ends where the tides sweep swiftly through Cuan Sound,
over which one is ferried to Luing. So greatly has road transport
improved in these parts in recent years, that one may arrive by
bus at one's destination in Luing, comfortably and expeditiously,
any weekday. The bus leaving Oban, metropolis of the Western
Highlands, conveys one speedily, and often hilariously, to the
Cuan ferry, having called on the way at several stopping-places in
Seil. At the jetty by the road-end, one alights to board the motor-
ferryboat which, in a few minutes, and despite the powerful
currents flowing in one direction or another, except at slack
water, reaches the Luing side of Cuan Sound, three hundred yards
away. There the 'Luing Local' awaits one. This compact
omnibus traverses the greater part of Luing, calling first at Cullipool, the populous quarrying centre by its western shore, and
proceeding thereafter to Toberonochy, the island's other centre
of population, situated by the eastern shore, and separated from
the lofty and well-timbered island of Shuna by the kyle of
the same name. All regular traffic for the island of Scarba
comes through Luing, branching westward for Black Mill Bay
where such as may be destined for Toberonochy branches eastward.

. . . .

Easdale is reached from Seil by a ferryboat constantly plying
the strait between these two islands. This strait, at its narrowest, is no more than four hundred feet wide. Easdale's village
of whitewashed, slated, one-storey cottages would seem to be a con-
tinuation of Ellenabeich, the corresponding village on the Seil
side of the strait. These cottages are occupied, often from generation to generation, by the quarrymen and their families. The
former are employed at such quarries among the Slate Islands
as have not already been denuded of slates commercially profitable to work and to market. On Easdale's more elevated reaches,
as well as on such of its lower parts as have not been stripped
entirely of verdure by quarryings and resultant slag-heaps, the
villagers' cows graze at will.

A weird atmosphere pervades these islands, with their precipitous cliffs of slate, and their numerous, abandoned quarries filled
with green, slimy water. To one accustomed to wild places un-
spoilt by commercial enterprise, they present an unattractive
appearance. Even the storm-beaches, where such are composed
of elongated dumps of broken and discarded slates, are apt to
be repellent.

Of the many slate quarries in the district, perhaps those on Easdale have been the most famous, partly on account of the quality of the rock and of the uniformity of the bedding, and partly owing to the length of time they have been worked. That the value of this island's slates was recognised even before Dean Munro journeyed through the Hebrides about the middle of the sixteenth century, is shown by their having been used to roof Castle Stalker, the old fortress of the Stewarts of Appin, built in the reign of James IV of Scotland. Easdale provided the slates with which Ardmaddy Castle was re-roofed in 1676, when the wood used for the purpose was resinous pine from a remnant of the Old Caledonian Forest. The pine was sawn into planks an inch thick. To these planks the slates were pinned down by oak pegs about three inches in length.

That the slate industry on Easdale was in a prosperous condition in 1772 is shown by Thomas Pennant. Slates split into what he describes as merchantable sizes were being shipped from the isle at twenty shillings per thousand; and he tells us that about 2,500,000 of them were being sold annually to England, Norway, Canada, and the West Indies. By 1794 the number had risen to 5,000,000. It was estimated that, between 1842 and 1862, no fewer than 140,000,000 slates of varying sizes were exported from Easdale alone—an average of 7,000,000 a year.

Scanning from Easdale's higher parts the great, deep basins of still, ominous water, and bearing in mind that quarrying began here centuries ago, one realizes how considerable a proportion of that island's surface has been chiselled away to within a few feet of sea-level.

In olden times there lay in the centre of the channel between Seil and Easdale an islet two acres in extent, known as *Eilean a' Beithich*, Island of the Birches. This isle disappeared gradually. It was wellnigh quarried out of existence. Nothing but its shell remained. Slate refuse and rubbish of all kinds, tipped into the channel separating it from Seil, completed the island's disappearance as such. According to Dr. Patrick Gillies,[1] this was probably the most lucrative quarry ever worked in the neighbourhood. For many years, its annual output of slates of the best roofing quality was seven to nine million.

The memory of the old channel is perpetuated in the name, *Caolas*, which is the Gaelic for a kyle or narrow strait. This is the name applied particularly to that part of the quarrymen's township of Ellenabeich where once the channel lay. Thus the township of to-day stands partly on territory artificially created,

[1] *Netherlorn*, by Dr. Patrick Gillies, London, 1909.

and partly on a raised shoreland of slate rock fringing the basaltic cliffs at the north-west corner of Seil.

Ellenabeich's prosperity vanished on the night of November 22nd, 1881—a date as significant among the older inhabitants of the Slate Islands as that of Bannockburn, or August 4th, 1914. That night, the Inner Hebrides experienced one of the worst storms in their history. A south-westerly gale of exceptional velocity drove before it the disastrous tide which demolished the buttress supporting the sea-wall of the great quarry, then being worked at a depth of 250 feet below sea-level. The tide, having made for itself a channel thirty feet wide, filled in an excavation roughly three hundred feet deep, and two-and-a-half acres in extent. Mountainous seas, breaking through the partition of rock between the quarry and the Atlantic, flooded the former irrecoverably. At the bottom of this drowned quarry lie the machinery, bogies, and rail-tracks which, in Seil's heyday, dealt annually with nearly a million slates. This calamity threw out of employment 250 men and boys, some of whom eventually found work on Easdale. Most of them, however, were obliged to seek alternative employment in the Clyde area.

The sad expanse of water filling this quarry is a locality prohibited to the Seil children, because of its being dangerous. Yet, not a single fatal accident has occurred there since the night the Atlantic tore its relentless way through the sea-wall. Toward the close of 1951, however, minor slate slides near the quarry's rim, precipitously close to which stand some of the quarriers' cottages, so increased the chances of drowning accidents that Seil's 150 inhabitants invited the Argyll County Council to close the quarry off entirely, in the interests of safety.

The slate industry in these isles of Lorne has known many vicissitudes. Some of the quarries have been abandoned and re-opened at varying intervals of years. As we go to press, we learn that, in order to meet the rising demand for West Highland slates in connection with various housing schemes, that at Balvicar, closed down in 1949, has just been re-opened.

.   .   .   .

Luing is certainly the island from which several of the lesser and more remote of the Inner Hebrides may be reached most conveniently. From Cullipool a lobster-fisherman may transport one west to Fladda and its lighthouse, to what the quarriers have left of deserted Belnahua, or to the Garvellach Isles, a couple of miles beyond. Anybody desirous of examining on Aileach an Naoimh, most celebrated of the Garvellachs, its ancient ecclesiological remains, would always be well advised to reach them from Cullipool. One should experience no difficulty in obtaining at Black Mill the services of a fisherman who will ferry one across to the lofty and arduous island of Scarba, or to Lunga, with its old site associated with the Chapel of St. Columba.

He who, with ample time at his disposal, arrives at Cuan Sound on a clear day, will be in no hurry to cross to Luing. The ferryboat, as he soon observes, plies as required, all day long. This affords anyone interested in islands and seaways an opportunity of ascending one of the neighbouring hillocks to view the racing and swirling tides. I know of nothing more alluring than this—nothing more thrilling than watching the ferryboat, powerfully engined though she is, being swept this way and that, moving diagonally across one rushing, gushing stream as best she can, seemingly borne helplessly out of her way, and then managing, somehow, to get into an equally swift and powerful current flowing in the opposite direction, carrying her back toward the jetty at which she eventually finds safe mooring. The crossing of Cuan Sound at slack water is, indeed, dull after having experienced a few trips when the tides were at their swiftest.

Having set foot on Luing, one is often as loth to proceed to one's destination as to quit the Seil side of the sound. The view of its turbulence from the Luing side is even more exciting. And what a panorama from the hillside above the jetty! I once sat half a day on a knoll just there. The firth and the isles of Lorne had me so much 'under enchantment' that the cattle grazing around me began to regard me as a fixture—as in integral part of the landscape. While I sat, spellbound, watching sunlight and shadow deploying over Mull, they advanced to crop my sandwiches with the grass!

.   .   .   .

Luing stretches six miles from Cuan Sound. Nowhere does its breadth exceed a mile and a half. The most southerly third of its 3,800 acres—the region known as Ard Luing—is rough and little frequented. Sheep and cattle graze upon it. The remaining two-thirds of the island have always carried a fair population, distributed among its villages, hamlets, small farms, and crofts. No quarrying has been pursued south of Toberonochy. Consequently, human habitations are not to be found beyond this village of small, whitewashed cottages.

In 1951 the only slate quarry operating in Luing was that at Cullipool, which then appeared to be employing most of its adult male population, and also a number of its youths. The workings in the Toberonochy neighbourhood have been abandoned, which explains how some of the cottages there are derelict or uninhabited. At Cullipool, much the larger community, nearly every habitable dwelling is occupied.

Luing is also industrious in the matter of agriculture. The Cadzows conduct at Ardlarach a splendid dairy farm, not only supplying with milk the island itself, but also sending daily a quantity to Oban. The dairy is run on the most modern lines. It is doubtful whether, elsewhere in the Western Highlands or Islands, milk is marketed under conditions so hygienic. At Ardlarach there is no unnecessary waste, such as one regrets to see almost everywhere around one nowadays. In a countryside where winter feeding is a perennial problem, it was heartening to find, in operation there, a modern silage system.

One must not omit to mention that Luing also specialises in potato-growing. Its early crop is usually excellent.

The Luing quarrymen were fully employed when I visited the island in 1951, and witnessed the departure of a coasting vessel carrying to Lerwick, for housing schemes in the Shetlands, no fewer than 180,000 Cullipool slates—one of the largest shipments by any single coaster throughout Luing's long association with the slate trade.

Luing is not rich in archæological remains, though the sites of some forts, probably of pre-historic origin, have been identified. Little survives of the old church of Kilchattan but part of its roofless walls. The burying-place in which it is set—the only one in Luing—is not without interest, however. Close to the inside wall along the outer side of which runs the road between Cullipool and Toberonochy, is a recumbent slab bearing the following inscription:

"I protest that none be buried after me in this grave which I have dug for myself as Jacob did Gen. 5, having adhered till death to the whole work of the second reformation in Scotland between the year 1638 and 1649 and died in full assurance of the heavenly inheritance Heb. VI. 11 & 19."

At the head of this recumbent slab is an upright stone built into the churchyard wall. On the side facing inward is this inscription:

"SACRED: It is a mervelous headstone in the eyes of builders, the Lord's doings,—Psal. cxviii. 22, 23. Also marvelous, to most that I digged my grave before I died, as Jacob

Gen. L. 5, & Joseph Arimathea, Matth. xxvii, 57-60, Israel would not bury evil men with good, 2 chr, xxi, 18, 19, 20. Jer. xxii. 17, 18, 19. Joseah King said, move not the man of God's bones, 2 king xxiii. 17, 18, its a bed of rest to the righteous, Isa. Lvii. 2, & no rest for the wicked, Isa. xLvii. 22, but a Prison & I protested that none go in my grave after me, if not have the earnest of spirit to be a child of God as I am of election sure, Rom. viii. 15, 16, 2 Petr. 1. 10, of the same principal of Pure Presbyterian Religion, the Covenanted cause of Christ, & church government adhering to the Confession of Faith, Second Reformation, Purity & Power of Covenents, & Noble Cloud of Witnesses Testimonies that Jesus Christ is the head King & Governor of the Church & not mortal man, as their King now is."

Thereunder, as one reads in smaller letters, "lies the Corp of Alex^r Campbell who lived in Achadnadure & died on 4th Nov^{m.} 1829. Aged 78 years."

Campbell carved these memorials for himself, years before he died. His age and the date of his death were, of course, added later.

This inscription, concluding with an invective against Popery, Prelacy, and other testifyings, might well provide one with a mental exercise in the realm of Bible Knowledge, or foster a desire to return to the scene with an Old and New Testament in one's hand.

The outer side of this upright headstone bears a lengthy inscription legible only from the roadside, which it faces. Lighting conditions were not sufficiently good to enable me to copy it the day I explored Kilchattan. On a dull day, the letters scarcely show up at all against the dull slate upon which they are carved. On a bright day, they may be equally difficult to read. The sun striking the stone's surface at a sharp angle may just supply the condition under which they can be distinguished most easily.

One could spend an entire day among Kilchattan's old stones reading and deciphering them, and even discovering, underfoot, recumbent specimens long since overgrown with mossy turf. The floor of the ruined church is as crammed with such as is the graveyard.

The Church's use as a place of worship must have ceased prior to 1685, the year in which its interior appears to have received its first interment. Its roof, however, did not collapse entirely until 1745. In 1670 John Duncanson and Alexander MacLean, two 'outed' ministers, were 'indulged' by the Privy Council, and permitted to preach and to exercise the functions of the ministry in the parish of Kilchattan. Fifteen years later, Duncanson, who would seem to have been the old church's last regular minister, was limited on a bond of five hundred merks from the restrictions of the Act of Council confining the 'indulged' ministers to the districts to which they had been appointed. Three days later, baselessly charged with contempt for the king's authority, he was put to the horn, and his bond declared forfeit. On September 29th, 1687, he died in prison at Campbeltown. He was described as a "good man, and useful in his day". The old Church at Kilchattan, it is thought, ceased to be used for worship with his imprisonment.

A large, granite headstone in Kilchattan kirkyard bears the names of several Latvian seamen buried here. They perished one wild night in October, 1935, when their ship, *Helena Faulbaums*, was wrecked on the west side of Belnahua. The few who survived managed to get ashore there, and sheltered as best they could in that islet's deserted and ruined houses. The Latvian authorities in Britain sent representatives to the funeral of their compatriots at Kilchattan; and, in recognition of the Luing people's kindness to the survivors, Latvian shipowners, in 1938, presented to the island's Parish Church its carved oak lectern, made in the Lord Roberts Memorial Workshop at Dundee. On the lectern appears the couplet recurring in that famous hymn by William Whiting—the hymn we sing, in time of disaster at sea, to Dr. Dykes's equally famous melody:

> *O hear us when we cry to Thee*
> *For those in peril on the sea!*

Within a foot or two of this stone is a curious one commemorating the loss, on this occasion, of Albert Sultcs, the vessel's radio telegraphist, whose likeness appears on the stone in the form of a cameo reproduced from his photograph. In tiny lettering under this reproduction is the name of B. Gerhards, a lady in Riga who designed this tombstone, and had it sent to Luing.

Belnahua lies a couple of miles west of Cullipool, a little beyond Fladda. It has been deserted for nearly forty years. In the heyday of the slate industry in Lorne, it was one of the most profitably worked of all the Slate Islands. The villagers, many of whom hailed from Luing, or from adjacent Seil, had their own store there. They also had a school for their children. The few cows pastured on such of the islet's surface as had not already been quarried away sustained the community in milk.

Belnahua's slates were known in Dean Monro's time. The Dean refers to this isle as one "quharin ther is fair Skailzie [Slate] aneuche". His allusion to Sklaitt, another isle "quharin ther is abundance of skailzie to be win", may well be to the Ellenabeich part of Seil.

In 1901, the number of quarrymen employed at Belnahua, and also at the quarries on Seil and Easdale, was considerably augmented by quarrymen from the Ballachulish district, where a trade dispute, culminating in a prolonged strike, threw out of employment many who, of necessity, were obliged to seek work elsewhere.

Slate-quarrying continued on Belnahua until 1914, when it ceased, owing, I understand, to financial difficulties. Work was resumed temporarily on a smaller scale a year or so later. In 1915 the island's quarries were finally abandoned. By the end of that year, the island itself was evacuated. It has been unoccupied ever since.

A Glasgow correspondent (a certain Angus Shaw, who was connected both on the paternal and the maternal side with the families concerned in the exploitation of Belnahua's slate resources) assures me that, until comparatively recently, it was possible to ride abandoned bogeys on the rails down to the pier there, now completely covered by slate debris washed up by the sea. It was at this pier that the S.S. *Sylph* shipped her slate cargoes for the Glasgow market. Many of these went to the roofing of Glasgow University, and also to the expansive covering in of that place of horror, the cattle market.

The wall built round the slaty heart of the island to seal out the sea remains a monument to those who, as Angus points out, carried on the industry without the benefit of public subsidies. He tells me that, when last he visited the island, the weighing-scales still reposed on the shop counter, while the power-house, with its rusted boiler and decrepit winding gear, told the story of an island suddenly stricken dead.

An uglier and more forlorn spot than Belnahua, it would be difficult to imagine. Even at the height of its prosperity, it must have been ugly. Now it is—sinister. Few set foot upon it. Not that it was ever too easy of access, except to skilly seamen. We have mentioned the great rush of waters in its vicinity, and also in that of Fladda.

In the days when people had less to spend, and when they saw in these parts scarcely any newspaper except *The Oban Times*, the inhabitants of Belnahua were, indeed, isolated. The story is told of one old resident who received this celebrated weekly paper with such regularity as weather conditions allowed. A neighbour of his called as regularly to have the reading of it, often wishing that the subscriber would permit him to take it home with him, that he might relate its contents to his household. "No! No!" said the subscriber, whenever his neighbour asked whether he might borrow his paper for a little. "You can sit there and read it all day long if you like; but you mustn't go outside the door with it!"

There came a day when the subscriber to *The Oban Times* entered his neighbour's cottage to ask whether he might borrow his bellows. "Certainly!" said the accommodating neighbour. The former was on the point of quitting the house with the bellows when their owner intercepted him. "No! No!" he said. "You can sit there and blow them all day long if you like; but you mustn't go outside the door with them!"

.   .   .   .

Though Luing is now one of the most accessible of the Inner Hebrides, many legends and traditions still survive there. The island is by no means devoid of inhabitants who can recite its folk-tales in the Gaelic manner.

There lies among its uplands a little sheet of water known as the Fiddler's Loch, close to which stand the ruins of an old fort said to have been built, centuries ago, for the protection of the inhabitants against the ravishing Northmen.

Now, there once lived in the Fiddler's Loch—"and maybe does to this day", my storyteller added—a sea-horse, which kept the natives in a constant state of panic. Unlike other horses, he did not care for a diet of grass and oats: he preferred to feed on the islanders' livestock, and, indeed, from time to time, on *themselves*! For this reason, the people of Luing kept good hours; and they insisted that their children should be indoors by sunset, lest the wily sea-horse devoured them.

In mounds by the shore of the Fiddler's Loch lived a community of the Little Folk who, at sundown, came forth from their dwellings to dance to the fiddler's playing—an enchanting sight which the older and bolder natives of Luing often watched! When there was a shower of rain, the Little Folk hurriedly retired to their mounds to have supper. And so, to this day, when a shower falls on Luing while the sun is shining, an islander may be heard remarking, " The Little Folk will be at their supper now."

.   .   .   .

Tales of the days when the natives of Luing and the neighbouring isles had a profitable hand in secretly distilling and shebeening are still told. The water on Shuna appears to have been particularly good for the making of whisky, a fact recognised by its inhabitants, many of whom were engaged in this illicit trade. Consequently, excise officials frequently descended upon Shuna, though seldom with anything to show for their trouble. Hairy Donald, Shuna's distiller-in-chief, saw to that! Sentries placed at vantage-points in the heather, or concealed among the rocks by the shore, soon apprised them of the gaugers'—of the excisemen's—approach. It was Donald himself whom the authorities really sought. However, he always managed to elude them. When word was carried to him that these formidable officials were again in the locality, he fled to a cave at the south end of the island. About the entrance to this cave grew heather and scrub which, to some extent, obscured it. But the entrance was so narrow that Hairy Donald's abnormally large head prevented his entering the cave in his entirety. He could get the remainder of his person out of sight by seeking to enter it feet first. His head, as it happened, was all that nature required by way of camouflage. His long hair, pulled down over his face to mingle with his long beard, merged so perfectly with the grey and russet background that the excisemen, though passing by the mouth of the cave, often within a few inches of his concealed face, never discovered him. The cave thus affording him immunity from arrest is still pointed out on Shuna.

Let me now give you a Luing account of a Ghost Light and of its sequel, as related to me by an old friend, Captain Alexander MacLachlan, himself a native of Luing, and master of one of the vessels operated by the Commissioners of Northern Lighthouses. One Sunday morning in November, 1906, Alexander, then a comparatively young man, accompanied to public worship at Achafolla an old elder of the Established Church of Scotland named James Campbell. As the two of them were passing through the small glen known locally at Duilleter, Campbell told him of the following incident. Through the entire length of the glen, one should add, runs a burn normally carrying a foot or two of water—a grand burn for guddling, Alexander tells me. The road traversing the glen is carried across the burn at several points by stone bridges rudely constructed, but each sufficiently strong to bear the weight of a horse and cart, with perhaps half a ton of load. As he and the elder approached one of these bridges, the latter halted to say that, when passing this spot one dark midnight many years previously (it was actually in May, 1890), he saw, at some considerable distance ahead of him, a bright and ominous illumination—a Ghost Light! The light was following the course of the burn, and travelling toward him at what he believed to have been a terrific speed. On reaching this particular bridge, it vanished.

Young MacLachlan, until then a little sceptical about such things, asked old Campbell what his reactions had been to this weird situation. "I wasn't frightened," Campbell answered; "but I *was* a little awed."

So much for the light. What of the sequel?

The following morning, Donald Livingstone, son of a local farmer, was returning home, astride a horse, from the island smithy, where the animal had just been shod. It was surmised that, on reaching this particular bridge, he had not dismounted to open the gate erected across it, but had urged the animal sufficiently close to it to enable him, by bending low, to unlatch it. Anyhow, the bridge collapsed, precipitating Donald and horse into the burn. The rider lay pinned under his mount, the bulky form of the latter damming the burn. Its waters rose. The lad was drowned before assistance reached the spot.

Was there any connection between the Ghost Light and the fatality of the following morning?

. . . .

To-day in Luing, as elsewhere, football is the all-absorbing diversion—a positive obsession. This small island recruits two teams, a junior and a senior, the latter being known throughout Argyll as the Luing United. The junior team, I was credibly informed by one of its numerous fans, is obliged to play nine aside, owing to a local shortage of boy power. Of the ups and downs of football as it obsesses so large a proportion of this countryside, both male and female, I learnt much from a lad staying in the cottage at Toberonochy where I was a guest last summer.[1] A

[1] A London friend with Luing associations tells me that the prospect of my spending a few days at Toberonochy filled the villagers with perplexity. How were they to cater for me, according to my station? The day before I was due to arrive, they organised a whip-round to see whether, between them, they could collect sufficient butcher meat to sustain me as amply as they thought seemly in the case of a stranger like myself. They were unaware that I had not partaken of the butchered beast since my early twenties.

I was but a few minutes in their midst when the matter of my nourishment arose. "And what will you eat?" I was asked.

"Anything simple," I am alleged to have replied. "Tomatoes at any time,

little fellow happened to pass by the cottage window, idly blowing at a mouth-organ. He was Wee Hughie Brown. Hughie, a day or two previously, had done an unheard-of thing! At a critical moment during a match against the junior team from Easdale, he had stood with his hands deep in the pockets of his shorts! Unforgivable! He was now under notice, although the goal he had scored on that occasion brought victory to the Luing team! This goal, everyone said, had been " a pure fluke ". Wee Hughie Brown had been seen to close his eyes as he advanced to the kick which scored it! Everybody declared it was by accident that the ball bounded between his opponents' goal-posts.

I tried to intercede on Wee Hughie's behalf, pointing out that, even if he had scored this goal accidentally, it more than compensated for his casualness on the field. The rest of the Luing Juniors were adamant, however. Wee Hughie Brown must never be forgiven his standing there with his hands deep in the pockets of his shorts!

The poor little lad may still be wandering listlessly among the cottages at Toberonochy, creating discordant notes on his mouth-organ, hoping that one day, perhaps, he may be re-instated.

and in any form," I continued, having observed, on a dresser near at hand, a dish containing three.

This innocent suggestion of mine precipitated a minor crisis among the inhabitants. Of this I was quite ignorant, of course. Secretly, a whip-round was now instituted in the hope of augmenting the three tomatoes. But only an additional two could be mustered throughout the community. Anxiety prevailed, my friend assures me, until someone managed to get a few pounds of them sent direct by bus and ferry from Oban. What happened to the supply of flesh so magnanimously assembled for my delectation, my informant never heard.

CHAPTER XI

THE GARVELLACH ISLES

Where is Hinba?

For centuries, the identification of this isle has been one of the desiderata of British topography. The name comes down to us from Adamnan, St. Columba's seventh-century biographer, who makes frequent mention of *Insula Hinbinae*, which would appear to have been derived from *Imbach*, or *Imbeh*, a word of ancient Gaelic origin denoting an encircling sea.

On Hinba, tradition says, Columba's mother, Eithne, was buried, at a spot still pointed out with confidence by the sea-going Gaels of western Argyll. Furthermore, though the creek at which they habitually land when disembarking at the isle they believe to be Hinba, is known as *Am Port*, The Haven, they sometimes refer to it as the *Geodha Eithne*, Eithne's Inlet. This would show that some, at least, feel fairly certain which isle Adamnan referred to. It is nothing short of extraordinary that the precise identity should be unknown of an isle to which Columba, as was the custom among the early Celtic monks and missionaries, withdrew from time to time for rest and meditation. Hinba was his *diseart*—his retreat—when seeking respite and solitude from exacting duties at Iona. This being so, one may assume its situation to be somewhere in the Inner Hebrides, and at a distance from Iona not too great.

It would seem that Columba, now established at Iona, and having had his residing there ratified by Bridei, the Pictish King, and also by Conall, King of the Scots of Dalriada, was soon to extend his missionary activities to other islands in this locality, and to build churches and found religious communities upon them, such as are known to have existed in Eigg, Skye, Tiree, and in Hinba. On the last named, according to Adamnan, Columba had a monastery to which he retreated on occasions, and in charge of which he placed Ernan, his maternal uncle. Here, as we also learn from Adamnan, the Saint had that divine inspiration, as the result of which " he remained three days and as many nights, neither eating nor drinking, within the house which was locked and filled with celestial brightness; and he would allow no one to approach him. And from this same house rays of intense brilliancy were seen at night bursting from the chinks of the doors and the keyholes. And certain hymns which had not been heard before were heard being sung by him. But he himself, as he afterwards declared in the presence of a very few persons, saw openly manifested many secrets hidden since the beginning of the world. And some obscure and most difficult passages of the Sacred Scriptures became plain and clearer than the light to the eyes of his most pure heart."

Whichever island was the Hinba of Columban days, such ecclesiological remains as exist on it must date back to the latter half of the sixth century.

. . . . . .

The location of Hinba has exercised the deductive faculties of historian, hagiologist, and topographer for many a day. From such sparse data as may be available, all have been desirous of identifying it.

It was not until 1824, the year in which Dr. John MacCulloch, geologist and littérateur, visited the Garvellach Isles, and discovered on the most southerly of the group a series of primitive, and presumably ancient, religious buildings and monuments, that scholars turned their attention to the likelihood of this being Adamnan's Hinba. *Ilachanu* is MacCulloch's rendering of its Gaelic name. This is obviously a corruption of *Eileach an Naoimh* (the Holy Isle, or the Saint's Isle), the name by which we now designate the second largest of the Garvellachs. At the time of MacCulloch's landing there it was uninhabited, and may have been so for some considerable time. To this, primarily, he and others have attributed the survival on Eileach an Naoimh of ruins which may well be among the oldest of Christian origin in Britain.

It does not necessarily follow, of course, that an island's uninhabited condition vouchsafes the existence upon it of ancient structures. Take, for example, the ruins on North Rona, an isle infinitely more remote than any of the Garvellachs. These ruins have been rendered more ruinous by shepherds and others who have dilapidated them in excess of what weather would have done, in order to construct pens and the like for the sheep pastured there, and attended to once every summer, if conditions permit the annual excursion from northern Lewis. On the other hand, archæologists are agreed that the survival of such ruins as are to be found on Eileach an Naoimh is due largely to the island's unpeopled condition.

132

Ruins of Dun Naomhaig, stronghold of the Lords of the Isles, Isle of Islay

MARY MAC CRAIN
Died in 1856 Aged 128.
Descendant of
GILLOUIR MAC CRAIN
who kept a Hundred y
Eighty christmasses in
his own house And who
died in the reign of
CHARLES 1.

The question *Is this Hinba?* was first put categorically, apropos Eileach an Naoimh, by Dr. Reeves, who visited that island in 1852, in company with the historian, W. F. Skene.[1] The grounds for supposing it to be Hinba were carefully stated by the latter, who believed the ruins we see there to-day to be those of a monastic settlement established by Columba himself, and supervised by Ernan, aforenamed. The ruined chapel Skene declared to be that in which Columba officiated when the four contemporary founders of monasteries—St. Congall, St. Cainnech, St. Cormac, and St. Brendan—visited him at Hinba.

Adamnan tells us that Columba, while staying on Hinba, was proceeding to ex-communicate some of the Christian Church's persecutors—the sons of Conall, the son of Domnail. One of the evildoers was Jo(h)an, of the race of Gabran. He was chief of the Scots of Dalriada, off the mainland of which lie the Garvellach Isles. A confederate of his, Lam-dess (a name derived from the Gaelic, the Latin equivalent of which is *Manus dextera*— right hand), instigated by the devil, it was said, rushed with a spear at Columba, who would have been injured, if not indeed killed, but for the intervention of one of the brothers named Findluganus. The following year Columba's assailant was killed with a javelin on the neighbouring island of Lunga. Twice had Joan ransacked the house of a friend of the Saint; and on his third attempt to do so Columba tried, but unsuccessfully, to dissuade him. The robber treated the Saint's intercession with derision. The Saint followed him and his plundering confederates up to his knees in the sea, praying to Christ, while they retired with their booty. When he returned to the shore, he prophesied that Joan and his roving crew would not reach land in safety. A sudden storm overwhelmed their ship; and they were drowned.

Dean Monro, writing of the Western Isles in 1549, refers but briefly to the Garvellachs. Aileach an Naoimh he renders as Nanaose. "Narrist to this iyle of Garowhellach—Nanronow," he writes, "layes ther a verey little iyle, callit in Erische Eluche Nanaose." He mentions Dunchonill, or Conall's fort, "ane iyle so namit from Conal Kernache, ane strenth, wich is alsmeike as to say in Englische, ane round castle". We have no difficulty in identifying the Dunchonill referred to by the Dean. It is the island at the north-eastern end of the Garvellach chain of islands, islets, and skerries. On our Ordnance Survey maps it appears as Dun Chonnuill; and upon it are the ruins of an ancient fort which may well have been Conall's round castle.

[1] *Life of St. Columba, Founder of Hy* (Iona), written by Adamnan, and edited by William Reeves, D.D., Edinburgh, 1874, p. 324.

ABOVE—LEFT: *Sanctuary Stone at Kilchomain, Islay*
        RIGHT: *Ancient Cross at Kilnave, Islay*
BELOW—LEFT: *Mary MacCrain's tombstone at Inverlussa, Jura*
        RIGHT: *Kildalton Cross, Islay*

Kernache, doubtless, is *cathernach*, the word from which we get
'cateran', a freebooter; and it is very probable that Dun Chonnuill, or Dunchonall, was the stronghold of Conall, Joan's father,
and of his piratical offspring. If this were so, as it well may have
been, it would seem to identify Eileach an Naoimh with Hinba.

. . . .

The Garvellach Isles lie off the Nether Lorne coast of Argyll,
at the seaward end of the Firth of Lorne. They are roughly five
miles south-west of Seil, and about the same distance west of
Luing, behind Lunga, as it were. Less than four miles of sea
separate Eileach an Naoimh, the most southerly of them, from
Scarba, looming loftily to the south-east. They are part of the
ecclesiastical parish of Jura; and they belong to the Craignish
Estates. Excluding the numerous islets and skerries with which
they are beset, they are four in number. At the north-east end,
as we have seen, comes Dun Chonnuill, next to which is Garbh
Eileach, the largest, and the one from which the group appropriately takes its name. Garbh Eileach is certainly a *rough* island,
as anyone traversing it readily discovers. Its greatest length,
from north-east to south-west, is $1\frac{1}{4}$ miles, almost exactly that of
Eileach an Naoimh; but, whereas the maximum breadth of the
latter is only a quarter of a mile, that of the former is twice as
much, which means that the area of Garbh Eileach is double that
of Eileach an Naoimh.

In the mile of sea between these two islands lies A' Chùli, the
fourth member of the group, and the only one which does not
appear to bear evidence of having been inhabited at some
time or other. Yet, tradition says that hither came St. Brendan
in time of retreat and meditation.

Dun Chonnuill has its ruined fort; Garbh Eileach has its ancient burying-ground, and a cottage, which is the only habitable
building on the Garvellachs: Eileach an Naoimh has its monastic
ruins, to which we shall turn in a moment or two.

Garbh Eileach, near the north-eastern extremity, attains its
maximum height of 362 feet. This is over a hundred feet higher
than the highest point on Eileach an Naoimh, which occurs towards its west side, where cliffs fall steeply to the sea about the
island's centre. The north-west shore of the latter isle is indeed
precipitous. Here the cliffs sheer to the tide, 200 feet below. The
site of the island's highest part is known as *Dun Bhreanain*, St.
Brendan's fort, or hill. Dun Chonnuill, by far the smallest of
the Garvellachs, attains, at 200 feet, a considerable altitude in
relation to its area.

These islands are composed for the most part of calcareous shale, though dykes of basalt are not uncommon among them. Geologically, they resemble the many isles in neighbouring waters known, for obvious reasons, as the Slate Islands—Luing, Seil, Easdale, and Belnahua. Slates have been quarried in this region for a very long time; and, indeed, Belnahua, on which stands the ruined village once occupied by the quarrymen, was almost chiselled down to sea-level!

The Garvellachs are treeless, of course. Apart from a little stunted and tenacious growth in clefts and hollows, they are shrubless too. Their less rocky and undulating acres, however, are richly covered with grass.

.   .   .   .

The ecclesiological remains on Eileach an Naoimh are grouped on a grassy slope near the middle of the south-east end of the island, not far from the shore. Their association with Columba is perpetuated in *Tobar Chaluim-cille*, the Gaelic name of a well nearby—St. Columba's Well. This, too, is the name of an ancient well on Lunga, the heathery isle lying between the Garvellachs and Luing, some three miles to the east of them.

Yet another reminder of the Columban associations of Eileach an Naoimh is provided by the name given to this day to a rock of hard quartzite standing out near its southern shore, at a height of 12 feet. It is referred to as *a' Chrannag Chaluim-cille*—Columba's Pulpit.

The remains on Eileach an Naoimh consist of a small, rectangular church or chapel, together with beehive cells of uncemented stones ancillary thereto. The chapel is built of undressed stones, without any trace of mortar. The exterior dimensions of its walls are 27 feet by 12. They still stand 8 feet in height, and are 3 feet thick. At the west end occurs the doorway, square-headed, its jambs sloping inwards from the perpendicular. At the east end is the chapel's only window, small, and, like the doorway, splay. The chapel is set almost due east and west.

To the eastward of it, and in a sheltered hollow at the foot of the slope, lies an ancient graveyard containing a few headstones, some of which are incised with crosses. These would appear to be fewer in number than when MacCulloch examined the site in 1824, since he tells us that this place of burial had "many ornamented stones, with remains of incised crosses". Their number and nature led him to suppose Eileach an Naoimh to have been an isle of great sanctity. The graveyard, which lies below the garden, is easily identified by such headstones as remain. They are of the slate quarried so abundantly in this locality.

Upon a grassy eminence 150 yards to the south-west of this graveyard is a loose cairn, with headstones, one of which bears what is believed to be a Greek cross somewhat crudely cut. This headstone, according to tradition, marks the grave of Eithne, Columba's mother.

The Greek cross has four arms equal in length, and at right angles to one another, differing from the ordinary Roman cross with which we are familiar in this country, the transverse of which is always much shorter than the upright shaft.

On a slope by the shore stand the remains of a double cell of the beehive order, to which the Gaels of western Argyll allude as the *Clochain*, a word obviously connected with *clach*, the Gaelic for a stone. The cell's diameter is 14 feet. Its doorway, placed in the south-west side, is largely in ruins. The roof is gone; but there survives of the edifice sufficient of its curved, though rudely built, walls to show its principal characteristics.

Attached to the outer wall of this cell, with a square communicating doorway between, and placed at the point of intersection, is a second cell but a foot less in diameter—a feature not uncommon among the ancient structures of its kind to be found in Ireland. I have seen the excellent example which survives on Skellig Michael, an isle off the coast of County Kerry—most westerly of Christ's Strongholds in the Ancient World.

As one side of the second cell is almost complete, it indicates clearly the beehive formation of the roof. The small opening close to the ground in one side of it could not have been a doorway if, at the time it was in use, the earth immediately outside it stood at its present level.

A third and smaller cell on Eileach an Naoimh, measuring 5 feet 4 by 4 feet 5, is oval in shape. Its roof is constructed of rough slabs laid horizontally, almost at ground-level.

Farther up the hillside is a building 15 feet by 10, with two doors opposite one another. Its east end is semi-circular; while two-thirds of its interior are occupied by a raised stone platform with a hollow in the centre, below which is a flue for allowing of the passage of air. This was the community's kiln: here it dried such corn as was grown on Eileach an Naoimh, and possibly on the other islands of the Garvellach group.

Nearby, on the south side of the chapel, there is a little underground cell containing two stone shelves. This is thought to have been the cellar for the wine used at the Eucharist.

One might mention, also, that the space of level ground enclosed by a ruined wall has been identified as the monks' garden. Botanists have found here some rare plants believed to be the descendants of exotic plants introducd by the monks for medicinal purposes.

No trace of a cashel's having existed on Eileach an Naoimh has been found; but, as that profound scholar and most competent archæologist, the late Dr. Joseph Anderson, pointed out in this connection, there is no rule without its exception, for, although the fortified enclosure was the rule where the site's natural features necessitated the building of a protective stone wall, it would appear as though this had been dispensed with where isolation, as in the case of the Garvellachs, lent to the site all the security it seemed to require.[1]

On Eileach an Naoimh there are other remains; but these, as Anderson tells us, present no features claiming attention. Those which he himself examined he pronounced as possessing neither the variety of form, nor yet the complexity of detail, warranting a lengthy description. All the remains here are typical of the early Christian structures found in Ireland.[2] One doubts, of course, whether any archæologist can say, or would *wish* to say, with any degree of certitude that they belong to Columban times. As Anderson succinctly puts it, specific dates are the exclusive property of history; and these cannot be ascribed except where specific records exist.

The settlement of Eileach an Naoimh probably flourished until early in the ninth century, when, doubtless, the marauding Northmen ravaged it, slaying such of its brethren as failed to escape from the isle.

In the nineteen-twenties the ruins on Eileach an Naoimh, together with their immediate surroundings, were bequeathed to the Ancient Monuments Department of the Office of Works, at Edinburgh, by Colonel Frederick Trench-Gascoigne, proprietor of the island. Shortly afterwards, an iron railing with a gate was erected round them; but, as yet, owing largely to the intervention of the Second World War, little has been done in the way of restoration, except to the *clochain*—the beehive cells. These received attention in 1937 under the supervision of J. S. Richardson of the Ancient Monuments Inspectorate. Something will have to be

---

[1] *Scotland in Early Christian Times*, by Dr. Joseph Anderson, Edinburgh, 1881. (The Rhind Lectures in Archaeology, 1879.)
[2] An exhaustive account of a survey of the antiquities on Eileach an Naoimh, by Thomas Bryce, M.D., F.R.S., and G. A. Frank Knight, D.D., F.R.S.E., appears in the *Transactions of the Glasgow Archaeological Society, New Series, Vol. VIII, part V (1933)*.

SKYE AND THE INNER HEBRIDES

done soon to retrieve for future generations these ancient structures on Eileach an Naoimh, which may well have been the
Columban hermitage alluded to by Adamnan as Hinba.

.   .   .   .

Weather permitting, the Garvellachs are most readily accessible
from Cullipool, in the Island of Luing, whence the distance,
westward to Dun Chonnuill, is 3½ miles. To the customary
landing-place close to the monastic ruins on Eileach an Naoimh, it
is, as the crow flies, twice as far. Following a course through the
tides swirling tumultuously about Fladda and Belnahua, and
steering clear thereafter of the islands and skerries besetting the
sea between Lunga and Garbh Eileach, the distance is no more
than eight miles.

On weekdays Cullipool may be reached easily from Oban. For
a few shillings, the bus crossing to the Island of Seil at Clachan
Bridge conveys one down through that island to the Cuan Ferry,
at its southern end. Here, in the matter of a few minutes, one
crosses the swift tide-race to Luing, where *that* island's bus awaits
passengers travelling either to Cullipool, or to Toberonochy, some
miles farther south. At Cullipool, if the weather be suitable, a
lobster-fisherman may transport you to the Garvellachs. It is
well to bear in mind that, propitious though the day may appear,
and comparatively calm the sea, it may be quite impossible to
effect a landing on any of them. The place of disembarkation on
Eileach an Naoimh is sometimes accessible, however, when that
on any of the other three members of the group is not. That at
Eileach an Naoimh is somewhat sheltered from winds and swelling seas by the series of islets and reefs known as the Black
Skerries.

A word of warning! When soliciting local help in the matter
of water transport to and from most of the Hebrid isles, remember
that the owner of the boat may charge exorbitantly. Be
precise with him as to what you expect him to do for an agreed
fare. Before you embark, see that he understands exactly the
services you propose paying him for. Do not let him harass or
hurry you by making all sorts of excuses why you should now be
returning. He will want to return when it suits *him*, just as he
will set out for your objective when it suits *him*, often after
having kept you hanging about an hour or two beyond the
appointed time. You will find that, although *you* have hired
him and his craft to enable you to accomplish a particular
mission, he will always make use of your hire by inviting his
friends to accompany him. Furthermore, at your expense and in

your time, he may visit his lobster-pots sunk in neighbouring waters, or deliver a message or a letter or a parcel to some special friend of his. He himself may even have some object in landing where you wish to land. For instance, he may be under obligation to find out whether all is well with somebody else's cattle pastures there—a task for which he is being paid in any case. If he can make the run at *your* expense, he will do so, stoutly asserting the while that he is transporting you as a great favour, and at considerable loss and inconvenience to himself.

If you be delayed twenty minutes or half an hour in returning to the boat from your investigations, he will start up a plaint that he never realized you wanted so much of his time and services for so little financial remuneration. This plaint—a form of unpleasantness when you have still to conclude the purpose for which you have hired him—can be very depressing, very troublesome. It has frequently been the means of extorting from one, already afloat among the Isles, a fare in excess of that which one had consented to pay before embarking.

Take a firm hand in seeing that your boatman fulfils the remaining obligations you have engaged him for. Maintain a calm and indifferent demeanour, bearing in mind that the literature of the Western Highlands and Islands during the last century and a half supplies several classical instances where travellers like yourself have been subjected to this kind of thing.[1]

Be emphatic when your boatman begins to whine at you his excuse that you cannot now do this and you cannot now do that, because you kept him waiting so long while you were ashore at this isle or on that. He is probably itching to get back for some village football match. Study time, tide, and weather for your-

---

[1] The instance which immediately springs to mind is that which John Wood, of Kinross, recorded in his *Diary*, just a century and a half ago. In 1801 Wood travelled through Mull in company with two friends. When they decided to return to the mainland, they agreed with the boatmen the sum for which they might be landed at Oban. As they neared their destination, however, the boatmen refused to proceed farther, and threatened to land their passengers on Kerrera unless they divested themselves of a further sum of money. "So they paid the enhanced price," writes the late Rev. Thomas Hannan, citing this case in his book, *The Beautiful Isle of Mull*, "just as people have to do in other matters in this highly favoured year of Our Lord, 1926 [the year his book was published]. It was in the years of turmoil following the French Revolution, and in the era of world war in which the nineteenth century was born, so that probably ideas were prevalent very similar to the Bolshevik doctrines of the present day."

Incidentally, one would like to know the whereabouts of John Wood's *Diary*, for it appears to have been lost sight of. One supposes it to exist, however. The description it contains of arrival and travel in Mull shows the extreme backwardness of the island at the beginning of the 19th century. The inhabitants were living in the most squalid way. There was scarcely a horse on the island; and the little cultivation attempted was conducted with the most primitive of implements.

self; and judge the situation accordingly. If you know anything about boats and about local conditions, you can sum up the position fairly accurately.

Do not allow yourself to be hurried, since a sense of repose is essential for the type of work which will have brought you to parts as remote as are many of the Hebrides. Remember, too, that the impatience of your boatman's friends, seated in boredom in the boat while you are pursuing your explorations, will accentuate *his* impatience to tarry longer, and at the same time magnify the confidence with which he will demand your augmenting the figure agreed upon for the trip.

Above all, do not pay the sum agreed until he has performed all the services agreed.

Adopt the same attitude when hiring a vehicle to transport you overland. You will certainly find those owning a car very willing indeed to oblige—*for a conseederaation*, as the saying is. Your inability to accomplish your journey otherwise, or to solicit the services of any competitor, will render you liable to monopoly exactions. Beware when your seeking such transport evokes from your proposed transporter the sigh and the pretended utterance that he really doesn't want to be hired, either because money means nothing to him, or because he is committed to doing something else precisely at the hour when you propose requisitioning his services. It is then that, having by this time convinced you of his indifference to your problem, he will make the customary gesture—"*I wouldn't see you stuck*". Do not be deceived into feeling that this is an expression of generosity worthy of being rewarded with additional pecuniary recompense. In being deceived, you merely encourage him to raise his monopoly charges, thus making it even more impossible for those less affluent to obtain any such services at all.

Chapter XII

SCARBA

How long ago is it since I sat by Frances Tolmie's fireside at Kilchoan Cottage, in Dunvegan, at autumn gloaming, listening to her stories of Mary MacLeod, the bardess known to Gaeldom as *Mairi Nighean Alasdair Ruadh*, Mary Daughter of Ruddy Alasdair! Of all the storytellers of Celtic Scotland, there was surely none more competent to recite the affairs of her native Isle of Skye, especially such as concerned the MacLeods of Dunvegan, than Frances Tolmie, that celebrated folklorist who died there, at Kilchoan Cottage, in 1926, in her eighty-sixth year. It was from her that I first learnt something of Scarba. She had been talking with me of Mary MacLeod's banishment from Dunvegan to Mull for her having included in one of her compositions some references to which her Chief took exception. Mary, in exile, seated one day on a knoll overlooking Scarba, wrote her *Luinneag MhicLeoid*, her famous clan lullaby, which made her Chief relent. He now sent a boat to bring her back to Dunvegan, where she was re-instated on her promising to compose no more songs—an undertaking she found it impossible to observe.

In subsequent years I was to learn more about Scarba through my interest in such natural phenomena as the Gulf of Corrievreckan, to which we shall revert later.

Scarba is a wild and mountainous isle lying but a mile north of Jura, to which parish it belongs. To the north of it, and at a distance of two or three hundred yards, is the isle the heathery condition of which gave it its name—Lunga. Not much more than a mile to the north-east lies Luing, one the many isles in the Firth of Lorne known as the Slate Islands, and for a reason instantly apparent to anybody arriving among them. Then, at a distance of three-and-a-half miles to the north-west lies that remote but interesting chain of uninhabited isles—the Garvellachs.

Scarba is conical in appearance, and attains, in Cruach Scarba, its greatest height at 1,470 feet. It has an area of 3,676 acres. Its shape is roughly circular. Its maximum length of 3½ miles is found in its northeasterly-southwestly axis. Its coast is penetrated by numerous caves; and several little lochs lie in folds about its mountainous centre. Down its eastern side, and close to the shore, there are pleasant woodlands of no great area. These are composed for the most part of deciduous trees. Old oaks and nut-trees are common among them. Two other plantations occur in the vicinity of Kilmory Lodge, one to the west of it, the other to the south. These help to relieve a scene of barren, windswept desolation. The Lodge, reached by a steep path running up from the shore nearest Luing, first through woods, and then through moorland, is perched on a comparatively flat piece of ground a few hundred feet up, and is backed by such of the island as rises to culminate in Cruach Scarba, the summit of which is two miles away. The Lodge and the precipitous hillside immediately behind it command a fine view in northerly and north-easterly directions. South-eastwards stretches the Craignish district of Argyll, with its numerous islets and skerries, not the least perilous of which being those off Craignish Point. Here intervenes that turbulent channel known as the *Dorus Mor,* or Great Door, where many a small vessel sailing between Crinan and Oban in a sou'-westerly gale has endured a tossing.

Scarba has long been noted for its deer, which explains Kilmory Lodge, now the only habitable dwelling on the island except that situated remotely by its eastern shore, and occupied as a rule by a stalker. When I visited Scarba in 1951, however, this latter abode was tenanted by three Irish labourers whom the proprietor, taking advantage of a public grant for the eradication of bracken, has imported. Bracken is as serious a menace on Scarba as elsewhere. Here it was being dealt with by a mechanical mower, and by scythe or sickle where the unevenness and stoniness of the ground required. Experts say that, if bracken be diligently mown down three years in succession, and before it has been afforded an opportunity of seeding, any area overrun with it is well under control by the fourth year.

Not for many years has Scarba been farmed. During its prolonged condition as a deer-forest, nearly all evidence of pristine agriculture has gone. However, in the autumn of 1951, the island was let to a certain Ronald Carmichael, an Argyllshire farmer, who announced his intention of re-stocking it with cattle and sheep, and of rehabilitating its old farm steadings.

. . . .

The Gulf of Corrievreckan is by no means the only channel in this locality famed for its treacherous tide-race. Indeed, all the waters of the southern part of Lorne are beset with tidal disturbance, owing to the manner in which so many islands, great and small, are distributed about them, impeding the free passage of the tides. We already have mentioned the *Dorus Mor*—the Great Door; and we might well mention the tide-race in the Cuan Sound, between the islands of Seil and Luing. Nothing could be more exciting than to watch, from the high ground overlooking the Cuan Ferry, how the tides sweep the ferryboat this way and that, in mid-channel, often carrying it irresistibly seaward, until, somehow or other, it seems to reach the edge of the current flowing as swiftly in the opposite direction. Diagonally across the latter current is it deftly steered to the wonted landing-place.

Then there is the tidal rush off Fladda and Belnahua, as well as that between the north end of Scarba and the south end of Lunga—the Pass of the Grey Dog, as this channel is called. When afloat in a small boat as distant as a mile from this strait, you can see the waters mounting there at half-ebb or at half-flow; and you can hear them too, since they rush and swirl noisily. Those who venture a-sea in these parts, such as do the Luing lobster-fishermen, often mention their having heard the Grey Dog's angry growl. They regard it as a prognostication of stormy weather.

More celebrated than any of these are the tide-race and whirlpool in the Gulf of Brecan—the Corrievreckan, as it is usually called—where the tides go racing by at ten knots. Awesome accounts of this West Highland Scylla and Charybdis are still related round the peatfires in Jura of a winter's evening; and one supposes that they were recounted likewise in Scarba when that island carried the population which tilled the acres over which heather and bracken have now spread once more.

The conflicting waters of the Corrievreckan—their hoarse roar —can be heard at a great distance, particularly in calm weather, and when there is a tinge of frost in the air.

Every Scot, sooner or later, gets to know about his country's maelstrom. He may first learn through Sir Walter Scott of——

> *Scarba's Isle, whose tortured shore*
> *Rings with Corrievreckan's roar.*

Or he may alight upon the allusion to it in Aytoun's *Lay of Charles Edward at Versailles*:

> *Let me feel the breezes blowing*
> *Fresh along the mountainside!*
> *Let me see the purple heather,*
> *Let me hear the thund'ring tide.*
> *Be it hoarse as Corrievreckan*
> *Spouting when the storm is high—*
> *Give me but one hour of Scotland,*
> *Let me see it ere I die.*

The channel through which such turbulent tides run east and west, unceasingly, is roughly two miles in length, and, as we have already seen, about a mile wide where the distance between Scarba and Jura is least. At its western end, and fairly close to the Scarba shore, is its famed whirlpool. Though ranging in depth from 50 fathom to 150, it is the scene of a mighty congestion of waters, especially at a flood spring tide, when, rushing westward, the whole of the Atlantic's increase in these seas, sweeping up between Jura and the mainland, would seem determined to press through, creating in their urgency not only the main whirlpool, but also several subsidiary ones. "An impetuous current," as Martin Martin (c. 1695) describes it, "not to be matched anywhere about the isle of Britain. The Sea begins to boil and ferment with the Tide of Flood, and resembles the boiling of a Pot; and then increases gradually, until it appears in many Whirlpools, which form themselves in sort of Pyramids, and immediately after spout up as high as the Mast of a little Vessel, and at the same time make a loud Report. . . . This boiling of the Sea is not above a Pistol-shot distant from the Coast of Scarba Isle, where the white Waves meet and spout up."

To-day, as in Martin's time, the Corrievreckan is referred to by the Gaels as the *Cailleach*, the Old Woman—the Hag. According to the many Celtic folk-tales concerning her, she dons white headgear, thus warning those who may approach that she is in no mood to be trifled with.

The name, Corrievreckan, is derived from *Coire*, the Gaelic for a kettle or cauldron, and from Brecan. Who Brecan was, we are not too certain. Martin speaks of him as having been a son of the King of Denmark, who was drowned here, and whose retrieved body was interred in the cave at the north end of Jura still bearing his name. According to Dr. Gillies, quoting in his book on Nether Lorne from that old, topographical work, the *Dinnseanchus*, Brecan was the son of the King of Lochlann—of Norway. But the Irish claim that he was the son of Maine, and therefore grandson of Neil of the Nine Hostages. However, tradition is agreed upon one point, namely, that Brecan was drowned here when his fleet of fifty galleys sank in the *coire* ever since bearing his name.

It is popularly supposed that *vreckan* has some connection with the English word, *wreck*. However, it seems much more probable that it is derived from the Gaelic, *breacan*, meaning tartan, or a tartan plaid, suggested by the speckled surface of this seaway.

The Corrievreckan's unsuitability for navigation has long been recognised. Adamnan may have been the first to allude, in writing, to its perils; and one recalls in this connection the following account of it, written about 1630: "Betwixt Scorba [*sic*] and Jura runns the most dangerous gulff called Coirrabreaggan. There can neither shipps, gallies, nor boatts goe nor saill between these two Ilands except it be in ane quarter of ane hour in respect of the strong streame of this gulff, nor go through the same unless it be ebbing or full sea."

Though fraught with peril, it may surprise many that the experienced can sail across this celebrated tideway in a small motor-boat, between Jura and Scarba, or in the opposite direction, at slack water, and that deer have often been seen to swim it when it was in a condition in which all but the stoutest of human swimmers would have perished. The recognised course adopted by a Jura boat is from Kinuachdrach, northward, to the bay at the south of Scarba, where the stalker's house is. Over this course, the waters are at all times less constricted. When the flood tide comes hurrying up the east coast of Jura to push its way through these narrows, one should never venture farther to the west. If one does, one's chance of being swept westwards, toward the Atlantic, and wrecked—and *drowned*—is anything but remote!

On calm days and at slack water, crossings between Jura and Scarba can be made almost anywhere. But the tide does not allow of any dallying. One must choose the right moment, and embark with resolution, for, once the tide begins to run again, it does so at an ever-increasing velocity until it creates not only a great whirlpool, but also what must be the greatest overfall anywhere around the coast of Britain.

. . . .

When staying at Toberonochy, in Luing, as recently as the summer of 1951, I proceeded westward a mile or so to Black Mill, a hamlet of three or four houses situated by the bay of the same name. Nearby, largely concealed by meadow-sweet and contemporaneous herbage, stood the ruined meal mill from which hamlet and bay derived their name. At Black Mill I engaged the services of John Livingstone, a lobster-fisherman who frequently crosses to Scarba in his motor-boat. For one pound he agreed to ferry me there and back the following day, adding that he would not do so for less, since His Majesty's Post-Office paid him as handsomely to cross with a letter addressed to one of the Mac-Kechnies, the keeper's household, whose dwelling is attached to Kilmory Lodge. The following morning, accompanied by my hostess, her little son, and a native lad living with them at the time, I returned to Black Mill, where Livingstone awaited us, as arranged. Since all three of them knew the MacKechnies, and had had no opportunity of paying them a visit at Scarba, it seemed reasonable that they should come too, and make as much as they could of the social occasion my desire to see the Corrievreckan from the Scarba side might afford them.

Instead of putting ashore at the usual landing-place, whence a track leads up through steep woodlands to Kilmory Lodge and the adjoining house in which MacKechnie resides with his wife and son, we landed a little to the east, on a stretch of shoreland beautifully fringed with irises in full flower, some hazel scrub, and bracken shoulder-high. Somewhere amongst the bracken at this spot, Livingstone informed me, were the island's burial-ground, long since in desuetude, and also the ruins of the ancient place of worship associated with it. Exactly where they lay, he could not tell; but he was certain that, had it not been for the height and density of the bracken, old tombstones, as well as the low, crumbling walls of the chapel, would have been located quite easily. We all pushed our way into the bracken at different points, and began to feel with our feet for anything which might be a recumbent stone. The entire site for which we were searching was so completely obscured by aggressive vegetation that our quest did not seem very hopeful of result. However, we continued zealously with this arduous enterprise for some time. When on the point of abandoning it, Livingstone announced that something underfoot felt like a gravestone. Sure enough, it was. We all joined in uncovering its surface of many years' vegetable accumulation. Thus the site was found—the site of St. Mary's. Hence Kilmory, the anglicised name of the Lodge.

Within a few feet of this stone were others, some recumbent, some standing. In order to photograph what we had found, a good deal of strenuous bracken-pulling now became necessary. Two able-bodied adults and an enthusiastic schoolboy of fifteen soon cleared sufficient of it to lay bare not only several old stones, but also the very dilapidated walls of the chapel, the floor of the interior of which proved to be as thickly strewn with recumbent slabs of native slate, hidden below bracken and bramble, as was the exterior. The only feature of this ruin readily distinguishable, even after the bracken had been cleared away from it, was the doorway, so very tumbledown.

A brief call at Kilmory made me the recipient, at Mrs. Mac-Kechnie's hands, of a cup of tea and a treacle scone. These fortified me for the strenuous hours now lying ahead of me. The long, stiff climb up the hillside behind Kilmory Lodge, following where possible the broken track leading over the lofty shoulder of the

island toward the Gulf of Corrievreckan, seemed to have no ending. At last there came in sight the cairn erected by the edge
of this track at its highest point—about 1,000 feet above sea-level.
Here, where the track changed direction, the north end of Jura
suddenly came into view. With every advancing step, one saw
more and more of the restless Gulf, swirling noisily far below.
For a mile or two thereafter, one pushed on, through rocky wastes
and over deep ravines, toward the main whirlpool. The view
of the Corrievreckan became more fascinating, and its roar louder
and louder, as one proceeded westward. An ebbing tide, flecked
with the foam churned by its own restlessness, was now racing past
with incredible speed. I had at last witnessed something I have
visualised for years—an ebb tide with a mighty overfall in the
Gulf of Corrievreckan, seen from Scarba.

The rest of the daylight at my disposal was occupied in climbing to the summit of Cruach Scarba, and in exploring thereafter
one or two caves by such parts of the shore as were accessible without incurring too much risk.

A steady trot brought me across the island to the timber-shaded
creek where it was agreed that Livingstone would pick me up at
dusk, and transport me and my three passengers back to Luing.
I reached the creek with a feeling of profound thankfulness, having accomplished all I had desired. Very, very tired, and with
the fingers of one hand so stiff that I could scarcely open them
to transfer my tripod and camera to the other hand, I was helped
into the boat. In a state of mild exhaustion, I slumped comfortably on a thoft. The wind began to rise, and the sea with it, as
we steered diagonally across the Sound of Luing toward Black
Mill. Lowering clouds soon hung menacingly overhead; and we
could hear distinctly the snarling of the Grey Dog. But we were
back at the fireside in Toberonochy before the storm broke.

Chapter XIII

ISLAY

WITH an area of 235 square miles, or approximately 150,000 acres, Islay, most southerly of all the Hebrides, is the third largest of the *Inner*. Only Skye and Mull exceed it in size. It lies roughly 14 miles west of Kintyre. From north by east to south by west, its utmost length falls but a few hundred yards short of 26 miles. Its greatest breadth, at right angles to this axis, is over 19. Measured from north to south, and from east to west, as is more usual, its maximum dimensions are about 25 and 20 miles, respectively. Loch Indaal, that great expanse of relatively shallow water reaching far inland to its broad head, and contributing on its eastern side the crescentic sweep of Laggan Bay, adds considerably to the length of its coast-line. Apart from Loch Indaal, the only appreciable coastal indentation is shallow Loch Gruinart, penetrating from the north for 5 miles. An isthmus less than half that distance separates the head of Loch Indaal from the head of Loch Gruinart. This isthmus connects the most westerly reaches with the parent isle, as it were. They comprise the barren, wind-swept peninsula known as the Rhinns of Islay, the historic and once populated region of Kilchomain, the fisherman's paradise of Loch Gorm, and the district of Kilnave.

Having mentioned Kilchomain, one of Islay's three parishes, one might as well add at this stage the names of the remaining two. Kildalton is one: Kilarrow and Kilmeny is the other. The former includes the Oa, the southernmost part of Islay, much of it regarded as being out of the reach of all but the sturdiest of travellers on foot. The latter embraces all the island's northern territory right up to the extremity called the Rudh' a' Mhail headland on which stands the lighthouse marking the Atlantic end of the Sound of Islay, that constricted tide-race separating hilly Islay from mountainous Jura.

Islay has little to offer the mountaineer or the rock-climber. Beinn Bheigeir, its highest hill, lying some 3 miles south-west of MacArthur's Head, and composed of quartzite rock, is only 1,609 feet. Several hills exceed a thousand feet, however. All the land which might be considered hilly is confined to the east side of

148

ABOVE: *The Donkey-cart at Bowmore, Isle of Islay*
BELOW: *Portaskaig, Isle of Islay*

the island. The bulk of it is situated well to the east of the road linking Port Ellen with Bridgend, by the head of Loch Indaal. Here the River Sorn, draining much of the moorland watershed in which lies Loch Finlaggan of historic memory, wimples its way through the woodlands at Islay House to join a shallow sea. The only other part of the island which might be deemed more than ordinarily hilly is that lying beyond Loch Finlaggan, occupying the centre of its northernmost peninsula, terminating in the Rudh' a' Mhail, the promontory already mentioned.

Rocks not altogether unworthy of the climber occur at Sanaig and at Smaull, near Saligo Bay, in the north-west of the island, and also at the Mull of Oa, a locality of tragic association, as we shall see later. Though I am aware that the serious 'rocker' considers Islay as devoid of cliffs deserving of his skill, those at the Oa would seem to provide climbs, or rather descents, sufficiently fraught with difficulty and danger to be scorned by none but the most experienced and intrepid. This I readily discovered a year or two ago, when attempting to photograph from perilous positions among them. The cliff scenery on the Atlantic side of the Oa is truly awesome.

.   .   .   .

Islay's comparative fertility and the general ameliorative qualities of climate have won for her the title of the Queen of the Hebrides. The bards sing of her as Green, Grassy Islay. Such fertility and greenness as she may display are confined to the southerly parts, rather than to the northerly. The more extensive stretches of land adapted to the plough or devoted to hill pasturing have produced farms larger than are to be found elsewhere in the Hebrides. Here the grain crops are heavier, and ripen earlier: here, too, strawberries, grown in the open, may be picked as early as midsummer's day.

Many writers have remarked upon Islay's greenness, and have been impressed, not only by her pastures, but also by her luxuriant growth of hydrangeas, rhododendrons, fuchsias, honeysuckle, and royal ferns. Much of the island is devoted to husbandry in the good, farming sense, rather than in the crofting and smallholding. The continued existence of several large and prosperous farms has retained for the island a stable and self-supporting economy which has disappeared entirely from those islands of the Outer Hebrides where, at various times during the present century, self-sufficing farms were indiscriminately broken up into what, in so many cases, proved to be uneconomic holdings. That this has not occurred in Islay has been all to the good. It explains how

ABOVE: *Crofting township of Keills, Isle of Jura*
BELOW: *Old Burial-place of Earnadail, Isle of Jura*

her agriculturists have managed to hold their own in marketing, elsewhere, their increase. The island is renowned for the dairy produce derived from its lovely Ayrshire cows. Dairying has given Islay's agriculture a cleanliness and tidiness not commonly found in the Highlands and Islands.

Eggs are also among the island's assets. So plentiful are they in the late spring and during the summer months that one never sees an islander step into the plane for Renfrew without a small, precious, fragile parcel in his hand—a dozen fresh eggs given by relatives at his departure, or purchased from some neighbour at 4/6 the dozen. Eggs are often plentiful in Islay when quite unobtainable elsewhere. In the days when tweed was abundant and uncontrolled, the visitor to Harris or to Skye was as unlikely to leave without a suit length as, to-day, the visitor returning from Islay is unlikely to embark or emplane without a few of the island's eggs.

Islay's retention of so much of the sound husbandry of former years has ensured the survival of many of the old arts and crafts associated with agriculture. One recalls in this connection the smithies to be found throughout the island. These are always busy with the repairing of agricultural machinery and implements, and with the shodding of the farmhorses which, as yet, have not been replaced by machines. Visit the smithy in Lennox Street, Port Ellen, any lawful day, and you will find half a dozen or more horses tied up outside it, waiting attention at the brawny hands and arms of Donald MacDougall, perhaps the bestknown of Islay's blacksmiths.

Once upon a time, Islay was famed for its horses, and for the Islayman's preference for travelling on horseback. This explains the persistence to this very day, despite the decline in horse traffic in favour of more humane mechanical means of transport, of an old Gaelic saying that an Islayman will walk a mile, carrying with him a saddle, for the purpose of riding half that distance.

One might mention, incidentally, that the motor-car is a mode of transport more agreeable in Islay than in most of the Highlands and Islands, because of the better condition of its principal roads. Fortunately, it is not as overrun with motor vehicles as are Mull and Skye. It lies too remote by sea for that. The journey between Oban and Craignure is negligible by comparison, both as regards distance and cost. Cars are continually being carried to and from Mull, therefore. The ferrying distance between the mainland of Wester Ross and Kyleakin, in Skye, is even smaller.

Islay's farming economy, I have been told, though vastly superior to that of other Hebrid isles, is by no means as stable as its industrious farmers would like. This being so, one can imagine the position of the crofting economy elsewhere! Though Islay, to all appearances, is an island of prosperous farms, several of them would seem to be in a condition none too secure. The farmers complain that, when they transfer their beasts by sea to the mainland marts, they do not get for them their value. The buyers, they say, know that, as island sellers, they are not in a position to bargain as can mainland sellers. The latter, if they feel they are not being offered a reasonable price for their beasts, can take them home if they so desire: the island seller, on the other hand, faced with the high cost of re-shipping his unsold beasts, finds himself with no alternative but to accept what he can get for them. This is a grievous matter to the Islay farmer who, while admitting that his island may not be too good for the *fattening* of livestock, is well aware of its excellence for the *rearing*.

Having made these points rather heartlessly, as it would seem, I cannot but feel it incumbent upon me to add what many of my readers already know, namely, that, to me, the whole business of breeding, transporting, marketing, and slaughtering of other animals, and the devouring thereafter of their cooked corpses, is cruel, crude, and degrading. It is, moreover, quite primitive, and lies at the root of much of that savagery to which we resort when dealing with members of our own species. Of the pleasantries associated with civilized, armed conflict, we have experienced much in recent decades. In time of war, we talk of atrocities without as much as a blush for the countless victims of our abattoirs in time of peace. When Christmas comes, we celebrate the birth of The Christ by getting our teeth into flayed carcases and strangulated fowls, obscenely dangling from hooks everywhere around us. The war is in our hearts, in our thoughtlessness, our indifference, our callousness. The strife finding such refined expression in high explosive and atomic bombs is but the logical sequence of those inhumanities we prefer to gloss over than to face. We get the type of society we are fit for.

.   .   .   .   .   .

Peat is burned extensively throughout Islay. Everywhere the aroma of its reek greets one. On a good, drying day, one may see, among the peat-hags bordering so many of the island's roads, groups of natives busily plying the peat-spade, or stacking such peats as have already been cut. After a recent visit to Barra, where, until a decade or two ago, everyone burned peats, and where to-day so few do, owing partly to laziness, partly to the lack of labour, and partly to the costliness of transporting from peat-moss to hearth, it seemed strange, and even commendable, to find in Islay so universal an appreciation of this indigenous fuel. In 1951 I had scarcely stepped out of the plane, which had brought me so speedily and comfortably from Renfrew to Glenegedale airport in less than an hour, when a whiff of peat-reek reached me. Whereas most of Britain had been complaining of months of continuous rain, Islay had been crying out for moisture—an unusual state of affairs in these parts. Farmers and crofters alike were deploring this drought, since it meant no summer hay. On the other hand, it did make possible the removal from the island's peat-mosses of huge quantities of fuel which the persistent wetness of previous seasons had rendered impracticable. The drought had at all events ensured for the more enterprising inhabitants a good peat-stack by the back door.

Islay's normal rainfall is more than adequate for all her purposes. Indeed, there are times when she could well be spared the drenchings she gets. One recalls in this connection the deluge that descended upon her the Sunday war was declared in 1939. In passing along the rough road between Port Ellen and Bridgend —the high road, as it is called, in order to distinguish it from the lower highway to Bowmore—one cannot but be struck by the number of temporary wooden bridges crossing streams and the merest burns. All the old stone bridges lie in ruins. The floods of that fateful Sunday swept them away. The gorge through which flows, under the highroad, a burn no more than a foot wide in normal times, became filled in a few minutes with a raging torrent. In tearing its way to lower ground, it carried with it not only the little bridge spanning it, but also thirty yards of roadway on either side of it. Three days later, under the direction of the local road surveyor, the present wooden structures were erected, temporarily. They carried all the island's greatly augmented war-time traffic; and they are still in use.

.   .   .   .

In addition to its use for domestic purposes, peat in Islay has the virtue of imparting a peaty flavour to the malt, under which it is allowed to smoulder away in low, open fires. In this island, which has so many distilleries as to have been nicknamed Whisky Island, the quantity of peat cut and transported in a manner properly organised is enormous. In order to differentiate between them and the peats won for private, domestic purposes, they are called the distillery peats. The gigantic stacks of them built within each distillery's precincts are continually being used and replenished. The winning of the distillery peats is as important a feature of Islay's calendar as is the gathering of the harvest. This one instantly realised when travelling the low road between Bowmore and Port Ellen at the time the peats are being cut and loaded. This road passes by that considerable deposit known as the Machrie Moss, whence the natives bear the peats away in horse-drawn carts, and in barrows. The latter have rubber-tyred wheels making them more resilient in soft ground.

Great quantities of the distillery peats at Machrie are transported to some convenient re-loading point in trucks run on narrow-gauge rails temporarily laid across a stretch of the moor where operations are being pursued at a speed which would be impeded were the peats allowed to accumulate there in any great numbers.

Communal life flourishes in the vicinity of those bays and creeks of Islay in which its distilleries lie. These are sometimes remotely situated, as in the case of the Caol Ila Distillery, or that at Bonahaven, both of which nestle by the shores of the Sound of Islay, to the north of Portaskaig. Between Port Ellen and Kildalton, at the south of the island, are the famous distilleries of Ardbeg and Lagavulin, each with its own pier, from which its potent product may be shipped direct. Port Ellen has its own distillery; and so has Bowmore, the island's chief centre. Hard by the short-road pursuing its course round Loch Indaal to Portnahaven and Port Wemyss, at the extremity of the Rhinns, stand two other famous distilleries, one of them at Bruichladdich, the other at Port Charlotte.

The natives are proud of their reputation as distillers; and they brag that, if ever a petrol shortage should render inoperable their internal means of transport, they could easily re-start it on a little of the proof-spirit barrelled away in their bonded warehouses.

. . . .

Only a fraction of Islay is wooded. Yet, among those woodlands at Kildalton, or at Bridgend and in the grounds of Islay House, one can lose oneself sufficiently to forfeit all idea of one's being on an island where anything in the nature of sylviculture is exceptional. A few minutes' wandering in the summertime through the deep shade at Bridgend, where ferns grow darkly, and to a stature more in keeping with conditions semi-tropical, soon robs one of the feeling that there lies so close at hand a hinterland of moors, barren, windswept, and rain-drenched throughout the greater part of the year. These very woodlands, in late winter, are as white with snowdrops as they are blue with wild hyacinths in springtime.

Late May or early June, when masses of daisies whiten the fields where the Ayrshires graze, is a lovely season for Islay. It is the time of the yellows and golds of gorse and of broom, of iris, of dandelion, of kingcup and buttercup, of tormentilla and lady's bedstraw, of the flower of the silverweed clinging so close to the ground—the time of the blues of lobelia and hyacinth, of speedwell and dog-violet—the time, also, of white, not merely of daisy, but, in addition, of the downy *canach* or cotton-grass. And it would, indeed, be ungracious to overlook the white of the tiny moss-roses unfolding by the primroses in nooks sheltered by the rocks.

One is astonished at finding, anywhere in the Hebrides, trees as mature as the oaks, planes, and beeches so long cared for at Kildalton by the Ramsays, its proprietors for so many years. Here, during the first few days of June, when the iris buds are beginning to unfold by the shorelands near at hand, the ferny floor beneath these trees is white with the flowers of garlic or blue with the bells of hyacinth:

> *Still on its bloom the mournful flower retains*
> *The lovely blue that dyed the stripling's veins,*

according to Virgil.

On the other hand, at Bridgend, and in much of the lower valley of the Sorn, the woodland's floor is as blue with hyacinth as it is green with fern and fresh-sprouting bracken.

The Kildalton woods were planted and nurtured with great devotion by the Ramsays, out of whose hands the Kildalton estate passed in 1922. To-day, for a variety of reasons, these woods are left largely to their own resources; and it would seem as though many rare and exquisite shrubs, such as Himalayan and Japanese rhododendrons may begin to deteriorate and revert if some attention be not shown them before long. The same applies, of course, to Kildalton's azaleas, magnolias, and hydrangeas.

It surprised me to find in Islay, and in such abundance, the dainty, maroon flower which one supposes to be the progenitor of all the dancing lady columbines in the world—surprising, also, to find the island's rushy places gilded with kingcups, or so faintly heliotrope with cuckoo-flowers, its moorlands and hill pastures splashed so generously with the gold of gorse. I know certain moist pastures there where the kingcups crowd so densely and prosperously as to give the impression that they are being cultivated for market-garden purposes. In an adjoining patch of ground the lady's smocks take over control, and the blue of speed-well gives way to the purple of orchid. The daisies are no longer wholly responsible for the whiteness of the banks fringing the roadside, since the tiny flowers of the wild strawberry now vie with them for preëminence.

As one proceeds toward Portaskaig, the Ayrshires become scarcer. By the time one has reached the inland village of Bally-grant, they have almost disappeared from the scene. Blackfaced sheep have taken their place, since the countryside now assumes a moorland aspect. All in an April evening, a year or two ago, I lingered long hereabouts among the sheep and their little lambs, having returned across the moors from exploring the historic ruins at Loch Finlaggan. Could any setting have recalled more appropriately—nay, more poignantly—Katherine Tynan's lovely lines?

> All in the April evening
> April airs were abroad;
> The sheep with their little lambs
> Pass'd me by on the road.
> The sheep with their little lambs
> Pass'd me by on the road,
> All in the April evening
> I thought of the Lamb of God.
>
> The lambs were weary and crying
> With a weak human cry;
> I thought of the Lamb of God
> Going meekly to die.
> Up in the blue, blue mountains
> Dewy pastures are sweet;
> Rest for the little bodies,
> Rest for the little feet.
>
> But for the Lamb of God
> Up on the hilltop green,
> Only a cross of shame,
> Two stark crosses between.
> All in the April evening
> April airs were abroad;
> I saw the sheep with their lambs
> And thought of the Lamb of God.

One of the most idyllic experiences to which I ever treated

myself was a cycle ride from Port Ellen to Portaskaig, early in June, just as the may and the blackthorn were thinking about breaking forth into flower. Wild blooms decked the wayside except where it traversed the peat-hags; and, even there, one could discern tiny, moorland plants anxious to proclaim, among the clusters of newly-spun cotton-grass, their infinitesimal existence. The cotton-grass, as yet, was unbent by wind, unsmutched by rain. Under the tall trees marshalled on the eastern slope, down which the road falls so very steeply to the tide's edge, just by Portaskaig's inn and pier, drifts of primroses were springing among young shoots of fern, and mosses livid green.

One of the most satisfying of island prospects with which I am familiar is that of the Sound of Islay, with Jura beyond, from the point where this precipitous road bends sharply among these trees. Immediately below lies the pier, scene of bustle and animation when the mail-steamer ties up for a few hectic minutes. Beyond stretches the Jura shore, backed by graceful peaks so alluring when contemplated from this vantage-point. Running the eye along the distant shore, the discerning readily pick out such features of interest as the raised beaches, about which he may have learnt something in the geological lecture-room of student days. He will also note the swift flowing of the tide at its turn, and realise how it is that, even with modern motive power and various aids to navigation, vessels still meet with disaster in the Sound of Islay. Trawlers often come to grief in it; but they are usually Fleetwood-owned, I am told. The masters of our Scottish trawlers know these waters better, and traverse them more cautiously. An Aberdeen trawler seldom has mishap in this strenuous tideway. So many trawlers have been lost in this sound of late years that, as recently as 1951, the Commissioners of Northern Lighthouses decided to place in it an additional lighted buoy with a bell.

.   .   .   .

On an island as large and diversified as Islay, it is only to be expected that bird-life should be varied. Never in all my experience of the Scottish Isles have I seen or heard so many species within so small a compass. I will not seek to enumerate them, lest some meticulous ornithologist should challenge me on the existence, there, of this one or of that. We have in Islay the birds of the mud-flats and the marsh-lands, the birds of the woodlands, the meadowlands, the moorlands, and of the rocky shorelands. Among the Sanaig Rocks, infrequently visited because of the swampy nature of the moors intervening between them and the road, is one of the chough's few nesting-places in Britain. The

Kiloran Bay, Isle of Colonsay
Robert Meechan, shepherd, on the tidal sands
between Colonsay and Oronsay

cuckoo, so often heard, so seldom seen, may easily be seen here in Islay, in time of cuckoo-call. All the commoner song-birds haunt the island's woodlands. The corncrake croaks by the way-side, almost underfoot, and yet so difficult to locate. The plaint of plover is heard as she rises from the reeds and cuckoo-flowers to gyrate overhead, fearful lest one should intrude upon her nest. The lark rings rapturously aloft.

In the summer of 1950, when lingering with my camera about the meadows near Islay House, listening to lark-song overhead, I was reminded of what I think must have been the most perfect melodic lines I have ever heard—the opening passages of the second movement of Brahms's *Concerto in D* for violin and orchestra, played in the Albert Hall by Szigeti, with the London Symphony Orchestra—gossamer-like cadences the more sensitive *saw*, as well as heard. I doubt whether in Heaven itself there awaits us, in the realm of sound, anything more spell-binding.

One need not specify here all the birds frequenting Islay's shore-lands, nor yet those seen so close at hand, in mating pairs, as one proceeds not too obtrusively along the moorland road near the airport, little disturbed, it would seem, by the noisier flyers with whom they now share the skies. These birds appeared remark-ably tame—as tame as the island's hares. Nowhere have I seen so many hares at such close range as among the farmlands of Islay at sundown in June.

Apropos the corncrake, it might be added that, numerically, this species is greatly on the decrease throughout the British country-side. It was certainly numerous enough in Ross and in Sutherland during my boyhood, forty years ago. I can scarcely remem-ber a hay-time in northern Scotland then, which one did not associate with the incessant craking and croaking of this elusive summer visitant.

My ornithological friends tell me that the corncrake has become relatively scarce in England too. In the Western Highlands and Hebrides, on the other hand, it is as common as ever, despite the absence of such knee-deep, or even waist-deep, meadow herbage as the species delights in. Investigation would seem to show that the corncrake, with its tendency to nest late, finds unsuitable as a haunt and nesting-place those hay-fields harvested early in the year—harvested during incubation and the first week or two of fledging. The earlier cutting of the meadows under newer methods of husbandry has driven the nesting corncrake to regions like the Outer Hebrides, where the hay and wild flower crops mature later in the season, thus enabling her to lay her eggs and hatch her brood before such cover is reaped away.

157

The Rev. Dr. Kenneth MacLeod in his boat in the Minister's Creek, just below his manse on Gigha
The ferryboat leaving the mail-steamer off Craignure, Isle of Mull, on an autumn morning

It is possible, too, that harvesting by mechanical reapers, taking in so wide a margin of herbage with each sweep, now denies her and her young sufficient time to seek cover elsewhere, whereas hand-reaping—reaping by scythe or by sickle—gives just the necessary warning. This, in part at least, may explain the corncrake's deserting highly cultivated localities for the remoter and less luscious pastures of the Western Highlands and Islands. On the other hand, she is more readily seen among the thinner hay-crops of the latter regions, which may account for her preferring to lay her eggs among the tall iris-flags and meadow-sweet growing in hollows and ditches seldom approached by human beings. For purposes of cover and nesting, the corncrake is fond of nettles, from which she may feel herself less likely to be disturbed. When she takes to the wing, she does so in a manner so uncertain that one wonders how she ever manages to migrate.

By the wayside in North Uist, where the species is comparatively common, I have found a corncrake's nest containing as many as ten eggs, and could not but ponder whether, in hatching so large a clutch, she did not have to cover with her wings such of them as her rather small body could not span.

A word about the grey-lag geese which come to Islay in the late autumn or early winter. One dull, November morning, when there was but little light in the rainy heavens, and the sombre land bore the colour of chocolate, except where patches of bracken, so recently frosted down and withered, relieved the monotony of the scene, I landed from Renfrew at Glenegedale, Islay's airport. By the alert of eye and of ear, despite the morning's dreichness, there was much to be seen and heard. Standing close to the runway, or flying low, parallel with its margins, were about forty greylags, but a fraction of the vast flocks of their kind newly arrived in the Hebrides from the Arctic, and now settling down in their wonted winter quarters. These bonnie birds seemed quite accustomed to the invasion of their own airy element by our latest means of transport. The drone of plane appeared to disturb them not at all. From the car conveying me from the airport to my destination at Bowmore, I spotted additional contingents of this mighty feathered force, lending to a scene otherwise rather drab and depressing, that sombre November morning, something of interest, even for the most amateurish of ornithologists.

·   ·   ·   ·   ·   ·   ·

According to the census returns of 1951, the population of Islay was 4,269. This showed a decrease of between 700 and 800 since the census of 1931. In 1911 the island's population was 6323.

This means that it has dropped by approximately a third in the last forty years. The decline has been greatest in the Kilchomain parish, and least in the Kildalton. The bulk of the island's population is distributed among Bowmore and the many 'ports'—Portaskaig, Port Charlotte, Port Ellen, Portnahaven, and Port Wemyss.

Nothing could be cleaner and more orderly than Bowmore's main thoroughfare, falling steeply and broadly from its round parish church, at the top of the brae, toward its principal shops and its small harbour. The shallowness of Loch Indaal, on the eastern shore of which it is situated, has rendered impracticable its development as a port capable of accommodating vessels larger than the Firth of Clyde puffers berthing there periodically with cargoes of coal, bricks, and the like. Yet, in the days when small sailing-smacks were common in these waters, it conducted its due share of the island's maritime business.

Paul Jones is said to have anchored off Bowmore as a preliminary to an attempt to despoil Islay House, seat of the Campbells of Islay. Owing to the shallowness of Loch Indaal, he could not bring his craft nearer his objective. So he and his men took to their cutters, and proceeded to row up to the head of the loch. As the cutters grounded with the ebbing tide about a mile from the shore, it was decided to return with them to the ship whenever the next tide refloated them. While they still lay stranded in this shallow sealoch, two local men, one named Currie, the other named MacNiven, curious to know what was afoot, rowed out to them in a coble of shallow draught. The pirates soon seized them and placed them in irons. When Paul Jones decided to quit Loch Indaal, he had them bound hand and foot, and cast adrift in their own boat. They eventually made land below the farmhouse of Gartbreck, a couple of miles to the seaward of Bowmore. Ever since that incident, the natives of Islay have referred to Paul Jones as the Bloody Yankee.

The story goes that Paul Jones was not yet finished with Islay. Shortly afterwards, it is said, he intercepted the packet sailing between West Loch Tarbert and the island, having learnt that aboard her was Major Campbell of Islay, a gallant who was returning to his native isle from his campaigns in foreign lands, taking with him not only his newly-wed bride, but also all the wealth he possessed in the form of money and jewellery, and of antiques collected abroad. The pirates decided to pursue the packet as she tacked off Gigha. Her captain, in an endeavour to reach the little harbour now known as Port Ellen, crowded on all sail. But soon the pirate vessel bore down upon the packet, sending a shot or two across her bows. "Heave to, or I'll sink you!" shouted Paul Jones. But Campbell of Islay was all for offering resistance to the Bloody Yankee, since he had everything to lose if the pirates succeeded in boarding the vessel. So he cocked his pistol, prepared to defend himself, his wife, and his treasure. The captain, however, thought discretion the better part of valour, and persuaded him to commit no rash act. The pirates duly boarded the packet, threatening to shoot anyone resisting them in their search. They robbed the major of all his treasure. Eventually, he and his wife landed in Islay, penniless. But, as the storyteller reminds us, Paul Jones could not rob the gallant major of his lands, with the result that, after a few years' residence among his sympathetic tenantry, he built up another fortune, enabling him and his wife to live prosperously for the remainder of their days.

Whether or not Paul Jones ever entered Loch Indaal during his piratical exploits, he was certainly active in the waters between Islay and Ireland in 1777. It was at this time that shore-forts were erected on Islay, especially about Islay House, as a protection against his acts of piracy. To this day, some of these forts, in crumbling condition, can be located in the vicinity of Islay House, where the guns once placed in them lie smothered in rank vegetation.

To outward appearances at all events, the main streets of Islay's villages exhibit a cleanliness conspicuously wanting in a town like Stornoway, where offal, garbage, and even sheep's heads and trotters sometimes litter pavement and gutter, so nauseatingly from the visitor's point of view. Islay's villages show a sense of order and tidiness in other ways too. The shop windows of the seaport village of Port Ellen, for instance, are dressed in a manner which might well attract one seeking an island holiday retreat reasonably provident, as well as reasonably accessible. And what island of the Hebrides is now more accessible than Islay? Twice daily, and sometimes even thrice, except on Sundays, a British European Airways' plane lands at Glenegedale from Renfrew, accomplishing in less than an hour a journey which, by sea, would occupy a whole day, and often a very stormy day at that.

Port Ellen, founded in 1844, was named after Lady Elinor Campbell. It lies at the south of the island, but four miles from the aerodrome which civil aviation inherited from the Second World War. A centre more ideally situated for an island holiday would be difficult to find. This explains the pressure on its accommodation throughout so much of the year. Of course, it has its less salubrious quarters, like any other village. These are to be found among its alleys, whence access may be obtained to many a back garden so full of junk, rickety outhouses, and dusty poultry as to have extinguished all vestige of verdure. The passer-by, unfamiliar with such economy, may be surprised when a cow, ruminating out of sight, suddenly pushes her head through a gap in a stone wall to scrutinise him. She may just have been milked in the low byre leaning in upon itself in a corner of such a back garden, so much of which would seem to be permanently occupied by manure, and possibly also by an old, propped boat long since home from sea. For all this, Port Ellen possesses attractions. It has its sandy bays, as well as its reefy shores, on the flat skerries off which the seals lie sunning themselves.

Then the Oa is within reach of those hardy enough to explore its remote places. The less energetic, however, will content themselves with the shoreland tracks enabling them to skirt Kilnaughton Bay, with its ancient chapel and burying-ground, and arrive at the somewhat unusual lighthouse known to seamen as the Port Ellen Light. This lighthouse is not round, but rectangular.

So much less accessible than Port Ellen is Portnahaven, at the extremity of the wild and distant Rhinns—land's-end in the truest sense. Its remoteness is shown by the fact that, although the Gaelic language is still widely understood, if not always spoken, throughout Islay, here it persists as the everyday tongue of the inhabitants. The farther afield one travels from centres like Bowmore and Port Ellen, the nearer one comes to communities essentially Gaelic-speaking, though bi-lingual. The natives of the Rhinns use English only when conversing with those who haven't the Gaelic, as the saying is. The male inhabitants of Portnahaven and of the adjacent township of Port Wemyss were once prosperously employed at cod-fishing, an industry which has now decayed in these parts. To-day many of the natives are merchant seamen. The harbours from which the fishermen used to operate are well protected from gale and surf by MacKenzie's Isle and by Oversay, or Orsay. On the latter stands a lighthouse erected in 1825.

The sturdy, stone-built cottages comprising Portnahaven and Port Wemyss are orderly and tidy; and in almost all of them electric lighting is installed. A little fishing, of course, is still prosecuted, as is evident from the number of small boats beached during stormy weather behind houses having their back to the sea. But the economic mainstay of the Rhinns, as of much of the rest of Islay, has been the making of whisky. The distilleries and bonded warehouses of Bruichladdich and Port Charlotte are in the Rhinns.

The failure of the City of Glasgow Bank, in a sum exceeding £6,000,000, brought much distress to Islay, as to other parts of the Highlands and Islands. This happened in 1878, a year remembered by the oldest inhabitants for its infelicities. It ruined not only great numbers of small people, but also the thrifty and industrious Islay farmers, many of whom were now obliged to quit. Such as had to go were succeeded, to some extent, by farming stock from Renfrewshire and Ayrshire—chiefly from the Cumnock district of the latter county. These incomers introduced new methods of agriculture, as well as their own Ayrshire cows. They devoted attention to dairying, an enterprise hitherto untried in these parts. Their descendants are dairy-farming in Islay at the present day.

On a rocky sea-girt promontory near Lagavulin, of White Horse fame, stand the ruins of Dun Naomhaig, or Dunyveg, as English writers usually render the name. Within this stronghold in early centuries, the great Clan Ranald chiefs—the Lords of the Isles—remained secure against enemies temerarious enough to assail it. Somehow or other, it got into the hands of the Earl of Argyll in 1519. But the MacDonalds were back in it before long, resisting, though not always successfully, attempts by the MacLeans of Duart to wrest it from them. The siege laid by the MacLeans in 1586 failed in its objective, although its defenders were hard pressed throughout.

The Lords of the Isles held on to this ancient keep of theirs until 1615, when it surrendered to Campbell of Calder. About thirty years later, it became a ruin. There is extant the pitiful letter written by Sir James MacDonald on July 1st, 1615, to Lord Binning, praying him to intervene on his behalf, lest his Campbell foes should root him and his out of Islay, where they had been in possession for so many centuries. Sir James promised to restore law and order in the island, to find surety for the rent, and also to guarantee the fealty of himself and his clan, if only he could be helped to remain at Dun Naomhaig as the king's tenant, failing which, as he added, he would acquiesce in Islay's becoming the absolute property of the crown, " for that is certane, I will die befoir I sie a Campbell posses it ". His pleadings went unheeded; and he was obliged to quit Dun Naomhaig and flee the island. Before long, the Earl of Argyll subjugated, in the king's name, such of his followers as were still in rebellion against the central authority.

Dun Naomhaig was the principal seat of the Lords of the Isles when at the height of their power. From it they administered their vast Lordship—the Lordship of the Isles, or the Kingdom of the Isles, as it is sometimes called. Their other resort in Islay was at Finlaggan, an island in the freshwater loch of the same name. On this island are ruins closely associated with their occupation, including those of the chapel standing in the midst of an ancient burying-place. It is held in Islay that in this chapel, as well as in this place of interment, many of the wives and descendants of the Lords of the Isles were buried. Many of the Lords themselves were carried to Iona for burial. Preserved among the chapel ruins are several stones exquisitely designed and beautifully carved. Once recumbent, they now lean against the chapel's roofless walls, the better to preserve them, and certainly to locate them. Some of these represent warriors in mail. This would seem to suggest that, perhaps, one or two of the Lords of the Isles may also have been interred here. The Celtic interlacing patterns on some of the stones are very fine; and the reader desirous of knowing more about them could not do better than consult Graham's exhaustive work, *The Carved Stones of Islay*.

Incidentally, Islay is famed for its ancient stone crosses. On the green sward at Kilchomain, so closely cropped by wandering livestock, stands a sanctuary cross of great antiquity. It is situated not far from the site of the house once occupied by the Mac-Eacherns, hereditary sword-makers to the Lords of the Isles. In a hollow in its pedestal was a round stone turned sunwise by those believing that, in so doing, they should offer up prayer for their personal safety and wellbeing. Several ancient crosses have a pedestal with such a hollow; but the stone would seem to have disappeared from each. It may well have been removed by those who, in later days, regarded such practice as idolatrous.

At Kildalton are the ruins of its ancient church; and in the churchyard surrounding it may be seen that beautiful specimen of Celtic art known as the Kildalton Cross, executed in a form not unlike that of St. John's Cross at Iona. Standing 8 feet in height, and measuring 4 feet across the arms, it bears representations of the Virgin and Child, Abraham sacrificing Isaac, and David rending the lion.

Tradition has it in Islay that Columba landed at Kildalton after quitting Ireland, and before reaching Iona. In Islay this saint is commemorated in the churchyard named after him at Keills, located little more than a mile from Portaskaig. The headstones here readily indicate the surnames commonest in the island—Campbell, Currie, MacEacharn and MacEachern, Mac-Dougall, MacQueen, and Shaw. A stone built into the outer wall of this burial-place, and dated 1820, shows how numerous were the offspring of a certain John Hill and his wives. To the right of this headstone, and similarly fitted into the wall, is another enumerating no fewer than fourteen members of this prolific clan—a remarkable example of Scots' thrift in the matter of gravestones! It bears the names of William Hill and Jane Rousfell, his spouse, together with those of twelve of their family. Flora, the last named, died at Keills in 1949, in her hundredth year. There is still room at the foot of this headstone for three or four additional names; but, whether others may fall to be included, I cannot say.

At Finlaggan, with impressive ceremony, the Lords of the Isles were proclaimed in hereditary succession. The following extract from the *Collectanea de Rebus Albanicis,* written by MacDonald of Sleat, conveys some idea of the importance of the Lordship:

"MacDonald had his council at Island-Finlaggan in Isla, to the number of sixteen, viz. four Thanes, four Armins, that is to say lords, or sub-thanes, four Squires, or men of competent estates, who could not come up with Armins of Thanes, that is freeholders or men that had their lands in factory, as Magee of the Rinns of Isla, MacNicholl in Portree in Sky, and Mac-Eachern, MacKay, and MacGillivray in Mull, Macillemhaoell or MacMillan, etc. Moreover, there was a judge in every Isle for the discussion of all controversies, who had lands from MacDonald for their trouble and likewise the eleventh part of every action decided. But there might still be an appeal to the Council of the Isles. MacFinnon was obliged to see weights and measures adjusted, and MacDuffe or MacPhie of Colonsay kept the records of the Isles."

The proclamation rites at Finlaggan were conducted by a bishop and several attendant priests, in the presence of the representatives of many West Highland and Island families then powerful and prominent. The bishop anointed the new Lord at a spot where lay a square stone bearing a deep imprint the size and shape of a man's foot. Robed in white, the legal claimant stood with his right foot upon it. A white wand was placed in his right hand, and in his left the claymore of the forebear whom he was now succeeding.

Ruins of Aros Castle, Isle of Mull

Fifty yards or so from this island in Loch Finlaggan is an islet covered with grass, upon which there nests every year a pair of swans. This islet goes by a Gaelic name denoting its having been the place where the Lords of the Isles held council. Here, in fact, sat the Lordship's central government, presided over by the Great MacDonald of the Isles Himself. There is now no trace of the stone seat from which he administered the law. Local tradition has it that all such relics were removed from the islet by the artful and all-conquering Campbells!

In 1951 I spent a memorable summer's day at Finlaggan, having wandered from the road at Ballygrant farm, and thence by a short-cut through daisied fields to the end of the loch at which lies the island whereon stand these historic ruins. The day was sultry and a little oppressive. A little disappointing, too, from the photographer's point of view. Groups of Ayrshires and of Highland cattle were standing for coolness well out in the loch, or by the edges of its sandy strands. Because of several weeks' drought, as I was soon to discover, it was possible to set foot on the island without wading and almost without as much as wetting the soles of one's footwear. The merest strip of the ground intervening was pleasantly marshy. In picking my way across this, by stepping on bleached stones usually submerged all the year round, I was not long in finding myself in the heart of the ruined chapel, examining the carved stones already mentioned as leaning against its inner walls. Underfoot I could feel several more, still recumbent, still buried beneath accumulations of mossy and grassy vegetation. As there seemed no position on the island itself from which it might have been possible to include, in a photograph, all the ruins at once, I decided to wade out to the islet about which I have told you. Having divested myself of footwear, and fastened it round my neck, anticipating a further use for it when confronted with the nettles I already had observed from the adjacent shore, I proceeded to wade with camera and extended tripod. But the loch's floor, underfoot, was composed of sharp, serrated rocks, their stratification almost vertical, rather than horizontal. It was like walking barefoot on the edges of upturned slates, closely packed, and sharply splintered. So painful was the going that I had to retreat to put on my shoes. Having tucked my trousers as high as they would go, I sallied forth a second time. When a third of the way across, I found the water reaching to my clothing. Returning to the shore yet again, I divested myself of everything except my shirt, and set off, determined to reach my objective even if it meant swimming with my camera held above the water. Upon the slippery stones about mid-channel, the going was pre-

Ben Buie, Isle of Mull, on a summer morning,
with the Memorial Cairn to Edward VII, raised
by MacLaine of Lochbuie

carious; and every now and then my shoes, but lightly laced in case of emergency, began to sink, with every outward step, deeper and deeper in the ooze. With the exercise of caution, I managed to reach the islet. Instantly, the curved neck of a swan among the greenery by the shore caught my eye. Ah! a nest, which I was not long in locating. The cob had already given the alarm to his partner, sitting sedately upon her eggs. Without showing resentment at my intrusion, both birds waddled to the shore, and went a-cruising in the channel across which I had just waded. Their nest in the immediate foreground, the swans themselves in the middle-distance, and the ruins of Finlaggan in the background would have made an ideal picture, had there been some cloud overhead, instead of a haze. The nettles everywhere around me stung legs and ankles. When it became necessary to change the film in my camera in this shadeless place, I could not get down on my uncovered haunches because of them. My shirt-tails were quite inadequate. Standing upright with my back to the sun, and employing as skilfully as I could my teeth, I succeeded in re-loading, without letting light either into the film I had exposed, or into the unexposed one now inserted. But what a trial it was! How irksome! And how stinging, those nettles at Finlaggan!

Though my limbs tingled for several days thereafter, this was one of the loveliest days I have ever spent alone with my camera. It reminded me of a somewhat similar excursion in sultriness to the Loch of Stenness. At Finlaggan, as at Stenness, plovers and oystercatchers, sandpipers and curlews, winged noisily about me, each employing, according to its kind, some decoy, lest I should happen upon its eggs or young. All these birds were nesting everywhere around me. So, also, were wild duck. On every side, when making my way homeward across meadow and moor-land at dusk, rabbits scurried, and hares went a-bounding. The hares seemed more plentiful than the rabbits.

.   .   .   .

The history of Islay, like that of the rest of the Hebrides, is largely concerned with the doings of the warring clans. Much of the strife which existed between the MacDonalds of Islay and the MacLeans of Duart found physical expression there. One of the most historic encounters of these two deadly rivals was that which took place, largely with bows and arrows, on the foreshore at the head of Loch Gruinart, in the latter half of the sixteenth century,[1]

[1] Notice how canny I am! I find myself in a quandary as to the exact year. Bartholomew's ½-inch map bears the legend, *Site of Battle, A.D.,1588.* The Ordnance Survey 1-inch, on the other hand, gives the year, 1598, which, I am told, is correct.

when Sir Lachlan MacLean sailed from Mull in the hope of wresting Islay from his redoubtable nephew, Sir James Mac-Donald. A pair of crossed swords on the map seeks to indicate the spot.

The Mull force is thought to have consisted of about 400 war-like MacLeans, more than half of whom were slain. Their rout was complete in no time. Out of a force half the size of Sir Lach-lan's, the Islay MacDonalds lost only 24 slain, and 60 wounded. These casualties were inflicted "all with arrowes", we are told. MacLean had come in strength to Islay to take from his nephew the Rhinns, which the latter had refused to give over to him. The stubborn uncle swore he would take by force what prolonged negotiations had failed to obtain for him. Sir Lachlan himself was among the slain at *Traigh Ghruineart*, or Gruinart Shore, as historians denote this sanguinary incident. There resides in this neighbourhood a crofter who has an old sword found here many years ago, and supposed to be one used at the battle. Per-haps a sword which once belonged to a MacDonald protagonist! If so, it may have been fashioned by a MacEachern, a patronymic still wellknown in Islay, and one with which I have been familiar since childhood, because of my father's friendship with a family of the name belonging to this island.

The natives of Islay point to a stone by the fringe of Loch Gruinart said to mark the spot where fell Sir Lachlan MacLean of Duart, leader of the defeated host from Mull. As the contest appears to have been in the nature of a running fight, no one can say just where it was fought. Precision in the matter is ren-dered impossible through the fact that, as so much of the loch dries out at low water, there was no way of deciding on which stretch of the tidal sandflats the major part of the conflict was fought.

This conflict bequeathed to Islay some of its folk-tales. With these we need not concern ourselves too much here, since Islay is fortunate in having had most of her tales adequately recorded by that indefatigable collector, John Francis Campbell, once pro-prietor of much of the island, and widely known as Campbell of Islay, author of *The Popular Tales of the West Highlands*. Campbell was born at Islay House, near the head of Loch Indaal, in 1821, and was buried at Cannes in 1885. He was an eminent Celtic scholar, which accounts for the excellence with which he set down so much folk-tale and tradition already being lost or for-gotten. This is evident from the work alluded to, and also from his *Leabhar na Feinne*, Book of the Fingalians. Matters Celtic did not absorb entirely his interests and literary energies: he also wrote a geological treatise, *Frost & Fire*; and he invented the sunshine recorder. His fame, however, rests mainly on his *Popular Tales*, regarded as one of the most important contributions ever made to the scientific study of folk-tales. In 1887 the Islay Association erected, conspicuously, on a grassy knowe at the head of Loch Indaal, a monument to him who, "loved alike by peer and peasant . . . preserved and rendered classic the Folklore of the Scottish Highlands".

. . . .

Hebrid seas have taken heavy tribute in human life. Of this one is given an optical reminder or two when making for the wild, high ground at the Mull of Oa. There, at the edge of the cliff-top, stands a monument of native stone. The inscription on the large, metal plaque set aslant under the American Eagle, close to the base of it, on the landward side, explains the cemetery:

SACRED
TO THE
IMMORTAL MEMORY
OF THOSE
AMERICAN SOLDIERS & SAILORS
WHO GAVE THEIR LIVES
FOR
THEIR COUNTRY
IN THE
WRECKS OF THE TRANSPORTS
"TUSCANIA" AND "OTRANTO"
FEBRUARY 5TH, 1918   OCTOBER 6TH, 1918

This Monument was erected by
The American National Red Cross
near the spot where so many of
The Victims of the Disasters
Sleep
In Everlasting Peace

On the barren warren at Kilchomain is an American walled cemetery, exposed to all the winds that blow, to the winter storms that descend upon the Hebrides, to the very spume and spindrift borne some hundreds of feet up the inhospitable cliffs, when heavy seas come crashing far below. Interred in this cemetery were the corpses recovered after these two disasters. The ground to the seaward of it drops precipitously in cliffs to a tumbled confusion of hillocks and immense, bent-covered sand-dunes stretching westward to a shore of sand golden and gleaming at sundown, with the Atlantic surging ceaselessly beyond.

Upon the rocks at the Mull of Oa the *Tuscania*'s life-boats were dashed to pieces when she was torpedoed midway between Islay and Ireland. Swept up by high seas and tempestuous winds into the more inaccessible clefts and hollows of the cliffs are fragments of bleached timber, long since deposited there. The natives of the Oa say they are bits of the *Tuscania*'s shattered life-boats.

The *Otranto*, in collision near the Irish coast, had her steering-gear put out of action. She drifted over to Islay to strike a sunken rock off Kilchiaran farm. The survivors got ashore on the Kil-chomain strand.

So wild and so sparsely peopled is the Oa that the undetected ransacking of drowned men's garments was common. It became a standing joke in Islay, when anyone left the island for a day or two about this time, to say, "Och, he's away to Glasgow to cash the dollars!"

Such corpses from these wrecks as came ashore in Loch Indaal were less liable to this. They were placed in the Port Charlotte Distillery, part of which had been converted into a mortuary.

On that February evening in 1941, when the *Politician* went ashore in the Sound of Eriskay,[1] the *Floristan*, a merchantman of 10,000 tons, struck a rock at Kilchiaran, on the Atlantic side of the Rhinns. There she broke her back, fortunately without any loss of life. She was one of twenty-eight vessels in convoy, which had left Liverpool some days earlier in a south-westerly gale and a thick fog. The captain, aware of his being in the vicinity of the Rhinns, hovered at a reduced speed of two knots to see whether he could spot the Oversay lighthouse. He was unaware, however, that his ship was in a contrary current of four knots, and was therefore drifting steadily inshore.

The *Floristan*'s cargo included nylons, Coty's powder, shirtings, suit lengths, cigarettes, wines, spirits, fountain-pens, 250 drums of tetrachloride, and a few locomotives. This mixed bag encouraged the natives of Islay to do a bit of salvaging on their own. Consequently, they also had their "Whisky Galore"! There was an epidemic of new suits made up by tailors and drapers visiting Islay. These suits, all to the same pattern, occasioned much amusement throughout the island.

As the wreck lay in deep water but a stone's-throw from the

[1] For a detailed account of this mishap and of all that followed, see our companion volume, *The Western Isles*, pp. 274-283.

shore, the Irish labourers, meanwhile employed in the construction of Islay's aerodrome, were able, *ad libitum*, to help themselves. They and others brought ashore great quantities of Brylcream. In this cloying commodity everybody now became as immersed as did the natives of Eriskay, Barra, and the Uists in the Kolynos tooth-paste retrieved from the *Politician*. Brylcream was used extensively for washing fuel oil from salvaged cigarette tins. More than sixty persons were prosecuted before the sheriff at Campbeltown, as the result of investigations made by police and by customs and excise officials. All were fined in small sums. Lightning raids were made by those searching for dutiable goods. Whisky secreted in rabbit-burrows was brought forth when the local 'All Clear' sounded. Those who found themselves in trouble with the authorities over the unlawful possession of a few tins of cigarettes were much aggrieved when they discovered that, with impunity, their neighbours had removed from the wreck enormous rolls of cloth! The tide, in a sense, has been generous to Islay.

By the way, there lies buried at Kilchomain Machir a cask of whisky which came ashore during the First World War, and was interred below a bush. But a storm and a particularly high tide carried away the bush, and, with it, all knowledge of the location of the cask. This occurred in 1917. No one looks for the cask now, since Islay's experts in matters of casks and their contents declare that the timbers of a buried cask, containing Islay whisky, disintegrate in five years!

But for a change in the direction of the prevailing wind, Islay would certainly have been the graveyard of hundreds more who lost their lives off these shores during the Second World War. The prevailing wind had always been the south-westerly. In November, 1939, it went round to the south-east. There, except for two weekends in May, 1940, it has remained. From the end of May, 1940, until December, 1947 (that is to say, until two-and-a half years after the cessation of hostilities), the prevailing wind was very definitely south-east. A similar change in direction was noted elsewhere down the west coast of Britain. So far as Islay was concerned, and indeed the whole of the western and north-western coasts of Scotland, this meant that the bodies of countless persons torpedoed in the North Atlantic were driven westwards, away from our shores. An old Portnahaven fisherman, who had served aboard naval patrol vessels off the Inner Hebrides, told me that, had there been no alteration in the direction of the prevailing wind, the shores of Islay and of the neighbouring isles would have been strewn with corpses. He himself had seen scores of them being wafted away from these very shores by a south-east wind.

The bodies of all American soldiers and sailors recovered from the sea during the First World War were buried initially at various points along our coasts, roughly where they were found. Between 1919 and 1923, the nearest of kin of all identifiable American dead were given the choice of having their war dead returned to their homes in the United States, or placed in the nearest permanent American military cemetery, which, in the case of Great Britain, is Brookwood, in Surrey. Approximately half requested that the bodies should be sent home: the others preferred that they should remain in Europe. I learn from the American Battle Monuments Commission, established in Paris by Congress in March, 1923, that, in the very few cases where the next of kin desired that bodies should be left at the original place of burial, their wish was acceded to; but they were asked to sign a waiver relieving the United States' Government of all responsibility for the upkeep of such graves. Records show, at the time of writing, that American soldiers and sailors still lie buried at Girvan, at Ayr, on the Argyllshire mainland, and in Islay.

.   .   .   .

To revert again to the Oa, this region is now so thinly peopled that, for ecclesiastical purposes, it has been joined with Kildalton. The last incumbent of the *quoad sacra* parish of the Oa was the Rev. Donald MacLean, a man who conducted public worship in his church just as and when he felt inclined. And *that* was seldom enough! So notorious did he become for his dereliction of parochial duty that, in response to complaints, investigators were sent to the Oa from the church offices in Edinburgh. As the result of their findings, he was deposed. During the latter years of his life, he wore the uniform of an American soldier—slouch hat, khaki tunic and breeches, and puttees. These he had taken off the bodies of some of the *Tuscania*'s victims.

After a fashion, he farmed the glebe. With him lived a sister not too strong in the upper part of her framework. He used to set her to work in the fields, tethering her to a post to prevent her running away from the various tasks he gave her. He was a bachelor. He was also a miser. He left over £4,000.

The story is told in Islay of an old friend of mine, the late Lachlan MacNeil Weir, a native of the island who, for several years, was Socialist member for one of the Scottish mining and industrial constituencies. One Sunday morning, while Lachie, then a pupil-teacher in Glasgow, was home in Port Ellen, recuperating after an operation for appendicitis, he and his family set out for the Oa with the idea of attending forenoon service, due to begin at MacLean's church at 11.30. Lachie was anxious to find out how the minister was behaving himself. He duly arrived at the church. It was closed; and there was nothing to indicate that a public diet was to be held. Knowing how perfunctorily MacLean performed his duties, and determined not to control his impatience beyond the stroke of noon, Lachie proceeded to toll the church bell. MacLean knew this could not be the beadle's doing, since he had mentioned to him the previous evening that he hardly thought he would hold a service that Sunday.

Down to the church hurried the half-dressed minister to find the convalescing Lachie summoning to worship the parishioners of the Oa, many of whom had already set out for the church in response to his bell-ringing. Rushing up to the offender in threatening fashion, the irate incumbent was heard to say: " They took the guts oot o' ye in Glesca, but they didna take the *cheek*! "

.   .   .   .

Quite recently the sea took toll in Islay, and in a manner poignant and personal. One Sunday evening in July, 1951, Barbara Patricia Price-Hughes, an artist of thirty-five summers, came to see me in order to discuss with me the manuscript of a book she was writing about Islay and her personal experiences there. She had spent several holidays at Portnahaven, where she had a cottage. She had planned that her text should be illustrated with a selection from her own paintings. Her mentioning Portnahaven prompted me to tell her that I had known intimately, since the age of ten, a certain Colonel George Cockburn Campbell, whose father, long ago, had been parish minister at Portnahaven. George was born in the manse there in 1897. He and I were enrolled as pupils at George Watson's College, Edinburgh, in 1909.

Forty years earlier, his father and mine had graduated at Glasgow. Furthermore, George's two sisters and my own began their careers at George Watson's Ladies' College on the same day in 1909—the day on which my father and their parents re-discovered one another, after a lapse of so many years. So, you see the basis of the friendship went back a long way.

Scarcely had I been given time to tell Barbara all this, and to add that my first knowledge of Green, Grassy Islay had been derived from the Campbells, when she exclaimed that she was actually leaving London the following evening for Portnahaven, where she had arranged to join George and his wife, Helen, already on their annual holiday there from Edinburgh.

On the evening of August 3rd, 1951, I happened to be standing by the tape-machine of a Fleet Street news agency, talking to an editor friend, and watching rather casually the news, as the machine ticked its way along. Suddenly the word, Islay, caught my eye; and then the names of George and Barbara. An hour or two before, while bathing in Saligo Bay, within a few miles of George's birthplace, both of them had been drowned. Helen had managed to extricate herself from the current which had swept husband and friend to their death. Barbara was thirty-five: George was fifty-four.

This tragedy shocked us all; and even now I cannot imagine how a fellow who had distinguished himself in various athletics, both in war and in peace, and had begun his swimming career with me in Edinburgh as long ago as 1909, should have perished thus.

The evening Barbara came to see me here, in Chelsea, she told me that she had left a duplicate key of her Islay cottage with the editor of Messrs. William Collins, the publisher. I asked her why. She answered that she had discussed with him, rather tentatively, the publication of her book, and thought she might like to leave the key as a sort of charm. She had no doubt that the key, in the keeping of Freddie Smith (another Watsonian, by the way), would 'charm' Collins into accepting for publication her manuscript, when she returned with it from Islay in the autumn, somewhat amplified. When I visited Freddie at St. James's Place the day after the tragedy, I asked him what the name, Barbara Patricia Price-Hughes, conveyed to him. "*That!*" he answered, pulling out a drawer of his desk, and extracting from it a key, which he now held out toward me. "Well, Freddie," I said, "I don't think the poor lassie will be wanting the key any more."

I cannot write further of this fatality now, but may want to revert to it one day in a volume of memoirs.

CHAPTER XIV

JURA

Like water-cress gathered fresh from cool streams,
Thy kiss, dear love, by the Bens of Jura;
Cold, cold the Bens, cold thy love as they,
Like water-cress gathered fresh from cool streams.

JURA!

The name which has fascinated ever since the sound of words
has conveyed anything to me! At varying intervals during most
of my life, I have viewed its comely peaks—its Paps, as they are
called—at a distance and from different angles. I have gazed upon
them, as if under enchantment, from Knapdale, from Kintyre,
from the shorelands of Gigha, from the highlands of Islay, from
the swirling edge of the sound of the same name, from the quiet
pastures of Colonsay, and from the deck of the good ship,
Hebrides, as she steered a course for Portaskaig on her circuit
between the Clyde and the Outer Isles. And I have also seen
them from the air.

Grouped like the three eternal Graces about the centre of the
southern half of the island, some four miles inland, the quartz
rock cone of each of them rises to approximately 2,500 feet, and is
crowned with a huge cairn. Beinn an Oir (2,571 feet), Beinn
Siantaidh (2,477 feet), and Beinn a' Chaolais (2,407 feet) are etched
upon my inward vision as clearly as are the Coolins of Skye,
at which I used to gaze, enrapt, from the windows of the home
of my infancy. If one have a regret about these three peaks,
it is that from most directions only two of them may be
seen.

With Beinn an Oir, as the name indicates (it means the Hill of
Gold), is associated one of the numerous legends of hidden
treasure. Down from *Loch an Oir,* that tiny Loch of Gold found
on its northern flank, flows *Allt nan Oir,* the Golden Brook, to
meet the Atlantic at one of the many stretches of Jura's coast interesting to geologists because of their raised beaches.

The prominence of the Paps is shown by their being visible
not only from the continent of Argyll, but also from Perthshire,
from Ayrshire and Bute, from Dunbartonshire, and even from

the uplands of Lanark. From their summits, owing to their isolated position, with little high ground intervening, the prospect is considerable. Most of the Inner Hebrides can be seen from them, and also a fair stretch of the Ulster coast. My mountaineering friends tell me that, under exceptionally good conditions, the Coolins of Skye are also visible, though dimly.

The summits and flanks of the Paps, comprising for the most part sheets of rock and the detritus of aeons, support little vegetation. The fine-grained quartzite of which they are composed weathers into fragments sharply angular. This one readily discovers when faced with the necessity of traversing their precipitous screes, the colour of ordinary pepper. The hill-climber will find his ascent of these screes as plodding and arduous as anything he is likely to undertake in Jura, for they roll away underfoot as would a treadmill. The few tufts of moss or heather scattered here and there among them are indeed a boon, since they enable him to stand still and rest for a moment or two, without a sense of insecurity. They are infinitesimal spots of *terra firma* amid acres of sliding, slithering detritus, such as will try the patience and endurance of any mountaineer, and at the same time test the quality of his footgear. The cragsman's boots are unavailing here. In fact, their clumsiness may only encourage the detritus to slip from under them.

However, one must not draw from all this the conclusion that Jura's peaks present anything really formidable. On the contrary, they may be ascended with comparative ease, and even with safety, as mountains go. Beinn an Oir lies but five miles of crow-flight from Craighouse, the island's port of call; while Beinn a' Chaolais (so called because of its relative proximity to the Sound of Islay) lies no more than four miles in a north-easterly direction from the ferrying-place at Feorlin—four miles, one ought to say, of very heavy going.

I should say, from experience, that these mountain-tops are most easily reached and explored from the north-east, particularly if one can get a lift from Craighouse to the point at which the road travelling northward along the east coast of Jura crosses the Corran River. Follow the Corran to its source at Loch an t-Sìob, less than a steep mile to the north of which lies the summit of Beinn Siantaidh. About the same distance to the west of this summit is that of Beinn an Oir, the col between which descends to about 1,500 feet above sea-level. This means a descent and a re-ascent of roughly 1,000 feet—not worth mentioning. South-westwards from Beinn an Oir, at a distance of about a mile and a half, lies Beinn a' Chaolais. Here the intervening col necessitates a drop to about 1,200 feet. Anybody moderately able-bodied can attain all three summits in a summer's day, without any excessive expenditure of energy. Such an expedition, I have calculated, entails a total ascent of not much more than 5,000 feet. This would present no hardship whatsoever to any aspiring mountaineer. Indeed, any hill-climber in reasonably good fettle could tackle it.

Mountains more enticing than the Paps of Jura I do not know. Almost every day during a week's sojourn in Islay in wintry weather, as recently as 1951, they drew me from Bowmore in the direction of the Sound of Islay. I could see two of them, afar off, from my bedroom window. Their allure involved me in a considerable expenditure of energy on a bicycle, and upon roads hilly and none too smooth. Five days in succession, they attracted me from the friendliest fireside to Portaskaig, merely to see whether their summits bore a little more of the first snows of winter than on the previous day. However, light conditions were uniformly poor throughout my stay in Islay, so that I found little opportunity for using the camera. Still, I felt compensated as long as two of the peaks, already lightly sprinkled with snow, remained in sight. Often against a head-wind, and as often obliged to dismount in face of the chilly, hail-laden showers passing over the isles from the Atlantic every quarter of an hour, I pushed on to the tide's edge at the Sound of Islay. The magnetism of the Bens was irresistible; and I could not but regret that, as a student, I had been so inattentive in the geology classroom, since I would have been able to appreciate more fully their petrological significance. Nevertheless, when afoot among them, I *was* in a position to trace, along ridges and across cliff faces, clearly marked quartzite stratifications, having remembered Sir Archibald Geikie's remark that nowhere in Scotland are the distinctive features of quartz rock scenery to be seen on so splendid a scale as among the mountains of Jura, and of the neighbouring isle of Islay—having remembered, moreover, that the raised beaches along the island's west coast range in height from 100 to 135 feet.

It was in Jura, in 1812, that Dr. Walker of Edinburgh carried out his experiments in the variation in temperature at which water boils at different levels. He took the boiling temperature at sea-level and compared it with that on the summit of Beinn an Oir. Roughly thirty years later, engineers surveying the west coast of Scotland were to get to know intimately this same peak. About 500 feet below its summit may still be seen the ruins of the rude dwelling they occupied while making numerous calculations in this locality. The track they trod so often between dwelling and summit is also clearly defined to this day.

· · · · · · · ·

Jura is as wild and barren as any isle of the Hebrides. Indeed, from the point of view of husbandry, it must be as intractable as any in Scotland. True, some plantations of trees thrive moderately at its southern and northern extremities; but the existence of these merely emphasises the island's status and condition as one vast, inhospitable deer-forest.

Jura has always been famed for its red deer. To-day they are so numerous that one seldom traverses its moorlands and hillsides without seeing a herd of them. One bright day in June, 1951, when proceeding along the course of the Corran River toward the mountains, I suddenly noticed, three-quarters of a mile ahead of me, two separate herds grazing on a stretch of moorland until then hidden from view by a low ridge. I sank slowly to the ground, and lay dead still. With great caution and a minimum of noticeable movement, I put the glass to my eye. This enabled me to estimate their number at not fewer than 250 stags, hinds, and calves. In the distant sunlight, with the purple of the Paps forming a royal back-cloth, as it were, they looked truly magnificent. I was moving toward them at crawling pace, in the hope of getting near enough to photograph them, when, on the horizon of a ridge no more than twenty yards up-wind, and ahead of me, I detected something move. It looked like a bifurcated twig momentarily disturbed by a whiff of passing breeze. Suddenly I realized it to be the tips of a stag's antlers. In a trice the bearer of them, a sentry on outpost duty, was on his feet and in full flight. I now dashed forward but a few paces to observe another herd of about eighty animals, bounding away from a deep fold in the moorland hitherto concealed. In their dash to join the main contingent, they travelled at a speed incredible, the youngsters keeping up with their panic-stricken parents, and, indeed, in most cases, fleeing a pace or two ahead of them. It was one of the most marvellous sights I have ever witnessed.

The sparse woods of Jura used to shelter the shy roe deer; and once upon a time the island was noted for its fallow. Neither roe nor fallow are to be found in Jura now. To-day, only the red deer, which are so numerous, roam its wild moors and barren mountain-sides.

In relation to area, Jura is one of the most thinly populated of all the isles of Britain. Its few inhabitants reside on the east side. Most of them are employed in some capacity on one or other of

the island's four estates—Ardfin, Jura Forest, Tarbert, and Ardlussa—and attend, between whiles, to their own crofts or smallholdings. The west side is too wild and inaccessible, too steep
and shoreless, too rent by torrent, to encourage the erection of
human habitation upon it. Here the eagle is monarch. Undisturbed, he has perched his eyrie among Jura's precipices for years
immemorial, sallying forth from it with destructive intent at
lambing-time. Even the deer find Jura's west side too inhospitable for them.

While mentioning the eagle, one might also mention the
ptarmigan. According to Seton Gordon, Jura is the ptarmigan's
most southerly haunt in Britain.[1]

Ornithologists tell me that, on the whole, the island's bird-life
presents few features of unusual interest. Yet, my own amateurish
knowledge of the subject might have been amplified, had I been
able to identify readily all the birds to be seen there. One of my
most vivid memories is of an evening I lingered unobtrusively
by the shores of the Lowlandman's Bay, watching the eiders as
they cruised close inshore among the seawrack, the duck so neat
and small in her dark brown plumage, the drake so large by
comparison, so richly feathered.

.   .   .   .

The island's west coast, characterised by the raised beaches
already alluded to, is honeycombed with caves, many of which
are of considerable size. In one or two of these, lobster-fishermen
from the neighbouring isles of Colonsay and Islay often reside
for several consecutive weeks when sinking their pots in these
waters.

It is said that in olden days, when weather prevented the transport of the corpses of persons sufficiently illustrious to be interred
in Colonsay, or, as is more probable, at the ancient Priory in
adjacent Oronsay, the coffins containing such were often deposited
in Jura's western caves until wind and sea moderated. Thus
some of the caves acquired a reputation for sanctity. Such was
the case, for example, with that which goes by a Gaelic name
denoting the Cave of the Iona Folk, and also with that at Corpach,
situated in the north-western part of the island. The latter cave,
according to Martin, " hath an altar in it."

So numerous are the caves and raised beaches occurring along
the western coast, particularly in the region of Loch Tarbert, that
one could devote, entirely, several weeks to exploring them. One
of the largest is that known as the King's Cave, located at the

[1] *Highways and Byways in the West Highlands.* (Macmillan, 1935.)

seaward end of Loch Tarbert. At its entrance is the well so greatly appreciated by those who, in former times, had occasion to occupy it.

Loch Tarbert runs so far inland toward the east side of Jura as to leave an isthmus no wider than a mile. Were it not for this narrow neck of land, Jura would be divided into two islands almost equal in area. The isthmus explains, of course, the name of the sealoch just mentioned, and also Tarbert Bay and the small township of the same name, situated halfway up the island's east coast. Hereabouts the topographical configuration is almost identical with that of the better known and certainly less inaccessible isthmus lying roughly eighteen miles to the south-east, across the Sound of Jura—between East Loch Tarbert and West Loch Tarbert, separating Kintyre from Knapdale.

. . . .

Jura has a maximum length of nearly thirty miles, and a maximum breadth of roughly eight. It has an area of 90,000 acres, few of which are not of poor quality. For its size, it is singularly lacking in archæological remains. Standing-stones of no great size are to be found here and there, and also the nondescript ruins of what may have been ecclesiological structures. But these are unimportant when compared with the remains on so many of our Scottish islands.

Early accounts of the island mention an unusual relic of antiquity. Here and there, along the declivity of a hill, are the ruins of an ancient wall that stood about five feet in height, and terminated sometimes in a loch, sometimes in an abrupt steep. At the lower end of this wall lay a deep pit, some twelve feet in diameter at its mouth, but considerably contracted at the bottom. According to local tradition, this contrivance was used in olden times for capturing the wild boar. The islanders, when boar-hunting, drove their victims along the wall, and caught them when, at length, they sought refuge in the pit.

. . . .

In a hollow among the heathery hills near the thatched township of Keills, where a gurgling burn falls steeply to the sea, is the ancient burying-ground of Earnadail. Here, in former days, stood the chapel referred to in old writings. Here, as a rule, are buried the islanders belonging to the southern half of Jura: those of the northern half are interred at Inverlussa, where stands a unique tombstone to which we shall allude later, when commenting on some remarkable cases of longevity among the natives.

The crofting clachan of Keills lies not much more than a mile from Craighouse. A stony road leads one from the clachan itself to the burial-ground, half a mile or so farther inland. This hallowed place of sepulture, dedicated to Earnadail, nestles in a corner of the glen, in a coomb among the hills, just beyond the high fence protecting the islanders' arable land from the herds of deer roaming the Bens. For the interment of the dead, it occupies one of the loveliest sites imaginable, a mountain stream perpetually singing nearby. The natives tell me that, even in the driest of seasons, this stream—the Minister's Burn, they call it, because it runs down from the graveyard, through the minister's glebe and past his manse, to join the sea a few hundred yards off—that, even in the driest of seasons, as I was saying, it flows melodiously, its banks in June, where they impinge upon the graveyard's mossy walls, covered to a height of eight or ten feet with whins in the densest blossom I have ever seen in the species. Here and there, the trunks of a few old ash-trees and their lithe saplings are succeeding in an endeavour to push these mossy, drystone walls away from their original alignment and symmetry.

Earnadail, who bequeathed his name to this spot, was one of our early Celtic saints. They say that he dwelt in Islay, and that, when dying, he expressed a wish to be buried in Jura, instructing his disciples to ferry his body over the Sound of Islay, and along the east of Jura, to a spot on the hillside, dependent over which they would find a ball of mist. There they must bury him. And this they did, at Keills, where one may see the burial-place and the site of the chapel, in the names of which his own is perpetuated.

The graveyard itself is a place of innumerable, grassy mounds, many of which are marked by no stone of any kind. Yet, several headstones of all ages and sizes declare the surnames commonest among the Jura people—Buie, Campbell, Darroch, MacCrain, MacDougall, MacIsaac, MacKay, MacKechnie, MacLean, and Shaw. A stone to Catherine MacLean testifies that she died in 1892 at Glasgow " through the result of an accident by falling over a window three stories high ". Catherine is reported to have been cleaning the window at the time.

A splendid stone of Aberdeen granite marks the grave of that goodly man, the Rev. John Donald Robertson, who, in 1947, in his seventy-eighth year, died at the manse of Jura, almost within calling-distance of his last resting-place here on earth. He had been parish minister for forty-four years. Above the inscription on his tombstone are the Robertson coat-of-arms, the date, 1451, and the motto, *Virtutis, Gloria, Merces*—Glory the Wages of

*The jetty at Iona, with the Ross of Mull
seen beyond the Sound of Iona*

Virtue. He was indeed proud of belonging to the Clan Robertson, to the ancient Clan Donnachaidh.

Here at Keills, too, is the grave pointed out as being that of
Gillouir MacCrain, who, according to Martin, "lived to have
kept a Hundred and Eighty christmasses in his own house".

A vault in this place of burial is the family tomb of the Campbells of Jura; and engraved therein, upon its marble tablets, are
the names of their kinsmen who died of wounds in France—at
Neuve Chapelle in the spring of 1915, and on the Somme the
following summer.

Misfortune overtook the Campbells of Jura, as it has done so
many other property owners of the name in recent decades. An
old woman—a spaewife, or soothsayer—was heard to say that,
before long, a cart drawn by a white horse would convey to the
pier all they would possess in the island. Her prediction grieved
many, since they recalled how there had come to pass several
other untoward things she had foretold.

"*Thainig an t-each ban!*" "The White Horse has arrived
anyway!" the spaewife's cronies were heard to remark when,
some little time later, two white horses were actually brought over
from the mainland. They now waited for the fulfilment of the
foretelling. Shortly afterwards, the Campbells sold Jura, together with Jura House and all therein; and it was commented
upon by the islanders that one of the two imported horses drew to
the pier at Craighouse just those few personal belongings they
took with them when leaving Jura in other hands.

Mention of the Campbells of Jura brings to mind Mary Campbell, an old native who lived at the village of Keills. Mary was
an authority on the old graveyard there. She knew more accurately where this one's and that one's relatives lay buried than they
themselves knew. When something untoward was about to occur,
she used to complain of a curious itch about her forehead. On
hearing a cock crow in a manner she thought unpropitious, she
would hurry out of her cottage to see which way the crower was
facing, that she might know the direction from which news of
death or other calamity was to be expected. Natives have assured
me that the things she prognosticated always came to pass.

Mary Campbell was not the only person in the island who
foretold by cock-crow. I know a delightful Jura family named
MacKay, most of whom now live furth of their native isle. When
John MacKay and I were staying at Craighouse recently with his
sister, John recalled an incident which the entire family remem-

*Iona: The Abbey, with the ruins of St. Oran's Chapel
to the right, and the Refectory (restored 1951) to the left*

bered quite clearly. It occurred in 1901, when they were living with their parents at Inver, in the days when such places were so remote that a newspaper reached them but once a week. Residing there with the MacKays at the time was an Edinburgh school-teacher named Alexander Keils. One evening, as the family was seated by the kitchen fireside, the cock on a spar high up in the adjoining byre began to crow.

"Mark the hour!" said Keils, with emphasis, pointing to the clock on the mantelshelf. "The Old Queen's just dead!"

This the young MacKays thought very odd, because Keils was an unsuperstitious Lowlander, from whom any such pronouncement was not to have been expected. When at length a newspaper arrived at Inver, it showed that Queen Victoria had died at that very moment.

. . . .

Next to the Rev. Donald John Robertson's grave (not forgetting the wooden cross denoting the spot where the body of an unknown sailor was buried in 1941) is that of one in whom I had a personal interest, since he was, *inter alia*, Professor of Education at Edinburgh University from 1903 until his death in 1924, at the age of 62. His name is Alexander Darroch; and his grave is marked by a simple cross of native stone. This weird Celt, born at Greenock in 1862, was of Jura parentage. Darroch, derived from the Gaelic for an oak-tree, is among the island's oldest surnames. The Professor's forebears hailed from Brosdale, at the south end of the island. In September, 1924, after he had been missing for a week, his body was found lying in one of Jura's burns. That he had died by his own hand did not surprise anyone who had known him intimately, nor anyone who had noted his other-worldliness as he crossed the Quadrangle of the Old University, a bulky tome or two tucked under his arm. There was a farawayness in his eyes that at times made one doubt whether he really existed in tangible form at all. I remember him at a graduation ceremony in the MacEwan Hall, where he was one of an illustrious company. The Senatus Academicus on this occasion was present in full force; and there was Darroch, an honoured member of it, boisterously blowing his nose on his fingers as the Senate strode in procession to the stirring strains of *The Robbers' March* from *Chu Chin Chow*, a piece of music very popular throughout the country at the time. For a moment, this nasal blast of his sounded like one of the bass pedals depressed in error by Tam Collinson, our university organist, perched away up in his loft.

My interest in our late Professor was revived recently through the publication of a book[1] by an old friend, the Very Reverend Dr. Norman MacLean. This book contains a dedication wrought in Norman's best style, and sufficiently unusual to warrant a wider knowledge of its existence. It concerns another member of the Darroch clan, a native of Jura, who may have been related to our tragic Professor of Education:

To
The Gracious Memory
of
JOHN DARROCH
A Native of Jura and a Graduate of Princeton,
Parish Minister of Portree, 1867-1893,
A Preacher, Narrow in Creed, but Great in Heart.

HIS CHURCH
was converted by strangers into a store.

HIS PORTRAIT
(Painted by Lockhart Bogle)
was thrown by them on its floor and left there for three
years, covered by grime, until attention having been
drawn to the sacrilege, it was salvaged and given a place
in the manse of the former Free Church.

THERE,
ESTABLISHED AND ENDOWED,
with security. in the Home of his former Opponent, He
now proclaims the folly of Sectarian Dissensions and the
heinous sin of rending and re-rending the Body of Christ,
which is The Church.

"He, being dead, yet speaketh."

The author of this dedication tells me that his old minister, though a lovable man, "was content that 99% of humanity should experience the pains of hell forever".

When Mr. MacRury, minister of the Snizort parish of Skye, mentioned to this patriarch, then on his deathbed, that Norman MacLean was to be the next Moderator of the General Assembly of the Church of Scotland, his comment was *"Impossible! I baptized him!"*[2]

.   .   .   .

[1] *Set Free*, published by Hodder and Stoughton in 1949.
[2] The Very Reverend Dr. Norman MacLean died at Portree House, in his native Isle of Skye, on January, 15th, 1952, at the age of 82.

If asked for what Jura is chiefly noted, one might instance its Paps, its deer, its seafaring record, longevity, and perhaps the water-cress growing in the streams that have their origin high up among its Bens. Water-cress is very sustaining, as I myself have often found when afoot in lonely, unpeopled places. To the Columban pilgrims journeying to Iona, it constituted both food and drink. It was, in fact, their manna. The Paps of Jura and the deer we have already mentioned. In the matter of seafaring, the island has been noted for the number of captains with which it has provided the mercantile service throughout the last century.

Apropos longevity, we have referred to the record of Gillouir MacCrain. Martin also instanced Bailiff Campbell, who attained the age of 106; and he tells us that, a couple of years prior to his visiting Jura (*circa* 1694), there died on the neighbouring Isle of Scarba a woman of seven score years, who enjoyed to the end of her days the full use of her senses and understanding.

Away up at Inverlussa, toward the north end of Jura, a stone marks the grave known in the Gaelic as *Uaigh Mhairi Rhiobach*, Hairy Mary's Grave. The inscription on this stone is as follows:

MARY MAC CRAIN
Died in 1856 Aged 128
Descendant of
GILLOUIR MAC CRAIN
who kept a Hundred &
Eighty christmasses in
his own house. And who
died in the reign of
CHARLES I.

Martin writes of Jura as "perhaps the wholesomest plot of ground either in the isles or continent of Scotland, as appears by the long life of the natives and their state of health, to which the height of the hills is believed to contribute in a large measure, by the fresh breezes of wind that come from them to purify the air".

Nevertheless, the inhabitants were not entirely free from the physical troubles assailing so large a proportion of mankind. According to the *Old Statistical Account*, they were prone to those disorders occasioned by their living much upon milk and fish. Many died of stomach troubles; and rheumatic complaints were general among those described as 'the lower orders'.

Whereas the Western Islanders boast the longevity of the Mac-Crains, the Irish like to compete by quoting the case of the Old

Countess of Desmond, who, they say, lived to 140. In fact, there are folks in County Cork who insist that she did not die until she was 162, and only then as the result of an accident. It appears that she fell from a hazel-tree which she had climbed in her old age in order to gather nuts. Sir Walter Raleigh, who knew this old dame personally, tells us of her having been married in the reign of Edward IV, and as having been alive in 1589—yea, and several years later, "as all the noblemen and gentlemen in Munster can witness". Edward IV died in 1483. That being so, and assuming the Countess married at the age of 16, she would have been 122 years of age in 1589. Raleigh says she lived "many years afterwards". If this mean even eight years afterwards, she must have reached 130 anyhow!

This case of longevity was also known to Francis Bacon, who, in his *History of Life and Death*, writes thus of the Countess's teeth: "They tell a tale of the Old Countess of Desmond, who lived until shee was seven score years old, that shee did dentize twice or thrice, casting her old teeth, and others coming in their place. . . . She might have lived much longer, had shee not mett with a kind of violent death, for shee must needs climb a nutt tree, to gather nutts; soe falling down, shee hurt her thigh, which brought on fever, and that brought death."

. . . .

While shore-wandering in Gigha one September afternoon just before the Second World War, the distant Bens of Jura put a spell so binding on me that I resolved to sail over to Craighouse the following day. At the north end of Gigha, where the steamer calls thrice weekly on the days she sails from West Loch Tarbert to Jura, instead of to Islay, I took the usual ferry. An hour or so later, I was stepping ashore at Craighouse in sunshine, making for what was then the island's inn, a large, whitewashed building situated close at hand. The sea about the pier lay as calm as the proverbial mill-pond. Any slight ripple upon the outer tide had been retained by the Small Isles, stretching in a reefy line some distance offshore, and providing, in time of storm, sheltered anchorage between them and Craighouse. The inn, a cosy and comfortable establishment, was run by the MacKechnies, an old Jura family. The briefest sojourn there served to convince the traveller that occasionally he may find among the Hebrides an inn as commendable and as reasonable as most of our inns are indifferent. The inn at Craighouse, in my view, gained appreciably from its having been a temperance concern. Here one was afforded concrete proof that comfort and homeliness are sometimes to be had *without* alcohol. There is no licence on Jura, though, oddly enough, the large buildings close by, most of them now gutted and stark, were once the famous Jura Distillery.

About the inn, moreover, there was an easy informality, without there being anything of the very casual air which now pervades most public places where the customer is treated so cursorily. Of a Sabbath morning, when many folks enjoy what is termed a long lie, you might have heard Miss MacKechnie climbing to the attics with a breakfast tray, and saying in a loud tone at the stair-head: "Listen, John! I've got your *brochan*[1] here! Now, don't be long till you're down! "

Then, about church-time, you might have listened to the little servant-lassie in the kitchen, lilting at her work the melody of *Once in Royal David's City*. Later, a bell would be heard across the shadowy bay, pealing for no more than a quarter of a minute, since Jura's beadle wasted neither time nor energy in ringing the church bell. Fifteen seconds were his usual: twenty seconds his maximum! One might have imagined that he performed this duty with a stop-watch in his hand. But the islesfolk turned out to church just the same.

Stepping from the inn porch on a tranquil September morning into the garden of fuchsias in drooping flower, of rambler roses, and of bee-hum among the last lingering blooms of summer, dew-wet and glistening in sunlight, to hear the burn wimpling by the ruined distillery on its way to join the tide by the old pier, and to find the white cottages of Craighouse reflected in the curved water of the bay, beyond the stooks of mellowing corn, backed by a vast moorland of heather and burnished deer-grass— well, it was like stepping out into dreamland.

One regrets in a way that the MacKechnies have now ceased to take visitors. They've made their handsome pile, one way or another, of course; and it is many a year since anything except the commercial instinct obliged them to continue with innkeeping, and with all the other gainful occupations with which they have been obsessed throughout their long and uneventful lives. Now the island, to all intents and purposes, is without an official threshold at which the wanderer among the Inner Hebrides can present himself with the reasonable assurance of finding accommodation. This need not deter him from disembarking at Craighouse, however. Within a hundred yards of the MacKechnies', and with the exercise of a little charm, he may obtain such simple bed and board as he requires.

One evening a young man employed about the inn motored me

[1] porridge.

northward by Lagg to Tarbert Bay, and to Inverlussa beyond, that I might see, in the old burial-place there, Mary MacCrain's tombstone; and I was grieved to find that, owing to weathering, a fragment of its face had fallen away, thus rendering a little incomplete its unique inscription. But I learnt from my driver that efforts were being made in Highland and Island circles to raise a fund for the repair and preservation of this interesting memorial.

As we travelled past Ardlussa, my informant became increasingly communicative. He bemoaned the fact that deer were occupying territory capable, he said, of carrying many thousand sheep.

"You'll know Nancy, no doubt," he observed, as we alighted at Tarbert to admire the view.

"Nancy! " I repeated. "You mean Nancy Astor? "

"Yes," he replied; "but she never gets anything but Nancy here. She owns about half of Jura, you know. The whole island calls her Nancy. She's a bit queer—got lots o' queer notions, you know. Och, but she's no' a baad sort too! Och, no. No' a baad sort. Yon wee building you're seeing, over a bittie from the big house, she put up for reading and sunning herself. A sun parlour, they call it. Just a sort o' notion she took, you know. She's always taking queer notions like that. But, man! she hasn't done much reading in it, so far as *I* can hear. And I doubt if she's got much sun in it either! Och, she's always flying here and there —here, there, and everywhere. Can't settle down anywhere. Always on the move. Always getting her name in the papers for something or other."

"I assume from what you say, then, that Nancy's not on the island at present? "

"No! But her sons are here, shooting all the time. Stalking deer on that hill you're seeing there, where there ought to be sheep! "

"And are the sons good shots? " I asked, "or do they merely wound their victims? "

"Good shots! " he repeated bitterly. "They're that good that they've nearly filled the natives with lead pellets more than once! "

. . . .

During my stay in Jura on this occasion, a jumble sale was held in the village hall at Craighouse. This synchronised with the departure of the Campbells of Jura, who recently had sold the last of their possessions, once so extensive, on this island. I attended the sale. A greater assortment of jumble and junk,

crammed into so limited a space, I never beheld in my life—
rotting poultry-coops, rusty oil-lamps, rustier skates, odd bits of
crockery (much of it chipped and handle-less), old books, discarded family albums and portraits, seared photographs, moth-
eaten blankets and mattresses. For the modest sum of a shilling, I
purchased twelve red-label recordings by Joseph Hislop, all of
which were in their cardboard containers, and looked as new as
on the day they left the premises of His Master's Voice. Then, to
my horror, I learnt that, a few minutes before my arrival, a copy
of the first volume of *The Songs of the North*, in perfect condition, had gone for threepence—the figure at which it had been
priced! Gone to somebody probably not the least capable of
estimating its value, nor of appreciating its musical excellence. A
secondhand copy of this volume, in good condition, cannot be
picked up in Charing Cross Road for less than ten shillings.

The sale realised about £18. This was sent to the Glasgow
Royal Infirmary, an institution upon which, for so many years
now, the communities of the Highlands and Islands, in cases of
serious accident and illness, have been so dependent.

When everything saleable had found a purchaser, there still
remained a residue of rubbish for which no one felt inclined to
offer anything. The rusty skates and wick-less lamps were un-
wanted. So was the officer's topee, complete with tin box, and
the rotting hen-coops, although the topee was priced at sixpence,
and the coops could have been had at a penny each! After a lull
of half an hour, while many of the natives were still assembled on
the grass outside the hall, surrounded by their purchases, one of
the conveners of the sale suddenly appeared at the hall door to
announce that anyone might re-enter and have, simply for the
taking, what remained unsold. A frightful scrimmage ensued.
The veriest trash now found half the population of Jura
scrambling to possess it. "It'll do for firewood, if for nothing
else!" was the remark of a woman struggling with a hen-coop
literally falling to bits from her hand as she made her exit.

A thin smoor was falling, as I returned to the inn with my
gramophone records, and made for my favourite corner by the
sitting-room fire. On the mantelshelf was a copy of Kenneth Mac-
Leod's poetic volume, *The Road to the Isles*. It lay open at his
verses on the Bens of Jura—"Like water-cress gathered fresh from
cool streams".

I picked the book up and, turning over its preliminary pages,
found Kenneth's inimitable handwriting. In response to the
owner's request that he might autograph her copy, he had inscribed upon the title-page his Riddle of the Isles:

Two youths went forth from the Isles to search for the Place of Unsurpassing Beauty, of which they had heard so many fine tales. They searched for it North and South, East and West, but found it not. When they returned home, Old Fate laughed uproariously at them both, whereupon they looked at each other and laughed too.

Can'st thou tell me why?

.   .   .   .

Early one overcast morning last November, when all colour seemed to have been washed from land and sea and sky, I set out for Jura with my good friend, Iain MacTaggart, who, in a professional capacity, travels thither from Bowmore, in Islay, once a fortnight. It was calm enough when we crossed the Sound of Islay from Portaskaig, and stepped ashore on that inviting beach at Feorlin, where stands a solitary cottage occupied from time to time by a writer who spells his Christian name with a ' t ' where I spell mine with a ' d '. By the jetty at Feorlin we were met by a lorry, the car usually conveying Iain to Ardfin, and later in the day to Craighouse, having been under repair. Across the sombre moors the lorry took us to Ardfin; and there, at Jura House, while Iain attended to his banking and factoring duties, I was afforded ample opportunity of seeing the garden cultivated commendably by Donald Shaw and his staff of under-gardeners. November is seldom a month when one would expect to see a northern garden in anything but an uninteresting state. Yet, it still displayed, especially of winter vegetables, sufficient to show how productive is this fine, walled garden, sloping toward the south to within calling distance of the sound. Through its centre, in a series of terraced cascades, falls a brook that, even in the bleakness of November, lent colour, as well as life, to a scene already dank and sear. In the maidenhair ferns clinging to crevices in the brook's walled channel, there lingered something of the splendour of the autumn so recently past. Donald told me how glad he was to have the opportunity of showing to anyone interested just what his garden was capable of producing in the way of flower, fruit, and vegetable, in an island notoriously barren. Of fruit—well, on my being taken into one of the potting-sheds, I instantly smelt the freshness of apples hidden from view. The lids lying loosely on boxes everywhere around me were soon lifted, that I might see for myself what can be grown even in Jura. Donald insisted that I should bear away with me two apples of each of the varieties he cultivates so creditably.

One could not but notice the profusion and luxuriance in

which there grew in this garden, and in its immediate environs, such shrubs as fuchsia, veronica, rhododendron, escallonia, jasmin, hydrangea, and another shrub, the name of which I forget, but which bears a flower resembling a Chinese lantern in veriest miniature.

Later in the day, and in time for lunch at the MacKechnies, we were conveyed from Ardfin to Craighouse by car. The time this three-mile journey took was occupied agreeably enough by Iain MacTaggart's reciting for my edification the traditional version of what happened at Gruinart the day the MacDonalds of Islay and the MacLeans of Duart joined bloody issue there, in 1596. I have read and listened to many accounts of this famous episode in clan warfare; but none of them has been as graphic—as arresting —as Iain's. It prompted me to bicycle off to this battle site a day or two later.

Rain and high wind and lowering cloud were our portion by the time we reached Craighouse. All of the Bens of Jura were obscured except their base; and even *that* at times was lost to view as the day wore on. The scene on every side became obliterated, though now and again one got a hazy glimpse of Gigha and of the Kintyre coast, sixteen or eighteen miles to the east. Nothing could be seen of Knapdale, which lay a few miles nearer. Mist and rain enveloped it completely. At no great distance, the waves were breaking white and noisily as I sat by the Mac-Kechnies' sitting-room window, watching for MacBrayne's boat, the *Lochnevis*, not in any spirit of anxiety, but interestedly, wondering how she was faring in such turbulent seas, against a strong head-wind. Only a few minutes behind scheduled time, she appeared from behind the Small Isles of Jura, and was soon alongside.

And what an exhilarating trip we had aboard her, that wild November afternoon! A spanking wind astern soon brought us within sight of the Kildalton hills, rising dimly behind the light-house on MacArthur's Head; and we were already altering our course, north-westwards, for the Sound of Islay. A wintry dusk had now fallen. A light or two, gleaming by the pier at Portaskaig, indicated how near we were to the anchorage at which the *Lochnevis* would remain overnight, before continuing to the Argyllshire mainland the following morning. That sail, of no more than an hour's duration, is indeed memorable. I felt some reluctance at quitting a little ship, so seaworthy, so admirably suited to these tempestuous seas.

As we slackened speed in approaching the narrows across which we had been ferried that morning, it became more than obvious that our decision to return to Islay by steamer had been a wise one. The ferryboat could never have crossed with us from Feorlin that evening. Consequently, we would have been obliged to tarry in Jura overnight, at least, had we sought Portaskaig by any other means than the *Lochnevis*. We stepped ashore, feeling as though we too, perhaps, had had a hand in navigating the vessel to this familiar destination. In a few minutes we were climbing, in Iain's car, the steep hill overlooking the pier and the chilly Sound of Islay. The moon was shining on Loch Indaal not too confidently by the time we reached Bridgend, and sped home to Bowmore, three miles farther on, along the wet shore-road.

Jura is one of the isles where depopulation has been most marked. A population of 1,097 in 1755 had fallen to 929 by 1792, when the island boasted as many as twenty-seven farms, fifteen of which were in tillage, and the remaining twelve in pasturage. By 1831, however, the population had risen to nearly 2,000. In 1911 it was 570. According to the 1951 Census, it has declined to 263. This represents a drop during the last forty years of 307—more than one half.

In all the nonsense written and uttered about Highland and Island depopulation, there is never any mention of what I believe to be one of the main contributory causes, namely, that there is no financial inducement to an outsider to come, nor to an insider to remain. Any little public office, such as might bring to a man, annually, just that pound or two of additional income he needs, goes immediately to one man in the island, or to some member of his family or household. This means that all economic gain finds its way into the same pocket. Here is a list of such offices as may be held by the same person in many an isle, to the rigorous exclusion of everyone else:

Farmer
Grocer
Draper
Motor hirer
Public Works contractor
Coal merchant
Registrar
Postmaster
Telephone Exchange operator
(usually handed on to wife, sister, or daughter)
Agent
Petrol retailer

Innkeeper
Licence holder
All other official or semi-official
appointments bringing further
perquisites from public funds.

Here the whole profit derivable through the community is concentrated in the same hands. And on top of all this, the recipient
is usually a county councillor, which means further business,
further perquisites, further pickings. It certainly means that he
travels at the public expense to the centre where, at statutory
intervals, the council convenes. There he is afforded a free opportunity of attending to his own private affairs. One has known
of several instances of this throughout the Highlands and Islands.

The other day, a workman approached me rather shyly in one
of the Inner Hebrides to tell me that he had arrived there with
his young family, in the hope of finding a living. "They talk
about depopulation," he said, with feeling. "Yet, not a penny
can an honest, industrious chap get. It all goes into old Duncan's
pocket. There are six of us; and we would stay if one of these
little jobs came my way. But no! They like to keep it all to
themselves! I've waited two years to see if I could get even one
of the small 'perks'. There's nothing doing. So we're leaving.
They needn't talk to *me* about depopulation, so long as this local
grasp and greed go on. Why should all the little official jobs be
always given to people already so rich that they don't know what
to do with their money? Of course, mind you, I daren't say a
word here. If it gets to the local boss's ears that I was talking to
you like this, I might not even get my groceries next week. You
see, I daren't quarrel wi' old Duncan!"

I told my enquirer that I had the deepest sympathy with him
in all he said, and that I had long been aware of this state of
affairs. This avarice certainly discourages anyone from remaining in areas where the introduction of fresh stock is so urgently
needed.

Postscript: Jura has not been altogether wanting in literary
associations; and in this connection one recalls the late George
Orwell, a genius dying of consumption, who went there with his
adopted son, Richard, in 1946. From that year until his death
in London toward the close of 1949, he rented from R. G. Fletcher, of Ardlussa, the house of Barnhill, situated remotely at the
north end of Jura. There, in isolation almost primitive and
savage, far removed from society, and certainly from any intellec-
tual and intimate circle, such as many a creative artist finds

essential, he spent his latter days—between violent hæmorrhages
—in writing.

It was at Barnhill, when so very ill, that he wrote his terrifying
vision, "1984", soon after the completion of which he became
permanently bedridden. Writing of him and of his heroism in
the *Sunday Times* shortly after his death, Arthur Koestler epitomised this brilliant rebel's progress by observing that, had he
adopted the advice of doctors and friends, and allowed them to
transfer him to a Swiss sanatorium, his great masterpiece could
never have been written. The greatness and tragedy of Orwell,
says Koestler, lay in his total rejection of any compromise. His
was a life which ought to find a competent and sympathetic
biographer.

Chapter XV

COLONSAY AND ORONSAY

COLONSAY lies eight miles west of the Sound of Islay, and twenty south of Mull. From the West Highland town and sea-port of Oban, it is thirty-seven. The sea-passage from Port Askaig, in Islay, to Scalasaig, Colonsay's port of call and parochial centre, can be very pleasant. It can also be very boisterous when a fresh south-westerly beats up the tide-races for which the surrounding seas are renowned. Except for the Blue Pool—the deep sea-basin where the channel between Colonsay and Oronsay contracts to but a few hundred yards—the ebb leaves uncovered between these two islands a vast expanse of sand known as *Am Faodhail*, the Strand. Together, these islands have an area of about twenty-four square miles, of which Oronsay occupies but an eighth. Together, too, they have a total length of eleven miles, and a breadth ranging from one to three. Until 1861, they formed part of the parish of Jura. That year they became a parish of their own. A celebrity among those who have been parish incumbents of Colonsay and Oronsay in recent years is the Rev. Dr. Kenneth MacLeod. Kenneth ministered here from 1917 until 1925, when he went to Gigha. The joint parish is divided into the following thirteen districts: Balnahard, Uragaig, Balavetchy, Kiloran, Kilchattan, Bonaveh, Scalasaig, Machrins, Balaruminmore, Bala-rumindubh, Ardskenish, Garvard, and Oronsay.

The census returns of 1951 gave the parish's population as 233, a decrease of only five since the previous census, twenty years earlier. Few island parishes have shown so negligible a decline in recent times. A century ago, however, the population was well over a thousand.

Most of Colonsay's inhabitants have been re-housed since the First World War, with the result that the thatched homes of for-mer years have gone completely from the island. In the Scalasaig and Kilchattan districts, where the majority of the population resides, many cottages have been rebuilt by the proprietor. In 1918 the old fishing-village of Riasg Buidhe, situated in the Bonaveh district, was evacuated. The villagers were moved to new homes at Glassard, roughly midway between their old ones

and Scalasaig. They are now more conveniently placed in relation to the harbour. The old, roofless, abandoned walls of Riasg
Buidhe are indeed eerie. One might think they stand as the reminder of some tragic visitation.

Colonsay is low-lying rather than hilly, especially when compared with Jura, its mountainous neighbour. None of its summits
exceeds 500 feet. Indeed, Carn nan Eoin, its highest eminence,
overshadowing the very beautiful bay of Kiloran, at the north
of the island, is but 470. Several hills attain an altitude of
thirty or forty feet less. Some of these, standing prominently, as
does Beinn Eibhne overlooking, at no more than 321 feet, the
Strand separating, at low water, Oronsay from Colonsay, provide,
under clear conditions, a view of several landmarks at considerable
distances. Heaval, the highest point of Barra, is sometimes
visible, seventy miles away. Dun I, Iona's modest summit, is seen
to the north-west. The famous rock-light of Dubh Heartach,
lying sixteen miles to the west, can usually be seen; and the lan-
tern-tower of the more famous and dramatic Skerryvore, rising
loftily from the surging seas to the south of Tiree, is discernible
when visibility is particularly good. I am told that, from Colonsay's higher parts, the hills of Donegal are sometimes visible on
the distant horizon, and that Goat Fell, Ben Nevis, and Ben
Cruachan are frequently seen.

.   .   .   .

Colonsay's interior, though bare and undulating, is not without its fertile patches. Upon these cattle and sheep are reared.
Meteorological records, which have been kept on the island since
1933, show the rainfall to be abundant and evenly distributed.
The pasture-lands, found mostly below the 250-foot contour, are
thus inclined to be mossy and spongy. The presence of water
above that level is indicated by the prevalence of rushes and
sedges.

Few islands of their size boast a greater number of wells and
springs than do Colonsay and Oronsay. John de Vere Loder (now
Lord Wakehurst) lists over forty of them in his monumental
work,[1] supplying with each its Gaelic name, together with a literal
translation in English. Wakehurst told me the other day that
the labour he expended on this great book of his afforded him
enormous pleasure. In it, he certainly bequeathed to those of us
having a major interest in islands the permanent fruits of his dili-
gence and scholarship.

Despite Colonsay's many wells, its chief drawback is the lack of

[1] *Colonsay and Oronsay*, published by Oliver and Boyd in 1935.

a good water supply. This may have deterred some from settling there to cultivate or to fish.

The absence of frost to any injurious degree explains how exotic plants survive and often flourish on Colonsay and Oronsay. The driest months are April, May, and June; and it may astonish those who know how very wet are Jura and Mull, to learn that these islands' crops sometimes suffer from actual drought during those months. In the summer of 1951, the ground was so parched that the beasts, many of them emaciated, were scarcely able to get enough to eat; and so dry were the roads that a passing vehicle raised a cloud of dust, leaving an ever thickening film on roadside vegetation, reminiscent of the country roads in the Highlands of one's childhood.

The sun is often shining brightly on Colonsay when heavy precipitation is taking place on Jura. Similarly, rain-clouds passing eastward over Iona may be seen in rapid descent upon Ben More and the other peaks of Mull.

On the whole, temperatures on Colonsay and Oronsay are fairly equable throughout the year. How far this is attributable to the Gulf Stream may be questioned. The Gulf Stream, one would suppose, has lost its warming influence before it reaches these shores. Yet, it cannot be denied that the seeds of tropical trees and plants are borne to them, as to the shores of the other isles of the Inner Hebrides, by the currents which the south-westerly winds create. These winds often reach gale-force, which they are apt to maintain for several consecutive days. One of the results of this is conspicuous in the eastward slant of the trees, and the sparsity of boughs and branches to windward. The south-westerlies, blowing persistently where shrubs hold on with tenacity in exposed positions, distort their growth unbelievably.

The winds and seas bring driftwood in plenty to these shores. This is appreciated particularly by the MacNeill family tenanting the farm on Oronsay. Unlike Colonsay, Oronsay has no peat. The MacNeills collect by its shores sufficient driftwood to keep the farm kitchen fire burning brightly all the year round. This fuel they supplement from time to time by a consignment of coal brought by puffer.

Colonsay is well favoured with driftwood, though much of it is cast up on parts of the Atlantic coast often inaccessible, and largely unknown except to the more daring of its lobster-fishers who sink their pots in every likely creek. The natives are expert in the matter of driftwood. They know its kind and the place of origin. I happened to speak to a man chopping kindling wood outside his cottage near the manse, between Scalasaig and Glas-

Two of the natives of Iona removing, as a labour of love, lichen and riotous valerian from the Nunnery walls

sard. He soon volunteered the information that he was chopping Oregon pine!

In the days of sail, ships were often wrecked off the coast of Colonsay and Oronsay. The records of what befell several of these survive. The Marquis of Argyll was granted a warrant to dispose in his own way of the cargo of a French barque wrecked there. In 1848 the barque, *Clydesdale*, on a voyage from South Carolina to the Clyde with a cargo of cotton, was wrecked on *Eilean nam Ban*, the Women's Isle, one of a cluster of islets not far from the shore at Lower Kilchattan. Six of her crew of twenty-six perished.

It is said that a shipwreck is commemorated in the name of each of the two sunken reefs lying off the west of Oronsay, only one of which—Cubaig—appears on the Ordnance Survey map. To the local fishermen it is known as the *Bogha Chubaig*, meaning the Quebec Reef. The other is the *Bogha Dale*, the Dale Reef, lying less than two miles to the north of it. Then, on reefy *Eilean nan Ròn*, the Seals' Isle, at the south-western extremity of Oronsay, the fishermen point out to one a number of stones said to mark the graves of sailors whose bodies were washed ashore there. It is thought that they may have been among those who lost their lives in 1885, when a schooner was wrecked on the Seals' Isle. Mrs. Murray, who published in 1887 her *Summer in the Hebrides* (a miscellany of information and impressions gathered from several holidays spent at Oronsay House), must have seen this wreck, since she writes of it as "sitting with all her sails up as yet. She is for no use to the place except firewood."

At Easdail, by the side of a tiny stream flowing into Kiloran Bay, the body of a drowned English sailor is said to have been buried. It was cast upon the shore nearby. Soon afterwards, the sailor's ghost began to intercept those passing homeward between Kilchattan and Balnahard; and a crofter, with whom the ghost insisted on shaking hands, lost the power of his right hand and arm in consequence. On another occasion the ghost waylaid an islander carrying a loaded gun, demanding that he should deliver the gun up to him. Recalling the case of his neighbour whose hand and arm had been rendered useless, he threatened to shoot if the phantom intruder did not instantly desist. The latter, now adopting a more reasonable attitude, explained that the stream had so undermined the bank, where the sailor had been buried, that many of his bones now lay exposed. The ghost promised never again to molest any of the living in Colonsay, once the sailor's bones had been gathered together and re-interred in a grave out of the reach of wearing water. So the bones were collected and carried some little distance inland from Kiloran Bay,

West side of St. Martin's Cross (tenth century), with the Sound of Iona in the middle-distance, and Fionaphort, in the Ross of Mull, beyond

and buried in the valley between Carn nan Eoin and Cnoc Ingibrig, at a spot marked by some stones. The ghost has troubled no one since.

The Norsemen must have known Kiloran well. Among the many relics of theirs found in this locality is a Viking burial-place which yielded several ninth-century coins, a pair of scales, a cauldron, sword, axe, and shield-boss.

Now to times more recent. Buried in the graveyards of most of the Inner Hebrides are sailors, merchant seamen, and soldiers, whose bodies were washed ashore from torpedoed vessels. The names of many of these victims remain unknown. Several crosses to unidentified men of the Royal Navy, and also to Danish and Norwegian seamen, whose corpses came ashore during 1940, 1941, and 1942, stand in the graveyard at Kilchattan, and at Oronsay Priory, where they were interred.

. . . .

Most of Colonsay's arable land is concentrated in two valleys fairly well sheltered by hills. The larger of these lies to the north. It comprises the crofting areas of Kilchattan and Kiloran, and also Colonsay House, and the pastures and woodlands among which it is set. It also includes Loch Fada, by far the largest freshwater lake in the island. The wooded policies of Colonsay House show what can be done in a region notoriously bare, where winds inimical to the growth of trees are so prevalent. Many of these trees were planted by a foreseeing proprietor about 1830. Woods old and stately have sheltered Colonsay House for many years. They were in a flourishing condition in 1776, when Thomas Pennant saw them.

On all the islands of the Hebrides where tree plantations have managed to attain any appreciable height, the Atlantic winds have stunted them, and often distorted their growth. But on Colonsay the trees seem to have withstood the winds' influences. There, in the vicinity of Colonsay House, they grow as erect and as little blasted as those in sheltered regions on the mainland. They are much haunted by the wood-pigeons which nest in them; and among them, in the sheltered shadows, the foxgloves attain giant stature.

The smaller valley is that running south-westwards across the island from the harbour at Scalasaig to Machrins and the machar beyond. It reaches the western shore in the vicinity of a series of well-marked raised beaches, a prominent characteristic of this side of the island.

In addition to the woodlands about Colonsay House, the island has two other wooded areas worthy of note, both of them situated where hilly ground falls to the eastern shore. The larger of these, known as the Big Wood, lies east of Colonsay House, in the region of the Raven's Ben—*Beinn nam Fitheach*. The smaller, half a mile to the north, is the Little Wood, near which is a hill of negligible size called *Dùnan nan Nighean*, Little Fort of the Daughters. On its summit are the ruins of a dwelling, the doorway and lintel of which still stand. Tradition has it that all the children of one of the MacPhee chiefs of Colonsay were born here, their mother leaving the family seat at Kiloran for each of her confinements. Here she is said to have given birth to seven daughters. Hence the name of the *Dùnan*.

. . . .

Everywhere on Colonsay one sees evidence of great geological changes. The many raised beaches indicate periods of land emergence and elevation: the many erratic boulders are but one of the proofs of extensive glaciation. One such boulder, weighing eight or ten tons, may be seen at Port Lobh, on the west side. It reposes at the foot of a series of natural steps descending through a crevice in the rock known as Fingal's Stair. The natives, tenacious here, as elsewhere in Celtic Britain, in their belief in a prehistoric race of giants possessing prodigious strength, speak of this boulder as having been Fingal's Putting Stone. It is not unlikely that the ice, moving westward across Colonsay, brought it from Jura. Here it has remained since the ice melted away. Evidence of inter-glacial periods, during which vegetation flourished on the island, are to be found in its peat deposits, and in the number of tree trunks preserved in the peat. Trees embedded in peat by the fringe of Loch Fada have been identified as a species of willow.

The rocky coast, where raised beaches are so common, is one out of which the sea has eaten many caves. The largest is the Pigeons' Cave, in the Uragaig district, by the southern shore of Kiloran Bay. It is 70 feet high, and at least 200 feet deep.

Better known is the Piper's Cave, less than two miles distant. Associated with it is that legend so often met with in connection with this cave or with that, in the West Highlands and Islands— the legend that a piper entered it, accompanied by his dog. The piper—a MacPhee—never returned, but his dog did, in a haggard, and even *singed*, condition. Those who witnessed the piper enter heard the strains of *MacCrimmon's Lament* gradually fade away as the player proceeded farther and farther into the dark and sinister recesses from which he never emerged.

Traditions concerning the MacPhees are numerous to this day in Colonsay, as might be expected in an island where so many of the inhabitants still bear this surname. Their patronymic is perpetrated in the island's toponomy—in MacPhee's Cave, for example. Here, in olden days, a MacPhee chief is said to have hidden from MacIain of Ardnamurchan. (Or was it from Mac-Laine of Lochbuie?) As the cave has two entrances, he placed his famous black dog on guard at the smaller, while he himself stood with drawn claymore at the larger. But his enemy outwitted him, they say, after a prolonged siege. Enlarging from above a hole in the cave's roof, he took him unawares, and slew him.

About 1934, Seton Gordon explored this cave in company with a native called MacPhee, who lived quite close to it, and worked the croft above it. He tells us that MacPhee, besides being courtly in manner, was swarthy of face. This called to mind Martin's description of the islanders nearly two-and-a-half centuries earlier: "The inhabitants are well-proportioned, and of a black complexion."

Both on Colonsay and Oronsay, archæological remains are common. Considerable quantities of stone implements made and used by Azilian men have been found. In 1881 Symington Grieve unearthed a great collection of these while excavating the mound on Oronsay known as the *Caisteal nan Gillean,* the Lads' (or, perhaps the Menservants') Castle. Several ancient sites were profitably explored about that time.

Numerous stone cists of the Bronze Age, some of which contained burial urns, have also been found. About 1885 three cists at Uragaig were opened by competent archæologists. Each contained a human skeleton. One of these is now in the museum of the Royal College of Surgeons, at Edinburgh.

Colonsay also has a good number of standing-stones. They occur all over the island. Many of them are indicated on the O.S. map. Perhaps the most remarkable are the two at Kilchattan, referred to among the Gaelic-speaking natives by a name signifying Fingal's Limpet Hammers. The larger stands 10 feet 8 inches high: the smaller is but 2 feet less.

Here and there, remains of stone-circles are also to be seen. A well-defined setting, roughly 10 feet in diameter, occurs at Scalasaig. The excavation of the site in 1881 brought to light a sword and a dagger. In the Garvard locality is a circle with a diameter of about 52 feet. Little of the stones composing it, however, is visible. Few of them stand as much as 18 inches above ground; most of them show no more than 6 inches.

If the traditions of Colonsay's giants be preserved in the names given to various stones and geological formations such as pits and gullies, its traditions of a pigmy race are likewise preserved in some of its place-names. On the hillside overlooking Scalasaig is a green mound marking the site of Dun Eibhinn (Eyvind's Fort) where the chiefs of the MacDuffies—of the MacPhees—are said to have resided in olden times. Here, too, according to a tradition cited by Martin, there once dwelt a very little generation of people known as Lusbirdan, "the same with pigmies". A similar tradition survives in connection with the Pigmies' Isle, situated near the Butt of Lewis.

As for the faeries, they abound everywhere, both on Colonsay and on Oronsay. The faeries of this island parish would provide more than adequate material for a long chapter devoted solely to them. Then, the Glaistig (the Grey, Sly One) and the Gruagach (the Long-haired One) are reputed to be among these islands' oldest residents. There are natives who, to this day, would not care to say that the Glaistig had entirely abandoned her interest in the occupants of their byres.

By far the most extensive, interesting, and valuable archæological monument in the parish is the Priory of St. Columba, at Oronsay, which flourished up to the time of the dissolution of the monasteries. This ancient foundation is believed to have been under the jurisdiction of Kiloran Abbey, the ruins of which are thought to have supplied the stones with which, in 1772, the present Colonsay House was built. This may explain the statement in the Old Statistical Account (1794) to the effect that "the remains of the Abbey were, with Gothic barbarity, torn asunder not many years ago, and the stones put into a new building".

Tradition has it that St. Columba landed on Oronsay when, in fulfilment of his vow that he would sail away to settle in some remote place whence Erin could not be seen, he reached the western coast of Scotland. From a hill on Oronsay he was able to see the Isle he had forsaken, as one can, on a particularly clear day. So he did not tarry long. but sailed on until he found in Iona what he had been seeking. One must assume from stories such as this that the sailors of olden times were possessed of a remarkable sense of geography and of direction. I sometimes ask myself whether they could have known quite so definitely whether, afar, they were seeing this island or that, this mainland or that, when I realize that, with my own geographical training and my fairly accurate reading of maps, I am often uncertain as to exactly what territory I see afar off. Even proper orientation and the aid of powerful field-glasses have left me in doubt. But maybe the saints of old knew in other ways. Anyhow, Columba is said to have remained on Oronsay long enough to have blessed it, and to have defined that part of it which long continued to be a sanctuary. The girth or garth—the boundary—of this sanctuary may still be traced by the knowledgeable and discerning.

Halfway between Colonsay and Oronsay, and visible at low water, is the foundation of what is believed to have been the sanctuary cross. The fugitive gaining the Oronsay side of this cross was safe, at any rate for a time, from the wrath of his pursuers. Residence on Oronsay itself for a year and a day vouchsafed to him immunity for all time.

In Colonsay, Columba is remembered by the wishing-well situated at Balnahard, bearing his name. It is one of the best known of the island's many wells. By its side is a little silver drinking-cup bearing the inscription, "A. M'N. F., 1894". It would be interesting to learn, perhaps through some reader, of the well's frequenter thus commemorated.

If Columba left his name on this well, the honour of having given to Oronsay its name fell to his companion, Oran, who landed there with him. Together they ascended the hill from which, according to Pennant's account, Ireland was to be seen.

While it is more than probable that a religious settlement was established on Oronsay in Columban days, it seems fairly certain that the Priory, the ruins of which now constitute so splendid a monument, was founded by John, Lord of the Isles, with the help of Augustinian monks from Holyrood. By his second marriage, *Good* John, as he was called, because of his beneficence to the church, became the son-in-law of Robert, the Steward of Scotland, who, in 1371, ascended the throne as Robert II. He was the first of the Stewart monarchs. John died in 1380. So the oldest parts of the Priory are certainly older than that. John of Fordun, writing about the time of Good John's death, mentions " Colounsy with an abbey of canons-regular ".

The ruins of Oronsay Priory, as they exist to-day, are extensive; and it would indeed be presumptive on my part, were I to attempt a description of them here when such may be read more profitably in Macgibbon & Ross.[1] No doubt, the farmhouse and appurtenant buildings impinging upon the Priory were constructed largely of material from it.

In the Priory's precincts are several ancient tombstones upon which are carved delicate Celtic patterns. One of these depicts

[1] *Ecclesiastical Architecture of Scotland.*

a galley under sail, with an emblematic bird—probably a raven—perched on the mast. The raven in olden times was believed, both by the Northmen and by the Celts, to be the most infallible indicator of the direction in which land, unseen from their galleys, lay. So they sometimes carried with them a raven or two, when making long voyages. When they released a raven, they noted carefully the direction in which it flew away. In that direction they then steered, knowing that, eventually, they would sight land where they could disembark.

In 1927 the Prior's House on Oronsay was restored and re-roofed for the purpose of accommodating the many carved tomb-stones which had been found lying scattered about the church's floor, and which, in 1891, had been placed upright against its walls, the better to preserve them. There are as many as thirty of these stones. Most of them measure about seven feet in length. The figures and designs carved upon them would seem to be fifteenth- and sixteenth-century workmanship.

At the south-west corner of the Priory stands Prior Colin's Cross, one of the most beautifully carved stones in Scotland. It consists of a single slab 5 inches thick, rising to a height of 12 feet from a pedestal of three steps. At the base it is 18 inches wide. Prior Colin died early in the sixteenth century. His Cross is supposed to have been erected in 1510.

Another carved stone worthy of mention is that standing on a mound a few yards from the north-east corner of the main church. It consists of the head of a cross carved with the figure of an ecclesiastic, and attached to part of the shaft of another cross different in material and in design. Stuart, in the second volume of *The Sculptured Stones of Scotland* (1867), deals with the two parts separately; and it is thought that they were united in this form when, early in the present century, through the munificence of the first Lord Strathcona, several repairs were carried out at the Priory.

An account of the many ruins and sites of ecclesiological interest on Colonsay itself would occupy more space than our immediate requirements would justify. Yet, there is the urge to mention, if only briefly, just one, and probably the most interesting—that at *Cill Chatriona*, Catriona's Church. This ancient Christian foundation is situated near Balnahard farm, almost at the extreme north of the island. Tradition has it that it was once a nunnery, the outline of several of the buildings composing which can be followed. The church itself, set within a rect-angular enclosure, measures 33 feet by 19. Its walls are much fallen. To-day they are represented by little more than uneven, turf-covered ridges. A number of stone slabs at the east end shows the position of the altar. A cupped stone near the doorway may have been the font. In the graveyard is a small cross no more than 3 feet high, rubbed smooth by wandering cattle. Another cross is preserved in the National Museum of Antiquities of Scotland.

A little distance to the north is a broad, sloping stone 4 feet in height, known as the Penance Stone, and believed to have been used by the nuns for flagellation purposes, after which they are said to have betaken themselves to a building called the Retreat of the Miserable Women, the remains of which may still be traced.

Many a curious relic from this site is preserved at Colonsay House. For details of these, could I possibly refer you to anything more authoritative than *Colonsay and Oronsay*, that great work to which I have already referred?

. . . .

In addition to all this, Colonsay possesses many natural objects well worth investigating. For instance, upon the green machar at Machrins, near the western shore, there lies a huge, rounded stone which may well be an erratic. It is termed the Lifting Stone, because the ability to raise it even slightly off the ground was, and indeed still is, regarded as an indication of great strength. Among the older inhabitants are men who declare that in their prime they lifted it, though never with ease. One man used to claim that he once lifted it into a cart, the back of which had been let down to facilitate his doing so. The islanders have the tradition that it found its way to the machar from the shore when a native, demonstrating his prodigious strength, carried it there in his plaid. The feat must also have demonstrated the enormous strength of the island's homespuns at the time! An old friend of my family (the late Professor William Watson, who occupied the Chair of Celtic at Edinburgh for so many years, and who, during his undergraduate days at Oxford, was an athlete of no mean order, especially when it came to throwing the hammer and tossing the caber) used to tell us of the occasion on which *he*, in an attempt to raise the Lifting Stone, " failed to put wind between it and the ground ".

According to Symington Grieve's ambitious volumes on Colonsay and Oronsay, which were the result of nearly half a century's research into matters archæological and historical,[1] the Lifting-Stone was conveyed from the beach about 1780 by a certain

[1] *The Book of Colonsay and Oronsay*, in 2 volumes (Edinburgh, 1923).

Donald MacFadyen in his younger days. Donald died about 1840. He is said to have removed the stone from the beach in a creel drawn by a horse. He deposited it on the golf-links, at the side of the road between Machrins and Kilchattan, where it still is. Once upon a time, no fellow on the island was regarded as having attained manhood until he had lifted it; and this ambition led to several ruptures. So Lord Colonsay gave instructions that the stone should be buried. Thus it remained out of sight for many years. Eventually it was dug up again, at the suggestion of Lord Colonsay's factor, Captain Archibald Stewart.

For centuries Colonsay and Oronsay were the proud patrimony of the Clan MacDuffie, or Clan MacPhee. One of their race witnessed a charter granted by John, Lord of the Isles, as long ago as 1463. They are said to have been descended from one whose Gaelic name indicated his having been the Son of the Black Faery, who, according to Irish tradition, was established in a scholastic capacity at Iona about 1160. This is the personage referred to by Martin where he writes: "On the south side of the church [Oronsay Priory] within lie the tombs of MacDuffie and of the cadets of his family; there is a ship under sail and a two-handed sword engraved on the principal tombstone and this inscription, *Hic jacit* [*sic*]*Malcolumbus MacDuffie de Collonsay*; his coat-of-arms and colour-staff is fixed in a stone, through which a hole is made to hold it."

The staff was believed to have been endued with magical powers. Upon it the MacDuffies—the MacPhees of Colonsay—depended for protection and prosperity. It disappeared in 1539, with the death (whether naturally or by violence, we know not) of Murdoch MacDuffie, last of the original lineage.

Martin also mentions that a quarter of a mile to the south of the Priory there was a cairn upholding a stone cross known as MacDuffie's Cross. It appears that upon it the corpse of each of the heads of the MacDuffie family was placed for a few moments on its way to interment.

. . . .

Early June is the time of year to visit Colonsay. It is then that the road leading northward to Kiloran, and on to Balnahard, abounds in delights, especially where it threads the considerable woodlands in the neighbourhood of Colonsay House. Scattered about one's feet are buttercups and kingcups, and at one's side the may, heavily scented, overhung by the first of the rhododendrons to break into flower, as if impatient to compete with the aspiring foxgloves. As for the woodlands themselves, their floors are thickly carpeted with wild hyacinths, lending to the scene a touch of ecclesiastical blue—of heavenly blue—the blue we associate with heaven and the saints.

No less enchanting is the road running southward to the Strand, by the margin of which it peters out. When one arrives at the road-end there, just at the hut used by the postman in the execution of duties as pleasant in summer as they must be exacting in winter, one may find the tide unsuitable to permit of a crossing to Oronsay. And in what way more delectable could this inter-tidal interval be whiled away than in shore-wandering about a locality the colouring of which has attracted to it so many artists? Come this way in early June, when one's approach prompts the oyster-catchers to petulant piping, lest their nests among these shore-lands be discovered and disturbed. Recline quietly here awhile, half-hidden among the iris-flags by the curves of dried seaweed and bleached driftwood, and a clutch of wild duck, but a day or two old, may go cruising by within a few feet of you, the colouring both of parents and of chicks so like that of their brown and bronze surroundings that you cannot distinguish them until they sail before you across a pool free from sea-tangle.

By mid-June, the irises are in full flower at the head of each baylet; and it is then that you will find, among the burgeoning bracken, a little farther inland, if not also upon the mossy pastures so closely cropped by the sheep, that little, blue gem, the vernal squill. This plant seems to enjoy the same habitat as the sea-thrift splashing with pink these exquisite shorelands.

The state of the tide may still leave ample time for your ascending the frowning cliffs of Beinn Eibhne in order to view to advantage the pastoral isle of your quest. But be careful how you proceed! Follow, where practicable, the sheep-tracks, for, although they may lead you deviously, and indeed at times so narrowly as to render irksome the placing of one foot in front of the other, they are eminently free from those hidden pitfalls common to territory strewn with heather and fallen rocks. Ascend and descend by the sheep-tracks where you can; and let nothing urge you to hasten. Safety is ensured only by strictly observing the old Latin motto, *Festina lente!*—Hurry slowly!

But let us return to the shorelands, for, much as I have traversed moorland and mountain in my time, shorelands have always appealed to me in a manner irresistible. To me, shore-wandering is one of the few completely unalloyed joys of life. Here, by the littoral pastures of Colonsay, I achieved something of an inward calm that cannot be described. These peaceful pastures, picked out so daintily in daisy, and in tiny, yellow flowers innumerable, bestowed a sense of restfulness, of repose. Their influence was immediate. It was a case of instantaneous transport; and it recalled the postscript to a letter written to me recently by a friend who thought that my anxiety to get these pages into the printer's hands was pressing rather heavily upon me. "Pop a bright chrome yellow or pale canary yellow scarf over your head while you are rushing to finish your book. It will help you to concentrate."

The impinging moorland also has its June-time treasures—wild violets, and butterwort, the latter standing erect on its leafless stalk above a miniature rosette as greeny-yellow as the tenderest shoots of fern or bracken. There is to be found hereabouts, by the way, that rarer butterwort which botanists call the western— a variety not so uncommon in Ireland, having a pale lilac corolla, with five almost equal lobes.

.   .   .   .

One June day in 1951, when desirous of crossing to Oronsay on foot, I sat high among the rocky clefts of Beinn Eibhne, watching the state of the tide, having just explored, near at hand, the Crooked Pinnacle, or Hangman's Rock, that projecting ledge overlooking the Strand, pierced by a hole through which the hangman's rope passed in the days when this was the island's place of execution. I was soon to find that I had left the domain of the wild duck for that of the buzzard. As I lay still, a huge buzzard rose from within a few feet of me to go planing down toward the sea, the sunlight on his wings helping me to pick out his hovering span in the great air-space far below. I wondered whether, perhaps, he was about to swoop down upon one of the little yellow-hammers I had seen among the lichened rocks at a lower altitude!

Harvey-Brown and T. E. Buckley, by the way, paint a pretty picture[1] of Colonsay's yellow-hammers sitting on the tops of the furze flowering luxuriantly on the rockier knolls, its petals vying with them in brilliancy and purity of colour. The first visit to Colonsay of these two indefatigable ornithologists was somewhat limited in result, owing partly to their having had no efficient guide, and partly to what they described as the constitutional slackness, uncertainty, and inconsequence of Highland directions. They discovered that no difficulties were ever prepared for, nor foreseen, even by the islander long resident in his insular home.

[1] *A Vertebrate Fauna of Argyll and the Inner Hebrides* (David Douglas, Edinburgh, 1892).

They discovered, too, that, if they omitted to put a leading question, they usually got an answer of no value. If, on the other hand, they *did* ask a leading question, the answer received usually conformed to the informant's own ideas. This difficulty, they thought, arose from pure indifference, or from a dislike of being questioned, or from their informant's not always understanding the questions put. They cite the following instance:

"How far is it from here to Scalasaig? "—No answer.

"Is it three miles? "—" Yes."

"Is it more? "—" No."

"Is it less? "—" Maybe."

"Will it be two miles? "—No answer.

"Is it two-and-a-half miles? "—" Yes."

From this the ornithologists deduced the distance to be not more than one mile. That was about seventy years ago. One experiences in these parts exactly the same vagueness to-day. To these Celts, precise information has never been of the slightest importance.

When on the subject of birds, one might add that here, on Colonsay, the herons nest on the reedy ground fringing the lochans. Can it be, as Seton Gordon asks, that these long-legged fishers, like the bittern, were once ground nesters, obliged by human intrusion to retreat at nesting-time to the greater safety of the tree-tops?

.   .   .   .   .   .

But I am still on my way to Oronsay, as you may remember.

Having quitted the buzzard-haunted heights of Beinn Eibhne, I descended speedily to the Strand, from which the tide had now receded, leaving no more than the shallowest pools among the worm-casts. So I was now able to pass over to Oronsay dryshod. As the previous day had been the full neap, I was not granted much time during which to explore the Priory—far less the geographical features of this grassy isle—and to return to the Strand before the incoming tide rendered impossible my swift, homeward passage across it. I did find time, however, to call on the MacNeills at the farmhouse, which the Priory walls all but embrace. By now, I was in a mild condition of fatigue; and it was comforting to be assured that I could relax and be refreshed without undue anxiety about the state of the tide. Angus Mac-Fadyen, the farmer's assistant, I was soon to learn, would be going over the Strand with the horse and trap anyway, to meet a relative living at Scalasaig. The relative, in due course, would be arriving by car at the road-end. This meant, in effect, that matters were being timed not merely to allow of Angus's getting over to Colonsay, but also to permit of the relative's taking the reins and returning in safety with the trap to Oronsay. All this put my mind at ease, enabling me to finish my tea none too hurriedly. Not that affairs of tide have ever given me a moment's anxiety in my life. But I wanted to get back to Colonsay in time to attend a function at which, apparently, Angus MacFadyen also proposed being present, for, when the horse was harnessed to the trap and we were about to set off for the Strand, he promptly fastened his bicycle to the back seat.

The *horse*, you will have noticed! Not the pony! The lightness of a pony, as I was soon to perceive, would not have been suitable for the purpose now ahead of us.

Down the white, sandy road from the farmhouse, something heavier and stronger, if perhaps slower, than a pony pulled us at a spanking trot. A backward glance showed that in a few minutes the farmhouse had passed out of sight behind a ridge of the green hills of Oronsay. Soon the horse was picking his way, undirected, through clefts cut in such sea-rocks as lay strewn about the route habitually adopted when the tide is already at the incoming. Onward the trap bumped, merrily, triumphantly, among these clefts, a single journey through which by a car would have immobilised it indefinitely. No motor vehicle could survive in conditions under which the MacNeills' horse and trap appear to thrive.

But for the splash of horse through the rising tide, but for the wobble of wheels on axle, the call of a pair of oystercatchers, and late cuckoo-call from the valleys we were approaching, all was silent. Now and again, however, young MacFadyen would break in to comment on the loveliness of the two islands between which he was now spending his days so contentedly, or to tell me something of the excellence of Oronsay's six hundred sheep and its thirty head of cattle.

Everything seemed completely in harmony and in synchrony as we crossed this sobering Strand. A family of eiders went cruising by, twenty yards ahead of us, and so leisurely that one might have thought their speed and distance had been determined by some mechanical timing device. It was interesting to observe how the horse, when he noticed ahead of us bunches of seaweed afloat, or even submerged, altered course slightly of his own accord, knowing the weed to be attached to hidden boulders, any one of which would have given the trap a severe jolt, had he allowed a wheel to come in contact with it. This was an excellent example of real horse-sense.

Having reached the Colonsay side of the Strand, Angus handed over horse and conveyance to a lady from Scalasaig, who had come by car to the road-end, and was proceeding alone to Oronsay. No time was to be wasted. Of this, even the horse seemed remarkably aware. No sooner had Angus released his bicycle from the back of the trap than he began to show his impatience to be cantering away across the Strand again. Angus was already off—off on his bicycle to a dance at Kiloran. As for myself, I was loth to quit a scene so colourful, so tranquil. For some little time I stood at the road-end, watching the trap's slow, steady progress through the rising tide. It was fascinating. The tide by now must have risen to the horse's belly; and I could not but reflect on the confidence with which the returning lady had taken the reins and driven off. It was obvious that she knew the Strand and its tides, its safe parts and its perils. It was obvious, also, that she knew all that was necessary about a horse and trap. Every now and then the vehicle seemed to vanish in the distant waters. Then, gradually, as if by dint of heroic effort, it emerged among the rocks, afar off. It was safely over. The scene filled me with admiration. This performance, to the performers, meant nothing. It was, for them, an everyday occurrence. Indeed, Angus had told me that four crossings a day were quite usual.

In accepting an invitation to step into the car which had brought the heroic lady to the road-end, I confess to having felt some reluctance about turning my back quite so readily on Oronsay. But I already had had a day pleasantly strenuous, and was now sufficiently weary to appreciate the gesture which was to save my limbs the necessity of carrying me and my camera back to Scalasaig.

Though the rough roads of Colonsay are reasonably fit for motors driven not too speedily, the horse still provides the island with its chief tractive power. Wherefore, in the vicinity of the hotel at Scalasaig, any lawful day, you may hear the clang of hammer on anvil, as Willie MacKenzie, Colonsay's blacksmith, shoes a horse, or re-tyres a cart-wheel.

· · · · · · · ·

There was much on Oronsay one might have explored with profit, had time and tide but waited. The island bears many traces of its earlier inhabitants—traces ranging from as far back as Azilian dwellings, like the Oban caves, to the beautiful Priory of medieval days.

In a corner of the Priory is a collection of unburied human

bones; and now and again, in the fields near the farmhouse, evidence of ancient interment is exposed in the course of ploughing.

Oronsay has long been the resort of university professors seeking a carefree holiday. Mr. MacNeill, the farmer, told a friend of mine that, on one occasion, when an ancient grave was opened in a mound in front of the farmhouse, a human skull was brought to light. This interested greatly a professor of anatomy who was his guest at the time, and who, on a subsequent visit to Oronsay, asked his host whether he might have the skull. Thereupon the farmer handed the professor a spade, led him to the spot where the skull had been re-interred, and told him that he could delve if he pleased. He was making sure that such untoward happenings as might arise from further interference with the skull should be the professor's responsibility, rather than *his*.

Many people have spent memorable holidays at Oronsay, and have returned with odd and interesting experiences to relate. Dr. Alan Macartney, however, writes me from Rutherglen that, when he and his wife were there, they neither heard nor saw anything worse than themselves. But he admits that when, on one occasion, the entire MacNeill family went to Colonsay for a wedding, leaving them in charge of the island, they were truly impressed by the atmosphere of the place, and were secretly relieved when the revellers returned—which they did by instalments!

. . . .

Late that evening, a concert and dance were being held at Kiloran, in the public hall, the upper, re-conditioned part of a long farm-building there. To these joint functions, by car, landrover, bicycle, or on foot, nearly everybody in the island seemed to have gone. That afternoon, the Kilmeny Choir had sailed over from Port Askaig, in Islay, to assist in the object of this double event, namely, the raising of money to establish a local sheepdog association. A bill posted prominently at Scalasaig pier already intimated that, under the auspices of the newly-formed Colonsay & Oronsay Sheep Dog Society, such a concert and dance had been arranged. "Admission 2/6. Tea 8 p.m."

As is usual in these parts, the concert was very late in beginning. By the time it did, several of the male members of the audience and of the visiting choir were certainly not without the benefit of drink. The customary hilarity therefore accompanied the proceedings throughout. As the evening wore on, this increased in volume until, at length, the visitors at the back of the hall were more audible than all the Islay choristers performing at their loudest. (A charitable report of these proceedings, published the following week in a wellknown Argyllshire newspaper, mentioned how the choir had held the attention of an appreciative audience!)

There were present many children, for whom, as usual, loud comments and interruptions provided diversion, if not also example. However, the local lads rendering solos and mouth-music in the Gaelic sustained their vocal obligations to the bitter end. The roisterous behaviour of their companions did not embarrass them in the slightest. Nor did the persistence with which certain people wandered freely among the audience during each performance, selling raffle tickets. One was invited to pay six-pence for the privilege of guessing the weight of a cake baked locally with real fresh eggs, and donated by the baker of it. Many had purchased their tickets before it occurred to someone that the public exhibition of the proposed award might at least facilitate an approximate estimate of its weight. So the cake was brought forth, and the raffle proceeded with renewed vigour. It did strike one that, having charged fairly heavily for admission to a performance well below mediocre standards, it was a bit of cheek to conduct, throughout the whole of the proceedings, a series of raffles and lotteries to augment a fund, the sufficiency of which, for the avowed purpose, the charge for admission must already have guaranteed. " Just taking a mean advantage of the audience! " a Glasgow visitor was heard to remark. And, as if this were not enough, a sale had to follow. Bottles of port, tins and packets of cigarettes, cheap glass receptacles of infinite variety— all donated, one presumed, by local shopkeepers and others— were put up to auction, and went at ridiculously high figures, especially when the more hilarious members of the audience got the notion that they must compete for this trinket or for that bottle. Bidding certainly became keen when the ' well oiled ' took a hand in it. Two local lads seated next to me (or standing, for never did they remain in the same attitude for more than a few seconds) spent two or three pounds each in outbidding one another for various objects. Their recklessness could not but suggest to one that, the sooner public grants and subsidies to such communities were examined, the better it would be for the tax-payer.

The concert (if such it might be termed in any sense but that of the revellers acting irresponsibly in concert) did not begin until well after 9 p.m. As the tea interval, advertised for 8 p.m., approached, there was passed round the audience, about 11 o'clock, while a songster continued to unburden himself of a particularly long wail in the Gaelic, a clothes-basket. Out of this

Doorway of St. Oran's Chapel, Iona

everyone took a teacup—and waited. The more potent type of 'celebration', for which the flimsiest pretext provides the occasion, was already well on its way toward culmination. But the real 'do' seldom begins before midnight, with the dance. By 12.30 a.m., therefore, the 'fun' was in full swing at Kiloran. Throughout all this, the young children present seemed mildly amused by the example of their elders. Small wonder so many of the lads in these parts succumb early to the bottle!

The Abbey's Sacristy Door, Iona

CHAPTER XVI

GIGHA

O F F the west coast of the Kintyre peninsula, and separated from it by the shallow Sound of Gigha, lies the Argyllshire island of Gigha, which, together with the islet of Cara, situated a mile or so to the south of it, forms the ecclesiastical parish of Gigha and Cara. Gigha—God's Island, as its Norse name would seem to denote—is one of the more accessible of the Inner Hebrides, its easternmost reach being no more than a mile and three-quarters from the Kintyre mainland. The mail-boat, sailing from West Loch Tarbert on an itinerary embracing Islay, Jura, and Colonsay, calls regularly, one day at the pier by the island's southern end, the next day at the northern, where she cruises offshore to communicate with the ferryboat at what is known as the North End Ferry. With the development of motor transport, however, most traffic to and from Gigha now goes by way of the ferry plying between Tayinloan, by the Kintyre shore, and the island's jetty at Ardminish. This passage of three miles, in water usually sheltered, is one of the pleasantest. Yet, under certain conditions, it can be boisterous enough. Even in midsummer, wind and sea in the sound may render impossible a crossing in either direction. On more than one occasion, when staying on Gigha, I have been unable to return by ferry to Tayinloan; and sometimes I have been held up overnight at Tayinloan when endeavouring to return to Gigha, after a day's wandering among the hills and valleys of Kintyre. Such conditions render inoperable, of course, the North End Ferry; but, as a rule, the comparative shelter of the pier near the island's southern extremity enables the mail-boat to make a cautious call.

The traveller to Gigha by road simply alights at Tayinloan to cross to the island by ferry, as just described. If he approach it by the alternative route, his journey will certainly be varied, as I well recall. In the days when I used to visit, at the manse there, its famous incumbent, the Rev. Dr. Kenneth MacLeod, D.D., it necessitated transport by train from Euston to Glasgow's Central Station, by train therefrom to Gourock, by steamer from Gourock to East Loch Tarbert, on Loch Fyne, by postal bus across the isthmus linking Knapdale and Kintyre, by mail-boat from West Loch Tarbert to the North End Ferry, by ferryboat to the jetty on Gigha, and, finally, by pony and trap to Kenneth's manse, at Ardminish.

. . . .

From north to south, Gigha measures six miles. Its greatest breadth from east to west is roughly a mile and a half. Its area is about 4,000 acres, which includes some 260 acres of foreshore. Its coast-line of 25 miles is not unlike that of Iona. Much of it is bold and rugged, affording modest adventure to those who delight in scrambling in steep places. Its western and south-western parts are characterised by caves, two of which—the Great Cave and the Pigeons'—are especially worthy of note. The latter, for centuries, has been the resort of countless wild pigeons. One must also mention the natural tunnel, 133 feet long, which the sea has eaten out at the island's south-western extremity. This tunnel has two vertical funnels through which the surging surf, in time of storm, comes booming with a great noise and commotion.

Lovely bays and tiny creeks, floored in sand smooth and clean, fret the island's east coast. The sands in a corner of Ardminish Bay, as also those fringing one side of Druimyeon Bay, are the delight of those who, every summer, holiday in their vicinity. Farther north, at Tarbert, where one finds the expected isthmus, are East Loch Tarbert and West Loch Tarbert, both of them lovely in their way, but lacking the elusive qualities of Ardminish, where the island's life, social and spiritual, would appear to have been lived all down the centuries.

The island, on the whole, is well favoured. Much of it is under tillage. Its farms are prosperous. Some of them are quite large. Trees grow in the neighbourhood of Achamore House, the proprietor's mansion. The peat deposits have been exhausted long since; and the natives are therefore obliged to import coal. This they do half-yearly. On very special occasions, a load of peats may be brought over the sea from Islay. Driftwood, cast up by storms, forms an asset by no means negligible. On the whole, Nature has dealt generously with Gigha, as regards both soil and climate.

. . . .

The island is well watered. Little lochs fill the hollows in its upper reaches; and springs are numerous. Among the more famous of Gigha's wells is that at the north end of the island, situated at the foot of a hill near the isthmus at Tarbert. It is called the Lucky Well of Bethia, or of Beathag—evidently a saint

of whom we now know nothing. In ancient days this well, referred to by Martin Martin as Mary's Well, was regarded as one
of the most sacred in the locality. Seamen desiring a favourable
wind consulted it regularly. A movable slab covered its water;
and there was a tradition that, if anyone forgot to replace the
slab after having taken from the well such water as he or she
required, a storm or flood would assuredly follow. Some years
ago, an exceptionally high tide visited Gigha, and began to inun-
date its littoral fields. The inhabitants immediately assumed that
someone had carelessly omitted to replace the slab over Beathag's
Lucky Well. Off to the north end of the island dashed the fleetest
of them to find the slab lying by the side of the well. He instantly
placed it as it should have been. And just in time, the natives
declared! The flooding tide then began to subside; and they
attributed their deliverance to the spirit of the well thus pro-
pitiated.

The belief that unfavourable winds could be altered for favourable ones by certain observances at this well was widely held
among the masters of foreign sailing-ships who found themselves
in this neighbourhood. The well had its custodian, who received
from strangers seeking its aid a piece of money. This was deposited on the slab covering it, together with such objects as pins,
needles, and variegated pebbles.

The natives of Gigha have always boasted of the excellence of
their island's water; and one recalls in this connection its reputation in olden times when illicit distilling was their forebears' pre-
occupation. On the farm of Druimyeon Beag is the site of what
is reputed to have been the last illicit 'pot' in the parish. The
water used in its celebrated blend came from the big loch behind
the farmhouse. A lade from this loch conducted the water which
drove the island's mill, the ruins of which, including the wheel,
may still be seen.

The whisky-makers were a family named Galbraith, a surname
closely associated with Gigha since ancient times. They were
the ancestors of the present occupiers of the farm of Druimyeon
Beag. Galbraiths have been connected with this farm, continuously, for many generations. Round the farmhouse kitchen fire,
tales of Old Galbraith's exploits as an unlawful maker of whisky
during the latter half of the nineteenth century are often recounted. The arrival on Gigha of excise and police officials, duly
armed with a warrant for his apprehension, frequently obliged
him to go into hiding. Somehow or other, he consistently
managed to evade them. They often searched farmhouse and
steading for him while he lay concealed in one of the island's

secret recesses. In later life he was a reformed character, having abandoned his law-breaking to deal with other law-breakers—as a policeman in Edinburgh!

The water on Gigha was noted for more than its excellence in the making of whisky. The old ferryman's wife, over yonder at Tayinloan, after an industrious spell at the churn, always washed her butter in Gigha water, though there lay within a few yards of her cottage a well clear as crystal. Over by ferry to Gigha she would cross, carrying a large pitcher, clearing dykes and ditches with the greatest zeal, on her way to the Minister's Well. Never was her butter-making so successful, she used to declare, as when washed in the blue water of the Minister's Well.

"We're fearfully fastidious about water," Kenneth once told me during one of my memorable sojourns with him at the manse of Gigha. The Minister's Well, situated on the glebe at no great distance from the manse, was a joyous source of sustenance. Though the manse has a proper water supply to its ample taps, affording such plenitude that one could enjoy a hot bath at any time of the day or of the night, in the whitest and brightest bathroom you ever beheld, its occupants always preferred the water from that well. Twice daily, I accompanied Kenneth to it with pails. In droughty summers the local people, when their own wells run dry, resort to the Minister's Well; and yachtsmen, at anchor in Ardminish Bay, replenish at it too. Its bluish water has been known to mariners for centuries; and one might believe that King Haco's seamen drank of it in the late summer of 1263.

. . . .

This brings us conveniently to a matter of history, since 1263 was the year Haco's proud fleet sailed southward to sustain irrevocable disaster off Largs. The Norse seamen ravished and plundered as they went. They travelled through Kintyre with fire and sword. Off Gigha, that late summer, the main part of their fleet lay at anchor, while they disembarked, not to plunder this time, but to bury one of their priests, who had died on the voyage south. The burial-service, according to one of the Sagas, was conducted with great pomp and ceremony. Friars from a neighbouring monastery attended with a pall. One assumes they were Grey Friars from Saddell Abbey. We know that, about this time, the Abbot of Saddell actually approached Haco to plead for peace on behalf of his brethren, and for the safety of the abbey and its holy precincts. The Norsemen landing on Gigha to inter their priest probably provided the occasion.

It is not unlikely that the Abbot who sought to interview Haco is he whose memory survives in the Abbot's Pool, the name given by the local fishermen to a sea-pool by the shore of the adjacent isle of Cara.

To this day, the natives of Gigha point out to one the anchorage where the Norwegian galleys lay, prior to their sailing southward to destruction; and they do so with the confidence to be expected from someone who had actually seen them there!

"This is where the Scandinavians anchored their war-galleys when they would be getting ready for their attack on Scotland," Kenneth once remarked as he and I wandered by Gigha's shorelands some years ago. Kenneth was at pains to point out the anchorage with his *cromag*—with his crook—defining its limits in detail, as though he himself had witnessed the war-galleys assembled there.

The Scandinavians' attack on *Scotland*, you will observe! Herein survives the ancient sentiment that the Hebrides are still part of the kingdom of Lochlann—of Norway o'er the foam—and that such of Scotland as never formed part of that kingdom is a foreign country.

"This manse was built for big men, for big Vikings," Kenneth once remarked, when drawing my attention to the inordinate height of the coat-pegs in its porch. "We're a lordship of our own," he continued, "the Lordship of the Isles. We're not really in Scotland at all. The law and order of the mainland are hardly applicable here, on Gigha. They're not needed. Nothing that happens on Gigha harms the King, away yonder in Buckingham Palace; and we never do anything here requiring a policeman."

The manse, incidentally, was built about 180 years ago, in the time of the old lairds, the MacNeils of Gigha. Its fine, thick walls could withstand the fury of the worst Hebridean winter. Below the manse lies the little inlet where the parish's incumbent moors his boat. Hence its name—the Minister's Creek.

That at one time Gigha must have known something even of the commercial usages of the Norsemen is suggested by a balance and weights of the Viking period now preserved in the Hunterian Museum, at Glasgow. These relics, recovered during excavations on the island in 1849, consist of a portion of the beam, the indicator, the pans of a balance, two suspension pieces in the shape of birds, three weights, and a leaden whorl.

.   .   .   .   .   .

The census of 1951 showed the population of Gigha and Cara to be 190. In 1931 it was 243—a decline of 53 in twenty years. In

1791, when the Rev. William Fraser, parish minister, was compiling his survey for inclusion in the *Old Statistical Account*, the population was 593. Nearly all the inhabitants at that time were either Galbraiths or MacNeils. According to tradition, the former clan waxed in prosperity among the seafaring communities of the West Highlands and Islands because there never was wrecked at sea a ship having more than two of this surname aboard her. Judging by Fraser's account, the islanders were in a flourishing condition. There were among them five weavers, four tailors, two innkeepers, two shoemakers, two pipers, two boat-carpenters, one mason, one fiddler, one blacksmith, one miller, and one distiller. Gigha's shoemaker at that time received a shilling for making a pair of shoes at home. If, however, he were employed to make them in the house of his customer, he received but sixpence.

How cheap commodities were on Gigha then! Sixpence was the recognised price of a good hen. A chicken could be had for threepence. A dozen eggs cost but twopence. A goose could be had for one-and-six. "A pig cost from 1s. 6d. to 2s. 6d., according to its age."

To-day, agriculture and lobster-fishing are the islanders' chief sources of revenue, though one must not leave out of account the island's increasing popularity as a summer holiday resort. Lobsters are lucrative; and even the sale of eggs is not to be sniffed at. In a century and a half, the price of eggs in Gigha has risen more than twenty times!

. . . .

Gigha is not lacking in antiquities. By the road to Ardlamey, and at no great distance from the present church and manse, are the ruins of the thirteenth-century church of Kilchattan, surrounded by the island's burying-ground. This is the *Ecclesia Sancti Catani* alluded to early in the sixteenth century in the Register of Privy Council. Little remains of it but the east wall, with its lancet window, and the stone font reclining at the base of this window. The altar has disappeared. It was there at the close of the seventeenth century, however. The floor of the old church is paved with tombstones, several of which are those of the MacNeils of Gigha, who, at the time of Martin's visit, were "the principal possessors of this Isle".

On a hillock just above the churchyard stands an Ogham stone —an upright stone bearing an Ogham inscription. Although such stones are not uncommon on the east coast of Scotland, this, I believe, is the only specimen known to exist on the west. Scotland has sixteen such stones. That on Gigha stands 5 feet 9 inches above ground, and measures nearly 4 feet round the base.

Ogham is the name given to ancient Irish writing in straight lines crossing each other. In the case of the Gigha specimen, this is incised along the stone's edges. MacAlister, in his *Irish Epigraphy*, gives as a translation ' Fiacal, son of Coemgen '.

The Ogham alphabet, by the way, is illustrated in that excellent publication on which I was so largely nurtured—*Chambers's Twentieth Century Dictionary*.

On the hillside above Ardminish Bay, and surrounded in autumn by fields heavy in ripening grain, stands the little parish church of Gigha, built between 1923 and 1924. It was opened and dedicated in the autumn of the latter year. It replaced the older church of 1870, which stood in front of the island's inn, and which was demolished. The present church is situated on a knoll known to the islanders as *Cnocan a' Chiuil*, Hillock of Music. Here the people of Gigha, when young, used to tarry to hear the faery music: here the same people, now old, say they used to hear the music which was an omen that one day, on this very site, they would be listening to the music of psalms and hymns.

To Gigha, from Colonsay, in 1923, came Kenneth MacLeod as parish minister. His induction synchronised with the laying of the foundation-stone of the new church, on either side of the gateway leading to which may be seen a rowan-tree planted as a sapling by Kenneth himself, to scare away ghosts and witches—" to lend a little paganism to the place," as he once told me, " for, though I'm supposed to be a Minister of the Gospel, there's a lot of the pagan in me yet! "

Kenneth remained minister of the parish of Gigha and Cara until 1947, when he resigned his charge to make room for a younger man.

This parish has had one or two incumbents of renown, though none more so than the elusive Kenneth. Among the old photographs and portraits in the church vestry is the likeness of the Rev. James Curdie, M.A., who occupied this charge for fifty years between 1827 and 1877, when he died, at the age of 87. A memorial tablet to him may be found in the wall of the present church. He left a large sum of money which, of course, he did not make on Gigha. He had inherited it from an uncle who was " very high up in the Church of England ".

Perhaps the most interesting point about Curdie is that, in his younger days, he had been Disraeli's tutor. In 1827, the year he became minister of Gigha, Disraeli gave him, for the manse there, his dining-room suite. The table of this suite was that upon which I always had my meals when staying with Kenneth. Disraeli's sideboard is to be seen at the island's post-office. Roughly a quarter of a century ago, it was bought by the post-master at a local sale of furniture. The auctioneer was unaware of its origin; and Kenneth tells me that he never mentioned the matter to him, lest his so doing put up the bidding to a figure at which no one on the island could have competed for it. After all, as Kenneth remarked, it might as well be in Gigha as any-where else!

In the Gaelic toponomy of Gigha is enshrined much of the island's history, legend, and tradition. A coomb known as the Hollow of the Mote perpetuates the memory of Haco's visit. Here the Norwegian king and his commanders, while their galleys rode at anchor in Ardminish Bay, are said to have held council. A knoll by the church goes by the name of the Little Hillock of the Oratory, for here, it is said, the monks of old had a private chapel. Upon the Hill of the Little Fox is the wishing-seat known as the Fox's Chair. The Fox, they say, was the name of an old chief who lived on Gigha long before the days of the Lordship of the Isles. From this rocky seat he administered the law, and granted wishes. At the north end of the island is the Kneeling Stone, to which pregnant women used to resort for prayer. The Irish held this stone in very special veneration. Well within living memory, when as many as forty Irish sailing-boats might have been seen at anchor off Gigha, their crews always made a point of visiting the Kneeling Stone. These boats came to Gigha for cargoes of the island's excellent potatoes.

On the hillside not far from the Kneeling Stone is a stone known as the Largie Rock, at the base of which, the natives say, a king or a chief—they know not which—lies buried.

Then there is *Cnoc nan Ordag*, Hillock of the Thumbs, which derived its name from an incident still included among the folk-tales recited on Gigha.

In the days when the island was occupied by two rival factions, the *Clann Fhamhair*, or the Sons of the Giant, and the Galbraiths, a man of the latter took unto himself a wife, and she a member of the Giant's clan. This marriage, it was thought, might have done something to reconcile the rivals. On the contrary, it but emphasised the wife's friends' hatred of the Galbraiths. Soon afterwards, her father fell into a decline. As he lay on his death-bed, his Galbraith son-in-law desired to visit him in the hope of patching up earlier misunderstandings. The dying man, resentful that so unworthy a son-in-law should have expected anything in the nature of deathbed forgiveness, sought his skean-dhu, and concealed it under the bedclothes, intent on dealing him a death-blow. Galbraith, suspicious of the old man's design, kept out of reach.

Scarcely was the latter in his grave when the rivals came to conflict on a little hill in Gigha. After this contest the victorious Galbraiths cut off the thumbs of their adversaries, before driving out of the island such of them as had survived. For a long time thereafter, the Clan Bhreatain—the Galbraiths—continued in un-disputed control of Gigha; and to this day the knoll where they routed the offspring of the Giant goes by the name of Hillock of the Thumbs.

.   .   .   .

For unnumbered years, a fairly good track linked the popu-lated part of Gigha with the ferry at the island's north end. In the middle of this track, and flush with it, lay a stone cist known as the *Uaigh na Caillich*, since it was believed to be the grave of a *cailleach*, or old woman.

Associated with this spot is an ancient Gaelic curse held to visit anybody desecrating it, or behaving there in an unseemly way. The Gaelic wording of the curse was given to Kenneth by the octogenarian beadle officiating at the parish church when he began his ministry there in 1924. Here is a literal translation:

> *An old wife, I, out of (?) Turkey,*
> *My Body in the Gateway of the Artizans (or Druids),*
> *If you lift not your burden off me,*
> *I will leave your heads on the field.*

In 1938, while this track was being elevated to the status of a road, such as would facilitate wheeled traffic between Ardminish and the North End Ferry, the workmen, when they came to the spot where the cist lay, were in doubt as to how to proceed. They were most reluctant about removing the top slab, over which countless feet had travelled all down the years. Yet, this was felt necessary in order that the cavity known to exist thereunder might be filled in, and the foundation of the road rendered firm at this point. Indeed, as a warning of what might befall, the ancient curse was recited by some of the natives. After much dissent, and not without serious misgiving, the slab was lifted, and the cavity packed with stones and gravel.

To-day the cist is incorporated in the road in as perfect a condition as when it lay across the original track. So far, no one concerned in these operations has been any the worse. The precise location of the cist is now marked by an uninscribed stone erected at the roadside. One day, people may ask just what that stone is doing there; and I feel flattered in the notion that they may not know until they have perused these pages!

.　　　.　　　.　　　.　　　.　　　.　　　.

And what of Kenneth? You will identify him whenever I tell you that he was Marjory Kennedy-Fraser's inspired collaborator in *The Songs of the Hebrides*, and that, in 1915, he wrote, for the Highland lads then serving in France, what has since become one of the most famous songs in the world—*The Road to the Isles*:

> *It's a far croonin' that is pullin' me away,*
> *   As take I wi' my cromag to the road:*
> *It's the far Coolins that are puttin' love on me,*
> *   As step I wi' the sunlight for my load.*

> *Sure, by Tummel an' Loch Rannoch an' Lochaber I will go,*
> *   By heather tracks wi' heaven in their wiles;*
> *If you're thinkin' in your inner heart braggart's in my step,*
> *   You've never smelt the tangle o' the Isles.*
> *It's the far Coolins that are puttin' love on me,*
> *   As step I wi' my cromag to the Isles.*

If you would know more about Kenneth, ponder his motto: *A boat to sail in, a sea to sail on, an isle to sail to, and never a day for leaving. . . .*

CHAPTER XVII

CARA

LESS than three-quarters of a mile to the south of Gigha—that elongated isle lying a mile or two off the west coast of Kintyre—is Cara. This isle is roughly a mile in length, and about half a mile at its broadest. "A treeless sheep-run, and a good deal of a rabbit warren" is the apt description given by a visitor who, a few years ago, made it the subject of an exhaustive archæological survey.[1] Except at the north-east end, which is the extremity adjacent to Gigha, and where one finds the customary landing-place, the shore-line of Cara is rocky and comparatively precipitous. At the south towers the Moyle, the island's only appreciable eminence, attaining a height of just under a hundred and twenty feet at mean water.

The name, Cara, is believed to be simply the Gaelic word for a corpse. Seen from the Kintyre shore, this island resembles for all the world a large corpse laid out, the Moyle representing its head.

In May and early June, the rocks of the Moyle, falling perpendicularly to the sea, are smothered in the nests of various species of seafowl. The Moyle itself is said to contain a great deposit of iron ore. Traditional accounts of the storm that, one night in the autumn of 1756, wreaked such havoc on Gigha and Cara, are still related by the older folks of this island parish. The lightning striking the Moyle on this occasion is said to have dislodged a great mass of iron ore. All the inhabitants of Cara heard the noise created by this mass in falling on the southern shore, and felt the shock in their cottages. A raging hurricane brought the sea over the rocks on the west side with such vehemence that the entire island was drenched in heavy showers of brine and foam. Houses were unroofed, and the stacks of corn overset and scattered. So serious was the inhabitants' plight that they were obliged to extinguish the fires in their hearths, and seek shelter in the only slated house on the island. This house, though now tenantless and in sorry disrepair, still stands. It belongs to the laird, MacDonald of Largie. Built about 1730, it consists of two storeys and attics. The tacksman, who occupied it in olden times,

[1] *The Antiquities of Gigha* by the Rev. R. S. G. Anderson, 1936.

possessed one horse and one plough. One of the attic rooms—the one to which daylight is admitted by the wee window high up in the gable—is inhabited to this day by the Brownie (or *Broonie*, as he is spoken of throughout Kintyre), who jealously guards the interests of the MacDonalds of Largie, and of whom I mean to tell you something later.

Except for the Brownie, for the livestock pastured on it, and for its flock of wild goats, Cara to-day is uninhabited.

.   .   .   .

Adjoining the tacksman's house is an ancient chapel with an arched doorway on the north side, in Gothic style. This chapel, now in crumbling ruins, was administered from Iona in ancient times. It constitutes Cara's chief object of antiquarian interest. It measures approximately twenty-four feet by fourteen, having had lancet-shaped windows with flat sills and splayed sides. Ten to twelve feet of its gables are still standing.

Tradition has it that this Chapel of St. Finla was used at one time as a burial-place, and that a priest or abbot lies interred in its north-east corner. Some years ago, a wellknown archæologist sailed over to Cara from Gigha, and commenced to delve in a corner of this ruin, in expectation of locating the tomb of an abbot mentioned in some old books and MSS. as having been buried there. But, delve as he might, he found nothing to satisfy him that his quest was not in vain. However, the association of an abbot with Cara persists in *Poll an Aba*, the Abbot's Port—the name given by local fishers and lobster-men to the little sandy bay below the house.

It is said that, by the close of the eighteenth century, the chapel had been converted into the kitchen of the laird's house. Prior to this date, no doubt, many of the stones composing its thick walls had been utilised in the building of the house itself. The population at this time was twenty-two, the majority of whom were Galbraiths and MacNeils. The Galbraiths are said to have been a tall people, who came originally to this island parish from Dumbarton. Their name in olden times was reckoned among the noblest in Scotland. And there is a tradition concerning them, to the effect that no ship was ever wrecked with three of them aboard.

That the chapel dates back at any rate to the fifteenth century is shown by a notarial document in the MacKintosh Muniments, dated 1456, wherein we read of a proposed meeting " in ye chapel of St. Finla, in ye Yle of Kara ". Finla, according to the Duke of Argyll, is none other than Fionnlaidh (Findlay), a saint contemporaneous with Columba, and closely associated with the ecclesiology of Islay.

* * *

Historical records of Cara and Gigha, her sister-isle, take us back to the centuries throughout which Norway dominated so much of our western seaboard and islands. Was it not in the anchorage between Gigha and Gigalum that, in the autumn of 1263, King Haco, resolved to decide with Alexander of Scotland, once and for all, the ownership of the Hebrides, assembled his ships, great and small—more than a hundred of them, including his long warship of thirty-eight benches, built of oak for him at Bergen? While Haco lay here at anchor with his fleet, he received the renewed allegiance of Angus and Murdoch of Kintyre, actually under threat of having their territories ravaged with fire and sword. And there also came to Haco at this time the Abbot of Saddell, seeking peace, and a guarantee that his abbey and lands would be immune from destruction. As it happened, the Saga tells us, the abbot's arrival at Gigha synchronised with the death aboard the the king's ship of one of the four priests accompanying him. The Abbot and the Grey Monks of Saddell conveyed the priest's corpse over to Kintyre, and buried it reverently in consecrated ground at Saddell Abbey.

* * *

Cara at one time shared with Gigha a reputation for the excellence of the spirits illicitly distilled locally, or smuggled there, and hidden away. To this very day the old folks of Kintyre are able to identify the caves in which smuggled goods were secreted; but no one as yet has found the spot on Cara where, according to the Highland saying, lie buried the seven rents of Kintyre. It is said that, within living memory, smugglers, under cover of night, have been seen to signal by light from the wee window in the Brownie's attic, high up in the north gable of the old house. From that window they scanned the Sound of Gigha—the Largie Sound, as the local fisher-folks call it—for the government sloop regularly searching the shores of Argyll for illicit stills and smugglers' hidie-holes.

* * *

Laird and parish minister, in deference to the Brownie, are expected to doff their headgear on disembarking at Cara. The Laird's Loft in the parish church that, in 1780, stood at Ardminish, on the Isle of Gigha, was referred to throughout the Kintyre peninsula as the Brownie's Gallery. Here the Brownie had a pew of his own. And the Rev. Dr. Kenneth MacLeod, minister of the parish of Gigha and Cara until 1947, assures me that the Brownie now has his special pew in the *new* church on Gigha. Moreover, carved out of rock on Cara is a wishing-chair known as the Brownie's Chair.

There is also a wishing-chair on Gigha. It is situated but a few yards from the manse, and is called the Fox's Chair. A wish is granted if the wisher wish thrice and, in so doing, undertake to keep his wish secret. "On more than one occasion," Kenneth tells me, "after a young lady has occupied this chair, and wished her wish, she has announced her engagement within a month. A few years ago, a young Highlander and myself went over to Cara with the laird's daughter. The two of them sat in the Brownie's Chair and, unbeknown to one another, wished the same wish. They were married shortly afterwards."

Concerning the Brownie, many tales are still recounted in Kintyre, and on the islands adjacent thereto. As with other members of his fraternity,

> *When ther wes corne to thresh or dichte,*
> *Or barne or byre to clene,*
> *He had a bizzy houre at nicht,*
> *Atween the twal an' ane.*

One tale associated with him describes the occasion when Mac-Donald of Largie despatched two of his men to Cara to carry away from the dark, mysterious cellar under the big house a cask of very special wine secretly deposited there for him by some smuggler friends. Careless of the fine susceptibilities of the Brownie, and perhaps even sceptical of his existence, the men entered the house and made for the cellar. There they duly found the cask. Having placed the gang-plank in position, they now attempted to roll the cask up to daylight. But, try as they might, somehow or other they could not move it. Perturbed by this unexpected delay, they eventually apologised to the Brownie for their rude behaviour, and requested him not to report it to their master. Thereupon the cask, as if of its own volition, bounded up the gang-plank, rolled out by the door, and, clearing banks and boulders, came to rest at a spot by the shore where, some hours previously, the two men had moored their boat in readiness.

Likewise related in this locality is the story concerning a cask of whisky stored by MacDonald of Largie in one of the upper rooms of this same house. The existence of this cask became known to some Gigha fishermen who were anxious to test the quality of its content. They proceeded to roll it downstairs; but, no sooner had they got it to the bottom, than it rolled upstairs again, apparently of its own accord. Scarcely believing their senses, the fishermen made another attempt. Again they brought the cask to the foot of the stairs: again it rolled back to its place in one of the upper rooms. To what was this due but to the power of the Brownie? Suddenly realising that he was at work, protecting the interests of the laird, the fishermen fled in panic. Instantly they put out to sea to escape the Brownie's influence, vowing at the same time that never again would they trespass on the rights or properties of MacDonald of Largie.

And one day, when the laird was expecting some guests to dine with him on Cara, the tablemaid found herself unable to open the cupboard in which the dishes were kept. Tug as she might, the cupboard door remained immovable. One of the guests expected was a person against whom the Brownie had a spite.

"Would you shame me before all the folks, after all the titbits I've given you?" cried the tablemaid in exasperation, as the laird's guests were seen landing on Cara, and she without a dish on the table.

The Brownie now took compassion on her; and not only did he allow her to open the cupboard, but he assisted her with the laying of the table.

On another occasion, a manservant in attendance on MacDonald, when in temporary residence on Cara, received from the Brownie a good, sharp slap on the jaw, as he passed through the house. This was in revenge for his having sneered at the suggestion that any such sprite existed on the island. That slap, as the manservant confessed, cured him for ever of his scepticism. Thereafter the Brownie extended to him the domestic assistance he had been in the habit of giving to the other servants employed by MacDonald, either on Cara, or at Largie Castle. Inmates guilty of untidiness often received from him a skelp in the dark.

Of nights, while the household slumbered, he washed up the supper dishes, tidied kitchen and scullery, removed ashes from the grates and relaid the fires, ground the meal, worked the churn, and filled the water-stoups. And sometimes, during the night, he stumbled noisily over stoups and the like, as a hint to those who carelessly had left them lying about in the passages.

At bed-time he took upon himself the responsibility for seeing that all the dogs were out of the house and tied up at their respective kennels. But his particular function was to make arrange-

Tomb of Abbot MacKenzie flanking the Holy Table in Iona Abbey. Behind are the Sedilia where, in Roman days, sat the Celebrant and his two assistants

ments for the arrival of strangers or of guests. Thus, he aired the beds, changed the linen when necessary, and assisted in the kitchen when the maids had rather much to do.

When he took the notion, he attended to the cattle. The herdswoman, delayed one evening in setting out to bring the cows home, could not locate them anywhere on Cara. When, in despair, she returned to the byre, she found them standing quietly in their stalls, waiting to be milked.

.   .   .   .

During the First World War, when this and similar localities were perpetually disturbed by rumours of the clandestine landing of enemy troops, there lived alone in the house on Cara a certain Mr. Kennedy, owner of Glencreggan, a small property situated about a mile or so south of Muasdale, by the Kintyre shore. Mr. Kennedy, who died some years ago, was employed at this time in a voluntary capacity by the government as a coast-watchman. It was his duty to report, among much else, mines or enemy submarines sighted in local waters.

One night, as he slept alone in the big house on Cara, an unusual noise awakened him. For a moment he lay uncertain whether it was attributable to warlike causes without, or to something, wind-disturbed, banging and rattling within. It then occurred to him that a ghost was responsible or, maybe, the Brownie. He immediately pulled on his trousers, and proceeded downstairs to investigate matters. With each downward step, he heard an even weirder sound. Whenever he paused to listen, there was silence but for the wind that, in sighing round the old house, brought a creaking to a door-hinge here, and shook a window there. With every step he took, this uncanny sound could be heard. As poor Mr. Kennedy himself often admitted afterwards, in the midst of all these strange ongoings he was terrified.

It was not until he reached the foot of the stair that he traced the sound to his dangling braces! In trailing them behind him their ends flopped noisily against the staircase, step by step!

.   .   .   .

One autumn noontide just before Kenneth retired from his ministry of this parish, he and I were put over to Cara from Gigha by a fisherman friend who, on leaving us there, arranged to return in the late afternoon, thus allowing us ample time to explore an island upon which, hitherto, I had not landed, but which Kenneth knew intimately. "There's Gigalum," he observed, meantime pointing with his cromag—his shepherd's crook

ABOVE: *The Reliquary of St. Columba*
BELOW: *St. Columba's Bay, Iona*

—in the direction of a rocky islet lying some distance off our course. "I often wonder why we should be asked to go to Jericho, when we might so easily go to Gigalum!"

On setting foot on Cara, Kenneth instantly doffed his hat in deference to the Brownie, and in conformity with the old custom, the observance of which, as I have already told you, is incumbent upon parish minister and laird. Our arrival was witnessed by a number of speckled heifers that hurried down to the shore to greet us, and followed us inquisitively as we proceeded, shore-wise, toward the island's house. The space in front of this solitary dwelling was yellow this calm September day with masses of the weed known as Stinking William, much of it reaching shoulder-high. By the shore, among nettles, lay a large knocking-stone, and also part of an ancient quern.

"You stand there, Alasdair, facing the door," said Kenneth with an air of solemnity, and he pointing to the door, "and tell the Broonie that you never have had any truck with the Campbells, and that you haven't a drop of Campbell blood in your veins!"

The door we found firmly barred, so as to prevent cattle from entering. But with ease we opened a window on the ground floor, and managed thus to gain admittance. We immediately climbed the creaking stair of the empty house to the Broonie's Room, and looked out across the sound to Largie Castle, ensconced among woods above the Kintyre shore. Then we descended to the secret cellar, which was so dark that the box of matches carried by Kenneth afforded us little or no illumination. This dark place, it is said, was used in olden times by smugglers for the concealment of their contraband. And it occurred to us that, perhaps, buried herein was the treasure believed to exist somewhere on Cara—the seven rents of Kintyre. "In Gigha, they say, lies some of Haco's treasure," Kenneth remarked while in this dark, eerie place. "And the seven rents of Kintyre lie buried in Cara, though no one seems to know what this strange saying means. But they say, also, that the seven rents of Islay are buried at Rudh' a' Mhail—at the Headland of the Rents, just by the lighthouse beyond Portaskaig."

When disembarking in the high-pitched noon, Cara was a soundless isle, except for the drone of bee among the heather and wild thyme—among the heart's-ease and lady's-bedstraw—except for the occasional screak of cormorant standing on a skerry offshore, and craning his long, sleek neck, as we passed on our way to the old house, except for the chug-chug of the mail-boat's paddles thrashing the shadowy brine over which she was travelling to Green Islay, for the hum somewhere overhead of a plane in flight between Renfrew and the outer Hebrides, and for a faint, striking noise as a couple of wild billy-goats, in butting one another, brought their long horns together in indifferent combat. So still was this September day that, when reclining on one of Cara's higher knolls, we could hear the drone of reaper-and-binder among the harvest fields of Gigha, dealing rhythmically with grain as robust as one might find anywhere in Scotland.

For a brief moment, too, one heard the tread of a pony's hooves on Gigha, and the noise of a trap's wheels moving laterally on their axle, as Mr. Wilkieson, the island postmaster, in delivering the mails brought from the mainland by the mail-boat an hour or two earlier, drove about the island's farmlands.

As we wandered over Cara in the direction of the Moyle, one was impressed by the amount of fresh water to be found on an isle of its size. It seemed to abound in springs, issuing from its verdant hillsides, and feeding the cool, clear streamlets meandering toward the shore through patches of moss and water-cress. For the greater part of the way, we followed the tracks made through brackens and tall, downy thistles by Cara's wild goats. Aware of our having landed, no doubt, the entire flock, numbering about thirty, had taken refuge among the sea-rocks under the Moyle, where their colouring blended so well with their surroundings that at times it was difficult to locate them. Their creamy-white coats however, stood out in sharp contrast against the greens and russets of brackens and the purple of heather, once they elected to leave the shorelands for higher ground. Here and there about the Isle, the tall growth of brackens and rushes lay flat in places, indicating where the flock had lain of nights. These goats were very timid. Probably, they were fairly unaccustomed to the intrusion of human beings. Two or three white kids skipped across the sea-boulders with incredible agility for wee, young things, endeavouring to keep up with the adults of the flock, as it stampeded on our approach.

"And now I've to perform another solemn duty as parish minister," whispered Kenneth in furtive tones, as we reached the rock protruding at a fair altitude from the grassy slopes near the Moyle. "I've to sit in the Broonie's Chair, and wish a wish. I'm fond of the Broonie!"

Thereupon he climbed into the Chair, and, gazing wistfully across to the Kintyre coast, proceeded to wish in prolonged silence.

"Seeing you've no Campbell blood in you, Alasdair," he eventually remarked, "the Broonie probably will be kind to you too. So you had better come up and occupy the Chair for a whilie."

This I did; and, when I had wished my wish, lo! by my side I found a banana!

"I mustn't leave Cara without making a boat—a water-flag boat," said Kenneth, in stooping to pluck an iris-flag in our return journey to the jetty, at which the Gigha fisherman had arranged to pick us up. "They sail well, you know—better even than those made from the logs of Lochlann."

So he pulled a strong water-flag in the marshy ground below the old house and, with his deft fingers, fashioned it into a wee, green boat. We now paused for a moment on the fringe of a sandy inlet. Here Kenneth committed his boat to the tide. "I love this tiny bay, Alasdair," he proceeded, "just because I can be making water-flag boats here to my heart's delight, and sailing them off on their own to Erin and all sorts of queer places like that."

"The child of the Isles, in his play hours and in his herding hours, makes for the nearest linn, and, building a boat out of iris leaves, he gives her prow to the sea and her stern to the shore, so to sail to a wonderland beyond the waves." So wrote Kenneth, the Sweet Singer of the Hebrides, in his mystical book, *The Road to the Isles*.

And whither would our flag-boat sail? Out to the Small Isles or to Colonsay or, perhaps, to Skye? We already had put place-names on all the objects lying in the linn of our launching. The linn itself represented the Western Sea. A low, flat slab, almost awash, we named Tiree. A stone with a steep, frowning precipice in very miniature we called Eigg, since it suggested the Scuir. Larger stones we designated the Coolins of Rum, and larger ones still the Coolins of Skye. Farther out, where the stones were big and numerous, and stretched in a line, lay all the Isles from Barra Head to the Butt of Lewis.

"She makes for Eigg of the Scuir and the Singing Sands—Clan Ranald's Country!" cried Kenneth in ecstasy, as we watched the water-flag boat sail out toward the west, with a faint wind astern. For a moment she anchored, until a touch of tide, turning her bow, carried her off toward the Lews.

I stood in silence as one entranced, watching Kenneth construct and launch yet another green boat. And I remembered a certain Malcolm MacInnes in the Sleat of Skye, who wrote of such tiny boats in the shape of egg-shells, having polished stem of daisy for mast, and butterfly wing for sail.

CHAPTER XVIII

MULL

The Isle of Mull is of isles the fairest,
Of ocean's gems 'tis the first and rarest;
Green, grassy island of sparkling fountains,
Of waving woods and high tow'ring mountains.

So runs the opening verse of that poetic translation by the late
Malcolm MacFarlane of Dugald MacPhail's celebrated Gaelic
poem, *An t-Eilean Muileach*, the Isle of Mull. Dugald, himself
a native of Mull, was born in 1818, and died in 1887. On a knoll
by the wayside at Ardura, just where the road to the Iona ferry
strikes westward across Mull by way of Glen More, there stands
a cairn commemorating him. Inscribed on each of the cairn's
four sides is a verse of his Gaelic poem, Malcolm MacFarlane's
English translation of which, sung to a Gaelic air from *The Minstrelsy of the Scottish Highlands* which Sir Hugh Roberton
arranged for choral purposes, has attained, through the Glasgow
Orpheus Choir, world renown. Nowadays one can scarcely hear
the name of Mull without recalling this translation, and the lovely
melody to which it is sung, a melody as perfect in construction as
The Londonderry Air, or that of *Ye Banks and Braes o' Bonnie
Doon*.

One recalls in this connection the wayside seat near the Ulva
ferry post-office, on the west coast of Mull, overlooking Ulva's
Isle and Inch Kenneth. This seat was placed there by the Glasgow
Orpheus Choir in memory of William Jackson, one of its most
devoted members—a devout lover of this spot. As the bronze
tablet affixed to it testifies, his ashes, at his own request, were
scattered here in 1937—while his soul goes marching on.

With an area of roughly a quarter of a million acres, Mull is the
third largest of the Hebrides. Of the Inner Hebrides, only Skye
is larger: of the Outer, only Lewis. On the north-east, it is
separated from the Morven district of the Argyllshire mainland by
the romantic Sound of Mull, and on the south-east by the resplen-
dent Firth of Lorne. The Ross, its western extremity, protruding
far into the waters known in ancient days as the Deucaledonian
Sea, terminates at the narrow Sound of Iona, beyond which lies

the hallowed Isle of that name. At Ardmore Point, in the extreme north, it is no more than four miles distant from Ardnamurchan, westernmost reach of the Scottish mainland; while the mouth of Loch Don and of Loch Spelve, on its eastern shore, are roughly the same distance from Kerrera, where the Firth of Lorne is narrowest.

Its coast, except in the north, is beset with islands and islets, reefs and skerries, many of them renowned. It has been estimated that no fewer than 468 islands, islets, and insulated rocks, lying adjacent to Mull, are included in its parishes. Having mentioned Iona and Kerrera, we might also specify some of the others, including those which fall to be treated separately in this volume. To the south-east lie the Slate Islands and the Garvellachs. Sprinkled upon the sea to the south of Iona are the black skerries known as the Torran Rocks, familiar to readers of R. L. S. Northward from Iona lie Staffa, Little Colonsay, the Treshnish Isles, Ulva and Gometra, Inch Kenneth and Eorsa. At no great distance from Duart Point lies Lismore, and, nearer at hand, the Lady's Rock of vindictive association.

The Tertiary and post-Tertiary formations of Mull, like those of Morven, have afforded geologists an interesting field. An account of these formations appears in the proceedings of the Scottish Geological Society. "It may safely be maintained," runs a pertinent passage, "that Mull includes the most complicated igneous centre as yet accorded detailed examination anywhere in the world."

Of Mull's stupendous volcanic origin we are reminded from time to time by its earthquakes. A friend of mine distinctly remembers a night in 1908 when his house on the island rocked and swayed. He imagined this to have been due to a terrific fall of rock, such as occurs at intervals in the Gribun and Carsaig localities, and to which we shall revert in greater detail. He was surprised to learn the following morning that the rocking and swaying he had experienced were the result of an earthquake shock—by no means an unusual occurrence in Mull, as he was now to discover. One recalls in this connection the pronounced quake recorded about noon on December 23rd, 1925, in the area between Tobermory and Salen. It was felt very distinctly at Salen, and was found to have synchronised with a considerable seismal disturbance recorded at Blairgowrie.

Mull's splendid mountains are but the denuded remnant not of several volcanoes, as might be imagined, but of a single volcano

40 to 50 miles in circumference—one stupendous volcanic outburst, of which they merely formed the centre. When at the height of its internal fury, this volcano's cone is thought to have attained an altitude of 15,000 feet—five times that of Ben More—now denuded by the epigene agencies of aeons—by heat and cold, snow and frost, wind and rain. The cliff faces present ample evidence of this.

The greater part of the island is composed of basalt. In the Ross, however, we find granite, and celebrated granite at that! Many famous structures are built of the red granite of the Ross of Mull. In Scotland, we have such splendid monuments as the Skerryvore and Dubh Heartach lighthouses: in London, we have the Albert Memorial, Holborn Viaduct, Blackfriars' Bridge, and much of the Thames Embankment. To-day the quarries of the Ross are derelict. We no longer build as did our grandfathers.

To the north of the village of Bunessan, in the Ross of Mull, is the modest peninsula of Ardtun, a locality known to palæontologists since 1850, the year in which the Duke of Argyll drew the attention of geologists to the fossil beds referred to ever since as the Leaf-beds of Ardtun. The find was originally made by a certain Mr. MacQuarrie of Bunessan, who duly informed the Duke about them. These beds lie beneath the basalt rocks comprising this particular part of the Ross. They are thought to have been deposited by streams, and perhaps by floods, carrying down from the slopes of Mull's great volcanic centre the débris of such vegetation as thrived before the creation of its basalts.

Just across the mouth of Loch Scridain, a couple of miles distant from Bunessan (the little port of the Ross, and centre of all local activity), lies the mountainous peninsula of Ardmeanach, territory so bleak and inhospitable that its seaward or western extremity is designated the Wilderness. Nevertheless, the Ardmeanach region is a favourite resort of the field geologist inured to hardship and fatigue. Here the sea has pierced the cliffs with several caves, two of which are wellknown—the Ladder Cave and MacKinnon's Cave. The former probably received its name from the necessity of a ladder to reach it, owing to the position of a slab of rock protruding below its entrance. It can accommodate nearly a hundred persons rather tightly packed together; and it is thought that in olden times it may have been used as a place of refuge. The latter cave is said to have derived its name from MacKinnon, paterfamilias of a family of the name believed to have owned lands at Gribun at one time. It is accessible only at low water, since the tide covers its entrance, greatly fortified by large boulders and seaweed. Once these have been negotiated, one reaches the cave's pebbly floor. Beyond the line of the flood, however, it is spread with smooth sand. A large, square boulder lying in its inner chamber goes by the name of Fingal's Table.

This is the cave to which Sir Allan MacLean conducted Dr. Johnson and James Boswell when accompanying them from Inch Kenneth to Iona in his strong boat, propelled by four stout rowers. Though the travellers admit to having already been disappointed by one cave they had seen, and were but little elevated by the expectation of another, Boswell tells us that the Doctor pronounced MacKinnon's Cave the greatest natural curiosity he had ever seen. In their endeavour to obtain some idea of its dimensions, they were nearly frustrated, for, as Johnson writes, " though we went to see a cave, and knew that caves are dark, we forgot to carry tapers, and did not discover our omission until we were wakened by our wants". Sir Alian immediately despatched one of the boatmen into the island's interior. He returned with one little candle. This enabled the party to go forward into the cave, but not to proceed far. " If we had been provided with torches," says the Doctor, " we should have proceeded in our search, though we had already gone as far as any former adventurer, except some who are reported never to have returned." According to tradition, the unreturning were a piper named MacKinnon, and twelve of his clansmen.

It is in connection with his visit to this cavern that Dr. Johnson, referring to his measurements being not critically exact, partly owing to penury of light, and partly to the absence of the necessary instruments, alludes so interestingly to the inaccuracy of the human memory. I quote the passage for the solace of those who, like myself, have experienced the great truth of it, and have been apt to blame themselves unduly for having unwittingly imparted particulars and details none too precise:

" There is yet another cause of errour not always easily surmounted, though more dangerous to the veracity of itinerary narratives, than imperfect mensuration. An observer deeply impressed by any remarkable spectacle, does not suppose, that the traces will soon vanish from his mind, and having commonly no great convenience for writing, defers the description to a time of more leisure, and better accommodation.

" He who has not made the experiment, or who is not accustomed to require rigorous accuracy from himself, will scarcely believe how much a few hours take from certainty of knowledge, and distinctness from imagery; how the succession of objects will be broken, how separate parts will be confused, and how many particular features and discriminations will be compressed and conglobated into one gross and general idea.

"To this dilatory notation must be imputed the false relations of travellers, where there is no imaginable motive to deceive. They trusted to memory, what cannot be trusted safely but to the eye, and told by guess what a few hours before they had known with certainty."

Before passing on to other matters, let me mention one remaining point of great geological interest in the Ardmeanach region. Near Rudha na h-Uamha, a western headland of Ardmeanach, Dr. John MacCulloch discovered, in the eighteen-twenties, one of the most remarkable of geological phenomena in Scotland, and undoubtedly the most remarkable natural object in Mull. I allude to the fossil tree, since known as MacCulloch's Tree. Rising like a pipe in the midst of the columnar basalt to a height of about 40 feet, it is roughly 5 in breadth. From this amazing spectacle, geologists draw their own conclusions. For a great number of years after MacCulloch found it, its location seems to have been forgotten. Even the natives of this part of Mull were unable to tell one anything about it, far less direct one to it. Now it is well and truly placed on the geological map, along with the prostrate fossilised tree seen in a cave a couple of hundred yards to the north of it.

. . . .

Measured from east-north-east to west-south-west, Mull attains a maximum length of thirty miles. At right angles to this axis, it finds its greatest breadth of but a mile less. No words, however, can convey as readily as a glance at the map an idea of its singular shape, in virtue of which it has been likened to a crayfish, the long and narrow peninsula of the Ross forming, as it were, its tail. The island certainly deserves its name, for the sea's numerous and often considerable indentations have bequeathed to it a coast in which mulls truly abound. (The word, mull, is derived from the Gaelic, *maol*, meaning a headland or promontory.) So extensively is it penetrated by sealochs that its coast-line measures nearly 300 miles. The greatest penetrations are Loch na Keal and Loch Scridain, occurring on the west coast. But for the narrow Sound of Ulva, separating Ulva's Isle from Mull, and for the extremely constricted channel detaching Gometra from Ulva, Loch

Tuath would have made a third, as it would appear to have done in past ages.

The northern and eastern shores, protected largely by the mainland, are less irregular than the west and south. The main inlets on the east are inclined to be curved bays, rather than penetrating fiords. Not far from Ardmore Point, in the extreme north, is Bloody Bay of sanguinary memory. A couple of miles to the southward is Tobermory Bay, the only really safe anchorage, in all weathers, on the Mull side of the Sound of Mull. Protected by Calve Island, stretching across the bay, and acting as a breakwater, it is a fine, natural harbour which would certainly have been improved and exploited, had it been situated in relation to a hinterland less barren and unproductive than the moors and mountains of Mull. Clustered round its head is the little town of Tobermory.

Tobermory Bay is probably the best known of Mull's inlets, on account of its historical associations with the sunken Spanish galleon, attempts to salvage treasure from which have been made at varying intervals throughout the last three-and-a-half centuries and more—some of them very recently. Halfway down this east coast and the Sound of Mull is Salen Bay, with its pier at which the mail-steamer calls twice daily, on her itinerary between Oban and Tobermory. Nearer Oban lies the wide curve of Scallastle Bay, and nearer still the Bay of Craignure, from the tiny township at which a ferry plies in conjunction with the mail-boat cruising offshore.

At Salen one disembarks for many of Mull's western reaches. Here an isthmus of three miles separates the Sound of Mull, on the east, from Loch na Keal, on the west. At Gruline, the road traversing this isthmus divides, the northern branch leading along the shore of Loch na Keal toward Ulva, and on thereafter to Kilninian, with the most lovely Bay of Calgary beyond. The southern route leaves Gruline for the other shore of Loch na Keal, passing in the shadow of great mountains, including that of Ben More itself. It also passes in the loom of the mighty cliffs at Gribun, from which there often fall enormous blocks rendering this road impassable for days, and sometimes even for weeks. Beyond the green pastures at Gribun, it turns sharply southward through the mountainous Ardmeanach region. At Kilfinichen it reaches the shores of Loch Scridain, round the head of which, by the inn at Kinloch, it runs on its way to Fionaphort, by the Sound of Iona, having by this time traversed the rocky, undulating Ross of Mull to its western extremity. This is the Pilgrims' Way—the overland route to Iona. When terrific falls of rock interrupt wheeled traffic

at Gribun, one is obliged to approach by the alternative route—
that by way of Craignure and Lochdonhead, thence through
strenuous Glen More to the headwaters of Loch Scridain.

Many instances of remarkable escape from landslide and
tumbling cliff at Gribun have been recorded. Great rocks have
come bounding down without the slightest warning. Seton Gordon relates the case of a friend of his who, while driving his car
along the narrow shore-road here, one wintry day, felt the road
tremble beneath him. He stopped to look back. An enormous
block now lay at rest on the roadway behind him. It had missed
him and his car by a few yards!

Shortly afterwards, the mail-van, proceeding toward the post-
office at Gribun, reached a landslide, beyond which the driver
found it impossible to go. No sooner had he alighted, in order
to see just where he might be able to turn, than a second landslide
descended at some little distance behind him. He now found
himself unable to travel either forwards or backwards. Much
arduous physical labour was necessary before the road could again
be opened to vehicles.

Rocks leaping down from the lofty bastions overhanging the
road at Gribun interrupted traffic in 1934, and again in 1950.
On the latter occasion, so great was the quantity of material in-
conveniently deposited that the Argyllshire County Council had
to employ special squads to remove it by blasting, and by toppling
it thereafter into the sea, so close at hand. More than a thousand
tons of rock and accompanying débris, it was estimated, blocked
the road. This was one of the worst falls of recent years in a
region notorious for them. It brought much of Mull's internal
transport to a standstill for several days. For many who had
occasion to drive overland to the Ross, and perhaps to the Iona
ferry, it meant a detour of nearly fifty miles, by way of Craignure
and Glen More. Fifty miles, I repeat, since this may give some
conception of distances commonly covered in an island no more
than 30 miles at its longest, and, as we already have seen, no more
than 29 at its broadest!

Many stories of tragedy at Gribun are recounted traditionally in
Mull; and I may be excused for interposing at this juncture one
of the best known. It concerns a tragedy said to have happened
so long ago that none in the island would care to pronounce on
the year. Some say it happened during the early years of the
nineteenth century. Others say it was at the close of the seventeenth. "Three hundred years ago, anyway," is the consensus.

According to a popular version, a young man named John, employed as a shepherd at a farm near Gribun, was about to marry Rachael, daughter of the local blacksmith. In anticipation of his marriage, John was installed in a cottage at a lone and awesome spot near the base of the great cliffs, where they tower several hundred feet. On the eve of the marriage, several islanders had the presentiment that something untoward was to occur at Gribun. Strange weather phenomena had been observed; and they say that, during the wedding-feast, a guest, noted in the locality as a seer, turned pale, as though he had 'seen' something.

Late that night, John and Rachael left for their lone cot at Gribun; and that was the last occasion upon which they were seen alive. That they had reached home safely, there was no doubt. But morning revealed that, during a storm in the night, a boulder as large as their cottage was dislodged from the cliffs above, and came hurtling down upon the cottage, which it crushed, together with its inmates. The boulder could not be moved away; and so, to this day, it remains just where it came to rest, " fitting the inside of the house so well," they say, " that one might think its walls had been built round it ".

Though the victims' bodies could not be recovered, a funeral service was held at the spot, conducted by the minister who so recently had married the couple. From miles away rode or walked the Mull folk to the funeral; and they tell one in this remarkable Isle that a dozen or more of its pipers convened at the funeral to play coronachs round the heartless boulder which had entombed them. To this day, the boulder goes by a Gaelic name signifying the Lovers' Stone.

.   .   .   .

The region of the Gribun Rocks is the haunt of the golden eagle, of the buzzard, and of the hoodie crow. Keep on the alert when passing this way, if you would see hoodies and buzzards in plenty. The latter have their retreats high up among the inaccessible precipices. Approach with caution, and you very likely will find them picking at carrion by the roadside, where they have slain an unsuspecting rabbit. They perch on the fence poles and telegraph posts at Gribun, waiting for the rabbits to cross, in the open, the road beneath them.

The eagle is by no means uncommon here. In travelling leisurely through Glen More, one seldom fails to see a specimen or two, hovering aloft. On a dull day they would seem to plane just above the cliffs' edge, under the lowest belt of cloud. Like the buzzards, they often remain apparently motionless in the damp and misty air, so high that only those with exceptional sight are able to spot them without the aid of glasses.

. . . .

And now a word or two about Mull's southern shore, before passing to an examination of its remarkable interior.

Nothing can give one a better general conception of its wildness than the downward view, on a clear day, from one of the planes passing daily high over its mountain-tops when flying between Renfrew and the Outer Isles. As a rule, however, the clouds are so low in this region for so great a part of the year that one is flying well above them, seeing nothing at all of Mull except, perhaps, the very summit of Ben More, afar off, a cone of deep purple in a sea of billowy vapours. Something of the wildness of Mull may also be seen from the deck of MacBrayne's splendid oil-burning vessel, *King George V*, on her passage between Oban and Iona, though one may require field-glasses to pick out such inlets as Carsaig Bay. The wider entrance to lovely Loch Buie, however, is easily seen. But only those with good eyesight and some local knowledge can locate, from this vessel's usual course, the very narrow entrance to Loch Spelve or to Loch Don. Certainly, the long, narrow opening to the former, no more than faintly discernible from the sea, gives no indication of the large and curiously shaped sealoch lying beyond.

The cliffs about Carsaig (incidentally, a locality rich in sapphires) are splendidly savage. Here they rise to a height of several hundred feet. Here, moreover, falls of rock are almost as notorious as at Gribun. The Innamore cliffs, quite close to Carsaig Bay, are nearly 800. Three or four miles to the west of this inlet, and in the midst of the wildest rock scenery, are the Carsaig Arches, two natural archways in the sea-cliffs, which have acquired a degree of celebrity in recent years. One of these phenomena is a tunnel 60 feet high, 50 wide, and 150 long. It passes through a mass of projecting rock, capped with a colonnade of basalt, and overhung by a cliff likewise capped, rising to a total altitude of over 900 feet. The other arch, although only a few feet in length, is 70 feet high. At an altitude of 170 feet, it pierces a rock crested with columned basalt.

From a quarry in the Carsaig neighbourhood came the freestone used in such restorations of Iona's ancient buildings as took place in 1874 and 1876.

. . . .

Mull is essentially an island of mountains. Apart from the

Ross, from the land situated at the head of its sealochs, and the valleys through which its rather secondary highways run, linking up almost every cultivable and habitable part, little of it lies at less than 500 feet above sea-level. Although various accounts, dating from earliest times, speak of cultivation, it must be remembered that, assessed according to standards known to agricultural communities more favourably situated and endowed, the yield per acre is low, and that, although perhaps a little less so in Mull than in most of our Hebrid isles, the cultivated portions are but the merest fraction of what is abandoned to mountain, moorland, rockland, and bogland. Judged by island standards, however, the cultivated proportion of Mull is quite considerable.

On the other hand, it should be borne in mind that, here as elsewhere in the Highlands and Islands, much land formerly tilled according to crofting standards, has gone out of cultivation during the past hundred years or so. Bracken has since laid its devastating hand on territory where, in olden times, were the little cornfields strenuously won from moorland by the inhabitants of a past age.

In this context we must mention Burg, a farm of 2,000 acres, situated in the Ardmeanach district, where lofty cliffs form much of its seaward boundary. In 1936, through the bequest of the late A. Campbell Blair, this typical West Highland farm was acquired by the National Trust for Scotland. For many years previously, it had been approaching, steadily, a derelict condition. The stock was poor, and the crop yield from its diminishing arable was becoming negligible. Bracken had gained the mastery.

The National Trust for Scotland, in conjuction with the West of Scotland College of Agriculture and the Pilgrim Trust, proceeded to carry out, on this property, experiments in the eradication of bracken, with a view to retrieving, for agricultural purposes more profitable, some of the farmland formerly cultivated. Bracken-cutting was rigorously pursued; and I understand that some crops were raised on land from which it had been uprooted, and that the farm's sheep stock was greatly improved. Moreover, the Trust renovated—and, indeed, largely reconstructed—the farmhouse and steading, built a pier, and also a landing-slip for the motor-boat provided for the purpose of enabling those installed at Burg to cross the mouth of Loch Scridain to the township of Bunessan, when necessary.

Whether these endeavours were in any way commensurate with the high cost entailed in reclamation is another matter. These costs, together with the difficulty of obtaining the necessary labour, must have presented the Trust with a problem wellnigh insoluble. The annual loss on the property was increasing, despite generous contributions toward the furtherance of the experiment. In 1948, therefore, the Trust announced that it had completed at Burg what it had sought to demonstrate, and that the property must now be let.

.   .   .   .

That Mull is an island more amenable than most of the Hebrides is reflected in the large number of fine mansions distributed over it, each installed long since with water and electric lighting. It is also reflected in the better condition of its farmhouses, farm buildings, and cottages. Furthermore, it possesses to a pleasing degree something of which most of the other isles are lacking almost entirely, namely, large and colourful gardens. Many of these lie in sunny hollows sheltered by the mountains. These mountains guarantee it an ample share of that rainfall for which the Western Highlands are noted, if not also eschewed. Yet, spells of prolonged drought are not altogether unknown even in these rainy regions. Remarkable to relate, in 1949 the watercart actually toured the houses of Fort William, one of the wettest places in Britain. Last autumn, when in Oban, another of our rainy spots, I asked a bookseller friend whether it had been a good season from an author's and bookseller's viewpoint. He regretted to have to say that it had not been as good as in past years. People hadn't been buying books and reading so much, he said, because the weather had been too fine! In *Oban*, mark you! In a town where the booksellers display prominently, in their premises, large notices requesting customers to remove their wet gloves before handling the books, and to see that raindrops do not drip from their hats on to the volumes below!

.   .   .   .

Ben More, Mull's highest peak, surrounded by many satellites roughly midway between the head of Loch na Keal and the head of Loch Scridain, is the only island summit exceeding 3,000 feet, apart from those of the Coolins of Skye. It is actually 3,169 feet. This beautiful mountain, by reason of its isolated position, is prominent from many parts of the island. It is easy of ascent from the north. A fairly steep climb from the roadside at Loch na Keal to the shoulder of An Gearna (1,848 feet) provides one thereafter with a comfortable ridge walk to its summit. Of course, there are other routes to the top of Ben More; but they are more fatiguing.

The island has another fine range of mountains lying roughly halfway between Glen Forsa and the Sound of Mull. Loftiest of these is Dun da Ghaoithe (2,512 feet), its top easily reached from Craignure by anyone reasonably fit. Any of the five or six peaks forming this group can be climbed from the track following the course of the river in Glen Forsa.

An island with so many fine mountains must needs have almost as many fine glens. The most noteworthy of these is Glen More, which we already have had occasion to mention. The northern half of the island has, in Glen Aros, the wide valley down which the river of the same name, draining a considerable watershed to the east, flows to the Sound of Mull, which it enters at an inlet of Salen Bay, near the ruins of Aros Castle. North-westward from the head of Glen Aros, the road runs down in gentle gradient to the village of Dervaig, at the head of Loch Cuan, having as company for the greater part of the way the River Bellart. This river reaches the sea through deep and sinuous channels fringed with reeds and bulrushes, What a volume of water flows seaward here, into Loch Cuan, after a couple of days' unceasing rain! The cataracts tumbling at right angles into the glen, many seen at considerable distances from the road, and the burns rushing and gushing garrulously by one's side, all add their quota to a river visibly increasing in volume as one proceeds downhill, scarcely able to keep pace with it in time of spate, even when awheel.

.   .   .   .

I well remember a day in 1951, spent in exploring the Aros and the Bellart, having hired at Salen a bicycle to enable me to reach Dervaig with a view to making enquiries there about a family named Paterson, of whom I had known a good deal in my boyhood. There, on a knoll in the old burying-ground of Kilmore, by the roadside above the village as one leaves it for the Mishnish Lochs and for Tobermory beyond, I came upon the fine, grey-granite Celtic cross erected to the memory of the Reverend Alexander Paterson by his congregation and friends. When he died at Dervaig in 1913, in his 76th year, he had been United Free Church minister of Kilninian and Kilmore for forty-one years. This memorial also commemorates Mary MacLeod, his wife, who died at Edinburgh in 1924, aged 71. Mrs. Paterson I recall clearly, having been taken to see her and her daughters on a number of occasions by the late Frederick Victor Branford, just after they had come from Mull to take up residence in Glengyle Terrace. Frederick Victor Branford (one of the two principal characters in my book, *The Goat-Wife: Portrait of a Village*) thought Mrs. Paterson's son, the late Reverend Hector Paterson, the most remarkable fellow he had ever known. I rather think I

Island Pastorale—Iona, with Ulva in the distance

may have seen the obituary of Hector, in South Africa, a year or two ago.

Since those Edinburgh days, the name of Dervaig has fascinated me; and, as this bicycle excursion was the first occasion on which I had visited this comely island village, I could not but feel tempted to enquire as to the whereabouts of any surviving members of the Paterson family. I made my way to the old U.F. church to find that one end of it had become a sordid storage-place for lumber, while the other end, converted into a dwelling several years ago, was occupied by a family named MacDonald. Roses rambled over the porch, at the entrance to their once dedicated abode. On the hillside, some little distance away, stands the old United Free manse, where the Paterson bairns were born, fifty or sixty years ago. Few were alive in Dervaig who could tell me anything about them, or about their parents. The space of nigh forty years had intervened since the reverend gentleman's death there. These years had blotted out all living memory of them. Only the Celtic cross testified to their having once walked these pleasant, if remote, pastures.

Reluctantly, I turned my thoughts from the lost Patersons to Dervaig's round-towered church, the old Established Kirk. Borrowing the key at the house of Mrs. MacFarquhar in the village, I let myself into this austere, but dignified and restful, interior. This is the old parish church of Kilninian and Kilmore: therein stands the pulpit from which Mr. Paterson's Auld Kirk rival held forth each Sabbath.

At the end of a long day, and with the Bellart now flowing toward me, I pedalled home to my quarters at Salen, anticipating the moment when I might reach the watershed to run freely downhill. Suddenly I realised that the stream by my side was flowing with me: I had arrived at the thread-like headwaters of the Aros. The crossing of a watershed always imparts a feeling of relief to the cyclist weary at the close of a long day. Downhill I now sped, with tiny, prognosticating raindrops flecking my cheeks. By the time I had pedalled past the nut-laden thickets fringing the shore-road between Aros Bridge and Salen, I knew the joy of being within a few minutes of journey's end.

.   .   .   .

Though indeed mountainous, Mull possesses only two inland lakes of any great size. The larger is Loch Frisa, lying in elongated fashion between hills, more or less parallel with the road after it begins to descend in the direction of Dervaig. The other, and by far the more beautiful, is Loch Bà, deep-set among the

R   245

Ann MacArthur and her pet lambs, Isle of Iona

mountains, sending its overflow by way of the short River Bà to the headwaters of Loch na Keal, which it reaches after running parallel with the shore for a good mile and a half.

As lovely as either of these is Loch Uisg, a lake small by comparison, situated midway between Loch Spelve and Loch Buie. The road linking these two sealochs traverses its northern shore. Then, a string of lovely, little lochs—of *lochans,* as the Gaels would term them—fills the rugged vale between Ben Creach and Ben Buie; and one might mention that the road between Tobermory and Dervaig, in the north of the island, skirts, throughout their entire length, the Mishnish Lochs.

The lochs and rivers of Mull, especially perhaps Loch Bà and the River Aros, are famed for their salmon and sea-trout. What these island waters yield to the piscatorial visitor enables him to tolerate such of its inns as are indifferently run—inns where the food is monotonous, coarsely cooked, none too plentiful, served crudely and in a manner exceeding in perfunctoriness even that experienced at most of the other hotels in the West Highlands and Islands, where, on the whole, the summer visitor, regarded largely as a nuisance, is catered for merely as a side-line, the sale of intoxicants at the hotel bar being, throughout the year, *the thing.*

.   .   .   .

Mull, by comparison with the Scottish islands as a whole, is well wooded—an isle of waving woods, as Malcolm MacFarlane describes it in the lines prefacing this chapter. However, such was not always the case; and in this connection we recall Dr. Johnson's remarks on the dreariness of the Mull scene, and his dissertation on matters of afforestation, suggesting that the island's gloom of desolation might be relieved by the planting of trees. Boswell tells us that Sir Allan MacLean, anxious for the honour of Mull, continued to talk to Dr. Johnson about the island's woods while accompanying them from Inch Kenneth to Iona in his boat, pointing out distant woods discernible on the skirts of the island as they sailed along. "Sir, I saw at Tobermorie," Johnson observed, "what they call a wood, which I unluckily took for a *heath.* If you shew me what I may take for a *furze,* it will be something."

It was the paucity of timber on Mull that made the Doctor despair of his ever retrieving the large, oak stick he lost while there. This stick, which he had brought with him from London, had stood him in good stead ever since his illness in 1766 had left him with weak knees, for which reason he had hoped to bequeath it to some museum. He had found it particularly helpful when, during his wild peregrinations in the Hebrides, he was obliged to dismount and walk. Two nails driven into it, one at a point denoting a foot, the other denoting a yard, rendered it useful as a standard measure, as well as a support when walking upon rough ground.

The stick had been entrusted to a fellow who ought to have given it to the baggage-man following at some distance. Boswell failed in his effort to convince the owner that it had not been stolen. But no man in Mull in possession of his stick, Johnson maintained, could be expected to part with it. " Consider, sir, the value of such a *piece of timber* here! "

That something by way of afforestation has been done in the years intervening is evident. The Forestry Commission has planted large tracts with various species of conifers; and there are considerable areas covered with native trees—with rowan or mountain-ash, birch, oak, and hazel. Splendid stands, both coniferous and deciduous, are to be found about Torosay and Lochbuie. The rocky steeps on either side of Loch Uisg are so densely clad in birches that one might imagine oneself in the Trossachs—somewhere in the vicinity of Loch Vennachar or, per-haps, of Loch Katrine. For these barren and insulated parts, woodlands of no mean order thrive at Craignure, at Scallastle, and between Salen and Aros. South of Tobermory a considerable stretch between road and coast is well wooded; and, indeed, the road itself, where it passes through part of this plantation, has all the lovelier attributes of the woodland scene—bird-song, for in-stance, in surroundings truly umbrageous. Woodlands also occur in the vicinity of Glengorm Castle, near the extreme north of Mull, and about Dervaig too; while those at Calgary, half a dozen miles to the west, contribute to its bay's being one of the sweetest settings in the whole island. Here, at Calgary Bay, are those alluring sands, fringed by a belt of typical machar-land, more reminiscent, perhaps, of the Outer Hebrides than of the Inner. The largest area under trees, however, is that about Gruline and the hillsides flanking the lower reaches of Loch Bà. Could any spot lie more deeply in shadow during the leafy months than the MacQuarrie mausoleum at Gruline? Of course, the total area under trees is only a negligible fraction of the island.

Mull is an island where, in past years, individual proprietors made some effort to ameliorate local conditions, and to give to nature the more cheerful face envisaged by Dr. Johnson. Even in parts of the island far inland and remote, one discovers, sur-prisingly and agreeably, gallant attempts at sylviculture. The result of one such effort may be seen halfway across the moorland waste between the little wood at Torloisk and the sylvan strip bordering Loch Frisa. Others are to be seen, though to a diminishing degree, in the sheltered vales and hollows about Loch Scridain. Little plantings at Kinloch and at Pennyghael, by the head of that wonderful sealoch, maintain against the inclemencies of the Hebridean winter their precarious hold on the shallow earth. One or two similar plantings grow about Tiroran and Kilfinichen Bay, in Ardmeanach, intractable territory on the opposite side of Loch Scridain. However, when we travel a few miles farther west, into the barren, windswept Ross of Mull, trees become increasingly scarce. The Ross hangs on tenaciously to its few negligible clusters.

Such woodlands have often been established in the face of climatic, geological, and other conditions little appreciated by those lacking any knowledge of the problems of afforestation in territory largely inimical to the survival of trees, let alone to their growth and maturity. Nevertheless, the measure of Mull's relative prosperity in the matter of native timber is the existence there of sawmills. One hears with surprise, and smells with delight, the roadside sawmill at Gruline when proceeding round the south shore of Loch na Keal. The panting of its engine, the hum of its saws, the smell of new-sawn timber and of sawdust slightly moistened by a passing shower, the aroma of the pines in its neighbourhood are, indeed, satisfying.

. . . .

The history of Mull, like that of the rest of the Highlands and Islands, is one of the warring clans. It is largely concerned with the occupants of such fortified places as were the castles of Duart, Aros, and Moy. Duart was the stronghold of the historic MacLeans of Duart. To-day it remains the possession of their descendants. Aros, now a ruin, belonged to the dauntless Lords of the Isles when in the zenith of their power and splendour. Moy Castle, likewise a ruin, gave security to the MacLaines of Lochbuie. With Mull, however, is associated the Clan Fingon—the MacKinnons. In olden times they flourished in the Gribun locality. The MacQuarries owned the island of Ulva. Campbells, MacDiarmids, Livingstones, MacGillivrays, MacPhails, and Beatons have also taken a hand in the affairs of Mull. The Beatons, a family famous in Islay and in Skye as well as in Mull, were hereditary physicians to the Lords of the Isles. Several of them were noted men of letters.

Preëminent among the island's internecine feuds was that

which, in 1480, culminated in the sanguinary sea-fight known as
the Battle of Bloody Bay. The principal protagonists were John,
Lord of the Isles, and Angus Og, his doughty and incalcitrant son.
Rebellion was in the very blood of Angus Og, as it had been in
that of his father and grandfather. Not only was he ready to
defy the Crown's authority, but also that of his father, in support
of whom one or two powerful chiefs now declared common cause.
But Angus Og prevailed against all such alliances. The coöperation of the Earls of Atholl, Crawford, and Huntly did not bring
John any nearer victory; and, in fact, there came a time when the
redoubtable Angus waxed so valiant in strength that the ardour
even of the more powerful of his father's allies began to cool.

What led to this feud, history does not seem to relate with
precision. Father and son are believed to have quarrelled over
the apportioning of certain lands. In some degree at least, all the
Hebridean chiefs were embroiled in this *cause célèbre* of theirs.
The MacDonalds took the son's part: the MacLeans, MacLeods,
and MacNeils sided with the father. At length the two opposing
factions, in their war-galleys, joined issue in waters since known
as Bloody Bay. In the sea-fight which ensued, Angus Og
triumphed yet again, and so decisively that the Clan Donald,
anxious to admit his prowess and valour, simply acquiesced in his
seizing his father's territories, and in his insistence that, *de facto*
at least, he was now their chief. This final test of strength left
the lawless John in a state of impotence for the rest of his days.
Twelve years later, he surrendered his title of Lord of the Isles.
A year afterwards, he appeared before the King to make full
submission for his lawlessness and contumacy over a great number of years. In 1498 he died at Paisley Abbey, whither he had
gone to spend, in tranquillity, the latter days of a life almost
unparalleled in dastardy and turbulence.

Angus Og, after his victory at Bloody Bay, did not survive
long to enjoy the fruits it might have brought him. According
to MacVurich, he was assassinated at Inverness by his own harper
—one named MacCaibre, or Art O'Carby. The harper, we are
told, cut his throat " with a long knife".

At the time of these ongoings, Aros Castle, which may well be
older than Duart, was probably the most important stronghold in
Mull. It was once a seat of the Lords of the Isles, whose history
is so involved, and from whom so many of the MacDonald families
claim descent. It was in 1608, during the castle's latter days, that
Lord Ochiltree held a court there, in order to receive, on behoof of
King James the Sixth and First, the submission of the clan chiefs.
Among the motley lot ostensibly tendering homage on that

occasion were Hector MacLean of Duart, and Lachlan, his brother, Rory MacLeod of Harris, and Alasdair, his brother, Donald MacAllan of Clan Ranald, Donald Gorm MacDonald of Sleat, and Angus MacDonald of Dunyveg.

With the history of Duart Castle and the MacLeans of Duart, I need not detain you unduly here, for is it not written copiously in works to which those interested in its details can now refer so readily? Suffice it to say that the present structure, occupying at Duart Point, on the Sound of Mull, so imposing a site, was restored in 1912 by the late Sir Donald Fitzroy MacLean, Chief of the MacLeans of Duart, a Crimean veteran whom I visited there a few years ago, when in his hundredth year.

Of Moy Castle, once the fortress of the MacLaines of Lochbuie, nothing remains but a tall, gaunt, square tower, roofless and empty, its walls partially clad with ivy. Its age no one knows, though the architecture of at least part of it would suggest a late sixteenth-century origin. It is situated in one of the loveliest and least frequented settings in all the Western Highlands. The waters of Loch Buie rise to within a stone's-throw of the outcropping rock on which it stands. Great mountains overshadow it, prominent among them Ben Buie itself. About these mountains I have seen the mists deploying in a manner suggesting that at any moment the Valkyries might ride out of them—suggesting, too, that the ghost of the headless horseman—that of Ewen of the Little Head—might emerge from them, foretelling yet another death in the already diminished family of the Lochbuie MacLaines.

The story goes that Ewen, son of one of the MacLaine chiefs— well, now, I see that, if I permit myself this digression, our Mull chapter will assuredly occupy more of this volume than a sense of proportion would warrant. Suffice it to say that Ewen and his ghost are to receive fuller treatment in a work dealing with occult matters, to which I mean to devote my attention shortly.

It seems unlikely that in early times Tobermory, situated at the head of its historic bay, did not have a stronghold of some kind. Ancient remains exist in its neighbourhood; but these appear to belong to an age pre-historic, rather than to the turbulent centuries when the rafters of Moy Castle, of Aros, and of Duart were ringing with the halloo of bloodthirsty Highlandmen.

The small town of Tobermory consists mainly of a street built along the harbour side of Tobermory Bay. Many fine houses occupy prominent sites on the steep hillside immediately behind.

On the west side of the town, where may be seen the ruins of an ancient chapel, there still exists the well, from the religious significance of which the town is said to have derived its name. Tobermory (the word is a corruption of the Gaelic, *tobar*, a well, and *Mairi*, Mary) means the Well of Mary—Mary's Well. The modern town was founded in 1788 by the society formed for the purpose of developing the fisheries and improving the sea coast of the kingdom at a time when the locality is said to have boasted no more than two primitive dwellings. According to the account the Rev. D. MacArthur, D.D., wrote of his parish in 1843, Tobermory then had a population of nearly 1,500. It was 1,566 nineteen years later. In 1951 the population of this small burgh was slightly under 700.

In 1851 the population of Mull was 7,485. In the century intervening, it has fallen by more than half, as has also that of such satellites as Ulva, formerly so populous. The clearings once rudely cultivated here and there about the island, the sodden and sunken shells of old homesteads, and the sites of the ancient chapels and burying-grounds of former years all testify to a large population, although not necessarily to times prosperous.

Tobermory's fame rests mainly on the several attempts made in recent centuries to retrieve treasure from the wreck of the Spanish galleon lying beneath the sand and silt of its bay, at no distance from the shore. With these attempts, as well as with the various objects recovered, I need not detain you here, since I dealt very fully with them in a recent book.[1] It should be added, however, if merely by way of bringing matters up to date, that the Tobermory galleon received some further attention in the spring of 1950, when the Admiralty entered into a contract with the Duke of Argyll, owner of the wreck, whereby the former undertook, on a repayment basis, some diving operations in an effort to locate the wreck of the galleon said to lie submerged there. Two small naval craft duly arrived at Tobermory from Port Edgar to carry out diving operations, which continued for some weeks. The Admiralty made it clear at the outset that it was concerned only in locating the wreck, and not in any subsequent operations. Its purpose was to provide a naval training exercise in diving and in the use of sweeping gear and echo-sounding equipment. It was soon announced that the poop of the galleon had been located.

The publicity which, at varying intervals throughout the past three centuries, has been accorded the galleon in Tobermory Bay would seem to have overshadowed completely the many other

[1] *The Buried Barony* (Robert Hale, 1949).

vessels of the kind known to have come to grief off the British Isles in Armada days. Several were lost off the Scottish coasts. In the Haddock Sands at Reawick, in Shetland, is said to lie the Levantine galleon, *La Annunciada*. In an inlet at the south-east of Fair Isle, *El Gran Grifon*, a ship of Rostock, was lost while Juan de Medina and his seamen were stranded there, in the winter of 1588. Tradition has it that several of the Spaniards married Fair Isle women, to whom they taught not only better methods of weaving and dyeing, but also the bright, colourful patterns which have distinguished Fair Isle woollen garments ever since. In 1727, a certain Jacob Rowe, who had designed an engine for salvaging wrecks, obtained permission to raise at Fair Isle "a Spanish ship or man-of-war called the *Grand Admiral of Spain*".

Guns have been recovered from one of the two Spanish ships wrecked at St. Catharine's Dub, on the Aberdeenshire coast. Indeed, according to tradition, the Dub received its name from the *St. Catharine*, one of the ships. The other is said to have been either the *St. Michael* or the *St. Martin*.

In 1740 (the year in which several relics were recovered at Tobermory) a cannon was salved from a galleon aground in relatively shallow water near the ruin of Portincross Castle, in Ayrshire. This cannon was afterwards mounted on the Castle Green.

Tradition tells of similar wrecks off Islay and off North Uist. In Easter Ross it is held that a galleon perished on a sandbank off the Doune of Creich, in the inner part of the Dornoch Firth.

The document bestowing upon the Marquis of Argyll, in 1641, rights in the wreck lying in Tobermory Bay mentions "divers ships and uther vessels of the Armada . . . cast away and sunk in the seaground on the coast of Mull, near Tobermory, where they lay, and still lie as lost". One recalls that, when, in 1909, a London syndicate was formed under the direction of the late Colonel Foss to search Tobermory Bay for Spanish treasure, the Duke of Argyll granted Foss permission to salvage another galleon said to lie off Lochaline, on the opposite shore of the Sound of Mull.

Mull's attraction for landowners and tenants domiciled in England, explains how, in the neighbourhood of some of its English-owned mansions, one finds an Episcopal Church, as well as a Presbyterian. The former, built and maintained by English Episcopalians, and by Scottish Episcopalians also, fall under the jurisdiction of the Bishop of Argyll and the Isles. These Episcopalians came to Mull with their Episcopalian retinues largely at a time when Episcopacy was being embraced by many old Scottish families—a religion regarded as more 'fashionable' than Presbyterianism, and thus thought to be more appropriate to those possessing property, and laying claim to social position and cultural status.

There were several Episcopalians in Lochbuie and elsewhere in the island of Mull in the time of Murdoch MacLaine, grandfather of the present MacLaine of Lochbuie, and also in the time of Sir Stephen Gatty, Murdoch's successor at Lochbuie House, all of whose staff came from England with him. Moreover, Mull's shooting-lodges at this time were let mostly to English tenants. The services held in St. Kilda's, the little Episcopal Church at Lochbuie, were well attended then. Now services are held there but seldom. This little church, standing picturesquely by the shore of Loch Buie, was consecrated in 1876, having been built largely with funds raised by the Lochbuie of the time—Murdoch Gillian MacLaine of Lochbuie, whom we have already mentioned. He was prime mover in the matter of its establishment. A bronze plate affixed to an interior wall of the church commemorates this loving laird of Lochbuie, who reigned there for forty-six years, who died in 1909, aged 63, and who, "after he had served his generation, fell on sleep".

The interior of St. Kilda's is quite lovely. Four of its ten stained-glass windows preserve the memory of a Celtic saint—St. Columba, St. Oran, St. Kilda, and St. Finnan. Built into the wall of the porch is a Celtic cross unearthed at a considerable depth while the church's foundations were being dug. The cross is of the simplest form, and is thought to be about 800 years old. The crucifix above the chancel was carved by Joseph Mayer, who played, no fewer than 114 times, the part of The Christ at Oberammergau, and who died in 1903. Murdoch MacLaine, aforenamed, purchased this crucifix, and had it placed in its present position.

Then, in the wall to the right of the altar is a fragment of the altar of the church of Merry-le-Hant—the slab which covered the relics of the Bishop of Metz, who died in 1851. When that church was set on fire by the retiring French troops in 1870, a French priest rushed into the conflagration to break the slab and to rescue from under it the relics. Murdoch Gillian MacLaine, then *The Times* war correspondent with the German Army, acquired the slab, and brought it home to Lochbuie.

St. Kilda's also contains a number of memorials to members

of the MacLaine family, as well as to others long and intimately associated with this lovely and sequestered part of Mull. As the church has no regular clergyman, because of the lack of funds for his maintenance, visitors cannot but feel tempted to place in the box a contribution toward the upkeep of church and parsonage.

At Gruline, by the head of Loch na Keal, is the little Episcopal Church of St. Columba. One sunlit Sunday morning in 1951, when about to cycle past it, I observed a great number of cars drawn up outside it. I alighted, and entered. The service, throughout which the door remained open, had just commenced. To the legitimate sound of worship there was now added at intervals the hum of a motor-car passing by, or the raucous roar of a motor-bicycle conveying a farm worker away among the distant hills on a visiting excursion, or the cackle of hen at a neighbouring farmyard, announcing something accomplished, something done. At times, too, one heard snatches of conversation, as a couple of Presbyterian islanders lingered by in the sunlight.

Seated by the organ and organist at the very back of the church was a lady with a voice so lovely that I could not but wonder what she was doing here. I was soon to discover that she was—and, indeed, is—a professor of music at the Guildhall, and that every summer she and her academic sisters visit Mull, an island with which they have filial associations. The organ was well played—surprisingly so, I thought, for in these parts, where the standard of musical appreciation is so low, both organs and organists are apt to be afflicted with organic disturbance just when their tuneful coöperation is most desired.

The interior of this little church, with its windows of stained glass, is inclined to be dark, even on the brightest day, and is restful in consequence, both to mind and to eye. So still was it that the candle burning at each end of the altar might have been luminants stilled by enchantment. Now and again, however, a faint whiff, reaching them from the open door, momentarily disturbed their flame. The oil-lamps suspended from the roof about the church's centre, were trimmed and polished in readiness for use in the event of descending darkness.

Who could quit this pretty, little Church of St. Columba without love and charity for his neighbour?

.   .   .   .   .

Unlike the other large islands of the Hebrides, such as Skye, Lewis, Harris, and the Uists, Mull has no regular internal transport service. Consequently, one is often obliged to hire a car—

and exorbitantly—to reach one's destination. Its roads, however, are reasonably serviceable for motor transport proceeding at reasonable speed. The surface of one road (that between Calgary and Dervaig) is a sheer boon to anyone awheel, since most of it is laid with two parallel tracks of concrete three feet apart, each about two feet wide, and runnelled at regular intervals to carry off the rains. A four-wheeled vehicle can speed along here without any jolting; and the cyclist, even where steep declivities necessitate caution when free-wheeling downhill, welcomes this stretch after the unevenness of the rest of the island's roads.

The introduction of the motor-car has enormously increased mobility in Mull, as elsewhere. People from Salen think nothing of travelling by car all the way to Bunessan, in the Ross, for a couple of hours' 'hop' in the village hall there, often leaving Salen after 10 p.m., and coming back about 5 a.m.—a return journey of 80 miles, roughly equivalent in distance to the return railway journey between Edinburgh and Glasgow, but a much more strenuous journey in every other way.

The road from the head of Loch Scridain, passing along the northern shore of the Ross to Bunessan, and to Fionaphort and the Iona ferry beyond, is surely one of the finest in the island. At the outset one's interest is focused largely on the cliffs and mountains of Ardmeanach. Although the road throughout the Ross runs at no distance from the sea, it is sufficiently elevated to afford one some of the finest panoramic views to be had in this locality. Once one has passed westward beyond Ardmeanach itself, the prospect to the north includes many lesser isles of interest—Ulva and Gometra, with Inch Kenneth, Little Colonsay, and Staffa nearer at hand. By the time one has arrived at Ardfenaig, that alluring group of islets known as the Treshnish may be seen to the north-west, one of them—the Bac Mor, or Dutchman's Cap— a ready landmark for seamen and landsmen alike, on account of its singular shape.

No road traversed the Ross of Mull even as late as 1843, the year in which the Glen More road was completed. The Rev. Duncan Clerk, minister of Torosay, mentions in his contribution to the *New Statistical Account* (1845) that plans were then being made for the extension, as far as the Sound of Iona, of the road through the Ross, that wild territory which, along with adjacent Erraid, is so wellknown to those who have followed David Balfour's adventures after the wreck of the brig, *Covenant*. To-day, when afoot or awheel in the Ross, one has it constantly in mind that this was the Pilgrims' Way of earlier centuries. Thus they travelled overland to Iona. The present road follows for the most part the track beaten in ancient days by bare or sandalled feet.

.   .   .   .

The remoteness of certain parts of Mull has preserved there a belief in much that is ancient. The island is rich in folk-tales and tradition; and few of its indwellers would deny—would be so *bold* as to deny—the existence of the faeries, having heard at cradle how Inary, housewife at a Mull farm, invoked their aid—how they arrived in great numbers to help her with the cloth-making, how they worked so feverishly all night that they developed appetites depriving her of every morsel in the house, and how, in the end, she had to resort to a ruse to get rid of them!

Mull's tales of faery have interested collectors of the like ever since John Gregorson Campbell's recording them made them so widely known. There are people in Mull to this day who declare that they have seen the faeries, that they have restrained their dogs from fighting with the faeries' dogs, which would assuredly have worsted them, and that they have heard—and, in fact, still hear—faery music at spots reputed to be the abodes of the Faery Folk.

The idea that an ordinary dog loses its hair after an encounter with a dog belonging to the faeries persists in the story told of one, Calum, who happened to come upon a cluster of St. John's wort when crossing the hills in the Ardmeanach district. This plant is said to have the magical power of endowing the unsolicitous finder with the faculty for seeing the faeries when others cannot.

No sooner had Calum found the precious plant than he sat down by a stream to contemplate such benefit as his discovery might afford him. Suddenly, a faery woman appeared on the scene to demand of him that he should surrender to her the sprigs of St. John's wort he carried in his hand. But Calum refused, and with a consequence none too happy. He did not return home from the hills that night, for he fell asleep, under spell, just where he was. The sun had again traversed the entire heavens ere his searching relatives found him there. When they roused him from his deep slumber to tell him that he had spent a day and a night in the open, he was greatly surprised. He thought he had been asleep for but a few minutes. It was not until he saw, by his side, his dog, and he completely hairless, that he realised what had befallen him!

At the farmhouse of Erray, a mile or so north of Tobermory, there used to reside one of that interesting species of faery known as a glaistig. As was usual with her kind, she performed in the farmhouse kitchen, during the small hours, all sorts of menial tasks left undone when the maids and menservants retired for the night. Outside the actual farmhouse, she confined her attention to the wellbeing of the byre's occupants. All the propitiation she expected was the little milk customarily left out for her. Failure to provide this none too exacting libation always explained the state of confusion in which were found various domestic apartments of farmhouse and outbuildings the following morning.

> But gone are now all those joys for ever,
> Like bubbles bursting on yonder river;
> Farewell, farewell, to thy sparkling fountains,
> Thy waving woods and high tow'ring mountains.

CHAPTER XIX

IONA

" We were now treading that illustrous Island, which was once the luminary of the Caledonian regions, whence savage clans and roving barbarians derived the benefits of knowledge, and the blessings of religion. To abstract the mind from all local emotion would be impossible, if it were endeavoured, and would be foolish, if it were possible. Whatever withdraws us from the power of our senses; whatever makes the past, the distant, or the future predominate over the present, advances us in the dignity of thinking beings. Far from me and from my friends be such rigid philosophy as may conduct us indifferent and unmoved over any ground which has been dignified by wisdom, bravery, or virtue. *That man is little to be envied, whose patriotism would not gain force upon the plain of Marathon, or whose piety would not grow warmer among the ruins of Iona!* "

T H U S wrote Dr. Johnson of an Isle that belongs not merely to all Christendom, but to all mankind. The portion reproduced in italics may be somewhat hackneyed. Yet, it forms part of what is surely one of the most memorable passages Johnson ever penned. The lover of Iona and of all things associated with the Old Celtic Church would readily concede that his journey to the Western Isles of Scotland, now nigh two centuries ago, had been worth while, had it evoked from so critical a Saxon nothing more than this passage. Boswell was so moved by it as to have commented in a footnote that, had their tour together produced nothing else but this sublime quotation, " the world must have acknowledged that it was not made in vain. The present respectable President of the Royal Society was so much struck on reading it that he clasped his hands together, and remained for some time in an attitude of silent admiration."

That Boswell himself was as deeply moved by Iona as was his great and pious friend is evident from his own *Journal*. Does he not tell us therein of his stealing back to its cathedral, there to indulge in solitude and devout meditation? While contemplating the island's venerable ruins, he reflected with much satisfaction that the solemn scenes of piety never lose their sanctity and influence. And what of that fervent hope of his, expressed in words as deserving of remembrance as Johnson's? " I hoped that, ever after having been in this holy place," he wrote, " I should maintain an exemplary conduct. One has a strange propensity to fix upon some point of time from whence a better course of life may begin."

Here, on Iona, as Fiona MacLeod, that devout lover of the Western Highlands and Islands reminds us, sacrosanct men have bowed in worship since the remotest days. Here was lit the lamp that sought to illumine Europe when the shadow of the pagan's sword still hung over so much of it. As for myself, I never disembark there without hearing in the inmost part of me the voice that spake unto Moses out of the burning bush: *Put off thy shoes from off thy feet, for the place whereon thou standest is holy ground.*

Upon no isle in all the world has so much homage been bestowed—an isle so small, so unassuming, physically so insignificant when compared with Mull, its mighty neighbour. Yet, its power has bound men in every Christian country, and even in heathen lands. Kings, princes, and chiefs have been carried thither at their latter end to lie where, in the heyday of the Old Celtic Church, the earth was consecrated by St. Columba, so long ago. Tombstones, sculptured in ancient days, mark their final resting-place in the precincts of St. Mary's Cathedral.

Nearly fourteen centuries ago—on May 12th, 563, to be as precise as the Christian Calendar will allow—St. Columba, then forty-two years of age, landed on Iona, at a spot known ever since to the Gaels as *Port na Curaich*, Haven of the Coracle. Accompanied by twelve of his brethren, he had sailed over from Derry in a frail coracle, "desiring to seek a foreign country for the sake of Christ," as Adamnan, his biographer, tells us. A small cairn situated on a hillock not far from this spot goes by the name of *Carn Cul ri Eirinn*, which is to say, the Cairn with its Back to Ireland. By its Gaelic name it is denoted on our Ordnance Survey maps. Tradition has it that Columba, in seeking for his missionary work a place from which, even on the clearest day, he could not see on the far horizon his beloved and alluring Erin, rejoiced at discovering Iona, raised this cairn and so named it in order to commemorate the island's suitability for his purpose, and buried near the beach where he had landed the coracle for which he and his fellow-emissaries were now to find no further use. They had come to Iona to stay.

An elongated mound at the head of the Haven of the Coracle, shown on the more intimate maps of Iona as *An Curach*, or as *An Curachan*, signifying The Little Coracle, was long supposed to contain the upturned craft of wicker framework, covered with hide, which bore St. Columba to the Isle with which his name, ever since, has been so fervently identified. However, shortly after the First World War, when the site of *An Curach* was excavated, nothing could be found there to substantiate this supposition. It is now thought to be a Stone Age barrow. Nevertheless, lovers of Iona and of Columba are loth to abandon the notion that, somewhere in this locality, the saint's coracle lies concealed.

That the coracle was known to the Celts from earliest times is shown by frequent references to it in their literature, as well as by frequent occurrences of the word in its Gaelic form as a place-name. On the west of Barra, for example, is an islet known as An Curachan. The Celt is fascinated with anything to do with a coracle. He applies the name, *curachan,* to a certain little shell in which, he says, the faeries put out to sea.

Thirty-four years after Columba landed at Iona, and on that very Sunday in June upon which Augustine reached Kent, he died on the Isle from which his name has become inseparable. "Unto this place, small and mean though it be," he said on the eve of his death, in 597, while ascending for the last time Dun I, Iona's modest hill, "great homage shall yet be paid, not only by the kings and peoples of the Scots, but also by the rulers of barbarous and distant nations with their peoples. The saints also, of other churches, shall regard it with no common reverence."

More than amply fulfilled has been this prophecy. All through the intervening centuries, men on pilgrimage have travelled the continents and the seas to reach Iona, Columba's Isle. In olden times they came, as do many even at the present day, by the Pilgrims' Way. They crossed the Sound of Mull from the mainland of Argyllshire, to land at Salen, whence they traversed on foot, and in a westerly direction, the many miles which eventually brought them to Fionaphort, at the seaward extremity of the rocky Ross of Mull. Less than a mile beyond, and on the opposite side of the Sound, lay the island of their quest. A route necessarily circuitous and arduous, I grant you, since the mountain mass of which Ben More forms the centre rendered unavoidable much travel by the shores of two of Mull's great sealochs, Loch na Keal and Loch Scridain, before one even reached the Ross. However, in good weather the pilgrims, journeying thus, subsisting, according to tradition, on the wayside water-cress, had one supreme consolation—incomparable scenery on every hand. And they had, moreover, that indescribable satisfaction still experienced by the westering traveller, be he afoot or awheel, when at last he achieves journey's end at Fionaphort, with Iona now so near at hand, and as a rule readily accessible.

Even those coming across Mull from Salen by motor-car experience at Fionaphort this peculiar satisfaction. I myself have

Fingal's Cave, Staffa

often felt, there, a complete abatement of hurry and anxiety, a resignation, a disinclination to cross too soon the Sound of Iona, aware that, except in very bad weather, one can do so by ferryboat at almost any time. Here time and tide do seem to wait for one. All sense of urgency is dissipated. One's piety is already warmer.

The ferry plying between Fionaphort and Iona must be one of the oldest in Britain. It has operated without intermission since Columban times. To-day, during the summer and autumn months, many thousands reach and leave the island by it.

A readier and certainly less arduous way to this alluring Isle, however, is provided by MacBrayne's *King George V*.[1] Every lawful day between the beginning of June and the end of September, this splendid craft, sailing from Oban and circumnavigating Mull, drops anchor in the colourful Sound of Iona, but a few hundred yards offshore. Her passengers are then transferred by speedy ferryboats to the jetty in the Martyrs' Bay, just by Iona's village, and are allowed roughly two hours ashore—sufficient time to enable even those who move tardily to visit, in comfort and with composure, the island's historic monuments, all of which are situated in close proximity to one another.

But there are times when the Sound of Iona cannot be crossed by ferryboat except at gravest peril—times when one is obliged to tarry at Fionaphort until the winds and the seas have abated— times, moreover, when one may be marooned on Iona. Such were the conditions prevailing when Columba died there, in 597, in his seventy-seventh year. News of his death travelled swiftly over Scotland; and multitudes set out for Iona to attend his funeral. But a tempest preternatural in its violence swept the Sound for the space of three days, confining them to the Mull shore, within sight of their sacred objective. Thus was Columba's sincere wish vouchsafed to him: he had asked that he might be laid to rest at Iona, quietly, with none present but members of his own island community.

No isle has remained so long, so intimately, and so reverentially identified with the name of an individual as has Iona. To the Scottish Gaels it has been known for centuries as *I*, a name pronounced like the English letter, e. Contemporary Erse chroniclers, who had frequent occasion to refer to it, rendered it as *Hy*, or merely as *Y*. The Gaelic word, *i*, means simply an island. When rendered as a capital, however, it denotes that sacred and very

---

[1] This vessel not only saw service in Dunkirk, but on one occasion made a trip to Ostend, and then carried out a shuttle service to Boulogne, followed by five trips to Dunkirk. She then returned to the Clyde to take up war service as a tender. In 1950 she was converted from coal-burning to oil-burning.

Staffa: The Great Face and the entrance to the Boat Cave

particular Isle—Iona. At a later date, and in order to emphasise Iona's true significance to them, the Gaels called it *I Chaluim-Chille*, Isle of Colum (or Calum) of the Cell.

And why Colum? one may ask. Why Columba? Is not *columba* the Latin for a dove? And is this not the word we know in Gaelic as *Calum*, a proper name, the better known equivalent of which is Malcolm?

The saint's mother called him her Columba—her Dove—because of his gentle disposition. It is remarkable, if not also impressive, that the Hebrew for a dove should be *Iona*.

In this context we remember that St. Columba, like Francis of Assisi at a later date, was known to the birds of the air. One day there came to his monastery at Iona a wounded swan. The wounded bird received succour at the saint's healing hands. When all was well with it again, the monks, assembled by the shore of the Sound of Iona, watched it as it rose from Columba's arms to wing out over the sea into the distant heavens.

The Gaelic-speaking natives of Iona, who take so great a pride in their island's history, and indeed in its geography and topography too, mention Columba to one as though their immediate forebears had known him, and as though these forebears had placed upon them some enchantment, as by sacred wand, obliging them to keep evergreen the traditions of the saint and his brethren, and to tend with loving and meticulous care everything on the island pertaining to the ancient Columban Church, so essentially missionary in its approach to Christianity. They know their history, the Presbyterian inhabitants of Iona. They know the significance of the Synod of Whitby, when Northumbria adopted Roman Christianity, and the Celtic missionaries retired to Columba's Isle. They are as well versed in what Adamnan has to say of our beloved Columba as they are in the Scriptures. They know by heart, and often sing to an ancient Irish melody, Hymn 179 in their Church Hymnary—the translation my clansman, Duncan MacGregor (1854-1923), made of Columba's *Christus Redemptor gentium*. Here are the first two of its four verses:

Christ is the world's Redeemer,
The lover of the pure,
The fount of heavenly wisdom,
Our trust and hope secure;
The armour of His soldiers,
The Lord of earth and sky;
Our health while we are living,
Our life when we shall die.

IONA

Christ hath our host surrounded
With clouds of martyrs bright,
We wave their palms in triumph,
And fire us for the fight.
Christ the red Cross ascended
To save a world undone,
And, suffering for the sinful,
Our full redemption won.[1]

Moreover, the islanders will tell you that, a day or two before Columba died, he put his blessing on the crops his monks had raised in the little fields about the monastery, and whispered appreciatively in the ear of the horse that daily brought the monks their milk from the adjacent farm—the old beast that, on resting its head in the saint's lap, emitted " plaintive cries, foaming and gently wailing ".

They assure one, too, that Columba, though old and ill, had been at his transcribing of the Scriptures the day he died, and that, as the hour of midnight approached, he struggled from the cold austerity of his couch of stone to be present as usual at Midnight Mass. A light, they say, was seen to rise from the little church whose foundations are now so truly incorporated in our Cathedral of St. Mary. The monks hastened to discover what portent was this. Diarmid, swiftest of them, found Columba on the altar steps, dying. He raised the saint's enfeebled hand, that he might pronounce his last benediction here on earth. "And thus," as Dr. George MacLeod told us so beautifully on St. Columba's Day, 1948, in a broadcast talk on the significance to Scotland of Columba, "he blessed them even as his soul was taken up into heaven; while the Grace of the Lord Jesus Christ remained with them."

Everywhere about Iona, Columba left his imprint. His name persists throughout its not inconsiderable toponomy. We have it in the Port of the Coracle, the inlet often referred to as Columba's Bay. In the Cathedral we have the stone with an incised Celtic cross known traditionally as Columba's Pillow—the stone that, according to Adamnan, was erected later to mark his tomb. In the Cathedral, too, and on the south side of the entrance to the

[1] According to a tradition in the Western Highlands, this hymn was the outcome of a difference Columba had had with the Pope over the latter's refusal to place in the Vatican library an earlier hymn the saint had sent him. The Pope's objection to it was that only one of its twenty-six verses concerned the Redemption. The others extolled the Creation, for Columba held that the whole of nature was made glorious. So, in a moment of inspired indignation, he delivered himself of his *Christus Redemptor gentium.*

nave, we have the spot designated Columba's Tomb. Tradition has it that here was located the shrine containing the saint's relics. During the ninth and tenth centuries, when the Danes and the Northmen were perpetually raiding Iona, the relics, it is said, were often transferred for safety, sometimes to the Scottish mainland, sometimes to Ireland.

About the year, 1200, when Reginald, Lord of the Isles, was establishing at Iona a monastery of Black Monks and a nunnery of Black Benedictine Nuns, the relics were lost sight of.

One should mention, however, that among the most precious of Scotland's treasures is that known as the Reliquary of St. Columba, or as the Monymusk Reliquary, since it was purchased from the Grants of Monymusk with the aid of the National Art Collections Fund. It may now be seen in the National Museum of Antiquities at Edinburgh. In olden times it was called the *Brecbennoch* of Columba, for it was said to have contained the relics of that saint. It consists of a house-shaped wooden box and lid, each cut out of the solid, and enclosed in bronze and, on the front, silver plates, the latter slightly incised with intertwined animals on a dotted background. The roof-tree is cast in bronze, with interlaced line and bird-head ornaments inset with blue glass. It was gilt, as were the six medallions on the front, bearing interlaced lines and red enamel inlay. Only four of the medallions remain. It still has one of the two large hinges for a carrying strap. This is decorated with red enamel and *champlevé* patterns of spirals, and a red and yellow star design. The box, which is empty, was fastened by an iron pin from one side. But long ago it was forced open, when the lower binding of the lid was wrenched off.

The ornamentation of the famous Brecbennoch, or Blessed Brec, suggests its having been made early in the eighth century— perhaps, a little more than a hundred years after Columba's death. Early in the thirteenth century, William the Lion bequeathed it to the Abbey of Arbroath, together with the lands of Forglen, in Aberdeenshire. These lands were conveyed for its adequate maintenance. Its owners and custodians were obliged to carry it "before the Scottish armies, wherever they went into battle". Proof of its having been regarded as the palladium of Scotland is surely shown by its having been carried into battle at Bannockburn in 1314 by the Abbot of Arbroath. The following year it passed into the possession of that wellknown Aberdeenshire family, the Grants of Monymusk, from whom it was purchased in 1923.

Let us now look more closely at Iona itself.

The island attains, from north to south, its maximum length of a little more than three miles. Its greatest breadth from east to west is about a mile and a half. Its area is roughly 2,000 acres, only a fourth of which is under cultivation. Compared with most of the islands in these western seas, it is low-lying. Toward the northern end it reaches, in Dun I, its greatest height at 332 feet, where stands the little cairn erected in 1897 to commemorate the thirteenth centenary of Columba's death.

For the most part, Iona is composed of Archæan rocks, overlain on the eastern side by sedimentary rocks of Torridonian times. In addition to these two pre-Cambrian formations, minor igneous intrusions of the Lower Old Red Sandstone and igneous Tertiary dykes are to be found. The former are related to the famed granites of the Ross of Mull: the latter belong to that period of igneous activity with which are associated the vast lava fields of Mull. Iona also has its erratic blocks, carried thither from the Ross during the Great Ice Age. Raised beach deposits of post-glacial times also occur. The areas of blown sand, such as one finds in the picturesque White Sands of Iona, at the island's northern end, as well as in the bays diversifying its western side, and in the plain known as the Machar, are, of course, of much more recent origin.[1]

[1] In September, 1951, a block of Iona marble of a delicate green colour, weighing three hundredweights, and hewn from the old quarry, not far from the rocky bay where St. Columba landed from his coracle, was presented by the Iona Abbey Trustees to the Church of Scotland congregation of St. Columba's at Pont Street, London, where it will appropriately form the base on one side of the main archway of the church's entrance. It is befitting, too, that the base on the other side should be of stone from the ruins of the ancient Cathedral of St. Regulus, at St. Andrews, bequeathed by the Office of Works.

St. Columba's, it may be remembered, was destroyed during an air raid on London in 1941. The foundation-stone of the new church on the same spot was laid by the Queen in July, 1950; and its restoration is expected to be complete by the end of 1952.

A graphic description of how the Iona marble was wrested from the island's disused quarry and transported to its jetty was contributed recently to *St. Columba's Church Magazine* by Mr. James R. Steele, the church's senior elder, and secretary of its building fund committee. A spell of fine weather and suitable sea conditions made possible the removal of the marble from the quarry on September 7th. Five skilled artificers from the Iona Community (about which I write at the end of this chapter) set out with Mr. Steele in a motor-boat on a calm and sunny afternoon, taking with them much simple tackle—logs, ropes, planks, wires, crowbars, saws, and other implements. It seemed just the day for a pleasant expedition; and everyone was in high spirits. A heavy swell at the south end of the island, however, hampered operations. Only with great skill was the boat brought sufficiently near to the rocks to enable the marble to be lowered into it, having already been moved across rocks and boulders and gaps into which it might well have slipped. One false step would have been fatal to the enterprise. It took everyone's skill, ingenuity, and patience to place the ponderous block securely and undamaged in the bow of the *Betty*. The task occupied several hours under a

The Machar, an arable tract situated on the west side of the island, is now a golf-course. Here a lovely turf, closely cropped by the islanders' livestock, provides the smoothest of greens: here the sand-dunes form natural bunkers. Golf is not pursued too seriously at Iona. The Machar supplies gentle recreation for those whose delight it is to wander leisurely after a ball over emerald velvet, in one of the most peaceful settings I know. Some may regard as sacrilegious, as profane, an attraction at Iona as modern as a golf-course. Yet, the royal and ancient game of golf, so indigenous to Scotland, is never likely to become anything more than a pleasant pastime there.

Iona also has marble outcroppings of great beauty, their calcareous parts streaked and mottled by serpentine of a yellowish-green colour. A small band of white tremolite intrudes between the Archæan or Lewisian gneiss and the Torridonian conglomerate. The island's marble was quarried at various times, though not too economically, from the considerable band occurring at its southern end. The quarry there was closed down during the first decade of the present century. Incidentally, the floor of the chancel in the rebuilt portion of the Cathedral of St. John the Divine, at Oban, is laid with Iona marble.[1]

Hillocks, ridges, and rocky knobs, running for the most part in the direction of the island's main axis, produce a topography of great variety, and, as the late Professor Jehu pointed out, supply in miniature several aspects of Highland mountain scenery. About its southern uplands lie those rocky protruberances which, in Fiona MacLeod's words, "wade in heather, and upon whose brows the sea-wind waves the yellow lichen".

Iona's northern, southern, and western shores are characterised by cliffs, rocky promontories, islets, and skerries. Its eastern shore is comparatively regular, as well as more sheltered. Innumerable islets and half-submerged reefs, lying at no distance offshore, do much to protect the island's coast from the full fury of the Atlantic swell.

Around Iona's coast the sea has hollowed out clefts and caves

grilling sun. Courage and determination, with a good seasoning of Scots humour, overcame every obstacle; and the adventurers must, indeed, have felt themselves handsomely repaid when, at last, they discharged their precious cargo at Iona's jetty. Its transference to London thereafter was a comparatively simple matter.

This block of the beautiful and delicate green marble of Iona is now in position at St. Columba's, Pont Street. I went to see it there the other day, since I live within a mile of it.

[1] A thoroughly competent sketch of the geology of Iona, written by one of my old professors, the late T. J. Jehu, and accompanied by an excellent geological map of the island, may be found in *Map of Iona*, published by Geo. Stewart and Co., Edinburgh, in 1928.

into which immense waves of the Atlantic dash violently during storms, and from which they recede with such suctional strength as often to bring down with them great rocks from the clefts, or from the roofs of the caves. Here and there about the island, several puffing-holes are thus being enlarged by this type of sea-erosion. On the west side a striking example is to be found in the famous Spouting Cave.

Iona's lovely White Sands are composed mainly of comminuted shells. They are the favourite haunt of artists who return to this island year after year. Nowhere does one find so remarkable a variety of bright colours as hereabouts—such emerald, such purple, such turquoise. At times the seas are coloured as if seen through a gigantic kaleidoscope. To those who do not know Iona, an artist's reproductions of its scenery, particularly of its sea-scapes, must at times appear fanciful. The colourings everywhere about the Isle, and especially toward its northern and north-eastern reaches, are indeed quite fantastic. The seas beyond the White Sands—those about Staffa and Little Colonsay and Ulva—are often the colour of the wild thyme, one of the commonest of Iona's wild flowers.

And how very white are the White Sands! Yet, they have historical associations with crimson, since that stretch of them known as the White Strand of the Monks is thought to have been the scene where the Danes, on their third invasion of Iona, slew its abbot and fifteen of its monks. The islanders say that a rock nearby derived its crimson colouring from its having been splashed with the monks' blood on that barbarous occasion, so long ago.

Here one might add that the monks' misfortunes at the hands of the Scandinavian rovers are commemorated not only in the name of the Martyrs' Bay, where the Danes slaughtered them in 806, but also in that of the old track leading up from this bay to the island's ancient place of burial, close by the Cathedral. To the Gaels this track, much of it no longer definable, is known traditionally as the *Sraid na Marbh*, the Street of the Dead. According to Pennant, it was, as recently as 1771, a broad, paved road leading up from the Martyrs' Bay, thence round the back of the Nunnery to the burial-ground. The remains of the illustrious dead of Scotland, ferried across the Sound from Fionaphort, were landed here. Hard by this spot is *An Ealadh*,[1] the sacred mound on which, tradition says, the mourners were wont to rest the bier before carrying it along the Street of the Dead to interment.

[1] A name the late W. J. Watson, Professor of Celtic at Edinburgh, believed to have been derived from *ailad*, an ancient Erse word for a grave or tomb.

Reverting for a moment to the matter of natural colour, one must not omit mention of the beautifully coloured stones found in Iona's southern and western bays and inlets, the most famous of which are the Iona Pebbles, a variety of serpentine ranging in colour from darkish green to light-greenish yellow. These stones occur in quantities in St. Columba's Bay, and are thought to be derived from serpentine nodules thrown up on the beach during storms from an under-sea extension of the island's marble formations. Half a century ago, the Iona children conducted a profitable business with summer tourists as they landed, holding out to them in the palms of their hands, or on plates or saucers, what they had gathered of these "Real Iona Stones". Many a gem of ocean, uncut, but beautifully rounded and polished by the rolling action of countless tides, left the island in this manner, to find its way eventually into some lovely piece of jewellery. I have a friend in Edinburgh who possesses a fine collection of Iona stones, the fruits of holidays diligently spent there. Exquisitely fashioned and smoothed in the watery caverns of their origin, they resemble the most precious of jewels. Their colours are as vivid and as varied as are their shapes and sizes—greens and yellows, purples and heliotropes, reds and pinks. When she touches them, as she does from time to time with reverence, they transport her in imagination, not merely to the little bays and gullies where she found them, but also to those parts of Iona so richly endowed with wild flowers—perhaps, to that marshy and limited part of the island's interior from which no sea is visible, but where, in June, orchids are plentiful—royal-purple ones, but most of them a pale heliotrope, and a few of them pure white— whiter even than the bog-cotton before the showers begin to smutch it. She sees in her precious pebbles the heather and the harebells, the sweet-scented thyme and the pungent bog-myrtle, the sea- pinks, the flowering stonecrop filling the crevices of the rocks beyond the Machar, near St. Columba's Bay. She hears in them the crooning tide of the Hebrides, and the drone of amber bees in Iona's creamy clover.

.   .   .   .

It is ironical that, in a region too well favoured in the matter of rainfall, one of Iona's chief problems should be the scarcity of fresh water for domestic purposes. The island's only piece of inland water is Loch Staonaig, a shallow tarn lying toward the south, in a hollow among the ancient gneisses. During a dry summer this little loch, unsheltered from the sun, becomes the merest marsh. No trees afford it shade. Indeed, Iona is as devoid of trees as it is of peat. Its very few trees are to be found on the east side, near the manse. In the absence of peat, the islanders' fuel consists of the coal brought to them twice a year by a Clyde puffer. This they supplement with driftwood washed up on their shores.

Though wanting in fresh-water lochs and ponds, the island has several springs. These supply its farms, crofts, and village with a modicum of excellent water throughout the year, but not in quantity sufficient to allow of any extension of premises likely to create an additional demand. Prolonged drought during the summer of 1951 caused some anxiety on the island, for its wells threatened to run dry. This I saw for myself. What the island requires is a reservoir.

In normal years Iona receives a rainfall more than adequate. Thus the harvesting of its crops, which consist mainly of oats, barley, and hay, together with some acres of roots for winter feed, is often precarious. Yet, the island's rainfall must be small when compared with that of Mull, so close at hand. I have watched rain-storms travel in from the Atlantic to pass eastwards over Iona, without shedding a drop until the lofty mountains of Mull have brought them down in deluging precipitancy. Wind can be as great a nuisance to husbandry in these parts as heavy and persistent rain. At harvest-time it often carries the islanders' sheaves and stooks and crescents of mown hay headlong into the sea.

.   .   .   .

In olden times Iona was famed for its wells. To these the natives resorted for a variety of reasons, as did also the seafarers seeking wind. Many of the wells of antiquity, such as St. Oran's, cannot now be located. The Well of the East Wind, the Well of the West Wind, and that of the South have been lost sight of, though not that of the North Wind, to which the mariners of old brought their votive offerings. Situated near St. Columba's Bay is a well known to those who fill at it the picnic kettle, to be boiled over a kindling of driftwood usually so plentiful hereabouts.

On the north side of Dun I, and half hidden at the foot of an overhanging rock not far from the summit, is *Tobar an h-Aoise*, the Well of Age, a small, triangular pool sometimes referred to as the Well of Youth. Thither came wishers in olden days, just before sunrise, " to touch the healing water the moment the first sun-ray quickens it ", thereafter to throw, over the shoulder and into it, a coin, preferably of silver. For countless generations, pilgrims to this Wishing Pool sought thus to recover at least a part of their lost youth.

. . . .

Iona is essentially a pastoral Isle—an Isle of small farms and little crofts. Its resident population during the winter months is about 120. In the summertime, apart from strangers holidaying there, it is about 150. In 1814, according to Sir Walter Scott, it was over 400. In 1881 it was 243. The census of 1931 showed a decline to 141. The young people leave their lovely Isle to seek employment elsewhere.

During the holiday season the population is considerably augmented by those who have come to Iona for many years, and whose parents, and even grandparents, holidayed there before them. A vacant bed is often scarcer than gold on Iona.

One is never able to resist the attraction of this Isle, never able to free oneself from its spell. Its open pastures are like emerald velvet; and the sheep-tracks intersecting them allure one from all sense of time and urgency. Sheep form an important part of the island's economy; and few of its ex-seafaring inhabitants are slow to augment their diet by fishing in the Sound, or even farther a-sea—by the Torran Rocks, for instance, or out toward Staffa or the Treshnish Isles.

One may ridicule the belief in faeries, but not when on Iona—just in case one's disregard for the Wee Folk should precipitate something untoward when in the vicinity of the knoll known as the *Sithean Mor,* or Great Faery-Mound. In walking westward across the island to the Machar, one passes by the farm called Shian before reaching this abode of theirs, where the road peters out. It is one of the many knolls in Iona reputed to belong to the Kingdom of Faerie; and I have spoken with natives who solemnly testify that from time to time they have heard the strains of faery music issuing from it.

That the *Sithean Mor* has another significance is shown by its also being known as *Cnoc na Aingeal,* the Angels' Hillock. It was here, Adamnan tells us, that an inquisitive monk, kneeling in prayer on an adjacent hillock, observed Columba in communion with a heavenly host. When the former lifted his eyes to heaven, " suddenly a marvellous thing appeared . . . for Holy Angels, citizens of the Celestial Country, clad in white garments, came flying to him with wonderful speed, and stood round the holy man as he prayed; and after some conversation with the blessed man, that heavenly band . . . sped swiftly back to the high heavens ".

Strange it must seem that, in later centuries, the Angels' Hillock should have been the venue of a pagan cavalcade at the Feast of St. Michael! The natives careering round it on horseback at the time of Pennant's visit in 1771 neither feared the faeries, nor respected the angels.

Iona's ecclesiological monuments, some of them in ruins, many of them restored or in course of restoration, are among the mediæval glories of Scotland. They include the Cathedral or Abbey Church, the monastic buildings associated therewith, the Nunnery, St. Oran's Chapel, several fine stone crosses, and the ancient burying-place known as the Reilig Odhrain, where the Kings and the Chiefs lie. With the exception of the Nunnery, the flowery ruins of which stand about a quarter of a mile to the south, nearer the island's village, they are to be found in close proximity to the Abbey, occupying a site that knew those earlier structures destroyed by the northern invaders, and rebuilt more than once.

The present Abbey, dedicated to the Virgin Mary, stands on the site of that which Reginald, Lord of the Isles, built about 1203 for the Benedictines. Reginald also founded, " in honour of God and St. Columkill "—God and Columba—the Benedictine Nunnery, placing in charge of it, as its first prioress, his sister, Beatrice. The Old Celtic Church was now in the final stages of decay. By the end of the twelfth century, the Roman order of things had displaced it everywhere except at Iona. There, owing to the island's remoteness, and to the steadfastness of the last of the Columban monks, vestiges of it still survived. With Reginald's establishing the Benedictines at Iona, such of the Columbans as remained were either expelled by the new order, or absorbed in it. Tradition says that, at the time of their final dispersal, many of their valuable manuscripts, vying in beauty with the priceless *Book of Kells*, were also scattered, some of them going to the Scots Colleges at Rome and at Douai, others to the Scots monastery at Ratisbon. Whether there is any foundation in fact for this tradition, one cannot say. One might add, however, that there also exists in the Western Highlands the somewhat similar tradition that the monks' library was secretly transferred to one of the remote Treshnish Isles, so as to prevent its falling into alien and desecrating hands.

Iona under Benedictine Rule does not appear to have been very inspiring. After 1247 its abbots acknowledged as their superior the Bishop of Dunkeld, even though the island, like the rest of the Hebrides, was still under the dominance of Norway, and indeed remained so until the defeat of Haco's galleys off Largs, sixteen years later. With the creation of a new Bishopric of the Isles about 1430, the Bishop came to reside at Iona, although the Abbey appears to have continued under the jurisdiction of Dunkeld until 1507, the year in which it was raised to the dignity of a Cathedral. This dignity it enjoyed for but a few decades, since the Reformation was now to deprive it of its ancient glory. By the Order of the Convention of the Estates of 1561, the Abbey and the monastery pertaining thereto were dismantled. At that time it was said that the island possessed over three hundred memorial crosses, only three of which would seem to survive. "So came the years of desolation prophesied by Columba," writes a friend of mine in a work he prepared for the Iona Community.[1] Was this the decline foreseen by Columba himself?

> *In Iona of my heart, Iona of my love,*
> *Instead of monks' voices shall be the lowing of cattle.*

Such ruins as we see to-day at Iona are mediæval. In 1899 they were gifted to the Iona Trustees, on behalf of the Church of Scotland, by George, 8th Duke of Argyll. Almost two centuries previously, the island, hitherto a possession of the warlike Mac-Leans, passed into the hands of the wilier Campbells. It remains the property of their descendant, the present Duke of Argyll. Between 1902 and 1910 the Trustees restored the Abbey, which long had lain a ruin. In 1905 the greater part of the nave was rebuilt, if not actually reconstructed.

The Abbey is Norman in architecture, cruciform in plan. From east to west it measures more than 148 feet, from north to south 70 feet. It consists, in the main, of a nave, south choir aisle, north and south transepts, crossing and tower, sacristy, and cloisters. Except for two arches at the north-west corner, erected from fragments by the Office of Works in 1923, the cloister arcades, originally occurring to the north of the nave, have disappeared. To the east of the cloisters were the chapter house and dormitories. The refectory stood at the north end of them. Apart from the east wall of the north transept, which appears to be late Norman, the oldest portions of the building date from the late fifteenth and early sixteenth centuries. The massive square tower is 70 feet high. Formerly it was capped with a gable roof containing a dovecot. On the abacus of the south-east capital at the tower crossing there occurs, in Lombardic characters, the inscription, *Donaldus O'Brolchan Fecit Hoc Opus.* The south belfry

---

[1] *Behold Iona! A Guide and Souvenir,* edited by John Morrison, and published in 1946 for the Iona Community.

window is a mediæval clock face. The bell of twenty-two hundred weights was presented in 1931. In 1940 the clock's hands were replaced. The sacristy is on the north side of the choir, the north wall of which exhibits traces of a crypt. Piscina and Gothic sedilia may be seen at the south wall, exquisitely fashioned, though somewhat weathered.

On either side of the choir is the recumbent effigy of an abbot—that of John MacKinnon, on the north, that of Kenneth Mac-Kenzie, on the south. The former, so excellently preserved, is dated 1500. MacKinnon became Abbot of Iona about 1490.

Space will hardly allow of our giving further details of the Abbey and of the monastic buildings adjacent thereto. These may be found in many of the works dealing with Iona published in recent years; and in this connection one must not overlook the substantial restoration now being carried out under the auspices of the Iona Community, to whose activities reference will be made later. However, some further mention ought to be accorded the Nunnery, the ruins of which are grouped round a quadrangle containing cloister garth, convent church, chapter house, and refectory. In St. Roman's Chapel, which adjoins the Nunnery, is the effigy, in low relief, of Anna, its last prioress. It bears the date, 1543.

In 1923, what remains of the Nunnery was beautifully preserved, in memory of Robina Jarvie Spencer, by her children, who also laid out so exquisitely, in the cloister garth, the rock garden which, to-day, is perhaps the most colourful scene in Iona.

The villagers bestow great esteem upon the Nunnery. They voluntarily tend its garden; and from time to time you may find them there with steps and ladders, diligently dislodging from its ancient crannied walls valerian and other plants growing wild and so luxuriantly as to jeopardise their preservation. One would scarcely believe it possible that such enormous clusters of valerian, crimson and white, could derive from the crannies of the Nunnery walls sufficient sustenance.

A little to the south-west of the Cathedral is situated that ancient, historic, and greatly revered enclosure known as the Reilig Odhrain, a name believed to signify the burying-place of Oran. This spot is not inaptly referred to at times as the Westminster Abbey of Scotland. It is thought that, even before Columba's arrival at Iona, it may have received royal remains. While the Columban Church was at the height of its power and influence, there were committed to earth at the Reilig Odhrain many kings, princes, chiefs, and ecclesiastical dignitaries. For more than a thousand years, people valorous, and famous in other

ways, have found here a last resting-place, among them Scottish
and Irish kings, and even Norwegian kings. And what better
evidence could one have of this than the following passage from
Dean Monro's account of these parts as they were when, in 1549,
he travelled through them in his capacity as High Dean of the
Isles?

"Within this ile," wrote the Dean about Iona, "ther is a
monastery of mounckes, and ane uther of nuns, with a paroche
kirke, and sundrie uther chapells, dotat [donated] of auld by
the kings of Scotland, and be Clandonald of the iyles. . . .
Within this ile of Colmkill, ther is ane sanctuary also, or kirkzaird, callit in Erische Religoran, quhilk is ane very fair
kirkzaird, and weill biggit [built] about with staine and lyme.
Into this sanctuary ther is three tombes of staine, formit like
little chapels, with ane braid gray marble or quhin staine in
the gavill of ilk ane of the tombes. In the staine of the ane
tombe ther is wretten in Latin letters, *Tumulus Regum
Scotiae*, that is, The Tombe ore grave of the Scotts Kinges.
Within this tombe, according to our Scotts and Erische
cronikels, ther layes fortey-eight crouned Scotts kings, through
the quhilk this ile hes been richlie dotat be the Scotts kinges,
as we have said. The tombe on the south syde forsaid hes this
inscriptioun, *Tumulus Regum Hyberniae*, that is, The tombe
of the Irland kinges; for we have in our auld Erische
cronickells, that ther wes foure Irland kinges eirded [buried]
in the said tombe. Upon the north syde of our Scotts tombe, the
inscriptione beares, *Tumulus Regum Norwegiae*, that is, The
tombe of the kings of Norroway; in the quhilk tombe, as we
find in our ancient Erishe cronickells, ther layes eight kings of
Norroway, and als we find, in our Erishe cronickells, that Coelus
king of Norroway commandit his nobils to take his bodey and
burey it in Colmkill, if it chancit him to die in the iles; bot he
wes so discomfitit, that ther remained not so maney of his armey
as wald burey him ther. . . . Within this sanctuary also lyes the
maist pairt of the Lords of the iles, with thair lineage . . .
with sundry uthers inhabitants of the hail iles, because this
sancturey wes wont to be the sepulture of the best men of all the
iles, and als of our kings, as we have said; becaus it was the
maist honourable and ancient place that was in Scotland in
thair dayes, as we reid."

In the Reilig Odhrain, in 860, was buried my ancestor, Kenneth
MacAlpin, first King of a united Scotland. His interment here

was regarded as a precedent which was followed for at least two centuries. Malcolm Canmore's burial at Dunfermline was the first break in it. Incidentally, the death of Malcolm's son, Duncan, provided Shakespeare with the opportunity for introducing into *Macbeth* our beloved Reilig Odhrain:

> ROSSE: *Where is Duncan's body?*
> MACDUFF: *Carried to Columskill,*
>   *The sacred storehouse of his predecessors,*
>   *And guardian of their bones.*

The tombs of the Reilig Odhrain were in a ruinous state, their inscriptions gone, when Pennant saw them in 1772. In 1868 the Iona Club, anxious for the preservation of the ancient stones defining them, gathered the majority of them within the low railing now surrounding them, laying them out in two parallel lines no distance apart. That to the west is known as the Ridge of the Kings: that to the east as the Ridge of the Chiefs. The former comprises twenty-one stones, most of which are unidentifiable. One of them is certainly that of Reginald, the Lord of the Isles who, as we have seen, founded at Iona the Benedictine Monastery and Nunnery. The latter Ridge consists of nineteen stones, fewer than half of which can be named. One commemorates a MacLeod of Lewis who died about 1532. Another, representing a fourteenth-century MacLean of Duart, is called The Rider because it depicts a knight on horseback charging with a spear in the thrust position. The stone of that notoriously wellknown member of the Clan MacLean, Allan of the Straw, is recognisable. This noted plunderer received his name from the partiality he had for setting on fire the thatch of his victims' homes. We can recognise, too, in the Ridge of the Chiefs, a MacLean of Coll, and two MacLaines of Lochbuie; while a stone with four panels is said to commemorate four Iona priors of the fifteenth century.

One of the Lochbuie MacLaines lying there is the chief known as Ewen of the Little Head, who was killed in a skirmish in 1538. The belief that the ghost of Ewen appears at Lochbuie, and indeed elsewhere also, when a Lochbuie MacLaine is about to die, is firmly believed in the Western Highlands, especially in Mull; and natives of Iona have declared that they have seen Ewen charging past them on a black steed, carrying under his arm his little head.

The nineteenth stone, numbered from left to right, is that of Dr. John Beaton, or Bethune, a member of the Skye family which

275

gave to the Lords of the Isles their hereditary physicians. John died in 1657.

A rough block of red granite lying to the east of the Ridge of the Kings, and bearing an incised cross, is said to denote the tomb of a French king whose name has been forgotten.

A stone erected by the United States Government toward the west of the Reilig Odhrain marks the grave of sixteen persons who lost their lives when, on New Year's Eve, 1865, the American ship, *Guy Mannering*, sank off the west coast of Iona.

In the Reilig Odhrain, among the kings and the chiefs and the illustrious of the Isles, there was interred in 1930 one whose name I must mention, for I knew her well, and her art has done much to sweeten my existence, to beautify my days. I refer to Marjory Kennedy-Fraser—*Marsaili nan Oran*, Marjory of the Songs—who died in her sixty-fourth year. A recumbent tomb-stone of grey granite marks her resting-place in the Reilig Odhrain. Round its edges is the Gaelic proverb:

> *Thig crioch air an t-saoghail;*
> *Ach mairidh gaol 'us ceol.*

> End will come on the earth;
> But love and music will abide.

It would certainly be no less fitting that, in course of time, Kenneth MacLeod, her collaborator in *The Songs of the Hebrides*, a man so generous—so distinguished—in his contribution to Celtic Scotland, should also lie here, among the illustrious dead.

Interred in the Reilig Odhrain in 1942 were Alexander Ritchie and his wife. The former died at Iona at the age of 84, a few days after his wife. Both of them were undisputed authorities on Celtic Art. In 1900 Ritchie, who, in his earlier days, had been a ship's engineer, and latterly acted as guide at the Abbey, began to make the jewellery which brought fame both to himself and to his wife, an artistic and accomplished woman who helped him greatly with his Celtic designs. To their reproductions of Celtic Art they applied themselves strictly and diligently for over forty years—indeed, up to the time of their death in 1942.

By 1913 their work was so much in demand that they sought, through newspaper advertisement, the assistance of a craftsman in metal. This brought them into touch with Fred J. Braddon, who, for the next twenty years, and at his own studio in Barn-staple, did the repoussé, chasing, and the setting of the stones,

ABOVE: *The Anchorage, Inch Kenneth*
BELOW: *The house on Inch Kenneth (1951)*

mostly in silver, following meticulously the Ritchies' patterns. Braddon was already established by this time, not only as a designer and skilled worker in metal, but also as an instructor, at various art schools, in the making of jewellery. He and the Ritchies produced between them the most beautiful crosses, brooches, pendants, paper knives, suède communion bags with silver crosses on the sides, rosaries, penannulars, and so on—for the most part in silver oxidised. Throughout their many happy years of coöperation, the reproductions of St. Martin's Cross were particularly popular. The bases of these were green Connemara.

"I have greatly missed this lovely Celtic Work," Braddon writes me. "But I am now getting old. Yet, the fascination of the work remains."

It must be some consolation to him in his old age (he is now 76) that jewellery he and the Ritchies produced is now being worn by people who made the pilgrimage to Iona from every corner of the globe.

One cannot pass from the Reilig Odhrain without making some brief reference to the small, hypaethral building within it, known as St. Oran's Chapel, believed to be the oldest of Iona's mediæval remains. It is roughly 29 feet by 15, and is thought to be "the smaller church of Columcille" which the saintly Margaret, Malcolm Canmore's queen, restored. If this be so, the original St. Oran's Chapel must be very old indeed, since Malcolm and Margaret visited Iona as long ago as 1072. Its Norman doorway, so beautifully carved, is probably of a date more recent than are the chapel walls, within and against which now rest several carved stones placed there for better preservation.

Older than St. Oran's Chapel by at least a century are some of Iona's magnificent stone crosses. Not far from the Abbey's west door stands St. Martin's Cross, a splendid example of tenth-century craftsmanship. A little to the north of it is all that survives of St. Matthew's Cross—part of the shaft, bearing a carved representation of Adam and Eve in the Garden. A little farther to the north, just beyond the old, walled well, stands St. John's Cross, another fine piece of tenth-century work, restored by Professor MacAlister in 1926 from fragments.

Then, on an elevated pedestal by the wayside, as one approaches the Abbey from the village, is MacLean's Cross, a thin slab of schist ten feet in height, the carvings on the west side of which depict the Crucified Christ in a long robe, with *fleurs-de-lis* above, and a chalice on one side, the carvings on the east being an ornamental pattern, below which are two animals and a mounted knight with lance and helmet. This cross is said to date from

Ruins of ancient Chapel on Inch Kenneth, with Gribun, Isle of Mull, in the background

about 1500, and to have received its name from one of the Mac-Leans of Duart who owned Iona at the time—perhaps, from the Rider, the chief depicted on horseback among the carved stones in the Reilig Odhrain, to whom we have already referred.

Iona has been much in the public eye during recent years on account of the aspirations and activities of the Iona Community, a Church of Scotland Brotherhood composed both of ministers and of laymen, married and single, who, while continuing in their chosen professions, are seeking the deeper meaning of Christian Community for the modern problems of the twentieth century. For three months each summer, they go to Iona, birth-place of Scottish Christianity, there to engage in a coöperative programme to re-build the ruined monastery. Believing that the peace of the world can be achieved through new efforts at coöperation, their work together is intended as a 'laboratory of living'. For the other nine months of the year they work at their jobs on the mainland—in industrial centres and other parishes, seeking to apply their Iona principles to actual modern situations, and living by an agreed daily discipline of devotion, economic witness, and planning of work.

The Community had its origin in 1938 in the Rev. Dr. George MacLeod's eight years' experience of one of the worst hit areas in one of the worst hit cities in Britain during 'The Hungry Thirties' of our own century. The city was Glasgow: the district was Govan. The experience revealed, among other things, the urgent and imperative necessity for the Ministry of the Church to find new ways to meet the clamant needs of men, if ever it was to re-establish that active relevance to the whole of life which formerly commanded the allegiance of their fathers. To preach of the Bread of Life to men without being actively concerned with the satisfaction of their physical needs, the Community holds, is a betrayal not only of them and of the Church, but of its Head.

It is the Community's belief that the primary problem before mankind in coming years is how to plan society, and at the same time preserve the rights of the individual. Its members claim that the tremendous truth emerges again that Christianity in its fulness alone can be relied on to conserve the individual as being of any moment at all.

The work of restoration at Iona proceeds apace. Idealists, who are skilled craftsmen or merely voluntary helpers, are re-building the ancient foundation with the generous assistance of well-wishers the world over. In 1947 the Norwegians, remembering the depredations their fathers had committed here in ancient times, sent across the North Sea to Iona a handsome gift of timber for the roofing of the Refectory, the restoration of which has just been completed. In the autumn of 1950, the builders laboured by moonlight to unload a cargo of New Zealand timber earmarked for the Dormitory. That same year, some two thousand of the Community's friends in the United States and in Canada provided the money for the restoration of the Cloisters, the timber necessary for which is expected to come from Canada. And so the Iona Community goes from strength to strength.

On August 11th, 1950, while members of the Community were digging a trench for a drain 20 feet south of the reredorter wall of the Old Abbey, they discovered, at about 21 inches below the present ground level, roughly 350 Anglo-Saxon silver pennies ranging from Athelstan's reign (925-939) to the early part of the reign of Ethelred the Unready (979-1016). This would seem to indicate their having been buried about the year A.D. 1000. Over 200 of them belong to Edgar's time (959-975), but only 6 to Ethelred's. Three are from Normandy; and 13 are York Viking coins. They are all in good preservation, and, except for a few duplicates, are now in the National Museum of Antiquities of Scotland, having been claimed by the Crown, and presented by the King's & Lord Treasurer's Remembrancer.

Along with the coins were a small, silver and gold strap ornament, diamond-shaped, with volutes at the corners, set with a green glass bead; part of a silver bracelet of Viking origin; and a fragment of gold wire.

Details of the coins will be given in a paper to be contributed shortly to the *Numismatic Chronicle* by R. B. K. Stevenson, keeper of the museum aforenamed. A further paper on them will appear in due course in the scholarly *Proceedings of the Society of Antiquaries of Scotland*.

Of the Iona Community's purpose and activities I know a certain amount through personal contact with it, having been its guest at Iona for a few days each summer during the past year or two. And this brings me to an amusing note upon which one might suitably conclude this chapter.

Each morning at eight, there is held in the Abbey a service, which many of the islanders now attend. The morning after my arrival at Iona in 1950, had not Dr. George MacLeod, the Community's leader, whom I have known intimately for the greater part of my life, selected, as the scriptural passage to be read by himself, Moffat's translation of the opening verses of the 14th chapter of Romans? I, the only vegetarian on the island, sat through this unpremeditated rebuke with composure, although one or two of the students then under George's guidance and instruction, recalling a discussion on vegetarianism we had had the previous evening, could not resist the urge to divert their gaze as unostentatiously as possible in my direction to see how I was reacting to these words: "Welcome a man of weak faith, but not to pass judgment upon his scruples. While one man has enough confidence to eat any food, *the man of weak faith eats only vegetables.*"

Even George saw the funny side of this, and assured me immediately afterwards of what I was already aware, namely, that the choice of this particular passage was quite accidental, that it had been made before he expected me at Iona, and that the coincidence was entirely free from anything which might have been regarded as malice aforethought.

Withal, it would seem as though the second part of Columba's prophecy, so cherished by lovers of this Isle, may be fulfilled:

> In Iona of my heart, Iona of my love,
> Instead of monks' voices shall be the lowing of cattle;
> *But, ere the world shall come to an end,*
> *Iona shall be as it was.*

CHAPTER XX

STAFFA

S I X miles north by east of Iona, and but a mile more to the west of the nearest point of Mull, lies Staffa, one of the most remarkable of all the isles of Britain. To the north-east of it, beyond Little Colonsay, and at a distance of four miles, is Ulva, the basaltic colannades of which are not much inferior to those which, together with Fingal's Cave, have bestowed upon Staffa a renown world-wide.

Staffa, with an area of seventy-one acres, is only a seventieth the size of Ulva. Its smallness renders all the more remarkable its phenomena. It is about three-quarters of a mile long, and a quarter broad. Its highest point, located at its southern end, is 135 feet above mean-tide mark. Its surface slopes gradually downwards to its northern extremity. So much for the more superficial of its dimensions.

The island is treeless, of course; and it supports nothing in the nature of a shrub but the few stunted bramble-bushes clinging precariously to life at a sheltered spot on the east side. A rich pasture, however, covers its entire surface, which is an uneven plateau. On this pasture graze sheep belonging to the owner. In the late springtime much of it is decked with primroses which, as the year advances, gradually give way to a profusion of daisies and buttercups.

The island's fauna is similar to that of its neighbours. All the commoner seabirds nest either upon its grassy surface, or on the ledges and crannies of its cliffs.

As the coast-line is composed almost entirely of shoreless cliffs, there are few spots, other than at the south-east end of the island, at which a landing is possible.

Close to the coast, and at a short distance to the south of the ruins of some ancient habitations, lies the island's only serviceable well—a point to be noted by anyone likely to land with the object of remaining ashore, maybe under canvas, for any length of time. Having been told of this well by a precise geological friend, who had surveyed the island, and having memorised its position, I found it soothing and satiating one day I remained long on Staffa, alone, with my camera, in hot sunshine, waiting for MacBrayne's steamer to transport me, in due course, to Iona. I had been afforded the solitude necessary for the fullest appreciation of Staffa's wonders; and it was reassuring to know that, in the event of the steamer's not arriving for a day or two, I could have survived on the water of this well and the few sandwiches I had in the rucksack containing my films and filters.

According to West Highland legend, Staffa originated with a mighty giant named Torquil MacLeod, who, when passing home from the Giant's Causeway to one of the Small Isles—to Eigg, it might have been—carrying in a sack much of the basalt coast of Antrim, felt his load rather ponderous as he waded across the sea. When off Iona, the sack began to give way; and, by the time he got a few miles farther north, it burst. Out of it and into the sea fell those massive columns, where they still lie, the topmost parts of them now forming the Isle of Staffa.

Geologists regard Staffa as a detached fragment of the great volcanic rocks found so extensively in Mull, the island of which, as in the case of Ulva, it may once have formed a part, and where there are some fine specimens of basaltic columnar formations. Indeed, petrologists believe Staffa's basalts to be identical with those of Mull, of Skye, of Antrim, and even of Iceland. All are said to have originated during the middle of the Cainozoic Age, which would mean that the dark, fine-grained basalt of Staffa— well, how old are they? A matter of between 35,000,000 and 40,000,000 years! (You will notice the readiness with which one allows for a margin of error amounting to a mere 5,000,000 years!) Their reputed age, in terms of geology, represents no time at all; and, even if we accept the greater figure of 40,000,000, Staffa's cliffs and caves are a good deal younger than our pre-Cambrian rocks—far younger, for instance, than the rocks of Iona, only six miles away.

What is now Staffa came into existence when Mull was one gigantic volcano, or at any rate the centre of colossal volcanic activity, discharging with every eruption, from a height of perhaps 12,000 feet, mighty floods of lava. With the disappearance, through subsidence and various types of epigene denudation, of large portions of the great basaltic plateau thus created, Staffa became the island it is to-day.

That Staffa has experienced mighty movements *since* the formation of its basalt colonnades is shown by such of them as are
curved, bent, or broken at numerous angles, and by portions of
them variously tilted.

The world must be full of such geological structures as one sees
in those outstanding examples at Staffa and at the Giant's Causeway, in Antrim. Yet, they remain invisible, buried away in the
earth's dark interior. These magnificent exposures in the Inner
Hebrides and in Northern Ireland may be attributable to aeons of
marine action which has worn away, and carried elsewhere, the
loose and softer rocks that otherwise would have obscured
them.

. . . .

Staffa's coast is penetrated by several caves, at least four of
which are worthy of note.

By the usual landing-place, and at a point comparatively sheltered from winds and tides, is the Clamshell, or Scallop, Cave,
so called because the basalt columns forming it have been bent
during the earth's building to resemble such a shell. Viewed
from certain angles, these columns appear even more like the grey
lichened ribs of a Viking galley long since cast upon the shore.
This formation well deserved that adjective so overworked
nowadays—amazing! Its quite extraordinary shape renders impossible any exact dimensional measurements. Donald B. Mac-
Culloch, in his useful little book on Staffa,[1] gives its approximate
inward length as 130 feet, its height as 18, and its breadth as
16 to 18. Both the cave and the landing-place, nearby, derive
considerable protection against the action of denuding seas from
the islet known to the Gaels as *Am Buachaille*—The Herdsman—
which high tide divides in two. This islet, separated by a channel
no more than 14 feet wide, consists entirely of fluted rocks set at
every angle. Though attaining a height of but 30 feet above mean
water, it is indeed spectacular, even when viewed at sea-level.
Seen from the adjacent cliff-tops, its appearance is fantastic. Much
of it resembles driftwood in the form of closely packed logs cast
up on one another by tempestuous seas driven against these rocks
by the prevailing sou'-westers.

Continuing sunwise round the island from the customary land-

[1] *The Island of Staffa.* (The Moray Press, Edinburgh, 1951.) The original
edition, published in 1927, was the outcome of a fortnight the author spent
there in June, 1922, along with his father and a certain Dan Cameron. The
three of them were put ashore by Messrs MacBrayne in order to install equipment for the safety of the tourists disembarking during the summer and
autumn months from the Mull and Iona steamer.

ing-place, one arrives almost immediately at the Causeway where, on every hand, columns of all shapes and sizes are to be found. The Causeway itself consists of the upper ends of innumerable columns, the tops of which have been wearing away for aeons. The ends we see are either concave or convex. Few, if indeed any, are completely flat. Most of the columns hereabouts are pentagonal or hexagonal, varying in diameter from 2 feet to $2\frac{1}{2}$ feet. Nonagonal examples are by no means rare.

Soon we come to that formation flanking the Causeway, and known, for a reason immediately apparent, as the Bending Columns. Here the cliffs' lower parts are regularly curved, suggesting that, as the material of which they are composed came pouring down in a molten state, it was suddenly arrested and hardened by rapid cooling.

But half a stone's-throw from the Bending Columns is Fingal's Cave, the caverns beyond the entrance to which can be reached only by boat, since the island's cliffs now tend to rise perpendicularly from the sea.

Fingal's dimensions are considerable. Its innermost reach is 230 feet from the entrance, where its breadth is 50 feet. Its height from mean water is 65 feet, above which rises a layer of cliff to a depth of 30 feet. This means that, from sea to skyline, one has nearly a hundred feet of architectural magnitude and magnificence.

People come from all parts of the earth to see Fingal's Cave; and experienced travellers declare that nowhere else in the world is there anything of its kind quite as splendid. Loftier cliffs and larger caves there are in plenty, of course; but none of these occurs in a setting so solemn, so awesome, so inspiring as Fingal's Cave. Come this way on a day of sun and flying cloud, of wind and dashing wave, when the cavern is sending forth such sea-music as inspired Mendelssohn to compose one of the most faithful descriptions in music extant, and you will never forget it as long as you live—nor thereafter. Here, within the compass of but a few hundred yards, is one of the most magnificent scenes in that part of Creation to which we have physical access.

When the seas come a-crashing at the entrance to Fingal's Cave before a strong sou'-westerly, all the world would seem to be in turmoil. Their reverberations can be heard many miles off; and one's only regret is that, when the cave is the centre of such dashing splendour, a landing on Staffa is impossible. In such conditions the cave's entrance, white with breaking wave and fawny-brown with effervescing spume, like the froth on *café au lait*, must needs be seen from afar, since the winds bringing sea-music to

Staffa's echoing caverns prevent even the powerful and responsive *King George V* from venturing too close inshore.

The commotion of mighty waters at Fingal's Cave may be heard on a ship sailing at a considerable distance. The volume of air driven into the interior by the impact of the water, wrote Sir Archibald Geikie, is at times under the pressure of several tons to the square inch of surface. When, with the wave's recession, the pressure is suddenly relaxed, " the imprisoned air at once rushes out, and in favourable chinks and passages gives rise to musical sounds as when a trumpet is blown ". How appropriate is this trumpeting when one gazes at those columns from which it issues, as from the pipes of some mighty organ! " I have seen the temple not made by hands," wrote Sir Robert Peel of his visit to Fingal's Cave in 1837, " and have felt the majestic swell of the ocean, the pulsation of the great Atlantic beating in its innermost sanctuary, and swelling a note of praise nobler far than ever pealed from human organ."

Fingal, by the way, left, in Staffa, his name on more than on this mighty cave. In the cliffs facing the south end of The Herdsman, a niche resembling a gigantic chair, such as a giant's ample proportions might find necessary, goes by the name of Fingal's Wishing Chair. The Gaels of old held that a wish thrice repeated by one seated there was instantly conceded.

. . . .

Extending westward from Fingal's Cave, and rising almost from sea-level, is that wonderful frontage of cliff usually known as the Colonnade, and often as the Great Face. Here the columns stand in dense formation, and nigh vertically. At a point roughly midway between Fingal's Cave and the Boat Cave (the next in importance as we move sunwise along the coast) the tallest components of the Colonnade reach a height of 112 feet above high water.

From the sea the Colonnade looks like an enormous array of lithe, blackened pit-props densely inserted to uphold, at the island's south-western corner, an immense, amorphous superstructure.

The Boat Cave's entrance occurs at sea-level, and is accessible only by boat, which explains its name. The distance from mouth to innermost wall is 150 feet. Its roof hangs 14 feet above high water. With a breadth of 12 feet at its entrance, it affords tolerably safe passage for a rowing-boat on a calm day, and in the absence of a swell. Having entered, however, one dare not tarry any length of time, since, even at low water, and on the calmest of days, the surge may come rolling in with disastrous result, swamping one's craft, or dashing it against the cave's walls, if not actually against its roof.

.   .   .   .

Almost as large as Fingal's Cave is MacKinnon's, the cliffs' ledges about which are the resort of countless seabirds. It recedes to a depth of 224 feet—just six feet less than does Fingal's. It has a height of 50 feet, and a breadth of 48. Doubtless, it received its name from John MacKinnon, who was Abbot of Iona at the close of the fifteenth century. Herein, according to tradition, the Abbot sought refuge at a time of schism. However, this retreat offered him sanctuary so inhospitable that he soon embarked for Mull, landing at Gribun, and finding there a cave more to his liking. This latter cave, no doubt, is that which Boswell mentions in a footnote to his *Tour of the Hebrides with Samuel Johnson, LL.D* as having got its name from a gentleman named MacKinnon, who entered it for purposes of exploration, but who never emerged!

"After noting the basaltic columns at its entrance," writes Donald B. MacCulloch of MacKinnon's Cave, "and the remarkable hooded formation over same, the most striking feature is the flatness of the roof, which, although slightly inclined from the horizontal, presents a surface as flat as that of many a dwelling-house, and slight markings might easily be taken to represent the impressions made by the plasterer's trowel. The walls glistening with dripping moisture complete a really wonderful sight."

.   .   .   .

Northward, at no great distance from MacKinnon's Cave, is the Cormorants', or Scarts', Cave, so called because of the preference of this species for nesting in and about it, the latter name being derived from *sgarbh*, the Gaelic for a cormorant. The cave is 100 feet in length, 18 in breadth, and 25 in height at mean water. A dark, subterranean corridor, 2 feet wide and 30 feet in length, branching off at right angles from its interior, leads into MacKinnon's Cave. Except that the corridor is apt to be slippery, it is easily traversed, since there is ample head-room. Nowhere is its height less than 6 feet.

.   .   .   .

Early references to Staffa do not seem to exist. Yet, the island must have been known to those Scandinavian rowers who gave to it its name, which would appear to be derived from the Norse,

stafr, signifying a column or pillar, and *ey*, an island. Having
regard to its proximity to Iona, it is very unlikely that it remained
unknown to those who, in the early centuries of Christianity in
Scotland, sailed these seas on their way to or from that isle, so
sacred and renowned.

The earliest mention of Staffa is probably that occurring in
George Buchanan's *Rerum Scoticarum Historia*—his history of
Scotland—first published in 1582. One is a little surprised at
finding no allusion to it in a work similarly entitled, written by
Bishop Leslie, and ante-dating Buchanan's by four years, since
Leslie does mention the Treshnish Isles, situated not very far off,
and no less remote. Buchanan's reference is terse enough.
"*Deinde a Gomatra quatuor millia passuum meridiem versus
Stafa, vtraque portuosa:* Four miles from Gometra, on the south,
stands Staffa. Both of these two last-named isles have many good
havens in them."

An Englishman (or was he an Irishman?) named Leach, while
on a visit to Drimnin, in Morven, in 1772, was among the first to
recognise the importance of Staffa, and to sing its praises. Observing how remarkable an isle it was when, fishing nearby that year,
he landed and explored it.

It was from Leach that Sir Joseph Banks, who arrived at Drimnin a few days later, learnt of the wonders of Staffa, an isle from a
distance resembling so many in these seas, but, on closer approach,
demonstrating features that instantly astound.

Banks visited Staffa in August, 1772, when on his way to Iceland
on a natural history expedition, six years before he became President of the Royal Society. He had accompanied Captain Cook as
naturalist on his first voyage round the world. The account of his
'discovery' of Staffa is included in Pennant's *Tour of Scotland in
1772*, first published in 1775, and dedicated to Banks. As Pennant
himself was unable to land on Staffa during his voyagings among
the Hebrides, he found it convenient to incorporate Banks's
account, part of which, at least, is well worth quoting:

"The impatience which everybody felt to see the wonders we
had heard so largely described, prevented our morning's rest;
everyone was up and in motion before the break of day, and
with the first light arrived at the S.W. part of the island, the
seat of the most remarkable pillars; where we no sooner arrived
than we were struck with a scene of magnificence which
exceeded our expectations, though formed, as we thought, upon
the most sanguine foundations: the whole of that end of the
island supported by ranges of natural pillars, mostly above

287

50 feet high, standing in natural colonnades, according as the bays or points of land formed themselves; upon a basis of solid unformed rock, above these, the stratum, which reaches to the soil or surface of the island, varied in thickness, as the island itself formed into hills and vallies; each hill, which hung over the columns below, forming an ample pediment; some of these above 60 feet in thickness, from the base to the point, formed by the sloping ot the hill on each side, almost into the shape of those used in architecture.

"Compared to this, what are the cathedrals or the palaces built by men! mere models or playthings, imitations as diminutive as his works will always be when compared to those of nature. Where is now the boast of the architect! regularity, the only part in which he fancied himself to exceed his mistress, Nature, is here found in her possession, and here it has been for ages undescribed.

"Staffa is taken notice of by Buchanan, but in the slightest manner; and among the thousands who have navigated these seas, none have paid the least attention to its grand and striking characteristic, till this present year.

"The island is the property of Mr. Lauchlan MacQuaire of Ulva, and is now to be disposed of. . . . With our minds full of such reflections we proceeded along the shore, treading up another Giant's Causeway, every stone being regularly formed into a certain number of sides and angles, till in a short time we arrived at the mouth of a cave, the most magnificent, I suppose, that has ever been described by travellers. The mind can hardly form an idea more magnificent than such a space, supported on each side by ranges of columns and roofed by the bottoms of those, which have been broke off in order to form it; between the angles of which a yellow stalagmitic matter has exuded, which serves to define the angles precisely, and at the same time vary the colour with a great deal of elegance, and to render it still more agreeable, the whole is lighted from without; so that the farthest extremity is very plainly seen from without, and the air within being agitated by the flux and reflux of the tides, is perfectly dry and wholesome, free entirely from the damp vapours with which natural caverns in general abound."

Staffa has had many interesting visitors during the last century and a half. Thomas Campbell, the Glasgow poet, came in 1795. In 1800, the year in which George Douglas, Advocate, visited it, he and his young companion, Norris, played in Fingal's Cave a duet on their German flutes, producing an effect "nearly equal to that of a full band of music", astonishing the boatmen at the mouth of the cave, and perhaps also the deer and the sheep grazing upon the island. They little thought that twenty-nine years later, in the person of Felix Mendelssohn, a German musician was to arrive, and afterwards give the name of this very cave to what has surely become one of the best known musical compositions in existence.

Staffa, but for its sheep and deer, Douglas tells us, was quite uninhabited. The latter, now so far removed from contact with human beings, appeared unaccountably tame. Far from being alarmed at their intrusion, while Douglas sat sketching, a deer on more than one occasion gave him a gentle nudge on the back as if to claim some notice.[1]

In 1803 Wordsworth landed at Fingal's Cave, but surely in company uncongenial!

> How could we feel it? each the other's blight,
> Hurried and hurrying, volatile and loud.

But the poet appears to have lingered there alone after the annoying and incongruous crowd had retired, so that he might review with undistracted reverence——

> . . . the effect
> Of these proportions where the Almighty Hand
> That made the world, the Sovereign Architect,
> Had deigned to work as if in human Art.

Sir Walter Scott, who landed at Staffa from the Lighthouse Commissioners' yacht in 1810, portrays in *The Lord of the Isles* this wondrous Isle of Staffa,

> And all the groups of islets gay
> That guard famed Staffa round.

In 1818 Staffa overwhelmed John Keats. "I am puzzled how to give an idea of Staffa," he wrote. "For solemnity and grandeur, it far surpasses the finest Cathedrals. . . . It is impossible to describe it."

.   .   .   .

Mendelssohn, who, as a young man of nineteen, arrived here

[1] *Tour in the Hebrides, A.D., 1800,* by George L. A. Douglas, Advocate. (Aberdeen: D. Wyllie and Son, 1927.)

in 1829, does not attempt, in words, a description of Fingal's Cave. He left that to his companion, Klingemann, who observed that a greener roar of waves never rushed into a stranger cavern—"its many pillars making it look like the inside of an immense organ, black and resounding, and absolutely without purpose, and quite alone, the wide gray sea within and without".

Music, rather than word-pictures, was Mendelssohn's pre-occupation. "In order to make you understand how extraordinarily the Hebrides affected me, the following came into my head there," he wrote. Thereafter follow the first twenty bars of his Hebrides overture, altered but slightly in the final version, which was to reach the musical ears of London in June, 1832.

When Mendelssohn's sister asked him, on his return to Germany, to tell members of the family about the Hebrides, he replied, "It cannot be told, only played." Thereupon he seated himself at the piano, and gave them the theme which, to-day, everybody in the world of music recognises as that of *Fingal's Cave*.

. . . .

The seas about Staffa must have been comparatively tranquil the day in 1847 on which Queen Victoria and Prince Albert landed from the royal yacht—tranquil enough, at any rate, to enable them to enter Fingal's Cave by barge. The cave, like the great entrance to a vaulted hall, "looked almost awful as we entered, and the barge heaved up and down in the swell of the sea ".[1]

Since those days, men and women of renown in every field have landed on Staffa and, between them, have set down with care and precision everything that is to be known about it.

. . . .

Though to-day Staffa is uninhabited, this was not always the case, despite its inaccessibility throughout so much of the year. In 1772, when Sir Joseph Banks visited it, there was upon it, according to U. Von Troil, one of his companions, a solitary hut tenanted by a solitary peasant, who looked after some cattle pastured there, and who was so overjoyed at the advent of human company that he sang Gaelic songs all through the night, and supplied the visitors with fish and milk. The island's lone occupant persuaded Banks to spend the night with him in his hut, rather than in the tent he and his companions had pitched. The following morning the distinguished physicist found himself in a

[1] *Leaves from a Journal of our Life in the Highlands.*

verminous condition, to which he mildly drew his host's attention. The host was infuriated, declaring that the guest had imported what he should have left behind in England!

The same solitary cattle-watcher was still on Staffa when the Bishop of Londonderry, arriving some years later, asked his guide to enquire of the island's Gaelic-speaking resident what he would like to possess above all else in the world. "A razor and soap" was the translation of his reply. The Bishop gave him, on the spot, a purse containing ten guineas, and afterwards sent him a considerable quantity of soap. History does not record whether the islander already had a looking-glass!

It seems incredible that, when the celebrated French geologist, Faujas de Saint Font, visited Staffa in the autumn of 1784, its population was 16. This number appears to have been distributed between two families dwelling apart in two huts, and in the most indescribable squalor. The huts were built of undressed blocks of stone, roofed with sods. A pyramidal opening in the middle of each served as a chimney, through which some daylight entered. Any further light was admitted by a door no more than three feet high. The islanders' fuel consisted of clods of bad turf; and they had a meagre sowing of oats and a planting of potatoes. They owned 8 cows, 1 bull, 2 horses, 12 sheep, 1 pig, 2 dogs, 1 cock, and 8 hens. "The women and children of the two families did not fail to come and see us," writes the Frenchman, "and invited us to their habitations; but, being already informed of their excessive dirt, we were inflexible; and preferred on good ground to receive their civilities and their compliments in the open air."[1]

When Abraham Mills, another geologist, visited Staffa in the summer of 1788, he found *three* dwelling-places, uninhabited, though he saw growing near the centre of the island quantities of oats, barley, and potatoes. These appear to have been planted by persons who, weather permitting, arrived in due season to harvest them. He learnt that 30 head of cattle, under the charge of a solitary herdsman, were sent each year to winter on the island, remaining there until the following seed-time.

Two wretched huts were found on Staffa by Professor Garnett, when he landed in July, 1798. One of these was occupied by a herd and his family: the other served as a barn or byre. "Upon the side of a hillock we sat down and partook of our provisions, and the herd's wife presented us with some milk in a large wooden bowl so heavy that we could scarcely lift it to our mouths; they had no smaller vessels, nor spoons. Indeed, their manner of

[1] *A Journey to the Hebrides* (1784).

life is extremely simple, their food consisting chiefly of milk and potatoes with, now and then, a little fish. There being no wood on the island, the only fuel used by these poor people is the sods of earth which they carefully dry."

Dr. John Leyden makes no reference to any inhabitants on Staffa when he landed in 1800, the year in which George Douglas, aforementioned, also found no one living there; and the island appears to have been deserted when Dr. John MacCulloch came this way twice or thrice between 1811 and 1822. Almost continuously throughout the last century and a half, Staffa has been without a human resident.

One's own landings on this Isle are among the most salient events of one's life. Whenever one sights it, long before one can expect to set foot upon it, the theme of Mendelssohn's *Hebridean Overture*, or perhaps that of Wotan's Farewell from *The Valkyrie*, begins to run through one's head, increasing in volume as one draws near and steps ashore, to be confronted so soon thereafter by the scene which inspired the former. Here time is timelessness. Here he who would look at his watch is instantly made to feel foolish—nay, contemptible—by some power imminent, infinite, invisible, eternal, unchangeable—something of that hidden Love of God, whose height, whose depth, unfathomed, no man knows.

Ulva Ferry with Mull in the background

Chapter XXI

INCH KENNETH

Situated near the mouth of Mull's great, tidal Loch na Keal, between the frowning precipices of Gribun, on the east, and Ulva's Isle, on the north and north-west, lies that grassy isle of the Kilfinichen and Kilvickeon parish of Argyll which John of Fordun, writing in the fourteenth century, refers to as the *insula sancti Kennethy*, Kenneth's sacred island. To-day it is known simply as Inch Kenneth, the first part of the name being derived from the Gaelic, *innis*, denoting an island of choice pasture, the latter part perpetuating the memory of Kenneth, the Irish missionary to whom Adamnan frequently alludes as Cainnech. It was he who, after years of goodly works with the Columban monks at Iona, became the head of Achabo Abbey, in Ireland, where he died in 600. Preserved on Inch Kenneth, under the provisions of the Ancient Monuments Protection Acts, are the ruins of St. Kenneth's Chapel, standing in an old burying-ground where, occasionally, interments still take place. The natives of the Gribun district of Mull, whose family place of burial it has been for centuries, still ferry their dead to Inch Kenneth, which explains how one finds in the old graveyard there so many tombstones to MacFadyens, a clan once numerous in this part of Mull. However, monuments may now be erected on Inch Kenneth only where prior approval has been obtained from the appropriate department of the Office of Works, at Edinburgh.

. . . .

Nine furlongs in length and but three in breadth are Inch Kenneth's maximum dimensions. These exclude the considerable areas at its northern end, as well as down the whole of its eastern side, occupied at ebb water by black reefs. The island is low and fertile. Only half a dozen of its 600 acres are tilled. On these are raised corn, potatoes, and a little hay. However, when traversing the island's interior, one cannot but notice the gentle banks and undulations which, in olden days, were the *feannagan* —the lazy-beds—on which a people long since vanquished grew its oats and potatoes, and at a period when Inch Kenneth in

U   293

Basalt columns by the southern shore of Ulva's Isle, with Mull in the distance

common with most of the isles of the Hebrides, carried a population in excess of what it could support, except on the meagrest level of subsistence.

.   .   .   .

According to the Ordnance Survey, Inch Kenneth's maximum altitude is 162 feet. This occurs where the cliffs rise precipitously at the western extremity. Yet, the island's cliffs appear formidable enough, even where only half that height. Down by the crescent of tide running landwards in that series of detached rocks which we call the Humpies, there lies scope for many an adventure. If, hereabouts, you be seeking such, tread cautiously, since the seaward walls of the cliffs in which the Humpies terminate are indeed in a shattered condition. So, also, are the gaps which the sea has eaten out between them. At the west end of the island, against which the Atlantic beats relentlessly in a south-west gale, the rocks overhanging the boulder-strown shore have weathered into the most fantastic shapes, many of them resembling a series of sinister gargoyles. Here the erosion is due largely to the action of wind-blown sand, carving the rocks curiously, often undercutting them at their base, where they wear more rapidly than at the top, until they resemble mighty mushrooms.

It is the Atlantic storms which bring to the shores of Inch Kenneth from occident lands all sorts of flotsam and jetsam—withering coconut shells, for instance, and quantities of bamboos. Enough timber is cast upon the beaches to provide Inch Kenneth's few inhabitants with fuel for an indefinite period, if only the labour were available to collect it and saw it into manageable sizes. This timber might be a considerable asset on a peatless and almost treeless isle, to which a certain amount of coal has to be ferried across from the Gribun shore from time to time.

When on Inch Kenneth, one is constantly aware that its detached rocks and cliff faces are as liable to topple as are those at Gribun—a region notorious for falling rocks which so often block the road running westward across Mull to the Ross and the Iona Ferry. Any day, rocks larger than a cottage may come leaping down from the lofty bastions of basalt overhanging so much of the southern shore of Loch na Keal. Veritable skyscrapers, these bastions, scraping shower from passing cloud, or torrent from dark, forboding sky.

Everywhere about Inch Kenneth, despite its pastoral aspect, huge masses of conglomerate occur—among the cliffs, on the shore, on the sward, deep down in the transparent sea—all so firmly cemented by nature. Many of these look like fortifications of concrete shattered by high explosive. The cliff-tops in places appear as though they had been put together by human hands. They have weathered into huge, almost rectangular blocks, piled so precariously one upon another as to suggest that at any moment they might go a-hurtling to the sea. They look as though they formed part of some gigantic Egyptian monument after some thousands of years' neglect and decay.

.   .   .   .

Almost treeless is this Isle, I have said, bearing in mind the few trees, coniferous and deciduous, growing in comparative shelter near the island's mansion-house, and by the lovely bay situated within calling distance of it—the bay fringed in June by clusters of irises in flower—the bay with the jetty at which one lands and embarks—the bay providing adequate anchorage for the pro-prietrix's motor-boat, wherewith she maintains with the world beyond just that minimum of contact necessary on an island not self-sufficing, and possessing not even a telephone.

That trees were once more numerous in the vicinity of the house, and not so long ago, is shown by the bleached stumps of many of them. Those which survive are old—old in the sense that the shallowness of the sub-soil will not allow of further maturity. Moreover, their lower parts are completely defoliated by a couple of white nannie-goats left to roam as freely among them as they are about the exterior of the house itself. Goats are remarkably destructive. Standing erect on their hind legs, and reaching upward with their forefeet, as one would with hands and upstretched arms, they are able to strip of their foliage branches at a great height. Thereafter they resort to nibbling the younger twigs, or to de-barking trunks and boughs, seriously to the detriment of anything in the nature of sylviculture. Watching these two nannies from the upper windows facing the steep, cliffy bank so close to the back of the house, perched, as it would seem, in perilous posture while reaching for the least accessible tufts of herbage upon it, was truly entertaining. Never once were these nimble-footed creatures unable to extricate themselves from positions apparently so devoid of foothold that even those familiar with goats and their agile ways might well marvel at their not tumbling to the concrete path at the back door. Had it not been for my own experience with Aunt Dorothy's fifty goats in the Highlands during my boyhood, their airy antics, witnessed from the upper windows, would have alarmed me for their safety.

Inch Kenneth's sub-human population at this time, in addition to its two nannies, consisted of 25 sheep, 14 stirks, 3 milking cows, 2 horses, an abundance of poultry, 3 dogs, 4 cats, and 2 kittens. Of all these, the most satisfying were the little, brown ducks and downy ducklings I used to watch each sundown, as they paddled about the shadowy fringe of the bay below the house, uttering little chirpings scarcely audible above the croon of the lulling tide. At sundown, then, in company with W. F. Harvey, the poet

> *From troubles of the world*
> *I turn to ducks,*
> *Beautiful, comical things. . . .*

If the brown ducks and ducklings were the most satisfying of Inch Kenneth's denizens, the kitten I christened Ferdinand (since he behaved as did his famous namesake, the bull) was the most diverting. Each evening, in the long, lambent twilight of the northern summer, as I adjusted the casement before turning in, I could see Ferdinand stalking with set purpose through the flower-beds below, smelling each bloom for an ecstatic second or two, with his eyes closed, before passing on to the next, purring loudly the while, and treading resolutely with his fore-paws. Though he and I knew one another well, all my efforts to draw his attention were futile. It seemed as though the flowers' scent had entranced him.

. . . .

Inch Kenneth is free from heather and, as yet, comparatively free from bracken. Rabbits are perhaps its greatest nuisance, for they have burrowed extensively in the marginal pastures, particularly near the cliff's edge. In proximity to the house, clusters of bracken have established themselves; and one cannot deny that in springtime their young, lemon shoots contrast appropriately with the blue of the wild hyacinths and the white of the narcissi. Nothing could be lovelier than the luscious greenlands through which there runs, between house and jetty, the pathway fringed with daisies and irises and sheaves of narcissi, among which frolic the first fall of the lambkins.

If the bracken on Inch Kenneth should show signs of getting beyond control, its owner will find herself fortunate in having as her boatman, resident on the island, Neil MacGillivray, who spent eighteen years at Burg, a farm on the west coast of Mull worked by his uncle, and now the property of the National Trust for Scotland. Neil is an expert eradicator, since the Trust's pre-occupation at Burg was the eradication of its bracken.

The distance from the shore at Gribun to the jetty at Inch Kenneth is just under a mile at high spring tide. The channel intervening, though stormy at times, is of no great depth, as the ebb shows. In fact, at a big ebb one could walk across its submerged reefs and banks of sand and gravel in no more than four feet of water. A crossing on horseback at such times would be easy for anyone knowing exactly where lay the sea-pools to be avoided.

Inch Kenneth abounds in springs. The house is supplied from a copious one situated by the shore, its water being raised periodically by motor-pump to a large, covered tank let into the green hillside behind and above it. A hot bath, one of life's greatest solaces, may be had on Inch Kenneth at any time of the day or night, for, even when the reserves of coal are low on the island, its shores, as we have seen, are strewn with an abundance of driftwood.

An excellent account of Inch Kenneth during the latter half of the eighteenth century is given by Dr. Johnson, and also by James Boswell. Here these travellers stayed for a few days in 1773 as the guests of Sir Allan MacLean, having arrived there from Ulva. "Romance," writes the former, "does not often exhibit a scene that strikes the imagination more than this little desert in these depths of Western obscurity, occupied not by a gross herdsman, or amphibious fisherman, but by a gentleman and two ladies, of high birth, polished manners and elegant conversation, who, in a habitation raised not very far above the ground, but furnished with unexpected neatness and convenience, practised all the kindness of hospitality, and refinement of courtesy. . . . He [Sir Allan] had then, for some time, resided with the young ladies in Inch Kenneth, where he lives not only with plenty, but with elegance, having conveyed to his cottage a collection of books, and what else is necessary to make his house pleasant."

Johnson and Boswell were met on arrival by Sir Allan and his two daughters. As they all walked up from the shore together, the Doctor rejoiced at finding, as on the mainland, a road marked with cart-wheels. Such a thing they had not seen for some time. Ulva, their previous place of sojourn, certainly exhibited no such amenity. This road gave them "a pleasure similar to that which a traveller feels, when, whilst wandering on what he fears is a desart [sic] island, he perceives the print of human feet".

The warmth of their reception at Inch Kenneth may have been due, in some measure at least, to the long and intimate friendship which had existed between Boswell's father and their host's predecessor, Sir Hector MacLean.

Sir Allan, his daughters, and their servants were Inch Kenneth's only inhabitants. Their host, who had been long in the army, and whose patrimony had now shrunk to almost negligible proportions, had retired to this delectable spot. There he had built for himself a commodious, single-storeyed dwelling, as well as excellent offices for his domestic staff. His own little apartment contained more objects of interest than the guests were able to enumerate. The house was well stocked with books, as indeed is the present mansion-house; and they were agreeably surprised to find a parcel of the *Caledonian Mercury*, published since they had left Edinburgh. From the perusal of these, Boswell derived that pleasure experienced by one long cut off from the animated scenes of the busy world.

Johnson and he visited together Inch Kenneth's ancient Chapel which, except that the roof was gone, then stood complete. It measured sixty feet by thirty. On one side of the altar was a bas-relief of the Virgin Mary. Close by it lay a little Celtic bell, cracked, and without a tongue. It had rested here, undisturbed, for centuries, guarded solely, Dr. Johnson tells us, by the venerableness of the place. The graveyard surrounding the Chapel was thick with recumbent tombstones. Burials were still taking place there. In contemplating, with some mournful emotion, these ruins, and the memorials to the dead lying everywhere around them, they found Inch Kenneth a suitable prelude to Iona, where they were to land a few days later. The day before their departure for this most celebrated of the Hebrides, Boswell took a spade and buried in the floor of the ruined Chapel some exposed bones he had found hereabouts—an act for which Dr. Johnson, who had a holy horror of dead men's bones, commended him.

Johnson referred to his Sunday on Inch Kenneth as the most agreeable he had ever passed. Sir Allan had told his guests that he and his household were in the habit of spending much of that day in religious devotion. So he invited his guests to join them at family worship, which they willingly did. The elder of the Misses MacLean conducted the evening service, at which Boswell read certain sermons of prayer. These observances made so deep an impression upon Dr. Johnson that he afterwards commemorated them in his poem, *Insula Sancti Kennethi*, the following translation of which was made by Sir Daniel Sandford, a Glasgow professor:

Scarce spied amid the west sea foam,
Yet once Religion's chosen home,
Appears the isle whose savage race
By Kenneth's voice was won to grace.
O'er glassy tides I thither flew,
The wonders of the spot to view.
In lowly cottage great MacLean
Held there his high ancestral reign,
With daughters fair whom love might deem
The Naiads of the ocean stream:
Yet not in chilly cavern rude
Were they, like Danube's lawless brood;
But all that charms a polish'd age,
The tuneful lyre, the learnèd page,
Combined to beautify and bless
That life of ease and loneliness.
Now dawn'd the day whose holy light
Puts human hopes and cares to flight;
Nor 'mid the hoarse waves' circling swell
Did worship here forget to dwell.
What though beneath a woman's hand
The sacred volume's leaves expand;
No need of priestly sanction there—
The sinless heart makes holy prayer!
Then wherefore further seek to rove,
While here is all our hearts approve—
Repose, security, and love?

The English celebrity and his Scots factotum were indeed loth
to quit Sir Allan's Isle. They found it so civilised, so endowed
with the graces. Here, to music played on the harpsichord by
one of his hostesses, Boswell danced a reel with the other. With
but little persuasion, the guests would have tarried. Yet they
had to remember that " life will not be all passed in delight ", and
that before long Boswell must needs be back in Edinburgh for the
impending session of the courts.

. . . .

Among the carved headstones, the inscription on which they
must have read, is that denoting the place of interment of a certain
Donald MacLean of Brolas, who died in 1725, at the age of 54,
" deservedly lamented by all who knew and understood his vir-
tuous and heroick mind ". They may also have glanced at the
stone nearby, under which " layeth the corps of Dame Mary Mac-

Pherson, Lady MacLean, daughter to Sir Aeneas MacPherson, who died the year 1717, aged 30 years". She was probably an ancestress of their host and hostesses.

A stone erected in recent years in this ancient chapel-yard marks the grave of Margaret, Lady Boulton, who died at Inch Kenneth in 1938. The inscription also records the death there, the following year, of her sister, Helen Brown Lyons, of Merriani. Lady Boulton was the widow of Sir Harold Boulton, Bart., my father's friend and contemporary. His name is familiar to everyone who knows *The Songs of the North*. We remember him especially, perhaps, for his inspiriting verses, *Maiden of Morven*, occurring at the end of the first volume, sung to an old Highland melody arranged by his collaborator, Malcolm Lawson:

> *Moan ye winds that never sleep,*
> *Howl ye spirits of the deep,*
> *Roar ye torrents down the steep,*
>   *Roll ye mists on Morven!*
> *May the tempest never rest,*
> *Nor the seas with peace be blessed,*
> *Since they tore thee from my breast,*
>   *Maiden of Morven!*

> *Oft I chased the deer of yore,*
> *Many a battle-brunt I bore,*
> *When the chiefs of Innistore*
>   *Hurled their might on Morven.*
> *Blunt my spear, and slack my bow,*
> *Like an empty ghost I go,*
> *Death the only hope I know,*
>   *Maiden of Morven!*

Sir Harold had purchased Inch Kenneth as a retreat for his wife, an incurable inebriate; and some of the natives of Gribun, put on their honour not to assist her in procuring alcohol, tell many a story of her antics when, somehow or other—probably by post—a bottle or two got into her hands.

When staying recently at Inch Kenneth, I could not but recall, in the midst of my own felicity there, the impression the MacLeans had made upon these two distinguished travellers, almost a century and three-quarters earlier. Strolling over the warm, springy velvet of its pastures in the sunshine of early summer, or in any direction which its devious sheep-tracks allured, I instantly became imbued with a consoling sense of solitude, rather than of loneliness. Though you may never meet a soul, you are pretty certain, in the late springtime and quite early summer, to disturb in your wanderings a nesting peewit; and she will demonstrate her resentment of your trespass by wheeling overhead with peevish plaint. Soon you will have passed beyond her temporary domicile to the larks' domain. There, with the exercise of a little patience and vigilance, you may see these palpitating specks soaring aloft in full-throated ecstasy.

A sense of solitude, did I say? Ah! yes! You can have solitude in plenty on Inch Kenneth. Its population, even when my hostess is entertaining a guest or two, seldom exceeds eight. When you realise that most of these are occupied with domestic and farming duties, and that Neil MacGillivray, the boatman, must necessarily be watchful in all that concerns wind and tide, lest the only means of communicating with the world beyond be rendered inoperable through lack of foresight, one realises how small is the likelihood of encountering anyone upon these succulent acres. Occasionally, however, a small boat may be sighted offshore, since the Loch na Keal lobster-fishermen sink their pots regularly, and indeed remuneratively, in the waters between Inch Kenneth and Ulva.

Chapter XXII

ULVA'S ISLE

A Chieftain to the Highlands bound
Cries " Boatman, do not tarry!
And I'll give thee a silver pound
To row us o'er the ferry! "

" Now who be ye, would cross Loch Gyle,
This dark and stormy water? "
" O, I'm the Chief of Ulva's Isle,
And this, Lord Ullin's daughter."

WHERE is Loch Gyle, that dark and stormy water mentioned by
Thomas Campbell in a poem, the fourteen verses of which every
Scottish school-child, well into the present century, was obliged
to learn by heart?   In one's early curriculum north of the Tweed
and Solway, this poem occupied, along with *Casabianca* and *The
Wreck of the Hesperus*, a position nothing could assail.   One
supped it with one's porridge, as one did the Shorter Catechism, or
the contents of the Family Bible.   It certainly familiarised us all
with Ulva, an Isle of which, otherwise, millions might never have
heard.

Almost perennial in Scotland is the controversy as to the
location of Loch Gyle.   Many assume, and not unnaturally, that the
loch the poet had in mind must lie in the region of Ulva—somewhere on the west coast of Mull.   They suggest that it is Loch na
Keal, that great sealoch along the entire northern shore of which
runs the road bearing one westward across Mull to the Sound of
Ulva and the Ulva Ferry.

Let me not disturb too many romantic illusions about the eloping couple by a passing mention that Campbell had envisaged no
sealoch of Mull, but Loch Goil, on the Firth of Clyde.   This is
shown by the fact that, at the time *Lord Ullin's Daughter* was
published, the Rev. Dr. Beattie of Glasgow, and the Rev. Mr. Mac-
Corkindale, parish minister of Lochgoilhead, were members of a
literary society, one of the topical debates of which concerned the
loch's identity.   Dr. Beattie, who had been Campbell's amanuensis,
agreed to ask the poet which loch he had in mind.   "Loch Goil,
on the Firth of Clyde, with, of course, a poet's licence," Campbell
replied.

In those days Dunbartonshire was regarded as Lowland, while even the now comparatively accessible parts of Argyllshire adjoining it were looked upon as Highland. A ferry plied regularly across the mouth of Loch Goil, between Portincaple, in the former, and Carrick Castle, in the latter. A chieftain to the Highlands bound would scarcely be standing by the shore of Loch na Keal, in Mull. Having arrived in the Highlands, however, he might well have asked a boatman to ferry him over to Ulva's Isle.

Though hardly the locality for which an eloping couple would make nowadays, Loch Goil, incidentally, *was* crossed some years ago by two runaway lovers who, pursued by wrathful parents, threw themselves on the mercy of the shepherd's wife. The latter, in a manner truly romantic, hid them in a cave, secretly supplying them with food and other symbols of Highland hospitality for more than a week, by the end of which time the parents, having abandoned the chase, had become a little more reconciled.

.   .   .   .

Ulva forms part of the Argyllshire parish of Kilninian and Kilmore. Its maximum length, measured from east to west, is just under five miles. Its greatest breadth from north to south is roughly three. Its area is less than eight square miles. Apart from the cultivated acres about Ulva House, situated near its eastern extremity, and from a few small, isolated woodlands in the same locality, it consists of hill and rough moorland. In Beinn Chreagach, almost at its centre, it attains its highest point at 1,025 feet. Like so much of the adjacent coast-line of Mull, and of Gometra and the other isles and islets near at hand, it is characterised by series of smooth, green terraces. These would seem to be interrupted only where tumbling water has cut small and almost perpendicular ravines down their faces, lending to the scene, when viewed at a distance, a touch of deep purple—green, steep terraces striped perpendicularly at irregular intervals in purple. During and after rain, the purple stripes become white ones by reason of the thin, impetuous bands of swiftly falling water, many of them resembling, afar, the thinnest of white threads.

Ulva possesses a series of basaltic colonnades but little inferior to those at Staffa, that spectacular neighbour lying four and a half miles to the south-west, beyond Little Colonsay. Among the first to draw attention to these was Dr. John MacCulloch, so well-known as a geologist and littérateur in the earlier part of the nineteenth century. MacCulloch observed that, although on a scale more modest than those at Staffa, they were almost as regular, and certainly as deserving of celebrity as the Giant's Causeway. Had Ulva's basalt formations been the only ones in this region, there is little doubt that they would have enjoyed something of the fame bestowed upon those at Fingal's Cave, off which David MacBrayne's swift and comely West Highland steamer, *King George V*, rides at anchor every lawful day during the tourist season, while those aboard her are ferried ashore.

. . . . . .

On Midsummer's Eve in 1951, when wandering about the uplands of Inch Kenneth with binoculars in my hand, I thought I discerned by the shore of Ulva, at a distance of about two miles in a north-easterly direction, these basalt columns, beautifully illumined at the sun's setting, the sunward side of each column a tall, thin streak of gold, sharply contrasting with the tall, thin, black lines denoting such parts as lay in shadow, and were broadening every moment with the sun's decline. The binoculars soon showed these to be Ulva's basalt cliffs. They stood out in that fantastic beauty one associates with the distant scenery of Wagnerian opera. For the first time I knew precisely where, on Ulva, they were to be found, since one might traverse the rough surface of an isle like this for days without discovering them. On the morrow my hostess put her motor-launch and boatman at my disposal. By noon I was ashore with camera, in bright sunlight, among these quite remarkable cliffs. They were indeed fascinating. I photographed them from every angle, and continued to do so until I ran out of film, for I had the feeling that never again might I be afforded the opportunity of capturing them under conditions so ideal. My hours among the basalts of Ulva's Isle that day are truly memorable. If, in 1773, the natives were appreciative of their own rocks, it may well have explained how, "when the islanders were reproached with their ignorance, or insensibility of the wonders of Staffa," to quote Dr. Johnson, "they had not much to reply. They had indeed considered it little, because they had always seen it."

. . . .

Ulva is the largest of the many isles situated off the west coast of Mull. Its setting is one of the most beautiful in the Western Highlands. To the north is Loch Tuath, beyond which lies the major part of the ecclesiastical parish to which it belongs. Across the southern horizon stretches the romantic Ross of Mull, with Iona at no distance from it. Away to the east, lovely Loch na Keal, with Eorsa Isle at its mouth, penetrates well into the heart of Mull itself, almost dividing that vast domain in two. To the south-east lies the sweet and historic isle of Inch Kenneth, backed by the lofty, eagle-haunted cliffs of Gribun. On the south-west, a sea peppered with islets and skerries intervenes between Ulva and Little Colonsay; and beyond, as far again in the same direction, lies renowned Staffa.

Due west of Ulva, and separated from it by a channel so narrow that a bridge but a few yards in length spans it, is Gometra, an isle less than a third its size. Three or four miles beyond Gometra stretches that interesting chain known as the Treshnish Isles.

Of the long road to Gometra I learnt something the other day when visiting, at Dervaig, in Mull, an elderly lady named Mrs. MacLean, who had been brought up at Howmore, in South Uist, where, many years ago, her father was parish minister. Mrs. Mac-Lean's husband once owned Gometra. There she had spent the greater part of her long life. "A goodly island," she told me. "Seven families on it then, three of whom were those of the lobster-fishermen inhabiting its western end." It was the seamen from these latter families who, until the outbreak of war in 1914, used to row or sail out in their big boat—their *red* boat—to meet MacBrayne's steamer off Staffa, and ferry its passengers ashore at Fingal's Cave. These seamen were said to have been the prototype of those brawny, jerseyed fellows depicted so conspicuously on posters in Glasgow and elsewhere, in the days when the Oban-Iona excursion first included a landing at Staffa, leaving sufficient time ashore to enable one to explore Fingal's Cave.

In Mrs. MacLean's time, as many as twenty pupils attended the little school on Gometra. With the exception of two or three who crossed from the adjacent part of Ulva, all of them were natives of the island. Though the channel between can usually be crossed dryshod at low water, a plank assisted the passage of the smaller children from that end of Ulva; but Mrs. MacLean's husband came to the view that this entailed some risk for the young people crossing regularly on their way to and from school, especially in the dark mornings and afternoons of winter. So he built the bridge now enabling one to reach Gometra from the Ulva ferry by motor or other vehicle, following throughout the length of Ulva the rough road twisting and turning, dipping and rising, until it brings one opposite Gometra. This is an arduous route even on foot; and the jolting in any vehicle traversing it can be good neither for man nor for mechanism. One would be interested to know how it suited that intrepid fellow, Hugh Ruttledge, leader of the 1933 Everest Expedition, who purchased Gometra that year.

305

Yet, how wildly beautiful, how primordial, is the scene every-where around one! And how sad, too, since Ulva's road threads its way through croft-lands long abandoned, through pastures rapidly reverting to ling and to bracken, among the derelict home-steads of a vanished people. Ulva and Gometra are but two of the many isles of the Inner Hebrides where, for reasons social and economic, population has decreased to negligible numbers. Nevertheless, they possess in their unpeopled acres a fascination, and a remoteness curiously emphasised by this very road. You might travel it day after day without meeting a soul. When, in one of the many hollow places into which it dips, you look around to find broken moorland and grey, lichened rock on every hand, you lose completely the sense of your being on a compara-tively small island. True, Mull's loftiest peak, a dozen or more miles away, would appear to dominate the scene. Yet, many of the ups and downs of Ulva occur in territory so rugged that from much of the island the considerable sealochs about it lie out of sight.

Of course, if you get among the bracken of Ulva in summer or in autumn, you cannot *expect* to see anything—not even the sky overhead. You might as well hope to see the heavens from the heart of a tropical jungle. Whatever Ulva and the other isles off Mull may lack in accumulations of fresh water, because of the porous nature of their surface, there would certainly be no ground for complaint if a *bracken* harvest were desired. In fact, it has been suggested that parts of Ulva might well be considered an exhibition ground for this almost ineradicable pest. Where it grows on the floor of shallow, gently-sloping gullies, it would seem to emulate in height the fronds thriving on the gullies' flanks. Here it may reach as high as fourteen feet, concealing absolutely the groups of shaggy Highland cattle often sheltering in its midst from sun and pestering fly. The cattle, even when standing, remain quite invisible. One becomes aware of their existence in such density of growth only when one happens to notice in the corner of the eye a faint movement—the upturned tips of horns as an unseen heifer looks round quietly to see who approaches.

Mull, to be sure, has its share of bracken. Yet, after experi-ence of Ulva's one can well appreciate the Mull natives' retort to observations about *their* bracken—"*You ought to see how it grows on Ulva!*"

A year or two ago, when traversing this island from north to south on a sunless day, I found myself pushing laboriously through acres of very tall bracken without appearing to be getting anywhere; and I could well imagine how readily the untried traveller might become panic-stricken in such a maze, with no sun to guide him, and aware that, consequently, his direction must have been altered unwittingly several times. It is always good practice to pause and rest at frequent intervals during such labyrinthine journeying, in order to regain just that element of self-confidence without which one might never emerge at all. To those unaccustomed to the trials, and indeed perils, of the unpeopled spaces, this may appear an exaggeration. If so, get yourself well into the midst of Ulva's bracken to experience the full reality of it! Nothing can be more alarming, more terrifying, to the untrained, to the uninitiated, whose physical endurance in such straits may already have been impaired by fear. You may trample your way through dense vegetation for a few yards with vigour: you won't be able to sustain anything like that vigour when it comes to a few *hundred* yards.

But for the modest plantations by the ferry, at Ormsaig, in the vicinity of Ulva House and of the vacant church and manse, all of them at the island's eastern end and at no great distance from one another, Ulva is treeless. Yet, how pleasant these little woodlands can be on a hot day, affording shelter from the sun after a trying journey across Mull! One autumn day recently, having cycled briskly all the way from Salen to the ferry in the hope of crossing to Ulva with as much good daylight as possible still ahead of me, I was indeed glad of their soothing and cooling embrace. They provided me with the much desired opportunity for rest and relaxation and general adjustment, before meeting, at Ulva House, my hostess, Edith, Lady Congleton, whom I was soon to find plying the hay-fork in one of the loveliest pastoral settings I have ever beheld. In the hay-field by the old house stood ricks but newly made. Upon the farmlands close by, the corn was still green, contrasting well with such of the island's vegetation as had already taken on the rich tints blazoning the incipience of autumn's decay. Everywhere around one was the fragrance of hay recently harvested, and of wild flowers in which the wild bees seemed more than usually audible. Overhead, between the old house and the summit of Ben More, white, blowzy clouds filled all the heavens. Their reflections on the sound, so near at hand, were as silent pools of pearl set in a sea of indigo, their edges tinctured like the faint blush of the dog-rose. To the distant mountains of Mull, as also to the cliffs at Gribun, seen just beyond Inch Kenneth and so much closer at hand, a heavy shower, now well on its way to the mainland of Argyll, had bequeathed, for an interlude all too brief, the most elusive greens and blues and purples imaginable. A glance in the direction of the loftier flanks of Ben More showed that the shower had deposited upon them a thin, opaque coating as of hail. Autumn, as if sickened with a surfeit of its own clover-scent and heather-fragrance, seemed prepared at any moment to surrender her taciturn splendour to the onset of winter.

The ferry between Mull and Ulva is public. One crosses and re-crosses for ninepence, never imagining for a moment that anything so tragic as is depicted in Thomas Campbell's poem could befall one with Neil Kennedy at the oars. No fear of shrieking water-wraith will divert the traveller from his objective once he has tolled the bell on the Mull side to summon Neil. Here the channel is only two hundred yards wide—"Two hundred yards, exactly," Neil informs one, *"when it's high water at both sides."* A path leads up from Ulva's jetty to Ulva House, half a mile away. This jetty, built of massive cubes of stone, dates from the years of want which followed the Potato Famine about the middle of last century. Prior to its construction, those who came from afar to visit the old MacQuarrie Chiefs of Ulva probably landed from a boat brought into the comparatively sheltered bay just below Ulva House.[1]

To Ulva, in 1773, came Johnson and Boswell. Since they arrived in the dark and were off to Inch Kenneth by noon the following day, Johnson asks us not to expect much from his pen on this ancient heritage of the Clan MacQuarrie. A servant was sent ahead of them in order to solicit, in advance, the ferryman's services. But the ferryman was on the Ulva side; and the night so dark and the wind so high that the servant found himself unable to attract his attention. But for the fact that there lay in the sound the Londonderry vessel, *Bonnetta*, the master of which—Captain MacClure—was paying the old MacQuarrie Chief a visit, they would have been in a sorry situation. MacClure's seamen ferried the travellers in their long-boat.

[1] According to the Valuation Roll for the year ending at Whitsun, 1950, Ulva House and farm, rated together as an agricultural subject, had an assessed value or rent of £190—a good deal less than I pay for my modest flat in Chelsea. The rent of Neil Kennedy's house, croft, and grazings, similarly rated, was but £6 a year. That of the vacant manse was just twice that figure. Residents in these parts little realise how well off they are in many ways.

Ulva House in autumn, with Ben More (Mull) in the distance

MacQuarrie's house, occupying a site about four hundred yards from the present mansion, was mean, according to Boswell. Yet, the travellers were hospitably entertained there by Lachlan MacQuarrie, XVIth Chief of Ulva's Isle, at whose appearance they were agreeably surprised. They found him intelligent, polite, and much a man of the world; and they were grieved to learn from him that, owing to mounting debts, Ulva and some of the isles adjacent thereto—the patrimony of his race for nine hundred years—were about to be sold. A lineage of nine hundred years by 1773 must have been something of an exaggeration, even for the oldest of the Highland clans. However, tradition supports the claim that MacQuarries were flourishing in these parts as early as the thirteenth century, about the middle of which a doughty ancestor of theirs was assisting Alexander II to wrest the Western Isles from the Norse, who, until 1263, the year of Haco's defeat off Largs, had dominated them for some hundreds of years.

With the forfeiture of the Lordship of the Isles in 1493, the suzerainty of the MacDonalds came to an end in Ulva, as elsewhere. According to a brochure of Lachlan MacQuarrie, aforesaid, published in 1945 by my friend, Robert Munro, an authority on the MacQuarries, it was about this time that the MacQuarrie Clan, at no period either numerous or powerful, became nominally independent, though in war it still followed the MacLeans, the MacDonalds' oldest and bitterest enemies.

Incidentally, it was on Ulva, in the heyday of the MacDonalds, that there resided that wellknown family, the MacArthurs, hereditary pipers to the Clan Donald. The MacArthurs are said to have had on Ulva a piping-college not unlike that which the Mac-Crimmons, hereditary pipers to the MacLeods of Dunvegan, conducted at Borreraig, in western Skye.

The MacLeans, in course of time, were displaced by the all-conquering Campbells, which explains how the Dukes of Argyll regarded themselves thereafter as the MacQuarries' overlords.

When Ulva was sold by public roup in Edinburgh in July, 1777, it fetched £9,080. Lachlan MacQuarrie, Dr. Johnson's host, was then 61. The following year he joined the 74th Regiment of Foot—the Argyll Highlanders—and embarked at Greenock to take part in the American war. Thereafter he returned to Scotland. In 1818 he died in Mull, at the age of 103, in straitened circumstances.

Perhaps the most distinguished member of the clan was Major-General Lachlan MacQuarrie, who was born in 1761, and died in 1824. At the age of 15 he entered the army. In 1800 he was

x   309

The road through Ulva. Mull in the distance

appointed Governor of New South Wales; and there are many of his clan in Australia at the present day. They are even more numerous in Canada.

MacQuarrie's name is writ large all over eastern Australia, where it is usually spelt Macquarie. It is to be found in the river of that name; in Macquarie Harbour, in Sydney; in Macquarie Street, Sydney, and also in Macquarie Street, Hobart; in the Sydney electorate of the name; and in MacQuarie Square, Sydney—the obelisk in the centre of this somewhat triangular space, surrounded by the commercial establishments of Macquarie Place, being that from which distances are calculated in New South Wales. The rock overlooking Sydney Harbour, on which the governor's wife used to sit, was known as Mrs. Macquarie's Chair. The Australians have now bestowed upon this rock the dignity of *Lady* Macquarie's Chair.

Lachlan MacQuarrie's name is greatly revered in New South Wales, not only for the great civil engineering enterprises he sponsored, such as road-making, but also for what he did to allay prejudice against ex-convicts making an effort to establish themselves honourably in the country of their banishment. Several notable deportees derived benefit from his magnanimity and friendship.

At the centre of a large, walled enclosure in the corner of a dark wood at Gruline, in Mull, stands the mausoleum containing Lachlan MacQuarrie's mortal remains, and also those of his wife and children. The inscription on a slab of polished red granite inserted at one end of the mausoleum provides all the necessary details of their birth and sojourn here on earth. A corresponding slab at the other end, bearing the MacQuarrie coat-of-arms and the motto, *Turris Fortis mihi Deus*, has a lengthy inscription testifying that here, in the hope of a glorious resurrection, lies the general. Then follows a lot of nonsense about his private virtues and the amiable disposition with which he was endowed—nonsense which only the most patient can decipher on polished granite in a dark wood. Even then, one must first squeeze through the outer railing before attempting to do so. If ever lettering were carved on stone so that no one should read it except with the greatest difficulty, it is the lettering people insist upon having on polished granite! Even in strong lighting, it is often quite illegible.

There is a tradition in Mull that a black servant employed in the general's household is also buried here at Gruline, and that until fairly recently her ghost might have been seen flitting through the dark wood. I have been told by natives of Mull that, when young, they would not venture near this mausoleum, either in daylight or in dark, for fear of encountering this ghost.

To return to the year, 1773, Boswell's account of Ulva is more interesting than is Johnson's. He tells us that when they were by themselves at night, each in an elegant bed in the same room, they talked to one another in Latin, "and with as much of the English accent as I could assume, so as not to be understood". They feared lest a conversation in English might have been over-heard and understood in MacQuarrie's small, Highland house.

Brief though their sojourn was, they derived much from it. In making enquiries about Ulva's customs, they were interested to learn of one which they believed survived nowhere else, namely, the payment of the *Mercheta Mulierum*, a fine due in olden times, Dr. Johnson tells us, to the laird at the marriage of a virgin. "It is pleasant to find ancient customs in old families," he adds. Mac-Quarrie told his guests that the *Mercheta Mulierum* mentioned in old charters was the overlord's privilege of having the first night of all his vassals' wives. The payment, like others of the kind, was anciently made in the produce of the land, because of the scarcity of money in these parts. MacQuarrie was in the habit of demand-ing a crown, in lieu of a sheep, regardless of the fact that the value of the latter might be constant, whereas that of the crown might fluctuate. "A sheep has always the same power of supply-ing human wants," is the lexicographer's comment; "but a crown will bring at one time more, at another less."

It was from MacQuarrie that Johnson and Boswell were to learn of a case of the Second-Sight which went far toward con-vincing them of the existence of this preternatural faculty, and certainly influenced the former when he came to setting down his views upon it. According to Boswell, who records the circum-stances, MacQuarrie had gone to Edinburgh, taking with him his manservant. One day during their absence, an old woman em-ployed by the Chief announced that on the morrow he would be returning with two gentlemen, and that the manservant would be attired in red and green. Sure enough, all four, as predicted, re-turned the following day. The manservant was in red and green livery which his master, in an impulsive moment, had bought for him in Edinburgh. When leaving Ulva, no such purchase had ever been contemplated. The old woman, he declared, could not have heard any previous mention of livery. MacQuarrie vouched for the authenticity of this instance of the Second-Sight.

Many another traveller of distinction visited Ulva in olden days, among them the Hon. Mrs. Murray of Kensington, one of the most redoubtable of woman-travellers in eighteenth-century Britain. In 1800, George Douglas, Advocate, and Sheriff of Kincardine, arrived here with two Oxford companions, during his tour of the Western Highlands and of as many of the islands of the Inner Hebrides as time and circumstances would permit. He writes of Ulva House as being large, but not graceful, and of its grounds as being quite in a state of nature. The views from the house he thought sublime, however; and he was astonished at the thriving condition of the young plantations in its vicinity, despite their exposed situation.[1]

When Sir Walter Scott came this way fourteen years later, his stepping ashore was greeted by a discharge of musketry. A distinguished contemporary of his—the Ettrick Shepherd—perpetuated the memory of a grievance he had in a scurrilous rhyme he entered in the visitors' book at the island's inn. Years later, there arrived at Ulva the most famous of his name surname—David Livingstone. He had come to see the Isle whence his grandfather had migrated to Blantyre. By this time, owing to the economic distress which had swept over so much of the Highlands and Islands in the nineteenth century, Ulva's population had dwindled considerably. A population of between 500 and 600 in the years before the Potato Famine and subsequent evictions and emigrations had been literally decimated. Those tragic years known as the Hungry Forties are commemorated on Ulva in the large number of ruined homesteads yet to be seen about its greener parts. A row of derelict cottages in one of its decayed townships is still referred to as Starvation Terrace. Further disaster was to befall the island when, in June, 1880, of the eight houses there, apart from the manse, and the mansion of Mr. Clark, the proprietor, all but the grocer's were destroyed by fire.

Ulva's decline is shown in the condition of its church, built in 1827 to accommodate its many parishioners then. To-day the island is without an incumbent; and the manse is vacant. Only by scrambling up to the church's windows one can see, and then but dimly, that feature of its interior which used to be regarded as remarkable. Under the unvarnished, unvisited pews lies no flooring, but the earth and stone upon which the church stands. Wooden slats kept the parishioners' feet off the bare ground during worship.

. . . .

[1] His description of a *Tour of the Hebrides, A.D., 1800*, together with an Introduction and Notes by John A. Fairley, was first printed in 1927, by D. Wyllie and Son, Aberdeen.

Ulva is rich in folklore and legend, much of which is now in danger of being lost or forgotten. Fragments of it are still recounted, however. Those who know the island intimately tell of the tragedy that occurred at the Shieling of the Maiden's Rock, for instance. Long ago, they say, when Ulva abounded in people, and had a score or more of summer shielings upon its hillsides, Christina, the dairymaid at this particular one, accused a young girl of the theft of a kebbock, which the latter denied having taken. In the hope of extracting a confession, she suspended the girl, a relative of her own, from an overhanging rock by tying a plaid round her neck. The plaid tightened: the girl was hanged. The women of Ulva were enraged. Seizing the heartless dairymaid, and tying her up in a sack, they deposited her on a skerry, there to await drowning with the incoming tide. So to this day one of the many reefs off Ulva's southern shore is called Christina's Skerry.

A happier association is that with the sprite spoken of as the Green Glaistig, or as the Glaistig of Ardnacallich—the name given to the site of the old house occupied for so many generations by the MacQuarrie Chiefs. This elusive creature, they say, still haunts this part of the island. In the MacQuarrie's heyday she tended their cattle. " Ho! ho! ho! " she might be heard shouting when she had failed in her self-imposed duties. " MacQuarrie's cows are in the corn, for the bad lass has slept in! Ho! ho! ho! "

INDEX

A' Chill, 55-6
A' Chrannag Chaluim-cille, 135
A' Chùli, 134
Abbey, 271
Abbot's Pool, 218
Abbot's Port, 225
Acha, 88, 90
Achabo Abbey, 293
Achadnadure, 124
Achafolla, 128
Achamore House, 215
Achnacree, 98
Achnacroish, 96, 97, 108
Achosnich, 28
Adamnan, 7, 67, 131, 133, 138, 144-5, 259, 262, 263, 270, 293
Admiralty, 93, 251
Adventures in Legend, 105
Ahmhor, 40
Aileach an Naoimh, 121-2, 133 (*see also* Eileach)
Ainort, Loch, 1, 2
Alexander II, 114, 309
Alexander III, 6, 115, 226
Allan of the Straw, 275
Allival, 30, 35, 37
Allt nan Oir, 174
Am Buachaille, 283
Am Faodhail (The Ford, Tiree), 73
Am Faodhail (The Strand, Colonsay), 194
Am Port, 131
American Battle Monuments Commission, 171
Amhuinn a' Mhuilinn, 69
An Caman, 104
An Curach(an), 259-60
An Ealadh, 267
An Gearna, 243
An Rioghachd Barr fo Thuinn, 74
An t-Eilean Muileach, 233
anam-chara, 103
Ancient Monuments Protection Acts, 293
Anderson, Dr. Joseph, 137
Anderson, Rev. R. S. G., 224
Angels' Hillock, 270-1
Angus of Kintyre, 226
Angus Og, 249
Antiquities of Gigha, The, 224
Antrim, 282-3
Appin, 96, 97, 120

Arbroath Abbey, 264
Ard Luing, 122
Ardachoirc, 109, 114
Ardbeg, 153
Ardchattan, 102
Ardclach, 102
Ardeer, 108
Ardentrive Bay, 111, 113, 114
Ardfenig, 255
Ardfin, 178, 189-90
Ardlamey, 219
Ardlarach, 123
Ardlussa, 178, 187
Ardmaddy Castle, 120
Ardmeanach, 235, 237, 238, 242, 248, 255, 256
Ardminish, 214, 215, 217, 220, 221, 222, 226
Ardmore Bay (Skye), 20
Ardmore (Kerrera), 110
Ardmore Point (Mull), 234, 238
Ardnacallich, 313
Ardnamurchan, 28, 30, 46, 60, 62, 68, 94, 200, 234
Ardskenish, 194
Ardtun, 235
Ardura, 233
Argyll, Duke of, 21, 75, 76, 80, 82, 94, 104-5, 225, 235, 251-2, 272, 309
Argyll, Earl of, 81, 162
Argyll, Marquis of, 197, 252
Argyll(shire), 28, 67, 96, 103, 109, 110, 116, 118, 121, 131, 134, 136, 142, 190, 212, 214, 226, 233, 239, 260, 293, 303, 308
Arileod, 88, 90, 91
Arinagour, 85, 86, 88, 89, 95
Arisaig, 28, 49, 59, 65
Armada, 252
Armadale, 11, 12, 15, 16, 22, 25
Arnibost, 88
Aros, Castle, Glen and River, 244, 245, 246, 247, 248, 249
Arroch, Glen, 25
Art O'Carby, 249
Artbranan, 7
Ashval, 32, 35
Askival, 35
Askval, 37
Astor, Nancy, 187
Atholl, Earl of, 249
Atlantic, 2, 12, 33, 62, 67, 89, 118,

144, 145, 148, 149, 169, 174, 196, 198, 266-7, 269, 285, 294
Augustine, 260
Augustinian, 202
Aunt Dorothy, 295
Australia, 310
Aytoun, W. E., 143
Azilian, 200, 210

Bà, Loch and River, 245-7
Bac Mor, 255
Bachull, 101, 103, 104
Baile a' Ghobhainn, Loch, 99
Bailegarve, 98
Balarumindubh, 194
Balaruminmore, 194
Balavetchy, 194
Balemartine, 72, 75
Balephetrish, Bay and Farm, 71, 75, 76
Ballachulish, 126
Balliemore, 113
Ballygrant, 145, 165
Ballyhaugh, 89, 90
Balnahard, 194, 197, 202, 203, 205
Balvicar, 119, 121
Banks, Sir Joseph, 287-8, 290
Bannockburn, 264
Barkeval, 35
Barnhill, 92-3
Barons of Bachull, 104
Barr Mor, 98
Barra, 38, 52, 68, 70, 72, 94, 151, 170, 195, 260
Barra Head, 38, 232
Barrapol, 68
Barrnamboc, 110, 114
Battle of Bloody Bay, 249
Battle of the Spoiling of the Dyke, 20
Baugh, 76
bean-nighe, 49
Bearreraig, Bay and River, 26
Beathag's Lucky Well, 215-16
Beaton, Dr. John, 275-6
Beatons, 248
Beautiful Isle of Mull, The, 139
Behold Iona! A Guide and Souvenir, 272
Beinn a' Chaolais, 174, 175
Beinn an Oir, 174, 175
Beinn Bheigeir, 148
Beinn Ceann a' Bharra, 68
Beinn Chreagach, 303
Beinn Eibhne, 195, 206, 207-8
Beinn Heynish, 68
Beinn Hough, 68
Beinn na Caillich, 6
Beinn nam Fitheach, 199
Beinn Siantaidh, 174, 175
Beinn Tighe, mountain and loch (Eigg), 39

Beinn Tighe (Canna), 56
Bellart, River, 244, 245
Belnahua, 121, 125-6, 135, 138, 143
Ben Buie, 246
Ben Creach, 246
Ben Cruachan, 109, 195
Ben Hogh, 84, 89
Ben More (in Mull), 109, 196, 235, 238, 241, 243, 260, 307, 308
Ben Nevis, 69, 195
Benbecula, 11, 12, 47
Benderloch, 96, 98, 99
Bending Columns, 284
Benedictines, 271, 275
Bens of Jura, 174, 185, 190
Beothail, 106
Bernera, 24, 101
Betty Burke, 12
Big Women, Isle and Loch of the, 44
Bilbao, 53
Binning, Lord, 162
Bioda Mor, 2
Birlinns (war-galleys), 29
Black Coolins, 6, 8
Black Mill, 119, 122, 145, 147
Black Skerries, 138
Blair, A. Campbell, 242
Blairgowrie, 234
Blaven, 8, 11
Bloodstone Hill, 31
Bloody Bay, 238, 249
Bloody Yankee, 159-60
Blue Pool, 194
Boat Cave, 285
Bogha Chubaig, 197
Bogha Dale, 197
Bonahaven, 153
Bonaveh, 194
Book of Colonsay and Oronsay, The, 204
Book of the Dean of Lismore, The, 107
Boreraig, 21, 22
Borreraig, 309
Boswell, James, 6, 8, 13-14, 17, 18, 21, 60-1, 84-5, 89-90, 236, 246-7, 258, 286, 297-9, 308-9, 311
Boulton, Sir Harold, Bart., 300
Bowmore, 152, 153, 158, 159, 161, 176, 189, 191
Bracadale, Loch, 1
Bracadale District, 7, 19
bracken, 55, 63, 98, 142, 143, 154, 158, 206-7, 231, 242, 296-7, 306
Braddon, Fred J., 276-7
Bragella, 15
Bragleen, 116
Branford, Frederick Victor, 244
Breachacha, 91-3
Brecan, 144
Brecan, Gulf of (*see* Corrievreckan)

Brecbennoch of Columba, 264
Bremner, Donald, 89
Breviary of Aberdeen, The, 102, 103
Bridei, 131
Bridge, Clachan, 118, 138
Bridgend, 149, 152, 153, 154, 191
British European Airways, 76, 160
Brittle, Glen, 24, 29
Broadford, 2, 25
Brock, 70
Bronze Age, 200
Brooch of Lorne, 116-17
Brosdale, 182
Brown, Hughie, 130
Brownie, 225-32
Bruce, General, 10
Bruce, King Robert the, 116
Bruichladdich, 153, 162
Bryce, Thomas, M.D., F.R.S., 137
Buchanan, George, 60, 287, 288
Buchanan, Dr. John, 91, 93
Buckley, T. E., 207
Buie, 180
Buie, Ben, 246, 250
Buie, Loch, 241, 246, 250
Bullough, Sir George, 32, 33
Bullough, John, 32, 33
Bunessan, 235, 242, 255
Burg, 242-3, 296-7
Burials and burial places, 14, 16, 22-
   23, 32, 33, 44, 58-9, 63, 65, 77-81,
   82, 102, 103, 114, 123-5, 131, 134-6,
   146, 161, 163, 168, 171, 179-82, 187,
   197, 198, 202-3, 205, 210-11, 217,
   219, 222, 226, 240, 244, 251, 259,
   261, 263, 267, 271, 273-6, 293, 298,
   299-300
Burial Cairn, 55, 65
Burial Urn, 44, 200
Buried Barony, The, 251
Bute, Marquis of, 54
Butt of Lewis, 201, 232

Cadzow, 123
Caesar, The, 94
Cailleach Point, 84
Cailleach, The, 144
Cairn, 65, 109, 233, 259, 265
Cairns of Coll, 84
Cairngorms, 7
Caisteal an Duin Bhain, 63
Caisteal nan Gillean, 200
Caldecott, Percy, 9-11
Caledonian Forest, 120
Caledonian Mercury, 298
Calgary Bay, 238, 247, 255
Calum, 256, 262
Calve Island, 238
Campbell, Alexander, 124
Campbell, Colin, 66
Campbell, Rev. Colin, 102

Campbell, Colin Buchanan, 91
Campbell, General Duncan, of Loch-
   nell, 116
Campbell, Lady Elinor, 160
Campbell, Colonel George Cockburn,
   172-3
Campbell, James, 128-9
Campbell, John Francis, 167
Campbell, John Gregorson, 256
Campbell, Lachlan, 53
Campbell, Malcolm, 93-4
Campbell, Major, of Islay, 159-60
Campbell, Mary, 181
Campbell, Nicholas, 106
Campbell, Samuel, 93
Campbell, Thomas, 82, 288, 302, 308
Campbells, 21, 164, 165, 180, 230,
   232, 272
Campbells, of Bragleen, 116
Campbells, of Calder, 162
Campbells, Clan, 104, 248, 309
Campbells, of Islay, 159, 167
Campbells, of Jura, 181, 187
Campbells, of Lochnell, 103, 116
Campbeltown, 125, 170
Cameron, Ewan, 93
Camerons, 93
Camus, Castle, 15
Camus Mòr, 63
Canna, 28, 29, 30-1, 47, 50-9, 61, 62
Cannach, 40
Caol Ila (distillery), 153
Caolas, 120
Caoles (Coll), 91, 93
Caoles (Tiree), 70
Cara, 214, 218, 220, 224-32
Carmichael, Dr. Alexander, 107
Carmichael, Ella, 107-8
Carmichael, Rev. Iain, 98, 100, 102,
   106
Carmichael, Ronald, 142
Carmina Gadelica, 107
Carn a' Ghaill, 50
Carn Breugach, 109
Carn Cul ri Eirinn, 259
Carn Mor, 68
Carn nan Eoin, 195, 198
Carsaig and Bay, 234, 241
Carsaig Arches, 241
Carved Stones of Islay, 163
Cashel, 55, 137
Castlebay, 70
Cathedral Cave, 40, 42-3
Cathedral of Iona, 271-2
Catholics, 31, 44, 47, 52, 53-4, 102
Catriona (MacQuarrie), 64-5
Catriona's Church, 203
Causeway, 284
Caves, 15, 25, 40-2, 51, 128, 141, 144,
   147, 178, 199-200, 210, 215, 226,
   235-6, 237, 266-7, 281-6, 303

Chalmers, MacGregor, 54
Charadale, Glen, 49
Charles I, 81, 116, 184
Charles Edward Stewart, Prince, the
    Young Pretender, 11-14, 107
Christie, Rev. James Reid, 36
Christina's Skerry, 313
Christus Redemptor gentium, 262-3
Cill Chatriona, 203
Cill Chriosd, 15
Cists, 200, 222-3
City of Glasgow Bank, 162
Clabhach, 86, 88, 89
Clachan, 102
Clachan Bridge, 118, 138
Clachan Seil, 118
Clamshell Cave, 283
Clan Bhreatain, 222
Clan Donald, 249, 309
Clan Donnachaidh, 181
Clan Ranald, 12, 20, 28-9, 44, 47, 50,
    52, 54, 57, 162, 232, 250
Clan Ranald Cave, 41
Clan Ranald, Reginald George, 52
Clann Fhamhair, 221
Cleadale, 40, 44, 45, 46, 47, 65
Clearances, Highland, 3, 31-2, 46
Clerk, Rev. Duncan, 255
Clochain, 136-7
Cluanie, 24
Cnoc Ingibrig, 198
Cnoc na Aingeal, 270
Cnoc nan Ordag, 221
Cnocan a' Chiuil, 220
Cocktail Isles, 28
Coeffin Castle, 105-6
Coins, 279
Coire, 144
Coll, 22, 30, 46, 63, 67, 68, 84-95
Collectanea de Rebus Albanicis, 164
Collie, Professor Norman, 7, 11, 38-9
Collins, publishers, 173
Colonnade, The, 285
Colonsay, 55, 68, 174, 178, 194-213,
    214, 220, 232
Colonsay and Oronsay, 195, 204
Colonsay House, 198, 201, 204, 205
Colonsay, Lord, 205
Columba, Saint, 7, 43, 55, 67, 74, 99-
    101, 114, 122, 131-3, 135, 136, 138,
    163, 201-2, 226, 253, 259-65, 270-1,
    273, 293
Columba's Bay, 263, 268
Columba's Pillow, 263
Columba's Tomb, 264
Commissioners of Northern Light-
    houses, 52, 128, 156
Compass Hill, 50
Conall, 131, 133-4
Congleton, Edith, Lady, 307
Connel, 97

Coolin Sound, 29
Coolins (of Rum), 33, 35, 232
Coolins (of Skye), 6, 8, 24-5, 35, 38,
    64, 174, 175, 232, 243
Coradale, 12
Cormorants' Cave, 286
Cornaig, 91, 94
Cornaigmore, 69
Coroghon Mòr, 56-8
Corpach, 178
Corran, River, 175, 177
Corrie Chatachan, 6
Corrievreckan, Gulf of, 141-7
Coruisk, Loch, 25
Craighouse, 175, 180, 181, 185-9, 190
Craignish, Estates and Point, 134, 142
Craignure and Bay, 87, 150, 238, 239,
    244, 247
Crawford, Earl of, 249
Creag nan Stàrdean, 31
Crinan, 142
Crofters' Act, 3
Crogary Mor, 40
Crooked Pinnacle, 207
Crossapol (Coll), 91
Crossapol (Tiree), 67, 82
Crotach, Alasdair, 15
Crozier, Celtic, 19, 103, 104
Cruach Scarba, 141-2, 147
Cruise of the Betsy, 31
Crusader, 31
Crusades, 19
Cuan, Ferry and Sound, 119, 122, 138,
    143
Cuan, Loch, 244
Cubaig, 197
Cuchullin, 15
Cullipool, 113, 119, 121-3, 125, 138
Culloden, 15, 47
Curdie, Rev. James, 220
Currie, 159, 164

Dalriada, 31, 133
Dalrigh (Kerrera), 114
Dalrigh (Perthshire), 116
Danes, 264, 267
Darroch, 180
Darroch, Professor Alexander, 182-3
Darroch, John, 183
Deer-forest, 177
Department of Agriculture for Scot-
    land, 75
Depopulation, 1, 5, 31, 67, 84, 108,
    143, 158-9, 191-2, 194, 218-19, 251,
    270, 306, 312
Dervaig, 244-7, 255, 305
Deucaledonian Sea, 233
Devon, Dr. Martha, 48
Diarmid, 263
Diatomite, 25
Dibidil, Glen, 32, 34

INDEX

Dinnseanchus, 144
Disraeli, 220-1
Don, Loch, 110
Dorus Mor, 142-3
Douglas, George, 288-9, 292, 312
dowser, 98
Drimnin, 287
Drinking horn, 21
Druimyeon Bay, 215
Druimyeon Beag, 216
Duart, 81, 87
Duart, Point and Castle, 97, 234, 248-249
Dubh Heartach, v, 69, 77, 195, 235
Duich, Loch, 24
Duilleter, Glen, 128
Duirinish, 1
Dumbarton, 225
Dun, 82
Dun Bhreanain, 134
Dun da Ghaoithe, 244
Dun Eibhinn, 201
Dun I, 135, 260, 265, 269
Dun Naomhaig, 162-3
Dunan nan Nighean, 199
Dunbartonshire, 303
Duncan, King, 275
Duncanson, John, 124-5
Dunchonill, or Dun Chonnuill or Dunchonall, 133-4, 138
Dundee, 125
Dunfermline, 275
Dunkeld, 271-2
Dunnett, Alastair M., 34
Dunollie, and Estates, 109, 111, 113, 116
Dunscaith, 15
Duntulm, 7, 23
Dunvegan, 4, 141, 309
Dunvegan Castle, 4, 10, 15-22
Dunvegan Cup, 20-1
Dunvegan Head, 2
Dunvegan, Loch, 1
Dunyveg, 162, 250
Dutchman's Cap, 255

Eagamol, 64
Eagle, 178, 240
Earnadail, 179-80
Earth houses, 56
Earthquakes, 234
Easdail, 197
Easdale, 118-21, 126, 130, 135
Ecclesiastical Architecture of Scotland, 202
Edinburgh, 18, 49, 75, 137, 171, 172, 182, 200, 204, 217, 244-5, 264, 266-267, 293, 298, 299, 309, 311
Education, Director of, 5
Eigg, 28, 29, 31, 36, 37, 38-49, 53-4, 60-2, 64-5, 68, 131, 232

Eileach an Naoimh, 102, 132-9 (*see also* Aileach . . .)
Eilean a' Beithich, 120
Eilean a' Cheo, 1
Eilean Ard nan Uan, 63
Eilean Donan, 43
Eilean Dubh, 100
Eilean nam Ban, 197
Eilean nan Each, 60, 63
Eilean nan Ròn, 197
Eirebal, 106
Eishort, Loch, 1, 11
Eithne, 131, 136
Ellenabeich, 119, 120-1, 126
Eorsa Isle, 234, 304
Episcopalians, 252-4
Eriskay, 169-70
Ernan, 131, 133
Erraid, 69, 255
Erray, 256
Ettrick Shepherd, The, 312
Ewen of the Little Head, 250, 275

Fada, Loch (Colonsay), 198-9
Fada, Loch (Skye), 26
Faeries, 26, 49, 66, 83, 201, 220, 256, 260, 270-1
Faery Bridge, 20
Faery Flag, 18-20
Faery Woman's Croon or Lullaby, 19
Fair Isle, 252
Falkirk, 24, 48
False Cairn, 109
feannagan, 297
Feorlin, 175, 189, 191
Ferguson, Captain, 47
Fiart, Loch, 99
Fiddler's Loch, 127
Findluganus, 133
Fingal, Fingalians, 15, 99, 167, 285
Fingal's Cave, 281, 284-6, 289-90, 304, 305
Fingal's Limpet Hammers, 200
Fingal's Putting Stone, 199
Fingal's Stair, 199
Fingal's Table, 236
Fingon, clan, 6, 248
Finlaggan and Loch, 149, 155, 163, 164-6
Finnan, Saint, 253
Fionaphort, 238, 255, 260-1, 267
Fionn Chrò, 30
Fionnlaidh, Saint, 225
Firth of Lorne, 109-10, 113, 118, 122, 141, 233, 234
Fladda, 121, 125, 126, 138, 139, 143
Flodigarry, 13
Forbes, Bishop, 47
Fordun, John of, 293
Forestry Commission, 247
Forglen, 264

INDEX

Fort William, 96
Forty-five, The, 22, 47-8
Foss, Colonel, 252
Fox's Chair, 221, 227
Fraser, David, 22
Fraser (Simon, Lord Fraser of Lovat), 22
Fraser, Rev. William, 219
Free Presbyterians (Wee Frees), 5
Frisa, Loch, 245, 248
Funeral, 240, 261 (see also Burials)

Gabran, 133
Galbraith, 216, 219, 221-2, 225
gale, March, 1921, 17
Gallanach (Argyll mainland), 112
Gallanach (Coll), 91
Gallanach (Muck), and Bay and House, 62-4
Galmisdale, 29, 40-1, 45-6, 49
Garbh Eileach, 134, 138
Garden of Skye, 1, 11
Garnett, Professor, 291
Garrisdale, Point, 56
garron, 84
Gartbreck, 159
Garvard, 194, 200
Garvellachs, v, 102, 121, 131-40, 141, 234
Geikie, Sir Archibald, 54, 59, 176, 285
Geodha Eithne, 131
George Watson's, Edinburgh, 28, 172, 173
ghosts, 26-7, 57, 128-9, 197, 250, 275, 310-11
Giant's Causeway, 282-3, 304
Giant's Clan, 221
Gigalum, 226, 229-30
Gigha, 159, 174, 185, 190, 194, 214-223, 224-30, 231
Gillies, Dr. Patrick, 120, 144
glaistig, 201, 256-7, 313
Glamaig, 9, 10
Glasgow, 88, 126, 169, 171-2, 180, 188, 212, 214, 218, 233, 278, 288, 298, 302, 305
Glassard, 194, 196-7
Glen Aros, 244
Glen Forsa, 243-4
Glen More, 233, 239, 240, 244, 255
Glencreggan, 229
Glendale, 2, 3, 4, 5
Glendale Martyr, The, 3
Glenegedale, 152, 158, 160
Glenelg, 21, 26, 28
Glengorm Castle, 247
Goat Fell, 195
Goat Wife, The, 244
gold, 42, 55
Gometra, 234, 237, 255, 287, 303, 305
Goorkha, 9

Gordon, John Wolrige, 24
Gorm, Loch, 148
Gott Bay, 70-3, 82-3
Gourock, 214
Graham, 163
Great Cave, 215
Great Face, The, 285
Great Glen, The, 96
Great Heroes, Port of the, 99
Gregorson, 101-2
Gregory, 81
Grey Dog, Pass of the, 143, 145
Gribun, 234-5, 238-41, 248, 286, 293-294, 297, 300, 305, 308
Grieve, Symington, 200, 204
Grishipoll, 86, 88
Gruagach, 26, 83, 201
Gruinart, Loch, 148, 166
Gruinart Shore, 167, 190
Grulin, 46, 64-5
Gruline, 238, 247, 254, 310
guano, 40
Guirdil Bay, 31-2
Gulf Stream, 196
Gunna, Isle, 91, 93
Gunna Sound, 68, 70
Gylen Castle, 109, 114-16
Gylen, Upper, 110

Haco, 5, 115, 217-18, 221, 226, 230, 271, 309
Hairy Donald, 128
Hairy Mary, 184
Hangman's Rock, 207
Hannan, Rev. Thomas, 139
Harris, 78, 150, 254
Harris, Glen, 32-5
Harvey, W. F., 296
Harvey-Brown, 207
Harvie-Brown, 45
heather, white, 2, 40
Heaval, 195
Hebrides (ship), 174
Hebrides Overture, 290
Herdsman, The, 283, 285
Herkia (Goorkha), 9-11
Heylipol, 75, 82
Heynish, and Bay, 69, 71, 75, 77
Heynish, Beinn, 68
Highland Clearances, 3, 312
Highways and Byways in the West Highlands, 94, 178
Hill, John, 164
Hill of the Little Fox, 221
Himalaya, 10
Hinba, 102, 131-3, 138
Hollow of the Mote, 221
Holy Women, Cliff of the, 55
Holyrood, 202
Horse's Isle, 60, 63-4
Hough, 75

320

House of Commons, 84
Humpies, 294
Hunterian Museum, 218
Huntly, Earl of, 249
Hutcheson, David, 111, 113
Hydro-electric, 26
Hyskeir, v

I (Iona), 261
I Chaluim-Chille, 262
Iain Ban Og MacLeod, 57-8
Iceland, 282, 287
Inary, 256
Inch Kenneth, 233-4, 236, 246, 255, 293-301, 304-5, 308
Indaal, Loch, 148-9, 153, 159, 167-8, 191
Innamore, 241
Insula Hinbinae, 131
Insula Sancti Kennethi, 298-9
Inventory of monuments and constructions, 39
Inver, 182
Inveraray, 21, 76, 104-5, 111
Inverlussa, 179, 184, 187
Inverness, 249
Inverness-shire, 5, 13, 24, 28, 38
Iona, 67-8, 72, 99, 101, 131, 163, 195, 201, 205, 215, 225, 233-4, 236, 238, 241, 246, 255, 258-80, 281-2, 286-7, 304-5
Iona Abbey Trustees, 265, 272
Iona Club, 275
Iona Community, 265, 272-3, 278-80
Iona Pebbles, 268
Ireland, 21, 77, 102, 136-7, 160, 163, 169, 185, 195, 201-2, 207, 221, 259, 264, 283, 293
Irish Epigraphy, 220
iron, 25, 50, 77, 224
Island of Staffa, The, 283
Islands of Scotland, The, 35
Islay, and Sound, 68, 148-73, 174, 176, 178, 180, 185, 190-1, 194, 211, 214-215, 230, 248, 252
Islay House, 149, 153, 157, 159, 160, 167
Isleburgh, 82
Isles of the Sea, The, 109, 140

Jackson, William, 233
Jacobite, 47
James IV, 120
James VI and I, 42, 81, 249
Janes, Mr., 16
Jehu, Professor T. J., 266
Jo(h)an, 133-4
John of Fordun, 202
John, Lord of the Isles, 202, 205, 249

Johnson, Dr. Samuel, 6, 8, 13-16, 18, 21, 22, 25, 31, 60, 85, 90, 92-3, 236, 246-7, 258, 297-8, 304, 308, 311
Jones, Paul, 159-60
Journal (Boswell), 13-14
Journey to the Hebrides, A, 291
Jura, 68, 109, 134, 141, 144-5, 147-8, 156, 174-93, 194-6, 199, 214
Jura Forest, 178
Jura House, 189

Keats, John, 289
Keills, 163, 179-81
Kennedy, Mr., 229
Kennedy, Neil, 308
Kennedy-Fraser, Marjory, 74, 223, 276
Kenneth, 293
Kernache, 133-4
Kerrera, Island and Sound, 109-17, 118, 139, 234
Kilarrow, 148
Kilchattan (Colonsay), 194, 197-8, 200, 205
Kilchattan (Gigha), 219
Kilchattan (Luing), 123-5
Kilcheran and Loch, 97-9
Kilchiaran, 169
Kilchoan, 94-5
Kilchoan Cottage, 15, 141
Kilchomain, 148, 159, 163, 168-70
Kilda, Saint, 253
Kildalton, 148, 153-4, 159, 163, 171, 190
Kildonan, 43
Kildonnan, 38, 42, 44, 65
Kilfinichen and Bay, 238, 248, 293
Kilmeny, 148, 211
Kilmore, 244-5, 303
Kilmory, 32
Kilmory Lodge, 142, 145-6
Kilmuir (Dunvegan), 16, 22
Kilmuir (of Trotternish), 14, 23
Kilnaughton Bay, 161
Kilnave, 148
Kilninian, 238, 244-5, 303
Kilninver, 118
Kiloran, 194-5, 197-9, 205, 210-13
Kiloran Abbey, 201
Kilvickeon, 293
King's Cave, 178
King's Field and Well, 114-15
Kingairloch, 98
Kingsburgh, 13, 14
Kinloch Castle (Skye), 29, 32-4, 36
Kinloch, River (Skye), 34
Kinloch (Mull), 238, 248
Kintail, 24, 43
Kintyre, 148, 174, 179, 190, 214-15, 217, 224-7, 229-31
Kinuachdrach, 145
Kirkmichael-Glassary, 103

INDEX

Klingemann, 290
Knapdale, 174, 179, 190, 215
Kneeling Stone, 221
Knight, G. A. Frank, D.D., 137
Knock Castle, 14
Knox, Thomas, Bishop of the Isles, 30, 61
Koestler, Arthur, 193
Kyle of Lochalsh, 2, 5, 24-5
Kyleakin, 5, 25, 150
Kylerhea, 24, 25

Ladder Cave, 235
Lady's Rock, 97, 234
Lagavulin, 153, 162
Lagg, 187
Laggan Bay, 148
Laig, 45, 49
Laig Bay, 38, 40, 45
Laird's Pew, 37
Lake-dwelling, 44
Lam-dess, 133
Lamont family, 83
Largie, Castle, Rock and Sound, 221, 224-8, 230
Largs, Battle of, 6, 115, 217, 271, 309
Latvians, 125
Lawson, Malcolm, 300
Lay of Charles Edward at Versailles, 143
Leabhar na Feinne, 167
Leach, 287
Leathan, Loch, 26
Leaves from a Journal of our Life in the Highlands, 290
Leith, 49
Lennox Street, 150
Lerwick, 123
Leslie, Alick, 112-13
Leslie, Bishop, 287
Lewis, 68, 78, 132, 201, 232, 233, 254
Leyden, Dr. John, 115, 292
Life of St. Columba, Founder of Hy (Iona), 133
Lifting Stone, 204
Linnhe, Loch, 96
Liosaich, 98
Lismore, 87, 96-108, 109, 234
Lismore in Alba, 98, 106
Little Colonsay, 234, 255, 267, 281, 303, 305
Little Folk, 127-8
Little Hillock of the Oratory, 221
Little Horse Shoe Bay, 109, 112-15
Livingstone, David, 104-5, 312
Livingstone, Donald, 129
Livingstone, John, 145-7
Livingstones, 248
Lobster King (of Kerrera), 112
Loch a' Phuill, 68, 69, 77
Loch an Oir, 174

Loch an t-Sìob, 175
Loch Bà, 245
Loch Bhasapol, 69
Loch Don, 34, 241
Loch Eishort, 1
Loch Fyne, 214
Loch Goil, 302-3
Loch Gyle, 302
Loch Mor Vaterstein, 2
Loch na Dal, 1
Loch na Keal, 237-8, 243, 246, 248, 254, 260, 293-4, 301-4
Loch nam Ban Mora, 44
Loch nam Dubhrachan, 26
Loch Tay, 117
Lochaline, 252
Lochan Nighinn Dughaill, 49
Lochboisdale, 29
Lochbuie, 200, 247, 253
Lochdonhead, 239
Locheil, 93
Lochlann, 19, 106, 144, 232
Lochnell, 116
Loder, John de Vere (Lord Wakehurst), 195
Londonderry, Bishop of, 291
Longevity, 184-5
Lord of the Isles, 57, 162-3, 202, 218, 221, 248, 264, 271, 275-6, 309
Lord of the Isles, The, 116, 289
Lord Lyon King of Arms, 24
Lord Ullin's Daughter, 82, 302
Lorne, 96, 118, 121, 125, 134, 142
Lorne, Brooch of, 116
Lorne, John, Lord of, 116
Lorne, Marquis of, 104-5
Lovat, Simon, Lord, 22
Lovers' Stone, 240
Lowlandman's Bay, 178
Luath, 15
Lucky Well of Bethia or Beathag, 215
Luing, 113, 118-19, 121-3, 125, 127-30, 134-5, 138, 141-3, 145, 147
Luinneag MhicLeoid, 141
Lunga, 122, 133-5, 138, 141, 143
Lusbirdan, 201
Lynn of Lorne, 96, 100, 109
Lynn of Morven, 96, 109
Lyon in Mourning, The, 47

Mac a' Phearson, 19, 20
MacAlister, 220, 277
MacAllan, Donald, 250
MacAlpin, Kenneth, 274
MacArthur, Rev. D., D.D., 251
MacArthur's Head, 148, 190
MacArthurs, 23, 309
Macartney, Dr. Alan, 211
Macaulay, 106-7
MacBrayne, 29, 96, 111-12, 190, 241, 261, 282-3, 304-5

322

MacCaibre, 249
MacCallum, Rev. Donald, 3
MacColl, John, 108
MacCrain, 180
MacCrain, Gillouir, 181, 184, 187
MacCrimmons, 21-3, 309
MacCrimmon's Lament, 199
MacCulloch, Canon John Arnott, D.D., 7, 132, 135, 237, 292, 303
MacCulloch, Donald B., 283, 286
MacCulloch's Tree, 237
MacDiarmids, 248
MacDonald, Alan, 49
MacDonald, Sir Alexander, 13, 15
MacDonald, Angus (of Dunyveg), 250
MacDonald, Angus (of Milton), 12
MacDonald, Flora, 11-14, 23
MacDonald, Flora (Mrs. Smith), 11
MacDonald, Hugh, 11
MacDonald, Captain James, 108
MacDonald, Sir James, 162, 167
MacDonald, Lady Margaret, 11-12
MacDonald, Mrs., 65
MacDonald family, 110
MacDonald of the Isles, 165
MacDonald of Largie, 224-5, 227-8
MacDonald of Sleat, 164, 250
MacDonald's Cave, 41
MacDonalds, The, 249, 309
MacDonalds of Eigg, 41-3, 45
MacDonalds of Islay, 162, 166-7, 190
MacDougall, 109, 111-13, 115-17, 164, 180
MacDougall, Donald, 150
MacDougall, Duncan, 116
MacDuffie, 201, 205
MacDuffie, Murdoch, 205
MacDuffie's Cross, 205
MacEachain, 12
MacEacharn, 164
MacEachern, 163-4, 167
MacEwan, Lawrence, 61-2
MacFadyen, Angus, 208-9
MacFadyen, Donald, 205
MacFadyens, 293
MacFarlane, Malcolm, 233, 246
MacFarquhar, Mrs., 245
Macgibbon and Ross, 202
MacGillivray, Neil, 296, 301
MacGillivrays, 248
MacGregor, Alasdair Alpin, 7
MacGregor, Duncan, 107, 262
MacGregor, Sir James, 101-2, 107
MacIain, 30, 200
MacIans, 11
MacInnes, Malcolm, 232
MacIntyre, 114
MacIsaac, 180
Mackarter, 23
MacKay, 180

MacKay, John, 69, 181
MacKechnies, 145-6, 180, 185, 190
MacKenzie, Clan, 15, 19
MacKenzie, Kenneth, 273
MacKenzie, Willie, 210
MacKenzie's Isle, 161
MacKenzie's Rock, 69
MacKinnon, 6, 248
MacKinnon, Hugh, 48, 65
MacKinnon, John, 273, 286
MacKinnon's Cave (Mull), 235-6
MacKinnon's Cave (Staffa), 286
MacKintosh Muniments, 225
MacLachlan, Captain Alexander, 128-129
MacLaine of Lochbuie, 200, 248, 250, 253
MacLaine, Murdoch Gillian, 253
MacLean, 180
MacLean, Alexander, 124-5
MacLean, Sir Allan, 236, 246, 297-8
MacLean, Catherine, 180
MacLean, Donald, 61
MacLean, Rev. Donald, 171-2
MacLean, Sir Donald Fitzroy, 250
MacLean, Rev. Hector, 85-6
MacLean, Sir Hector, 298
MacLean, Hector and Lachlan, 250
MacLean, Sir Lachlan, 167
MacLean, Mrs., 305
MacLean, the Very Reverend Dr. Norman, 183
MacLeans, 249, 272, 299-300, 309
MacLeans of Coll, 30-2, 91-3
MacLeans of Duart, 81, 91, 116, 162, 166-7, 190, 248, 250, 278
MacLean's Cross, 277
MacLellan, John Roy, 47-8
MacLeod, Alan, 46
MacLeod, Alasdair, 250
MacLeod, Fiona, 259, 266
MacLeod, General, 17
MacLeod, Rev. Dr. George, 263, 278-280
MacLeod, Rev. Dr. Kenneth, D.D., 48-9, 65, 74, 188, 194, 214, 215, 217-18, 220-3, 227, 229-32, 276
MacLeod, Malcolm, 21
MacLeod, Mary, 141
MacLeod, Miss, 18
MacLeod, Norman Magnus, 4
MacLeod, Sir Reginald, 17, 22
MacLeod, Rory, 250
MacLeod, Torquil, 282
MacLeod of MacLeod, 9-10, 29
MacLeod of MacLeod, Flora, Mrs., 4
MacLeod Cave, 41
MacLeods, The, 23-4, 28-9, 41-3, 46, 57, 249, 309
MacLeods, The, of Eigg, 42
MacLonich, Clan, 92-3

MacMartins, 93
Macnabb, 24
MacNeil, Donald, 52
MacNeils of Gigha, 218-19, 225
MacNeils, The, 249
MacNeill, John, 103
MacNeill family, 196, 208-11
MacNicol, Rev. Donald, 107
MacNiven, 159
MacPhail, Dugald, 233
MacPhails, 248
MacPhee, 199-201, 205
MacPhee's Cave, 200
MacPherson, John, 3
Macquarie, 310
MacQuarrie, Donald, 48, 64-5
MacQuarrie, Lachlan, 309, 311
MacQuarrie, Major-General Lachlan,
  309-10
MacQuarrie, Mr., 235
MacQuarrie Mausoleum, 247
MacQuarries, The, 248, 308-9, 313
MacQueen, 164
MacRae, John, 26
MacRae country, 43
MacRury, Rev. Mr., 183
MacTaggart, Iain, 189-91
Macvurich, 249
Machar, The, 265-6, 268, 270
Machrie Moss, 153
Machrins, 194, 198, 204-5
Maiden of Morven, 300
Mairi Nighean Alasdair Ruadh, 141
Malcolm Canmore, 275
Mallaig, 25, 29, 51, 52
Mam Ratagan, 24
Maol Castle, 6
Maolrubha, Saint, 114
Map of Iona, 266
marble, 25, 76, 265-6
Margaret, Queen, 277
Martin, Martin, 30, 39, 43, 44, 50,
  60, 144, 178, 181, 184, 200, 201,
  205, 216, 219
Martyrs' Bay, 261, 267
Mary Queen of Scots, 81, 115
Mary's Well, 216
Mary Stewart, The, 70
Mausoleum, 33, 247, 310-11
Mayer, Joseph, 253
Meggernie, 32
Melrose, 115
Mendelssohn, Felix, 284, 289-90
Mercheta Mulierum, 311
Merry-le-Hant, 253
Michael, Feast of Saint, 271
Miller, Hugh, 31, 45
Mills, Abraham, 291
Milovaig, 2, 16
Minch, The, 38, 52, 55
Minginish, 28

Mingulay, 38
Minister's Burn, 180
Minister's Creek, 218
Minister's Well, 217
Minstrelsy of the Scottish Highlands,
  The, 233
Mishnish Lochs, 244, 246
Misty Isle of Skye, The, 7
Moidart, 47
Moidart, John of, 44
Moluag, Saint, 99-103
Moluag's Well, 106
Monastery, 275
Monro, (Dean) Donald, 30, 60, 120,
  126, 133, 274
monster, 49
Monymusk Reliquary, 264
Morar, 28, 47
Morrison, John, 272
Morrison, Mrs., 36
Morven, 87, 96, 98, 233, 287
Moy Castle, 248, 250
Moyle, The, 224, 231
Muasdale, 229
Muck, 28-30, 36, 46, 60-6
Mudzartsonne, Angus John, 42
muinntir, 102
Mull, 22, 30, 68, 72, 73, 75, 77, 84,
  86-7, 91, 95, 109, 110, 122, 139, 141,
  148, 150, 167, 194, 196, 233-57, 261,
  269, 275, 281-2, 286, 293, 294, 296-7,
  308
Mull of Oa, 149, 168-9
Munro, Robert, 309
Murdoch of Kintyre, 226
Murray, Mrs., 197
Murray, Mrs., of Kensington, 312

National Art Collections Fund, 264
National Museum of Antiquities of
  Scotland, 103, 204, 264, 279
National Trust for Scotland, 34, 242-
  243, 296-7
Netherlorn, 120
Nettleton, M. B., 35
New Statistical Account, 255
Newton, Isaac, 102
Nicholas, Donald, 39
Nicolson, Sheriff Alexander, 8
Norse and Norway, 5, 6, 38, 43, 54,
  105-6, 114-15, 127, 137, 198, 203,
  214, 217-18, 221, 226, 264, 271, 286-
  287, 309
North Carolina, 108
North End Ferry (Gigha), 214-15, 222
North End Ferry (Lismore), 96-7,
  108
North of Scotland Hydro-Electric
  Board, 26
Nova Scotia, 46, 93
Numismatic Chronicle, 279

INDEX

Nunnery, 55, 203-4, 264, 267, 273, 275

Oa, The, 148, 149, 161, 171-2
Oban, 69, 73, 80, 84, 86-8, 94, 96-7, 109-14, 118-19, 123, 127, 130, 138-9, 150, 194, 210, 238, 241, 243, 261, 266, 305
Oban Times, The, 127
Obelisk (Hutcheson), 113
O'Brolchan, Donaldus, 272
Ochiltree, Lord, 249
Ogham Stone, 219-20
Old Statistical Account of Scotland, 99, 184, 201, 219
O'Neil, 12
Oran, 202
Oran, Saint, 253, 269, 273
Oran, Saint's Chapel, 271, 277
Ord, 6, 11
Ordnance Survey, 9, 197, 200, 259, 294
Ormacleit, 12
Ormsaig, 307
Oronsay, 178, 194-213
Oronsay House, 197
Oronsay Priory, 198
Orpheus Choir, 233
Orsay, 161
Orval, 35
Orwell, George, 192-3
Oscar, Bay and Inlet, 99
Ossian, 15
Over the Sea to Skye, 7, 9
Oversay, 161, 169
Oxford University Mountaineering Club, 35

Pabbay, 2
Paisley Abbey, 249
Papadil, 32
Paps of Jura, 109, 174-6, 177
Pass of the Grey Dog, 143, 145
Paterson, Rev. Alexander, 244
Paterson, Rev. Hector, 244-5
peat, 2, 62, 75, 85, 98, 151-3, 156, 196, 199, 215, 269, 294
Peel, Sir Robert, 285
Peingown, 23
Penance Stone, 204
Pennant, Thomas, 8, 20, 31, 53, 112, 198, 202, 267, 271, 275, 287
Pennyghael, 248
Perthshire, 33
Picts, 131
Pigeon's Cave (Colonsay), 199
Pigeon's Cave (Eigg), 40
Pigeon's Cave (Gigha), 215
Pigmies' Isle, 201
Pigmy, 201
Pilgrim Trust, 242

Pilgrims' Way, 238, 255, 260
Piper's Cave, 199
Piping College, 21-3, 309
Pittenweem, 81
Politician, The, 169-70
Poll an Aba, 225
Pooltiel, Loch, 16
Pope, The, 263
Popular Tales of the West Highlands, The, 167-8
Port Appin, 96
Port Askaig, 194, 211 (*see also* Portaskaig)
Port Ban, 70
Port Chaisteil, 106
Port Charlotte, 153, 159, 162, 169
Port Edgar, 251
Port Ellen, 149, 152, 153, 156, 159-61, 171
Port Lobh, 199
Port Moluag, 100, 102
Port Mòr, 62-3
Port na Curaich, 259
Port of the Coracle, 259, 263
Port of the Great Heroes, 99
Port Ramsay, 96
Port Wemyss, 153, 159, 161
Portaskaig, 153, 155, 156, 159, 163, 174, 176, 189, 190-1, 230 (*see also* Port Askaig)
Portnahaven, 153, 159, 161, 170, 172
Portree, 1, 2, 26, 27, 183
Price-Hughes, Barbara Patricia, 172-3
Prince Albert, 290
Prince Charlie, 11-13, 14, 47
Prince Charlie's country, 38
Prior Colin's Cross, 203
Prior's House, 203
Priory of St. Columba, 201-2, 205, 208, 210
Proceedings of the Society of Antiquaries of Scotland, 279
ptarmigan, 178

Queen of the Hebrides, 149
Queen of the Pirates, 43
quern, 230
Quest by Canoe, 34
Quirang, 2, 47

Raasay, 1, 2, 13, 25
raised beach, 39, 156, 174, 176, 178, 198, 199, 265
Ramasaig, 2
Ramsays, 154
Rankins, 22, 91
Red Coolins, or Red Hills, 6, 8
Reef, The, 73, 75, 77
Reeves, Professor, 101, 133
Reginald, Lord of the Isles, 264, 271, 275

Reilig Odhrain, 271, 273-8
Reliquary of St. Columba, 264
Remarks on Dr. Samuel Johnson's Journey to the Hebrides, 107
Renfrew, 76, 150, 152, 158, 160, 231, 241
Rerum Scoticarum Historia, 287
Retreat of the Miserable Women, 204
Rhinns of Islay, 148, 153, 161-2, 167, 169
Riasg Buidhe, 194-5
Richardson, J. S., 137
Ringing Stone, The, 82
Ritchie, Alexander, 276
Road to the Isles, The, 188, 223, 232
Robert, Steward of Scotland (Robert II), 202
Roberton, Sir Hugh, 233
Robertson, Rev. John Donald, 180
Robertson, Rev. Mr., 89
Robertson, Clan, 181
Rodil (Harris), 15
Rona, 1
Rona, North, 132
Ronin, 30
Rorie More's Cascade, 18
Rory Mòr, Sir, 21
Rory Mor's Nurse, 17
Rosemarkie, 102
Ross, The (of Mull), 233, 235, 237-9, 242, 248, 255, 260, 265, 294, 304
Rossinish, 12
Ross-shire, 150, 157
Royal College of Surgeons, 200
Royal Commission Report (1886), 3
Royal Highland Club, 111
Royal Society, President of the, 258, 287
Ruaig, 70, 83
Rudh' a' Mhail, 148, 149, 230
Rudh' an Dunain, 29
Rudha Langaninnis, 55
Rudha na h-Uamha, 237
Rum, 28-37, 38, 45, 50, 61, 64, 68
Runcimans, 39, 48
Ruttledge, Hugh, 305

Saddell, Abbey and Abbot, 217, 226
St. Andrews, 18
St. Brendan, 133, 134
St. Cainnech, 133
St. Congall, 133
St. Cormac, 133
St. Donnon, 42-4
St. Finla, 225
Saint Font, Faujas de, 291
St. Francis (Cave of), 41-3, 45
St. Kenneth's Chapel, 293, 298
St. Kilda, 68
St. Kilda's, 253

St. Martin's Cross, 277
St. Mary's (Scarba), 146
St. Mary's Cathedral (Iona), 259, 263
St. Roman's Chapel, 273
Salen and Bay, 234, 238, 244-5, 247, 255, 260, 307
Saligo Bay, 149, 173
Salisbury, Marquis of, 32
Salmon King (of Kerrera), 114
Sanaig, 149, 156
Sanctuary, 202
Sanday, 28, 50-1, 54-5
Sandford, Sir Daniel, 298-9
Sanna, 28
sapphires, 241
Saucy Mary, 6
Scalasaig, 194-6, 198, 200-1, 208, 210-211
Scallastle Bay, 238, 247
Scallop Cave, 283
Scalpay, 1, 2
Scamadale, 116
Scarba, 109, 119, 122, 134, 141-7, 184
Scarinish, 69, 77, 95
Scarts' Cave, 286
Scavaig, Loch, 25
Scian (Skye), 7
Sconser, 26-7
Scotland in Early Christian Times, 137
Scott, Sir Walter, 8, 17, 42, 57, 116, 143, 270, 289, 312
Scottish Airways, 24
Scottish Council of Social Service, 5
Scottish Gaelic Texts Society, 107
Scottish Geological Society, 234
Scottish Land Court, 75
Scottish Mountaineering Club, 7
Scottish Mountaineering Club Journal, 34-5
Scottish National Library, 107
Scottish Reminiscences, 59
Scresort, Loch, 28-9, 32-7
Scridain, Loch, 235, 237-9, 242-3, 248, 255, 260
Scuir of Eigg, 38-40, 47, 64, 232
Sculptured Stones of Scotland, The, 203
Sea Horse, 107
Sea Horse (man o' war), 127
seals, 51, 161
Seaweed Industry, 76
Second-sight, 311
Seil, 118-19, 120-2, 125, 134, 135, 138, 143
Seilisdeir, Glen, 30
Set Free, 183
Seton Gordon, 7, 30, 94, 178, 200, 208, 239
Sgòr nam Ban Naomha, 55
Sgurr Alasdair, 8

Sgurr Dubh, 8
Sgùrr nan Gillean, 32, 33, 35
Sgùrr nan Gobhar, 33
Sgùrr Sgaileach, 47
Shaw, 164, 180
Shaw, Angus, 126
Shaw, Donald, 189
Shian, 270
Shiel, Glen, 24
Shieling of the Maiden's Rock, 313
Shuna, Island and Kyle, 119, 128
singing sands, 40, 45, 232
Sithean Mor, 270
Skeabost, 17
Skene, W. F., 133
Skerryvore, v, 67, 69, 77, 195, 235
Sklaitt, 126
Skokholm, 31
Skye, v, 1-27, 28, 50, 57, 68, 131, 141,
    148, 150, 183, 232, 233, 248, 254,
    275, 282, 309
Skye Week, The, 7
Slapin, Loch, 1
Slate Islands, 109, 113, 118-30, 135,
    141, 234
Slatrach, 114
Slatrich, 110
Sleat, 1, 11, 14-15, 25, 26, 28, 232,
    250
Sleat, Sound of, 1
Sligachan, Glen, 8
Sligachan Inn, 9, 11, 26
Sligachan, Loch, 2
Slugan Burn, 36
Small Isles, The, 28-66
Small Isles of Jura, 155, 190, 232
smallpox, 61
Smaull, 149
Smith, Adam, 31
Smith, Alexander, 7. 8, 11
Smith, Freddie, 173
Snizort, Loch, 1
Snizort, Parish, 183
Soa, 70-1
Soay, 1
Somerled, 21
Somewhere in Scotland, 26
Songs of the Hebrides, The, 74, 223
Songs of the North, The, 188, 300
Sound of Iona, 233, 238, 260-1, 270
Sound of Islay, 148, 153, 156
Sound of Mull, 233, 238, 243-4, 260
Sound of Ulva, 237
Sorn, River, 149, 154
spaewife, 181
Spanish galleon, 251
Spar Cave, 25
Spelve, Loch, 110, 234, 241, 246
Spencer, Robina Jarvie, 273
Spouting Cave, 267
Sraid na Marbh, 267

Staffa, 234, 255, 267, 270, 281-92, 303-
    305
Staffin Bay, 1
Stalker Castle, 120
standing stones, 56, 82, 179, 200
Staonaig, Loch, 268
Starvation Terrace, 312
Steele, James R., 265
Stenness, 166
Stevenson, Alan, 69
Stevenson, R. B. K., 279
Stevenson, R. L., 234, 255
Stevenson's Rock, 69
Steward of Scotland, 202
Stewart, Captain Archibald, 205
Stewart, James, 42
Stewart, Kenneth, 91
Stewart, Brigadier Paul, C.B., 93
Stewart Kings, 202
Stewarts of Appin, 120
Stone Age, 260
stone implements, 200
Stornaway, 160
Storr Lochs, 26
Storr, Old Man of, 26
Strand, 194, 206-10
Strath, 6, 25
Strath Mor, 1
Strathaird, 11, 25
Strathcona, Lord, 203
Street of the Dead, 267
Stuart, 203
Stuarts, 13, 48
Suilven, 38
Summer in the Hebrides, 197
Summer in Skye, A, 7
Sunart, 32
Sutherland, 157
Swynes Ile, 60

Tales of a Grandfather, The, 116
Talisker, 16, 17, 25
Tarbert (Gigha), 215
Tarbert (Jura), 178-9, 187
Tarbert, Loch (East) (Gigha), 215
Tarbert, Loch (West) (Gigha), 215
Tarbert, Loch (East) (Kintyre), 214
Tarbert, Loch (West) (Kintyre), 159,
    179, 185, 214-15
Tarskavaig, 11
Tayinloan, 214, 217
temperance, 4, 46, 77-81, 185, 211-13,
    300
Thom, 50, 52-5, 58
Thumbs, Hill of the, 221-2
Tianavaig, 2
Tignernach, 102
Tiree, 67-83, 84-5, 94-5, 131, 195, 232
Tiroran, 248
Tobar an h-Aoise, 269
Tobar Chaluim-cille, 135

INDEX

Tobar Cnamh Bheothail, 106
Tobermory and Bay, 59, 77, 87, 94, 234, 238, 244, 246-7, 250-2, 256
Toberonochy, 119, 122-3, 129-30, 138, 145, 147
Tokavaig, 11
Tolmie, Frances, 15, 19, 141
Tomdoun, 24
Torloisk, 248
Torosay, 247, 255
Torran Rocks, 234, 270
Totarder, 7
Totronald, 88, 90
Tour of the Hebrides with Samuel Johnson, LL.D., 286
Tour of Scotland in 1772, 287
Tour in the Hebrides, A.D. 1800, 289, 312
Traigh Mhor, 71
Traigh Sorobaidh, 71
Trallval, 35
trawlers, 156
Trench-Gascoigne, Colonel Frederick, 137
Treshnish Isles, v, 234, 255, 270-1, 287, 305
Trossachs, 247
Trotternish, 1, 8, 13, 23
Trumpan, 20, 42
Tuath, Loch, 238, 304
Tynan, Katherine, 155

Uaigh na Caillich, 222
Uamh Mhic 'ic Ailein nan Eilean, 47
Uisg, Loch, 246, 247
Uist, North, 40, 68, 107, 158, 170, 252, 254
Uist, South, 12, 38, 47, 51-2, 68, 170, 254
Ulva, v, 233, 234, 237, 238, 248, 250, 255, 267, 281, 293, 297, 301, 302-3

Uragaig, 194, 199, 200
Urray, 15

Varrigil, Glen, 27
Vaternish, 3, 13, 20
Vertebrate Fauna of Argyll and the Inner Hebrides, A, 207
Victoria, Queen, 31, 117, 182, 290
Viking, 54, 55, 198, 218

Wakehurst, Lord, 195
Walker, Dr., 176
Walter, Mrs. (Flora, Mrs. MacLeod of MacLeod), 23
Water-horse, 2, 26, 49
Watson, Professor William J., 204, 267
Weir, Lachlan MacNeil, 171-2
Well of Age, 269
Well of the North Wind, 269
West of Scotland College of Agriculture, 242
Western Isles, The, 23, 169
Whisky, 4, 14, 16, 25, 49, 54, 77-8, 128, 162, 169-70, 211-13, 216, 226, 227-8, 246
Whisky Island, 152
White Sands of Iona, 265, 267
Wigmund, 55
Wilderness, The, 235
Wilkieson, Mr., 231
William the Lion, 264
Wilson, Dr. Hubert, 104
Windsor Great Park, 42
Wishing Chair, 227, 285
Wishing Pool, 270
Wood, John, 139
Wood, Miss M. I., 101
Wordsworth, 289

Yellow Stick, 31, 104, 105